Delano's Voyages of Commerce
and Discovery

Books in the AMERICAN CLASSICS™ Series

AMERICAN CLASSICS™

DELANO'S VOYAGES OF COMMERCE AND DISCOVERY

*Amasa Delano in China, the Pacific Islands,
Australia, and South America, 1789–1807*

Edited and with an Introduction by
ELEANOR ROOSEVELT SEAGRAVES

Foreword by William T. La Moy
Peabody Essex Museum

Berkshire House Publishers
Stockbridge, Massachusetts

DELANO'S VOYAGES OF COMMERCE AND DISCOVERY
Edited by Eleanor Roosevelt Seagraves

Originally published in 1817 as *A Narrative of voyages and travels in the Northern and Southern hemispheres*. Boston, 1817.

Grateful acknowledgment is made to the Peabody Essex Museum, Salem, Massachusetts, and to the Library of Congress for illustrations in this book. A complete list of sources begins on page 423.

Front cover art ©1994 by Michael McCurdy
Cover design by Joyce C. Weston
Book design by Catharyn Tivy
Maps by Ron Toelke

Library of Congress Cataloging-in-Publication Data
Delano, Amasa, 1763–1823.
[Narrative of voyages and travels in the Northern and Southern hemispheres]
Delano's voyages of commerce and discovery : Amasa Delano in China, the Pacific Islands, Australia, and South America, 1789–1807 / edited and with an introduction by Eleanor Roosevelt Seagraves: foreword by William T. La Moy.
p.   cm. — (American classics)
Originally published: A narrative of voyages and travels in the Northern and Southern hemispheres. Boston, 1817.
Includes bibliographical references.
ISBN 0-936399-56-2 (pbk.) : $14.95
1. Voyages around the world. I. Seagraves, Eleanor II. Title. III. Title: Voyages of commerce and discovery. IV. Series: American classics (Stockbridge, Mass.)
G420.D35D35   1994   94-23
910.4'1'09033–dc20   CIP

Berkshire House Publishers
Box 297, Stockbridge MA 01262
800-321-8526

Printed in the United States of America
10 9 8 7 6 5 4 3 2 1

A

NARRATIVE

OF

VOYAGES AND TRAVELS.

IN THE

NORTHERN AND SOUTHERN HEMISPHERES:

COMPRISING

THREE VOYAGES ROUND THE WORLD;

TOGETHER WITH A

VOYAGE OF SURVEY AND DISCOVERY,

IN THE

PACIFIC OCEAN AND ORIENTAL ISLANDS.

....

BY AMASA DELANO.

....

BOSTON:

PRINTED BY E. G. HOUSE, FOR THE AUTHOR.

1817.

TITLE PAGE FROM THE 1817 EDITION

Contents

VOYAGE   OF   1790 – 1794

Delano's Voyages of Commerce and Discovery

Contents

VOYAGE OF 1803 – 1807

Delano's Voyages of Commerce and Discovery

Maps and Illustrations

Delano's Voyages of Commerce and Discovery

Foreword

THE REISSUING of the account of Amasa Delano's voyages of commerce and discovery by Berkshire House is, indeed, a most welcome and worthy endeavor. The original account was published privately in Boston in 1817 and entitled *A Narrative of Voyages and Travels, in the Northern and Southern Hemispheres: Comprising Three Voyages round the World; Together with a Voyage of Survey and Discovery, in the Pacific Ocean and Oriental Islands.* The James Duncan Phillips Library of the Peabody Essex Museum in Salem, Massachusetts, has two copies of this edition as well as one copy of the second edition, released in 1818.

The presence of several of these volumes in this institution, however, should not be misconstrued; the original editions are available in only a few scattered rare book and manuscript libraries throughout the world. Also, the volume as it was first produced consisted of 599 pages, a considerable mass with which to contend. Eleanor R. Seagraves has performed the valuable service of reducing the quantity of entries that are less pertinent to the core of the story. One should realize that, when the book first appeared, this detailed level of documentation was expected as the United States began the task of defining itself as a new nation in the midst of an expanding world. With the present publication, a new generation of readers will now benefit from the judicious editing of Eleanor Seagraves.

To put Captain Delano's exploits in their proper context, it should be pointed out that his commercial and exploratory activities commenced aboard the *Massachusetts,* a vessel "built expressly for the Canton trade" and launched in September of 1789. It was the "largest merchant ship built at that time in the United States, and excited a considerable sensation in the commercial part of the community. Parties of people in every rank of society frequently came on board to gratify their curiosity and express their admiration" (p. 5). The *Massachusetts* was eventually sold, and several other vessels would be employed in the course of Delano's fascinating travels between 1789 and 1807.

The content of this book is highly pertinent for our own volatile times. It describes some of the early interactions of European and Western cultures with the people of the Pacific islands. Amasa Delano, of course, carried the mind-set of his society with him, but he displayed genuine admiration for the heritage and traditions of other peoples he encountered. An example of this may be observed in the following account he makes of the principled actions of Abba Thulle, a king in the Palau Islands:

> The king, according to his usual generosity, had sent word to the people of Artingal, that we should be there in three days for war. Although I was a Christian, and was in the habit of supposing the Christians superior to these pagans in the principles of virtue and benevolence, yet I could not refrain from remonstrating against this conduct on the part of the king. I told him that Christian nations considered it as within the acknowledged system of lawful and honourable warfare, to use stratagems against enemies, and to fall upon them whenever it was possible, and take them by surprise. He replied that war was horrid enough when pursued in the most open and magnanimous manner; and that although he thought very highly of the English, still their principles in this respect did not obtain his approbation, and he believed his own mode of warfare more politic as well as more just. He said, that if he were

to destroy his enemies when they were asleep, others would have a good reason to retaliate the same base conduct upon his subjects, and thus multiply evils, where regular and open warfare might be the means of a speedy peace without barbarity. Should he subdue his rebellious subjects by stratagem and surprise, they would hate both him and his measures, and would never be faithful and happy, although they might fear his power, and unwillingly obey his laws. Sentiments of this elevated character excited my admiration the more for this excellent pagan, and made an impression upon my mind, which time will never efface. Christians might learn of Abba Thulle a fair comment upon the best principles of their own religion (pp. 34–35).

THE PEABODY ESSEX MUSEUM is always willing to support the dissemination of material that is linked to its collections, and the reader will note that several illustrations occur courtesy of the museum. This volume, more importantly, contributes to an understanding of our global interrelatedness, and its edited format will enhance the accessibility of what is clearly a valuable contribution to the literature of maritime history.

William T. La Moy
Peabody Essex Museum
Salem, Massachusetts
January 1994

Introduction and Acknowledgments

"**M**ANY WERE the perils and dangers we three brothers encountered during this long, extraordinary and tedious voyage. We built both the vessels we were in ourselves and navigated them two and three times round the globe. Each one of the brothers has been master builder, master rigger, and navigator of ships and vessels in all quarters of the world." So Amasa Delano wrote later in life when he set down the record of his third and final voyage — beginning in Australian and Tasmanian waters in search of seals for the Canton market.

He could not have guessed that his narrative of sea life, business enterprise, and exploration, beginning in 1789 and concluding around 1810, is probably the most interesting and lively first-hand account of an American man's ventures at sea that 18th- to early 19th-century history has provided. This chronicle, which includes personal observations and commentary, is startling for the immediacy of the action as well as for the author's unpretentious examination of human beings, himself included, in many kinds of situations in many lands.

Delano, not without previous experience as a sailor, and already acquainted with misfortune, personal and financial, began the first of the long voyages at age twenty-six as third officer aboard the new merchant vessel *Massachusetts*. For a time, he had considered farming near his native village of Duxbury, Massachusetts, but having gained skills as a shipbuilder under the tutelage of his father, his ambition and hunger for knowledge led him outward. He wrote that he hoped "particularly to know how far myself and others were imposed upon with exaggerated accounts of the world, and false statements of things a great way from home." In many ways, the Delano narrative reflects our own late 20th century: global encounters in a fast-changing world, clashes of culture and belief, and great economic and political uncertainties.

It was an age when new enterprise, philosophies, and exploration stirred throughout Europe, the Americas, and much of the rest of the world. Our own Declaration of Independence was thirteen years old and France was beset by violent revolution. The same year of 1789, the United States federal government began to function under its own Constitution, the Bill of Rights ratified two years later. George Washington had just been elected to his first term as President. The Pacific Northwest fur trade was in full swing, and American merchants were testing the Canton market for the first time.

Though her first voyage was not commercially successful, the *Massachusetts* was launched with fanfare in New England. At "almost eight hundred tons burthen," she was "the largest vessel constructed to that date in an American shipyard — built at Quincy in 1789 for Samuel Shaw and other Boston merchants," wrote Samuel Eliot Morison. "Her dimensions were taken from a British East-Indiaman, and her equipment and roster, with midshipmen and captain's servants, imitated the Honourable Company as far as Yankee economy permitted."[1] The ship was launched in September 1789 and sailed from "Boston on Sunday the 28th of March 1790." Though the *Massachusetts* was constructed on English design, she was manned by a crew that represented many nations who were a part of a continuing flow of immigrants being added to the predominant English among Yankees. Morison tell us that "Were I asked to mention two Massachusetts families who generation after generation sent their sons to sea, I should name the Devereux and the Delano, both of French origin."[2]

The noted mutiny in 1789 aboard the English ship *Bounty* was of particular interest to Delano. In his travels he became a good friend to Captain Mayhew Folger of the American ship *Topaz* who, in 1808, was the first person to bring news to the world of the fate of some of the men who had rebelled against Captain Bligh. Of those mutineers (led by Fletcher Christian) who escaped English search parties, one survivor and his colony of women and children were discovered accidentally by Folger on "Pitcairn's Island." Folger, though he spent only a few hours with Alexander Smith of the original *Bounty* crew, was fascinated by this long-lost colony of people, and his story along with several letters corroborating his evidence was told many times to Delano, who included it in his own book.

Perhaps the most poignant chapter for modern readers is one Delano entitled "Particulars of the Capture of the Spanish ship *Tryal* at the island of St. Maria" (Isla Santa Maria, off the coast of Chile). The year was 1805. The unknown ship carried African slaves — men, women, and children destined for the Spanish kingdoms of western South America. A key group of male captives had seized control of the crew and captain Benito Cereno. Such a situation was far from the thoughts of Delano and his men when they first viewed the ship, or even when several of them boarded the *Tryal* to offer assistance. Indeed, physical need was apparent, and Delano sent to have food and water brought over from his own vessel. However, as the hours passed, the unusual state of affairs came

1. *The Maritime History of Massachusetts, 1783–1860*, Samuel Eliot Morison (Boston: Houghton Mifflin Company: 1941), p. 52.
2. Ibid., p. 21.

to a head with a battle to retake the ship. In acting against mutiny and salvaging "property," Delano's action coincided with historical law of the period. And, of course, he and his men thought they would receive a fair reward from the *Tryal*'s owners, if they succeeded. The outcome, when the *Tryal* and her "cargo" were delivered to port, is filled with tragedy and irony.

American novelist Herman Melville fictionalized the *Tryal* story, altered the characters of people involved, while frequently retaining the exact language and descriptive details Delano supplied. His "Benito Cereno" is one of six novellas published in 1856 in a collection entitled *The Piazza Tales*. It is interesting to note that 72 years passed before the Amasa Delano account was publicly identified as Melville's source.[3]

American poet Robert Lowell wrote three short plays which were published as a trilogy, *The Old Glory*, in 1964. "Benito Cereno" is the final play, and it is based on Melville's novella. While Amasa Delano is a main character in the play, there is no mention of his own 1817 chronicle. Columbia Records recorded the original cast of "Benito Cereno" in 1965.

Amasa Delano's book was privately printed in Boston in 1817. In the Berkshire House edition, the words are Delano's own, except where noted: italicized parenthetical explanations are provided to summarize eliminated passages or to define an unfamiliar term. Some punctuation and paragraph adjustments have also been made for easier transition; and headings of many chapters simplified to reflect the contents. His adventures, observations, descriptions of people and

---

3. See Harold H. Scudder,"Melville's Benito Cereno and Captain Delano's Voyages," PMLA, XLIII (June 1928): 502–532; reprinted in Herman Melville, *The Piazza Tales*, ed. Egbert S. Oliver (New York: Hendricks House, Inc., 1962).

places, animals and plants are all here, occasionally abbreviated. Much reduced in length are long navigational explanations, such as landmarks, shoal and reef locations, exact passages taken, or conjectures about possible alternatives — all written up by the author who hoped they would aid other navigators of the day. Less important documents attesting to adequately described events, and a number of lengthy dissertations from university encyclopedias of the period which the author used to elaborate his material at the time of compilation, are almost entirely eliminated.

We have retained the original orthography nearly entirely. However, for the convenience of a new audience, current place names are used wherever possible. The modern name is given in parentheses after the place name used by Delano, the first time it occurs; then the modern term is used throughout — for example, Batavia (*Jakarta*). The one exception is the ancient port of Canton, now Guangzhou. Notes have also been added to satisfy modern curiosity about current population figures and to update or clarify other information. On the other hand, there has been no attempt to change a few observations and comments that would naturally appear inaccurate or awkward to us. We have greatly increased the number of illustrations, and designed two essential maps which give the outline of the three major voyages. A glossary of nautical and other terms has also been supplied.

A complete facsimile of the original work was issued by Praeger Press in 1970, and also by The Gregg Press the same year. The original length and format of the book, plus the fine print of the earlier age, lost this fascinating narrative to the large audience it should have. Most major libraries today do not even possess a facsimile, and as a result, this first-hand, historical experience — encounters with alien social and natural environments, different habits of culture, religion, and measures of justice that figure in our American genesis, down to the present time — has not been available.

C. Hartley Grattan, general editor of the Praeger Scholarly Reprints series, wrote an interesting introduction to the facsimile in which he points out that Delano "is considered a distant relative of the Delanos of Franklin Delano Roosevelt's line, although the connection is not certainly known. He died in Boston on April 21, 1823, at the age of sixty. He had married, but he left no children."[4]

Recently, the archives at the Franklin D. Roosevelt Library at Hyde Park, New York, sent me a section of a genealogy chart which shows a distant cousinship, going back about five generations, between F.D.R. and Amasa, the common ancestor being Jonathan de Lannoy, 1647–1720. Of special interest are the two opening paragraphs of an article from the same archive. The August 1939 issue of the *Andean Monthly*, published by the Chile-United States Cultural Institute includes a paper by Professor Eugenio Pereira S., Secretary, Instituto Chileno-Norteamericano de Cultura, Santiago, Chile. It is entitled "The Colonial Houses and Domestic

---

4. C. Hartley Grattan, ed. Introduction to *Narrative of Voyages and Travels...* (Facsimile edition, New York: Praeger Publisher, Inc., 1970).

For an explanation of the Delano lineage, I am indebted to Elizabeth Denier, archivist at the F.D.R. Library, who located the following information from *The Genealogy History and Alliances of the American House of Delano, 1621 to 1899*, compiled by Joel Andrew Delano, New York, 1899: "The mutual ancestor of Franklin D. Roosevelt and Captain Amasa Delano was Jonathan (I), the seventh child of Philippe de Lannoy. Jonathan (I) was born in 1647 and died in 1720. The second son of Jonathan (I), Jonathan (II), was the father of Samuel, his sixth child, who was born May 11, 1739 and died November 6, 1814. In 1762, Samuel married Abigail Drew. Their first child was Captain Amasa Delano who was born on February 21, 1763. Captain Amasa Delano married a widow named Hannah Appleton, but the couple had no children. Amasa died c. 1823. The thirteenth child of Jonathan (I), Thomas, born in 1704, was the ancestor of Franklin D. Roosevelt.

Life," and quotes paragraphs from Amasa Delano's *Narrative of Voyages and Travels* that deal with Chilean family and domestic life.

The paper is introduced as follows: "Among the books of our University Library this is one of special significance on the relations between Chile and the United States; the first page bears the following inscription by Franklin D. Roosevelt: 'May the modest part which my kinsman, Amasa Delano, played in the building up of Chile encourage further fruitful cooperation between our peoples, who share the common ideals of justice, peace and humanity.'

"Amasa Delano and his brother Samuel were the first members of the family to come to Chile. They came in 1800 on board the ship *Perseverance*. Some years later, in 1818, during the war of our independence, Pablo Delano established himself in Valparaíso. He was the founder of this representative Chilean family, which is related to the same North American branch as is President Franklin Delano Roosevelt."

F.D.R. must have been delighted when this kinship corroboration was brought to his attention. There is no way of knowing whether or not he had ever heard of the Pablo connection before this. But here was a fact of life not to be ignored. One imagines F.D.R. looking up at his informant, catching the eyes of others surrounding him, throwing his head back, and with a broad grin, exclaiming his happiest phrase, "Don't you *love* it?"

Today we are bombarded, and sometimes bewildered, by a welter of instant communication. Two hundred years ago, it took weeks, months, even years for most news to travel across several counties, let alone between continents. The chroniclers, writers of history, literature, and everyday letters were the journalists and commentators of Delano's day. They lived in their own present, as we do in ours; and like us, they struggled to make sense of what they knew and what they feared. Many people kept diaries or journals, and wrote poems and songs of commemoration. Most were so-called "ordinary" folk — wanderers, surveyors, seafarers, pioneers, soldiers, slaves or ex-slaves, women and men who had something to tell about life because they lived it hard, and gave thought to their experiences. Most of them died young, or barely middle-aged.

We share with them those mirrors to human nature, behavior, and events, large and small, and make the connections necessary to extend our own humanity. Philosopher Karl Jaspers wrote in *Reason and Anti-Reason in Our Time* (1971), "We know nothing essential of one another except when we enter into communication."

*   *   *

I AM GRATEFUL TO MANY PEOPLE who responded with enthusiasm to the idea of editing Amasa Delano's remarkable book for a modern audience while retaining its original language. They offered advice, provided contacts, or sent letters confirming a growing interest among Americans to "view" history through the eyes of the people who actually took part in the events.

I extend thanks to the following institutions and their staff members who assisted my research:

The National Archives: Emily Soapes; and in the division of National Historical Publications and Records Commission: Roger Bruns and Mary Giunta.

The Library of Congress: The Reading Room staff; John McDonough, Manuscripts, for his interest and for referring me to Virginia Steele Wood, who saw me on the spur of the moment, provided books, including her own scholarly work with its excellent historical bibliography; Clark Evans and the staff of Rare Books and Special Collections; and the Geography & Map reference rooms where I spent many happy hours. *The Peabody Essex Museum*, Salem, Massachusetts: Paul Winfisky and Kathy Flynn expedited my search for illustrations; and the staff at the *Essex Institute* Library, now joined with the Peabody Essex Museum, were very helpful. *The Franklin D. Roosevelt Library*, Hyde Park, New York: Verne Newton, Director; Frances Seeber; Susan Elter; and Elizabeth Denier, whose special search turned up the material on the Delanos in Chile.

Appreciation is also extended to the staffs of several other institutional libraries in Washington, D.C: *The World Wildlife Fund*; *The National Geographic Society*; *The Population Reference Bureau, Inc.*

A NUMBER OF FRIENDS generously responded to my inquiries: Dr. William R. Emerson, former Director of the Franklin D. Roosevelt Library; Christopher duPont Roosevelt; Dr. Frank B. Poyas; Dr. Isabella Halsted; Thomas A. Halsted; Maureen Corr. In the Washington area: Steven L. Carson of the Manuscript Society; author Luree Miller; Ruth and Charles Holstein; David Katcher and Gladys Uhl Katcher.

Some people whom Berkshire House contacted also helped: William T. La Moy, Director of the James Duncan Phillips Library at the Peabody Essex Museum, generously contributed the Foreword; Ron Toelke of Chatham, New York, drew the maps; Marcia Perry and the reference staff of the Berkshire Athenaeum, Pittsfield, Massachusetts, assisted with the glossary; and Michael McCurdy of Great Barrington, Massachusetts, created the cover illustration.

To my husband, Van H. Seagraves, as well as to author Roger MacBride Allen, I am most grateful for patient assistance in my tugs-of-war with several computers that were new to me. Van's business at home, entailing his well-equipped office, is a delightful luxury that has eased my work enormously.

I am especially indebted to my wise friend Katherine S. Cohn of Washington, D.C., who took on the task of going through the entire edited manuscript, saved me from a number of errors, raised the right questions, and offered helpful suggestions.

To Professor Jeanette S. Roosevelt, now of Berkshire County, Massachusetts, I am boundlessly grateful. Her many friendships and myriad contacts, among them Molly Geraghty of the School of Law, Western New England College, led me to Carolyn Banfield, Director of the Berkshire County Historical Society, thence ultimately to Jean Rousseau, publisher, and editors Sarah Novak and Philip Rich at Berkshire House Publishers. It was Berkshire House's enthusiastic reception that got the project definitively under way as a book, and Sarah's and Philip's sensitive guidance that put it into final editorial shape.

Eleanor Roosevelt Seagraves
Washington, D.C.
January 1994

Preface

BY AMASA DELANO

IN PREPARING this book for the public, I have had several objects in view. The principal one was the hope and belief that a large part of the information, which it contains, would be new and interesting to the community. In regard to the Oriental Islands particularly, remarks are made, anecdotes are told, customs are described, and principles and traits of character among the natives are brought to light, which, I trust, my readers will find worthy of their attention.

Having kept journals of my voyages and travels, which were made at the time minute and full upon whatever was extraordinary, and being satisfied that the publication of what I had seen and experienced would be useful, especially to seamen, I also desired to employ and amuse my mind in this work, and to spend, in a rational and profitable manner, a number of months which might otherwise have been left a prey to melancholy and painful meditations. I esteem it an occasion of peculiar gratitude to Providence when a man, depressed in his spirits, can fall upon a mode of beguiling his sadness which is equally reasonable and useful in regard to the community, and at the same time agreeable and reputable in regard to himself.

My friends too were solicitous that I should draw up this narrative, and give it to the press. It is hoped that their partiality will not be greatly mortified by the compliance with their advice, and the respect to their opinions which I have here shown. No seaman from the United States has enjoyed the same opportunity for observation and discovery in the Eastern Ocean, which was afforded to me by the voyage I made with Commodore McClure. My remarks upon the navigation along the coast of New Holland, Van Diemen's Land, New Zealand, and round Cape Horn, will also be new to my readers, and I am confident, of great real value. Although I have to regret that my book is not better, I trust that my countrymen will find it containing information and exhibiting a spirit, of which, not withstanding its faults, they need not be ashamed. There are many suggestions made in it on the various subjects connected with ship building, with practical navigation, with the management of crews, with the conduct of seamen on shore and in port, and with the duties of owners and masters, which I am confident are deserving of the notice, recollection, and attention of persons employed in these departments of life. It was also thought expedient to introduce such information concerning the places which I visited, as might render the book interesting and instructive to landsmen, and as should give me an opportunity to offer my sentiments, as they occurred, upon various topics in morals, condition, and character.

In undertaking this work, I was aware of the difficulties which I should have to encounter, in consequence of my want of an early and academic education, although I have always seized every possible opportunity during my whole life for the improvement of my mind in the knowledge of useful literature and those sciences that are immediately connected with the pursuits to which I have been professionally devoted. My efforts have not been without success; and I have been often employed in giving instructions to midshipmen, other subordinate officers, and seamen, in mathematics, astronomy, and navigation. These difficulties therefore were not greater in regard to me than they have been in regard to many other voyagers and travellers, who have very properly and usefully employed their pens in writing accounts of their observations and discoveries for the public. I wished this narrative to have my own character, sentiments, and manner, subject only to such a revision by some of my friends, before the manuscript went to press, as would free it from any gross errors in grammar, and peculiar obscurity in the construction of the sentences. I know that the book is unequally written, that the order is not always as happy as it might have been, that the facts and observations are miscellaneously presented to the reader, and that sometimes those belonging to the same subject are separated from each other at too great a distance.

My manuscript was very nearly completed for the whole work before it was offered to any one for correction. It has undergone no alteration in respect to the facts, the general arrangement, the matter introduced, or the spirit and tenor of the sentiments and reflections. Although I am but little qualified to appear before the public in this way, yet the responsibility of every thing in the book, where credit is not given, is entirely my own. A number of my friends have been successively employed to revise the different parts of the manuscript, and in consequence of this, the style is in a degree varied according to the several hands. In the first part of my narrative, that which is included in the period when I was with McClure, the reflections are the most numerous, as I made them the most frequently myself in the narrative, and the thoughts were considerably filled out in the correction of the sheets for the press.

The names are spelled differently in different books. The orthography in this work is supported in every instance by some printed authority. The whole is written with a spirit of independence, without wounding the feelings, as I trust, of any good man. Perhaps my remarks may sometimes appear to pay too little deference to popular prejudice. I hope however, that what I have always felt may always appear in my expressions, and that is a uniform respect and attachment to all the good and generous qualities of our nature, and an unaffected veneration for the laws of Providence and the principles of true religion.

It may be considered by some of my readers that I have been at times too minute in giving details in this narrative concerning officers and crews, the manner in which they were treated, and the attention paid to their effects after their death. But notices of this kind are valuable to the cause of morality and humanity, and will help, I trust, to stimulate others to do the same things for their fellow men which are recommended here. What I have neglected myself, and what I have seen deficient in other commanders of vessels, have led me to make such remarks in the course of this work as I thought would be useful to the community, and particularly to those who are called upon, not only for acts of justice, but for those of disinterestedness, at sea.

Chronology
1790–1807

the American ship Eliza, *bound for Holland, April 10. Spends weeks beating a way south through the China Sea to the Sunda Strait and the Indian Ocean. Reaches Mauritius on July 10. He is held up there for months, finally leaving Mauritius on board the* Hector, *February 1794.*

CHAPTER XII: *With a new partner, Captain Stewart, Delano sails for Bombay, by way of Mahé Island, Seychelles; along the coasts on the northern Arabian Sea; then southeast to Bombay, arriving end of April.*

CHAPTER XIII: *Not long afterwards, Delano, with Stewart in the* Hector, *sails southeast along Malabar coast to the Coromandel coast, southeast India. Stops at Madras; then on to Calcutta. Delano and Stewart seek refuge at Serampore, about 18 miles upriver from Calcutta. The ship* Hector *is sold.*

CHAPTER XIV: *In late summer or early autumn, Delano, nearly penniless, sails for Boston with Captain Jeremiah Stimson on the* Three Brothers, *from Calcutta. Arrives Boston the latter part of 1794.*

V O Y A G E   O F   1 7 9 9 – 1 8 0 2

CHAPTER XV: *Leaves Boston November 10, 1799, in the ship* Perseverance, *to sail around Cape Horn to the Pacific Ocean. In the early part of voyage, languishes for some time in the equatorial doldrums. Lands at St. Peter and St. Paul Rocks. Passes west of the Fernando de Noronha Islands and reaches the Falkland (Malvinas) Islands January 1800. At Strait Le Maire February 8; against heavy seas, rounds Cape Horn March 12.*

CHAPTERS XVI AND XVII: *Reaches Juan Fernández Islands March 26, and Más Afuero on March 31. In the course of this second voyage, as well as the third, Delano visits the coastal and island possessions of both Peru and Chile many times. Main ports of call in Chile are Concepción, Talcahuano, Valparaíso, Coquimbo. Principal islands visited are Santa Maria, the San Ambrosio and San Felix Islands, Juan Fernández Islands, and the Bird Islands. In Peru, the ports of Lima and Callao, Pisco Bay, and various islands.*

CHAPTER XVIII: *Encounter with the Spanish ship* Tryal *off the island of Santa Maria, February through April 1805.*

Chronology

VOYAGE OF 1803–1807

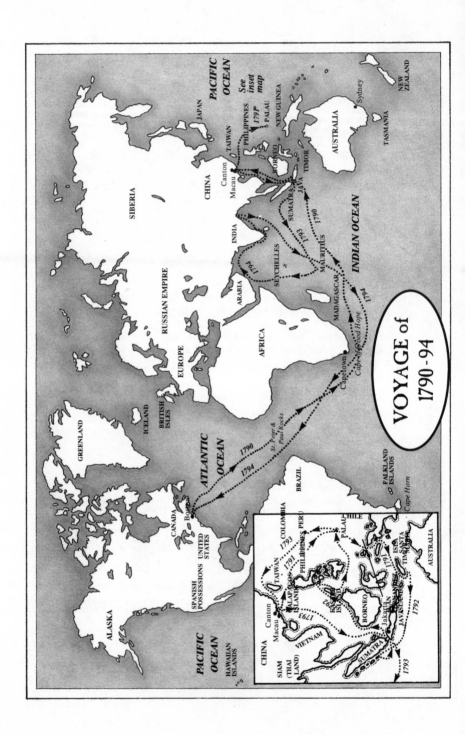

VOYAGE of 1790-94

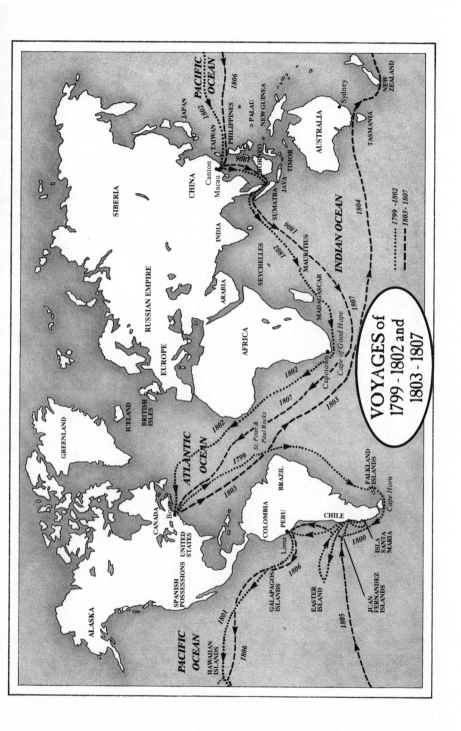

VOYAGES of 1799 - 1802 and 1803 - 1807

Delano's Voyages of Commerce and Discovery

VOYAGE OF 1790–1794

The Ship Massachusetts; Superstitions and Ghosts; Happenings at Sea; Passage to China

THE VOYAGE, with which I shall commence my narrative, was made in the ship *Massachusetts*. She was built at Quincy in one of the branches of Boston harbour, and was launched in September 1789. An agreement was made at Canton in China, with major Samuel Shaw, a Bostonian, to build the *Massachusetts* for the firm of Shaw & Randall, both of whom had been officers in the American army during the revolution, and had travelled to India after the peace of 1783, when the army was disbanded. Shaw was a man of fine talents and considerable cultivation; he placed so high a value upon sentiments of honour that some of his friends thought it was carried to excess.

The name of the master builder of the ship was Daniel Briggs. He was one of the best men I ever knew to keep a large company of men at work, and to make their labour productive. The family of Briggs in Pembroke, Plymouth county, was celebrated for extraordinary merit. There were five brothers. Elisha continued in his native town an excellent ship builder. Alden was brought up a blacksmith, and was remarkable for the talents he showed in the heavy work of a ship. Afterwards he became a merchant. Enos is a ship builder at Salem, and built the *Essex* frigate. Daniel united mercantile speculations with ship building, and has lived many years in Milton. Thomas was educated a ship builder also, went to sea afterwards as captain, and transacted business as a merchant in Boston for many years. The five brothers were employed upon the *Massachusetts*.

The ship was as well built as any ship could be under the circumstances. The timber was cut, and used immediately while perfectly green. It was white oak, and would have been very durable had it been docked, or properly seasoned.

Notwithstanding the unprepared state of the materials, the *Massachusetts* was so well built, that on her arrival in Batavia (*Jakarta*) and Canton the commanders of English, Dutch, and other European ships were continually coming on board to examine her, and to admire the model and the work. She was acknowledged to be the handsomest vessel in two ports.

She was however rotten when we first arrived in China. She was loaded principally with green masts and spars, taken on board in winter directly out of water, with ice and mud on them. The lower hold was thus filled, and the lower deck hatches caulked down in Boston, and never opened till we were in Canton. The air was found to be so corrupt that a lighted candle was put out by it nearly as soon as by water.

A mistaken idea prevailed at that time regarding the best mode of preserving a ship and her cargo. Air was prevented as much as possible from circulating freely through the hold. Precisely the opposite of this ought to be practiced. Whether in hot or cold climates, wind sails should be employed in fair weather, and the air sent into every part of the ship, for the benefit of the timbers as well as the cargo. We had between four and five hundred barrels of beef in the lower hold. When fresh air was admitted, the beef was found almost boiled, the hoops were rotted and fallen off, and the inside of the ship was covered with a blue mould more than half an inch thick.

Green wood should never be used in a vessel, especially above the navel timber heads. It will not last half as long in

4

low altitudes as that which is docked or properly seasoned. It is not of so much consequence as is generally imagined what kind of wood is used. The great object to be secured is the suitable preparation of the wood before it is wrought. White oak is thought to be the best, but the hacmetac, which grows in our eastern country, is the most durable, and is sufficiently strong. Black and yellow birch, hard pine, black spruce, and some sorts of maple, are good timber for ships.

In regard to spars, it is not necessary to have spruce seasoned, if no part of it is to be covered or to go under deck; but particular care should be taken to have it guarded with hot tar as soon as it is made. The tar should be put on three times at least. A pine mast should always be seasoned, and if checked, its supporters should be oak. To dock spars is the best method to preserve them. Salt water is peculiarly serviceable to pine, to render it both durable and tough. Spruce spars soon rot, if they are not docked, or covered with hot tar.

The pumps should be made of the best hard pine, hooped with iron, with good composition chambers, plain boxes, and well constructed. A ship as large as a thousand tons should have one good chain pump. The pumps are of the very first consideration with a prudent sailor, and yet I have been in ships at sea where little attention was paid to them. The leather employed in them ought to be of the best quality, and a number of spare sets of boxes well fitted with iron should be furnished.

THE *MASSACHUSETTS* WAS BUILT expressly for the Canton trade. She was the largest merchant ship built at that time in the United States, and excited a considerable sensation in the commercial part of the community.[1] Parties of people in every rank of society frequently came on board to gratify their curiosity and express their admiration. The voyage she was to

5

make was almost new to Americans. A station on board her was an object of consequence. Hundreds of applications were made by persons of the best character.

Job Prince, Esq. was appointed commander. He was not only a seaman but was well qualified to do business as a merchant. Josiah Roberts, a native of Portsmouth, New Hampshire, was first officer. I was appointed second officer and belonged to her from the beginning, hoisted the first colours that she wore, and continued with her till she was sold to the Danish East India Company at Canton. I hauled her colours down for the Danes to raise theirs. I never lost a day by sickness while I was with her.

Jeremiah Parker of Portsmouth was third officer. He died on his homeward passage, and was thrown overboard.

John Owen, the fourth officer, died with the scurvy on the North West Coast of America. All these officers had commanded vessels on foreign service previous to their entering on board the *Massachusetts*.

Nathaniel Shaw, purser, and brother to the owner, died and was thrown overboard, on a voyage from Canton to Bombay in an English ship in 1791. He was a good accountant, and of an excellent character.

Joseph Loring was surgeon, and was well qualified for his profession. He left America many years since, and has been travelling in different parts of Europe.

Thomas French, midshipman, as we were going into Jakarta, fell from the main yard and was killed by the fall. He was buried on a small island outside of Jakarta roads.

Samuel Proctor was another midshipman. He died in 1792 and was buried under the walls of Macao (*Macau*).

John Prince was also a midshipman, a son of the captain. He had a good education, and was a man of worth. He died four or five years since (*c. 1811–12*).

The Ship Massachusetts

Daniel Malcomb, a man well known in this town, was taken on board as a passenger by Major Shaw from motive of pure benevolence. He was of an extraordinary character, noble, brave, and generous, and yet intemperate, rash, and fickle in his attachments. He died and was thrown overboard in the Straits of Sunda, 1791.

For the satisfaction of the friends of the crew, I shall give a list of their names and stations, and of the events which happened to them as far as my knowledge extends. (*Delano's list shows that of approximately 61 regular members of the crew, 37 were born on American soil, 14 were English, seven from Ireland, and there were two Scots and one Swede. At the time Delano was writing, 1814–17, he recorded that 48 of the crew were known dead, many from disease, or accidents at sea; four had been murdered in other parts of the world, and one man was said to be a slave in Algiers.*)[2]

THE *MASSACHUSETTS* HAD MORE THAN three crews shipped before she sailed from Boston. The greatest part of them left the ship in consequence of a prediction by an old woman, a fortune teller, Moll Pitcher of Lynn, that the *Massachusetts*, and all aboard her, would be lost. Such was the superstition of our seamen at that time, that the majority of them believed the prophecy. It seems strange that a class of men, who are continually exposed to storms, hardships, and dangers, should be so powerfully affected by the traditions which are handed down from generation to generation concerning omens, charms, predictions, and the agency of invisible spirits. Perhaps they are more superstitious than landsmen because they are more subject to what they call luck in the weather and the elements, and are more dependent upon changes and agents which they cannot control.

In 1787, I commanded a ship, the *Jane* of Boston, be-

longing to Benjamin Beale Esq. of Quincy, which was famous
for being haunted. My people could not be persuaded that
ghosts had not been seen on board the *Jane*, although I tried
every expedient, which reason or ridicule could suggest to
dissuade them. They saw no force in the idea that the Deity
would not violate the laws of nature, and employ old women
as his supernatural agents. They were always ready to be disturbed by apparitions, and always showed the power of superstition to be paramount in their minds.

One pleasant evening, as we were running with the
trade winds in latitude 25° north, I heard the second mate
and some of the people talking about ghosts. Although
doubts were expressed of the existence of such personages, yet
many were full in the faith that they were common in all
ages.

It occurred to me that it was a favorable time to show
them a ghost, and make one more attempt to cure them of
their folly. They were sitting far aft upon the quarter deck. I
stepped down the companion way, went to the state room of
the chief mate, and asked him to lend me a hand in showing
the people a ghost.

He readily consented, and we took two mops, lashed
the handles together, made them long enough to reach from
a cabin window to the top of the tafferel rail. We put a bar
across a suitable distance from the mop-head for arms, dressed
it with jackets to give it proportion and shape, put a white
shirt over the whole, tied a string round the neck leaving the
top of the shirt like a hood on the head, the "face" looking
through the opening in the bosom of the shirt, and gave the
whole the appearance of a woman, because this was the kind
of ghost most generally expected.

A string under the arms easily aided the delusion that
it was the slender waist of a female. A cabin window was

THE SHIP *THREE SISTERS*, BUILT IN CHARLESTOWN, MASSACHUSETTS, IN 1795. (COURTESY OF THE PEABODY ESSEX MUSEUM)

opened while I took my station in the gang-way to see the people without being seen. The chief mate raised up the ghost so that it might be seen above the ship's stern. It immediately caught the attention of the men on the quarter deck. Never did I see human beings more frightened than they were.

They were struck dumb, fixed immovable with terror, and seemed like so many breathless but gazing petrifactions. The ghost gently rose and again sank out of sight, till the chief mate was weary with the labour, and withdrew it at a given signal. I remained to hear what would be said. The men remained motionless and speechless for some time.

After they recovered themselves a little, one of the boldest broke silence and began to question what it could be.

They concluded it was a ghost, and determined to speak to it if it should appear again. Upon this I went to the chief mate, and he agreed to hold it up once more. I resumed my station, the ghost appeared, and one of them made an attempt to speak, but his courage and his voice failed him. Another attempted, and failed. A third, but without success. The sounds were inarticulate and feeble.

The question was to be "In the name of the holy God, who are you, and what to do you want?" The image was taken down; we undressed it, and restored the mops to their proper shape. I went to bed without permitting the secret to be known. At 12 o'clock at night, the chief mate came to me and said that the second officer and people were extremely frightened, and wanted to see me on deck.

I got up and went above where all the crew were collected and filled with anxiety and alarm. I asked them what was the matter. They huddled round me like a brood of chickens, and said they had seen a ghost. I inquired why they were frightened at that, since their stories taught them that ghosts were so common, and so many had been seen already. They answered that they had never been sure of having seen any before, but now they were sure, and the evidence was irresistible. I told them that I had always disbelieved their stories on this subject, and did still; that it was weakness and folly for them to be agitated at the sight which they pretended to have seen; and that they would one day be ashamed of it. This produced no effect upon them.

Their sufferings were extreme, and I found it difficult to tell them the trick that I had played. As they had never been deceived by me in any thing before, and as I feared that some embarrassment might be brought on me in return, I determined not to disclose the truth till the end of the voyage, and then to declare it in such a manner as to remove if possible this error from their minds. It is a hazardous experiment for the master of a vessel to make, and no cause can justify playing tricks upon his people even for the best purposes. This affair caused me a great deal of anxiety afterward, and did not accomplish the good that I designed by it.

THE *MASSACHUSETTS* SET SAIL from Boston on Sunday the 28th of March, 1790. The weather was clear and pleasant, and the wind in the north west. Off Hancock's wharf, we got under way with all sail set, topgallant sails and royals. The anchor was hauled to the cat-head, and when the block was brought up suddenly against the under side of it, the hook of the cat-block snapped short, and the anchor ran to the bottom stopping the ship's way, giving us not a little mortification under the eyes of such an immense crowd. We soon recovered our anchor, and proceeded down the harbour as far as Congress Road, where we came in to seven fathoms water.

We fired a salute after getting under way a second time near the Wharf. At the time, I was standing on what is called the davit, a piece of timber used to keep off the anchor from the side of the ship as it is hoisted upon the gun wale. The first gun was fired immediately under the davit, and I was at the end of it a few feet further out than the muzzle of the gun. The shock was so great upon my ears, as to give me great pain, and almost to prevent me from hearing any one speak for fifteen or twenty days. I think that my hearing has been somewhat affected by this ever since.

Our ship was pierced for thirty-six guns, but our armament was 20 six-pounders and musketry. (*They sailed east and south, crossing the equator off the coast of Africa on the 18th of May.*)

ON THE 23RD, AT NINE in the evening, one of the people

Ship Massachusetts Built In Quiet Little Cove In Germantown District

Quincy Patriot Ledger — July 26, 1940

THE COVE WHERE THE *MASSACHUSETTS* WAS BUILT
WAS PICTURED IN THE *QUINCY PATRIOT LEDGER* IN 1940.
(COURTESY OF THE PEABODY ESSEX MUSEUM)

struck a porpoise off the forecastle, and being anxious to save it for food, he called out "a man overboard," that the ship might be brought to. The helm was instantly put to lee, and all hands were in agitation.

I was in command of the watch that was then below and not on duty. I jumped out of bed with nothing on but my shirt, ran up on deck, and made for the gangway ladder to the poop deck. The men there were going to clear away the jolly boat that was hanging by a tackle. As soon as I was in the boat, four men with me, I gave the order to lower it down.

She was lowered a little way when we were stopped, the boat swinging very much as the ship rolled with the motion of the sea. I called to the men who were tending the tackle to know what the matter was. I was answered that the fall was foul. I ordered it to be cut when the ship was on the roll so as to lift the boat highest from the water. The boat was at least fifteen feet high at the time she was cut away, but luckily she hit on her bottom. The fall however was so great that it knocked every man down as suddenly as if his legs had been cut off.

After we recovered, we got out the oars and pulled astern, setting up as loud a hallooing as we could, with a view to make the man whom we supposed overboard, hear us. We rowed round in different directions till the ship began to fire signal guns; we then pulled for her, but found ourselves making poor headway as her progress was not wholly stopped. We pulled for some time, when at length we got so near as to hear the bell ringing, which was of an excellent tone for a ship's bell. After being absent nearly an hour, we arrived along side, and found the pinnace in the yard tackles just lowering into the water to come in search of us. For such false alarms, that occasion so much anxiety and trouble, people should be punished.

NOTHING OF ANY CONSEQUENCE took place on our passage in crossing the Indian Ocean. The winds blew strong nearly all the time from the westward, with a heavy rolling sea from that quarter, till the 21st of July. The people were then scraping the sides of the ship in order to paint and varnish them to make the ship show to the best advantage when we should enter the port of Jakarta. The men so employed were on a stage slung over the ship's side, and some careless person cast off the ropes and let them fall overboard. One caught hold of something along side the ship; the other three went astern. The jolly boat was immediately lowered down, and was with them in five minutes, but before she arrived, one of them sank; the other two were taken up. The man lost was Samuel Tripe. An extract from the captain's journal: "Ordered Messrs. Roberts and Delano to appraise the affects of Samuel Tripe, which they did. Entered on the books their appraisement."

On the third of August we found ourselves in latitude 6° 52' south, that being nearly the latitude of Java Head; and by reckoning, in 103° 00' east longitude. We saw no signs of land. (*They tacked to the south and east, having concluded they were "westward of reckoning," and did not find their port till nearly three weeks later.*)

All this loss of time, happened on account of our not having any chronometer on board, nor any officer who knew any thing about lunar observations. Every commander should furnish himself with a good brass sextant, and so should every chief officer of any ship bound round Cape Horn, or the Cape of Good Hope. A wooden sextant is worse than nothing, as it will not keep the adjustment so that it can be depended on. The books necessary are no more than a requisite table, and a nautical almanack, or an ephemeris. It makes a sailor very happy after being at sea for a hundred days or more, to know that he can take his books and instrument, and ascertain his situation on the globe within ten or a dozen miles. It is not delay only that is occasioned by not knowing the longitude, but the loss of hundreds of ships and lives.

ON MAKING THE WESTERLY PART of Java, and drawing near to the land, it will be found that the Javans will come off in their canoes to the ship to trade. They will bring fowls, parrots, monkies and sometimes pigs, plantains, melons, sweet potatoes, cocoa-nuts, oranges, and green turtles. But as soon as a Dutch boat is seen coming off from Anger point, every one of the canoes will leave the ship, as they are in fear of the Dutch.

On the 30th of August we anchored off Pigeon Island. Whilst handling the main-sail, Thomas French, midshipman, fell from the main yard and was killed instantaneously. On the following morning we buried him on the above island, with decency and honour, firing minute guns all the time, from the boats leaving the ship with the corpse till it was interred. We anchored in Jakarta Roads the same afternoon, where we were received politely on account of Major Shaw's being consul for India and China — the first we ever had to the eastward of the Cape of Good Hope.

Our ship was a credit to us every where, but we found no favor in trade here, and were obliged to leave the port without selling any of our cargo, although it had been expressly laid in for this port. Major Shaw took apartments in the hotel for as many of his officers as could be spared from the ship, and kept four or five of us with him on shore all the time of our stay, allowing us every indulgence.

On the 7th of September we sailed from Jakarta for Canton, (*Guangzhou, China*), and crossed over the Java sea. (*They encountered difficult shoals, necessitating constant look out from the mast head, and many dangerous tacks through shallow waters.*) On the 27th of September, we experienced a severe typhoon, split the main sail, foretop sail, and foretopmast staysail. But owing to our ship's being an excellent sea boat, we weathered the gale, and suffered only trifling damage compared with some other ships. One Dutch ship was totally lost amongst the islands in Canton Bay, together with all the crew. She had three or four hundred thousand dollars in specie on board.

A Danish ship, which I was afterwards employed to repair, was totally dismasted in this gale, as were several other European and country ships. The gale did great damage to the Chinese craft. Many of their junks were lost, many torn to pieces in their sails and rigging, and many driven on shore. This typhoon took place at the change of the monsoon; it commenced from the south west, hauled round to the west and north, and took its place at north east. We arrived at Macau the 30th, took a pilot and proceeded up the river for Canton.

On our arrival it was found by the owner, Shaw, that his partner, Captain Randall, had been at Canton the previous season, and had contracted more debt than was owing before, and that was considerably large. The cargo we had would not sell for any thing, and our specie amounted only to about $15,000. All things considered, he thought best to sell the ship, as the Danish Company wanted to sell the one they had dismasted in the typhoon, and buy the *Massachusetts*. The bargain was accordingly settled, and the ship was sold for $65,000, Major Shaw paying the port charges, which were calculated to be $5,000. We were then settled with, and all set adrift, some going one way and some another. I was the highest officer that remained in the country.

English Service under Commodore McClure;
"Fool's Gold"; A Treacherous Incident

AFTER THE *Massachusetts* was sold, and I had obtained an honourable settlement with the owner for myself and my brother, I undertook the superintendency of the repairs of the large ship belonging to the Danish East India Company. For a supply of such materials and mechanics as are wanted to heave a ship down, and furnish her with masts and spars, reliance must be chiefly placed upon European or American vessels. The Chinese have no hard timber, iron, or copper, of the proper kind, and no mechanics qualified to do the work. If shipmasters, when bound to China, would provide a surplus of all the materials requisite for such repairs, they would not only be enabled to assist each other, but would always find a profitable market for whatever might remain. Had it not been for the aid which I obtained from other vessels at Wampoa (*Whampoa or Huangpu*), it would not have been in my power to accomplish the important work upon the Danish ship. The surplus materials should consist of hard timber, from twenty to fifty feet long, fifteen inches wide, and seven or eight thick; large bar iron, spikes of all sizes, hemp-rope, canvass, blocks, anchors, and cables.

My brother Samuel, who had been with me constantly, with whom I shared in all things, and kept one purse, was my principal support in the arduous task of repairing the ship. After the completion of this, and a settlement with the owner, we all separated. My brother went to the North West Coast of

A HUANGPU SCENE IN DELANO'S DAY.
(FROM THE COLLECTIONS OF THE LIBRARY OF CONGRESS)

America with Capt. William Douglas.

Huangpu, where the Danish ship was repaired, is the port, or anchoring place, for all vessels in the China trade, and is an island nine miles below Canton, on the river Tigris (*Pearl or Zhu*). Taking leave of all on board the Danish ship, I proceeded to Macau. There I found many friends, whom Major Shaw had procured for me before he left Canton. They were the English, Dutch, Danish and Swedish supercargoes, besides others. They remove from Canton to Macau every spring for the benefit of the wholesome sea air during the summer months. Commodore John McClure and myself soon became intimately acquainted with each other, and were friends. He wanted both officers and men for his expeditions with the English East India Company, having lost several of the former by sickness, and of the latter by desertion. (*Two vessels comprised this expedition fitted out from Bombay: the* Panther, *a snow of about two hundred tons — a snow is a small vessel resem-*

bling a brig — and the Endeavor, *a small snow.*)

McClure indicated I should be very useful to him as a seaman, an officer, or a ship builder; and if it was agreeable to me to go on board the *Panther* with him, "I should receive the same pay and emoluments with his lieutenants and astronomers; I should not be subject to any command but his; and as he was out on survey and discovery, if I liked such a trip, he would make the circumstances pleasant to me." The service was just that for which I had always entertained a strong desire, and I did not hesitate a moment.

The 14th of April 1791, I went on board the *Panther* as a volunteer officer, doing duty as lieutenant, and subject to none but the Commodore's command. This last article made it very unpleasant to me for a short time, for the Bombay Marine was as regular as any public service whatever. The officers, who were to obey me, did not all think the regulation proper, and were not satisfied. This however was but for a short period. We all soon became friends. They found in me a man able and willing to do his duty at all times in any capacity, for which he professed to be qualified, and one who was evidently desirous of being their friend and companion. I found in them gentlemen who were just and generous; and after the prejudice was removed, which had arisen from my admission to office out of order, and from my character as an American, with all the associations of the late war, they were kind and cordial to me, and I was more happy than I had ever been in any service, or with any set of officers before.

MY COMPANIONS IN THIS EXPEDITION were all North and South Britons by birth, had been educated in good schools in England and Scotland, and entered young into the Navy, or into the Bombay Marine. They had never known any but public service. From the youngest midshipman to the

Commodore, not one had arrived at the age of thirty. They had not been exposed to any degradation of sentiment or moral feeling, by that miscellaneous intercourse with nations, in the pursuits of trade, which has too often corrupted the mind and character through the temptations of avarice and commercial policy, especially when at a distance from home. They were in principle and practice honest, ingenuous and honorable; despisers of meanness and duplicity in every form; just and generous in the common duties of life; respectful to each other in their familiarity and playfulness, and faithful in their friendships. They encouraged in their conversation, and regarded in their conduct, high and honourable sentiments toward women. Their ideas of the importance and sacredness of the marriage relation, and of the character of a wife, were such as wise and good men, in a pure state of society, would rejoice to approve and disseminate. In the variety of countries and people where they visited, and the effects of different manners and institutions upon the communities, they had an opportunity to acquire a practical liberality of mind, while their estimate of the pre-eminent value of the domestic virtues was continually exalted. Let it not be supposed, under the dominion of prejudices, which are too common on shore, that this is a kind of praise but ill adapted to a sailor's life and habits. From my own observation, and the virtues of more fellow seamen than I have room to name, I affirm the extensive influence which moral, domestic and religious feelings have over their hearts, their conversation, their actions and their hopes.

There is also another article in the conduct of this expedition, which ought to be mentioned as equally honourable to my companions and worthy of imitation from others. Their treatment of the natives was uniformly just, honest, generous and friendly; no impositions were practised upon their credulity; no mercenary advantages were taken of their ignorance; and no treachery was used toward their interests. The impression left upon the minds of the natives in every place which our expedition visited, must have been favorable to us, and useful to them. It could not but have excited in their minds many reflections, and probably some resolutions, upon the subject of using the means of civilization, and seeking the blessings of such a religion as ours. It is my deliberate opinion, that most of that of which we complain in the character and conduct of natives of different countries toward us, is owing to ourselves, to our avarice and cupidity, to our selfishness, and the disregard of our own principles as we have at first announced them.

If all voyages, travellers, and missionaries had treated the natives as honourably and wisely as they were treated by Commodore McClure and his companions, we should not only have enjoyed uninterrupted friendship with them, but should have gone very far toward the accomplishment of their civilization, and the introductions among them of our own forms of society and religion.

I RETURN TO MY NARRATIVE. We continued the preparation of our vessel for sea, and were also employed in taking on board provisions and stock till April 27th, 1791, when we sailed out of the Typa, or bay at Macau.

We sailed eastward, anchoring in port San Pio Quinto, one of the Babuyan Islands, on May 14th. No island is more convenient than this for taking in wood or water. Ships may anchor in fifteen fathoms water, half a mile distant southwest from the watering place, which is at a river running several miles into the island, and large enough to sail a loaded boat. This river is associated in my story with a hoax played off upon me by my companions.

Delano's Voyages of Commerce and Discovery

When I joined this expedition for survey and discovery, my imagination was not a little fired with the strange things I was to see. My fellow officers jocularly called me Jonathan, as I had the curiosity which is considered characteristic of my countrymen. On the 15th, while we were taking in wood and water, Lieut. Drummond, and Dr. Nicholson, the surgeon, having been on shore all day, and knowing that it would be my turn to head a party the next day, reported that they had been up the river a long way, and had discovered what they believed to be *gold ore*. When they had fixed my attention by the story, and warmed my mind to credulity, they produced a shining yellow stone, which they had obtained before we came to the island, and a piece of antimony out of the medicine chest, and other substances of which I had no knowledge, and said they had found all of them up the river. As however they knew so little of minerals, and did not much like to labour for nothing in collecting what might subject them to ridicule when they should return home, they doubted whether they should go out again to increase their specimens. They appeared to me not confident enough in the evidence before them and to have too great a dread of ridicule.

I determined to pursue the subject next day, and to make a more liberal collection of the ore. When Drummond, who was a Scotchman and my friend, but still willing to enjoy a frolic, with the characteristic shrewdness of his nation, perceived that my ardour was sufficient, he slapped me on the shoulder and said, "*Odds mon*, if you are set upon this, there is my large canvas bag, which will hold two or three bushels. Take that and my Malabar boy with you for a guide. He knows the place where we found these curious ores, and you can return with a back load of gold." Every time this world *gold* was pronounced, my imagination became more heated, and I was soon ripe for the enterprise.

22

After a night of South Sea dreams, our party was ready for the shore. The Malabar boy could not speak English, and I could not speak any thing else. He therefore received his instructions from his master without suspicion on my part. The Commodore also gave very liberal instructions to me, as the head of the party, allowing me liberty to go all over the island if I chose, only leaving a midshipman to take charge of the companies for procuring wood and water. He observed at the same time that he always wished his officers to make every discovery in their power while on land duty.

At the firing of the gun, we mustered, and on landing at the watering place, I gave the midshipman his orders, took my gun and the boy with his bag and proceeded up the river with great exhilaration. The first mile was tolerably level and easy, and I was able to pass comfortably along the side of the river which was about 10 yards wide and knee deep, winding its course through a most delightful landscape. After this, the land rose abruptly, the river was filled with falls, its banks were broken with rocks, and a passage in any way became exceedingly difficult. But *gold* inspired me, and banished all sense of hardship.

At last the Malabar boy cried out, and sank down with fatigue. When I tried to make inquiries of him, he shook his head, and I supposed his meaning was that he did not understand me. As we were sitting on the rocks to rest ourselves, I saw a number of wild cocks and hens coming from the wood and lighting on the trees over our heads. I shot five or six, and found them so like our barn door fowls that I did not know but the place might be inhabited by beings like ourselves.

The boy had been instructed to point up the river whenever I asked for the place of gold ore, and he was to go with me as far as we found water. With much difficulty and after repeated stops and rests, we made our way more than six miles according to the channel of the river, and found it then divided into two or three branches near its sources. Here, after a very solicitous examination of the boy, I discovered that neither he nor his master had been up the river before. The boy appeared not to have been let into the plot, but began to be alarmed and anxious. And from the very moment that the idea of a hoax entered my mind, all the evidence on this subject struck me in a new light. The intrigue unfolded itself with perfect clearness, and I saw myself in a wilderness, a fatigued, disappointed, and ridiculous dupe. In the midst of my vexation, I could not help laughing, and almost crying at the same moment.

The trick was a severe one for me, but it had been well managed, and my ardor and credulity were fairly chargeable to myself. After a hard struggle with my mortification, I determined to take it in good part.

To relieve my mind, and to carry back something to check the force of the laugh against me, I employed myself in making observations upon the scenery, the soil, the products, the insects, and the reptiles about me. From the rock in the middle of the stream, where I had been sitting to think over my disappointment, and which I had chosen in order to avoid being bitten or stung by the numerous enemies of a discoverer's peace, I rose and penetrated into the wood ten or twelve rods, but the underbrush was too thick and thorny. The river was the only way to return.

The banks of the stream however were rich and variegated with all the flowers and colours of the spring. These formed a striking contrast with the reptiles concealed beneath them — scorpions, centipedes, iguanas and tarantulas. The soil was excellent and produced in great abundance the beetle nut, the cocoa-nut, various other tropical fruits, and fine timber for ships. As we proceeded down the river we were able to make little excursions further from its sides, and occasionally discovered pleasant lawns, some of which had been burnt over, and were not covered with high coarse grass. It was fine amusement traversing these lawns, and shooting the variety of birds which we found in them. We soon filled Drummond's large bag, not indeed with golden ore, which I might not have been able to carry, but with fowls of different kinds, and of a plumage surpassing in beauty and richness, the finest colours of the mineral kingdom. The large blue pigeon,[3] which Captain Henry Wilson saw at the Palau Islands, we saw here, and carried one to the ship as a specimen. It is three times as large as the pigeon of home; its blue is deep and rich except that upon the breast, which is changeable with red, producing with its graceful motions the most agreeable effect. Among the handsomest birds I ever saw, was one which I shot at this time, as large as an American pigeon, having a bright yellow about the neck, breast, and part of the back, while the upper side of the head and wings was a deep crimson. The hens had chosen the high grass for nests, which were filled with eggs, and we often started them in flocks, sometimes accompanied by numerous broods of half-grown chicks.

About four o'clock in the afternoon, I reached the shore again, completely worn down with fatigue, but in much better spirits than I was when at the sources of the river, in a trackless wood, revolving the rise, progress, development, and possible consequences of the plot which had been laid and executed at my expense.

When I had been seated in perfect silence, on a rock in the river, and could hear the echo of the waters through the awful stillness, mingled with occasional but unintelligible expressions of anxiety by the poor Malabar boy; and when I remembered that I was at an almost immeasurable distance from my native country, in the service of a foreign power, and now in a savage spot where the natives might be every moment upon me, I confess I was not very far from that mixed mood of melancholy, mortification, and terror, which required but little more to overcome me for the hour. Had I been attacked, desperation might have roused me, and made me brave, but the feelings which I then experienced have taught me how to judge of the sufferings and wants of men, whose spirits fail when they are at a distance from home, and appear to themselves to be cast out from the sympathies of the human family.

It is an evidence of as much folly as it is of inhumanity, to say that none but weak and dastardly minds are subject to these impressions. Good talents, a lively imagination, a temperament of ingenuousness and honesty, and those qualities of the soul which give charm to decisive and efficient characters, serve only to add bitterness to the feeling of desolation.

Whoever may have the command of men abroad, let him not, when he finds any of them oppressed with these feelings, begin to despise and reproach them as mean and pusillanimous. Let him learn human nature better; and by kindness, by increased manifestations of sympathy, by diversifying their employments, and appointing such as are adapted to their condition, let him gradually raise their hearts, invigorate their resolution, and bind them to duty, virtue, and friendship. Many are the instances in which generous and feeling minds have been ruined, and only relieved by death, when they were subject to the command of others, and during a period of depression were inhumanly treated without the means of redress. Sailors, and all men, even of the meanest education, have the essential qualities of high minds, and are exalted and improved, at the same time that they are won by generosity and kindness.

These remarks lose none of their force by the manner in

which I was received at the shore, after my return from my *golden* enterprise. Drummond and Nicholson, who had heard by the boats from the watering place, that I had been gone nearly the whole day up the river, and knowing that their scheme must have had its full effect, were willing to relieve my fatigue and soothe my temper by every act of friendship. They wished to mingle so much kindness with the trick they had played, that while it should afford the crew the full measure of amusement, it should not do me a real and permanent injury.

They came on shore at the hour when they thought they should meet me, and had liberally furnished themselves with every article of food and liquor which could tempt the appetite and exhilarate the spirits. Their countenances and their conversation were irresistibly pleasant and conciliating; and while I saw all the humour which they had in store to use against me at a future time, they still succeeded in allaying my irritation and persuading me to join in the common laugh. Whatever suspicions of malice might have lurked in my thoughts about the design were dismissed, and I never jumped into the boat for the ship with a lighter heart.

With the wood we carried on board at dusk, a large centipede eight or nine inches long had been taken, and unfortunately gave me a most venomous bite upon my throat. It swelled very much, and caused an extremely painful night. Bathing it with hot vinegar and salt afforded me some relief, but the swelling continued for two or three days, with pain. The bite of this odious reptile is said to be sometimes mortal, and always as dangerous as that of a scorpion.

THE SHORES ROUND THE ISLAND at port Pio Quinto were indented with small bays, some of which we visited for turtle whose tracks we saw, and for which as well as for fishing, the people of Luzon, at a distance of eight or ten leagues to the south, come to this place.

One night we observed a fire on the island, and sent a party to learn what might be discovered from it. The party landed in a boat, with a native of the Palau Islands, whom we had with us whose name was Cockawocky. They saw Indians engaged in cooking round the fire, and our Palau Island-man crept close to them before they discovered him. The moment they did, they ran with the greatest consternation, leaving every thing they had behind them. Cockawocky followed to assure them that we would do them no harm, and that we had been thus cautious in making our approach that we might ascertain their numbers and be sure of safety for ourselves. But they fled the faster for his pursuit, and we lost the opportunity to have in interview with them, a loss which we particularly regretted, as our Commodore always made it a point to establish a friendly intercourse with the natives wherever he could to leave benevolent impressions upon their minds in regard to white people, and especially the English.

We afterwards found that they were from Luzon. Cockawocky, by whom they had been so much alarmed, was brought from the Palau Islands in the *Panther* when she came last to Macau. His name, as it sounds to our ears, might be thought indicative of his character, for he was a forward, officious, and blustering fellow, quite unlike his countrymen generally, who are mild and modest.

ON THE 17TH OF MAY, the evening previous to our weighing anchor to leave San Pio, my friend Drummond proposed to me to visit some of the bays about the island in search of turtle, if we could get consent of the Commodore. This was granted, and I did not hesitate to comply with it.

We took two boats in order to increase our chance of

success. I called the boatswain, and told him that I wanted a party of volunteers to go with me, who should find good stores provided, and plenty of grog. The party was soon made up. Drummond collected his crew in his own way. We put two muskets and ammunition into our boat. He went to a small island westward, and I to a small bay, south of our anchoring place. As on the following night my life was in jeopardy from the boatswain it ought here to be mentioned that he was the only American besides myself in the expedition, and yet had a malicious spirit towards me. He was skillful in his office, vain of his ability and consequence, and had been much indulged by the Commodore. He was inclined to take great liberties in doing his duty, and had exceeded, or fallen short of my orders several times in following his own judgment. He seemed to be determined on obeying me no further than his humour led him.

This evil I felt myself bound to check, and made him do his work over again according to my orders. He said he had never been compelled to do his work twice over before, and murmured against my directions. I replied that while I was in command, I was responsible for the execution of my duty, and that my orders must be strictly obeyed in all instances, or I could not know on what to rely for the necessary results. Notwithstanding my reasonableness and my desire to conciliate him, he was my enemy.

This boatswain, with some of the most desperate fellows we had, was of my boat's crew. As it was not common for him to go in a boat on duty, I asked him how he came to be of the party. He said he had nothing to do till morning and wished to enjoy the sport with the rest of us. As it might be the means of reconciling him to me, the arrangement was not without its recommendations. Fear was not apt to sway my mind, nor in those days, to enter into it.

The bay which we sought was narrow at the entrance, but spread out much wider within, and extended about a third of a mile in depth. We landed at the head of it, except a boy who had come for a boat keeper. He was ordered to take the boat off a short distance, and to wait there till I should call him.

Thinking that possibly we might shoot a wild hog, I gave to the boatswain one of the muskets and spread the men round the bay. To the mouth of it I went myself, supposing that to be the best place for turtle. I watched there two or three hours and then walked round the beach to see what the people had done. I could find none of them; and when I called to the boy in the boat, he said he had not seen any of the party.

I waited two or three hours longer, took another walk in search, but saw no body. I searched a third time, and found no one. I made myself as easy as possible till day light, but none of the crew appeared. I walked the beach again, and discovered a path leading into the bushes, which I followed. In one of those grass plots made by burning of trees and shrubs, I found them all seated, apparently in consultation. They were surprised at my approach, and the actions of the boatswain, as well as his remarks, were particularly suspicious. When I interrogated them about their absence, they made out a story altogether unsatisfactory.

I told them to go to the boat, and that we must be immediately on board. I stood with my gun across my arm, and my thumb on the cock, till they all passed me, keeping my eye on the boatswain, who had his gun in the same position with mine. I made them go before, and we arrived at the beach. The boatswain ran a little distance as though he saw something to shoot at, and then laid down apparently to take aim. I watched him, keeping myself ready to fire at the first symptom of danger. I asked him sternly if he was turning fool, and manifested such a decision that at length he arose and I got them all into the boat, with the two muskets behind in my own power. We were soon safe on board, and it was a long time afterwards when I learned the true account of this conspiracy against me. The boatswain and the gunner quarrelled, and this brought out the proof that the boatswain had picked the crew for the purpose of going off to Luzon with the boat after they had landed me. But when I had stationed myself at the entrance of the bay, this plan was frustrated. He then collected the men while I was watching for turtle, and held a council on the grass plot, debating all night what they should do with me. They wished me out of the way, but believing me to be a good shot and a determined man, they did not expect easily to frighten me or to escape from the contents of my musket.

The boatswain said he had a musket as well as I, and could use it before I knew their designs. To this diabolical suggestion all agreed, except one man named Gibbs. Although he was a quarrelsome and desperate fellow, who had been trained as a sail maker, yet he refused to take my life in cold blood, and he succeeded in dividing their counsels till I burst upon them by surprise, and got them on board before their conspiracy was harmonized and ripe.

After all this was proved before a council of all the officers of both vessels, it was proposed to me to confine the boatswain and carry him as soon as convenient to some English port to be dealt with according to the law. But I knew his importance to the expedition, that he did not intend to take my life if he could have got away without it, and I interceded for him to be continued on duty in the ship under strict government, and never trusted with opportunities he could abuse to endanger the peace of any individual. The pride of magnanimity, the calculation of interest for the expedition, and other motives, may have mingled with my hope of his reformation and conciliation, to induce me to take the part I did. The council complied with my request, and after two or three of the forty were flogged, the matter was dropped.

We sailed for the Palau Islands May 18th, 1791, working round the north east side of Luzon till the 1st of June. The winds were light between east and south. On the 2nd, in latitude 15° 10' north, the wind hauled to the north east, and on the 5th, to the north and west, where we remained until we anchored under one of the islands, on the 10th.

Palau Islands; Abba Thulle, the King; Warfare; The People

THE NEXT DAY, June 11, our vessel was crowded with natives of both sexes and the water covered for forty or fifty yards round with canoes. They came on board with great eagerness and with as little fear or suspicion as a child would enter a parent's house. Interest, cordiality and happiness seemed to reign among all parties. It was delightful to witnesses such an expedition of benevolent emotions, and still more to partake in them with an active curiosity and lively sympathy.

Abba Thulle, their king, was a wise and benevolent leader. I often thought I could see more in his countenance than in that of any other man I ever knew. All who were acquainted with him were fully satisfied that he possessed the very first natural abilities.

As proof of his magnanimity, it should be stated that he always gave notice to an enemy at least three days before going to war with him. This was told to me by some of the chiefs among his enemies when I went out with a part of our own men to aid the king against them. They spoke well of him and said that Abba Thulle never lied. He was considered when he was young as the greatest warrior ever bred in the Palau Islands, and yet as eminent for his justice and humanity. His subjects were in general strongly attached to him; but some of them who lived in the distant islands were ungrateful and unwise enough to revolt from him.

As Captain Wilson had done before us, we joined the

king and went against the inhabitants of Artingall (*Artingal*), one of the islands under his dominion. The expedition for this purpose was fitted out the 21st of June, and was quite powerful. Some thousands of men were embarked. Two of our officers, the surgeon, a number of sailors, and a detachment of sepoys, were among them. I was assigned to the command of the launch with a crew of Europeans. We had a six pound brass cannon, several swivels, a chest of ammunition, and each man a musket.

The king, according to his usual generosity, had sent word to the people of Artingal, that we should be there in three days for war. Although I was a Christian, and was in the habit of supposing the Christians superior to these pagans in the principles of virtue and benevolence, yet I could not refrain from remonstrating against this conduct on the part of the king. I told him that Christian nations considered it as within the acknowledged system of lawful and honourable warfare to use stratagems against enemies, and to fall upon them whenever it was possible, and take them by surprise. He replied that war was horrid enough when pursued in the most open and magnanimous manner; and that although he thought very highly of the English, still their principles in this respect did not obtain his approbation, and he believed his own mode of warfare more politic as well as more just. He said that if he were to destroy his enemies when they were asleep, others would have good reason to retaliate the same base conduct upon his subjects, and thus multiply evils, where regular and open warfare might be the means of a speedy peace without barbarity. Should he subdue his rebellious subjects by stratagem and surprise, they would hate both him and his measures, and would never be faithful and happy, although they might fear his power, and unwillingly obey his laws. Sentiments of this elevated character excited

AN 18TH-CENTURY DEPICTION OF KING ABBA THULLE, WHICH ALSO
APPEARED IN DELANO'S ORIGINAL 1817 EDITION; LUDEE, A WIFE OF
ABBA THULLE. (FROM THE COLLECTIONS OF THE LIBRARY OF CONGRESS)

my admiration the more for this excellent pagan, and made
an impression upon my mind, which time will never efface.
Christians might learn of Abba Thulle a fair comment upon
the best principles of their own religion.

The king assembled all his force at Palau, and made all
the necessary preparation of provisions and arms. We moved
in the evening, pursued our course through the night, and on
the morning of the 22nd arrived off Artingal. The day was
fair and pleasant. The canoes formed three lines, front, centre,
and rear. The launch, with English colours flying, was in the
centre; the canoes pulled abreast in lines, with each a flag or
banner resembling ours as much as possible. With our spy-
glass we saw that the beach was covered with armed natives
for a quarter of a mile near to the town.

The king requested that a gun be fired, and a signal

made for some one to come off to us. We complied, and immediately we observed people go to a stone pier and enter a canoe which was paddled directly to our boat at the astonishing rate of eight or nine miles an hour. When they were within our lines, the king's canoe being made fast along side the launch, they drew up at about four yards' distance from us, and then, at the clapping of hands by the steersman, they all at once backed water with their paddles, and stopped as suddenly as if they had struck a rock. After this, they came along side the king's canoe, and we saw the chief, who sat distinguished from all the rest upon a seat in the centre. Their conduct upon this occasion attracted my attention and excited my admiration. With bold and fearless countenances, and with simple but determined manners, they looked round on all the instruments of death which we had brought with us, and preserved a uniform air of indifference and courage.

No signs of fear or doubt were betrayed by them, notwithstanding our expedition and various European arms must have appeared formidable. In addition to the articles already named, we had pistols, boarding lances, cutlasses, and a Chinese rocket which resembled our torpedoes. Although the rockets were not very destructive, they had an alarming appearance, and made a great parade of death to those who saw them approaching with smoke and fire, and threatening leaps upon the water.

The king said to the chief, "Are you ready to fight? Are you willing?"

The chief answered frankly, "We are not, but we will sooner fight than have any laws imposed upon us which we think unjust and disgraceful."

The king told him that we came prepared to give battle if they would not yield their rebellion, accept of pardon upon proper terms, and submit to the laws of their sovereign.

It was proposed to the chief that he should go on shore, confer with the people, and if they were resolved on war, a signal should be made for hostilities to commence; but if they were inclined to peace and reconciliation, word must be sent us, and we must be invited to go up to the pier. The proposal was accepted and they immediately started for the shore.

They made ready to put their canoes under way. According to custom, one man of the crew pronounces a kind of chant, and instantly they all flourish their paddles over their heads with a perfectly uniform motion, and with the greatest dexterity. The exercise is as regular as that of a military company, and much more difficult to perform. As our treble line of canoes approached Artingal that morning, this flourish of paddles by our crews was beautiful and impressive; but I thought that the rebels, who were now returning with their chief, executed it with still more grace and majesty. A strong interest for them was excited in my mind. Their open, candid, and admirable behavior secured my partiality and won my best hopes for their prosperity.

When the chief and his party arrived at the pier, they were met by the crowds on shore, and after a short consultation returned to us as before. They brought a message for the king and the fleet to come to the pier, and declared their readiness to enter into a negotiation. I was much delighted with this message. We were soon under way, drew up to the pier, and were received with every mark of respect. Refreshments were pressed upon us, and were as cordially received.

The terms which Abba Thulle proposed were that the people of Artingal should carry him from his canoe on a kind of litter to their place of state, and set him on the throne; that the two highest chiefs, who had been named kings of the two islands in rebellion, would bring him several valuable jewels which they held at that time, and which had descended from his ancestors; that they should acknowledge him to be their lawful sovereign, and promise never more to revolt on pain of death; that the under chiefs should prostrate themselves before him with their faces to the ground and make the same promise as the two first chiefs; and that they should exchange sixty women as hostages to secure the observance of peace. The king remarked that this exchange of women as hostages had generally been followed by a long period of tranquillity and good order.

When these terms were made known to the chiefs of Artingal, they seemed very unwilling to comply with them, and at first I thought they never would. They however took them into consideration.

At this time it was low water, and many hundred acres of the reef were bare. Abba Thulle gave his people liberty to go out upon the reef and collect shell fish. Crowds of Artingal men were also on the reef, and our people mingled with them in all directions, so that it was impossible to distinguish them from each other. This produced not a little anxiety in the minds of some of us who were not accustomed to such a mingling of enemies in a time of war. We remonstrated with the king against such unguarded conduct, but he said that it was the best way to forward the negotiation, that his own people were safe, and knew how to act, that they would become familiar with each other and remove animosity; and that the object was not to subdue the rebels merely, but to make them good subjects.

I now saw, from the actual experiment, the advantage of an open and generous policy, especially when united with such terms of submission on the part of the rebels as would leave no doubt of the king's power to conquer them by force if he chose. This naked savage had introduced such a spirit of confidence among the inhabitants of these islands, that treachery was never feared. We were left so unguarded that it appeared to me the men of Artingal might have taken us by surprise and have made us captives had they consented to violate the laws which rendered the suspension of hostilities sacred. The launch was aground and the natives might have come down opposite the pier with stones and spears and have got possession of her. But no symptoms of treachery appeared.

WE LAY AT THIS PLACE three days and nights during the negotiation, and were treated with every kind of hospitality. I was indeed many times uneasy, and thought the king's terms hard; but his reasonings were always good, and his policy effectual. What he had required was indeed a great deal for the people of Artingal to do, but he could not require less, and more would be inconsistent with the future contentment and obedience of the people. He said further, he should think that we were destitute of humanity and mere pretenders to the virtues of the heart, if we were not willing to protract the negotiation as long as there was a reasonable prospect of success. He assured us that those who now appeared so kind and friendly would fly to arms and fight desperately should we show that we were really haughty and vindictive, and seeking concessions beyond the justice of the case. He would not wantonly shed the blood of any of his fellow creatures, and much less of any of his subjects, although they might be in the wrong.

This policy at length succeeded; the people of both islands had agreed to all the articles which the king had proposed. The litter, which looked much like a bier to carry the dead, was brought. The pier of which I have spoken was about a quarter of a mile long, from twelve to fifteen feet wide at the top, and spreading out at the bottom, from fifteen to eighteen feet high, and was built solid with rocks. The king was taken out of his canoe by the arms of his returning subjects, set upon the litter and carried off the pier by eight men of Artingal, who lifted it to their shoulders. They enthroned him on a high seat made of wood and covered with mats. My fellow officer, the surgeon, and myself followed and stood by the throne. The two first chiefs approached, half bent, holding the jewels suspended by strings, and presented them to his majesty. He received them with dignity and grace and afterward bade them stand erect. He put such questions to them as he thought proper and they answered to his satisfaction. The under chiefs were then called, twenty-five in number. They also approached half bent, kneeled, brought their breasts to the ground and kissed the king's feet. He then bade them rise and questioned them as he had done the others.

After this ceremony was over, the women were brought according to the treaty. When they were collected, the king told each Englishman, if he saw any woman with whom he was pleased, he might take her. Next he said the same to his officers, who were denominated rupacks; and last he gave the same liberty to his common men, till the sixty were selected. I was curious to know whether any of the women would be unwilling to go with those by whom they were chosen, but I discovered in their countenances only cheerfulness and pleasure.

The articles of the treaty being settled, the people of both parties assembled round the square where the seat of the king was, and partook of the various refreshments, which the bounty of the island could supply. They amused themselves in dancing, and in different plays, for several hours, while the king was settling the details of the future conduct of this portion of his subjects. One rupack only was removed from his office in Artingal. When every thing was arranged to the satisfaction of the king, we re-embarked for Palau, and took the broken rupack and the sixty women with us.

This was not the first time that our people had gone out with Abba Thulle against the people of Artingal. The crew of the *Endeavor*, now with us, had been engaged in the same way while the *Panther* had gone to China. The officers told me that the men of Artingal had fought terribly hard and that no people were more brave. The inhabitants of Palau had taken several of them prisoners and had put them to death in a manner not agreeing with their general character for humanity. I cannot account for the degree of cruelty which on that occasion, was practiced by those who had so many good sentiments and real virtues in most of the departments of life.

The Palaus seemed to think themselves at liberty to disregard feelings of humanity toward prisoners, when they would treat an open enemy with magnanimity and justice. When they were asked why they were so barbarous toward their captives, and yet so generous and honourable toward the same persons as enemies, they answered that an enemy would meet them face to face, but captives would be plotting destruction under the appearance of contentment and good will. It is certainly inhuman beyond any apology or extenuation, to cut off the leg of a prisoner and beat his own face with it while he is yet living, although this is intended to be a mode of death, and not of protracted torment. The maxim handed down from their forefathers was that more is to be feared from one prisoner than from five open enemies. From the testimony of my predecessors at these islands, I am compelled to believe that the sentiments of Abba Thulle have not always had the same good influence over his subjects as they appeared to have when I was with them.

THE PALAU ISLANDS ABOUND with cocoa-nuts, sugar cane, sweet potatoes, yams, tarra (*taro*) root, bread fruit, limes and bananas. Wild fowls, the same as those we have about the barn door, a large kind of blue pigeon, and a bat of enormous size, called by the crew the flying fox, are found there in great numbers.[4]

They are supplied also with several kinds of fish, with sea-turtles, and with various species of oyster, among which is the pearl oyster in great abundance. There is one kind which has a shell each half of which is large enough to hold thirty gallons of water. Notwithstanding the size of the oyster, the meat is excellent. It is cut into pieces, and boiled, stewed, or fried. The utensils for cooking are made of clay, and are burnt in the same manner as our coarse pottery. The inhabitants wear no clothes, and drink only water, or the juice of the cocoa-nut and of the sugar cane without distillation.

Canoes for fishing, and houses of a small, unexpensive, but comfortable kind of shelter, complete their list of wants, all of which are easily supplied. Unhappily for the Palau islanders, they have lost much of their early simplicity and goodness, and have not yet gained the intelligence and virtue of a civilized people. They have mixed their native character and habits with those of the Europeans, and have not the excellencies or the enjoyments of either. When I saw them on our first visit, under Abba Thulle, they were far more interesting than they are at this writing.

In regard to their religion, I learned that they believe in one God, in the unlimited extent of his government, in the most important moral distinctions and religious duties as taught by the light of nature; in the immortality of the soul, and in future rewards and punishments. They have very few forms of religion, little ceremony in their worship, and no houses or temples devoted to this purpose. That their creed was not merely speculative, and that the want of houses of worship did not proceed from a disregard of God or his laws,

A Palau scene, showing dwellings and the place of council.
(From the collections of the Library of Congress)

may be inferred from the benevolence and humanity of their hearts, from the honesty and fidelity of their lives, and from the actual fruits of their principles in their mutual confidence and happiness. Had their virtues been as vigorous and permanent, after their intercourse with Europeans, as they were unaffected and genuine at the period of their discovery, and had they continued to be happy under an increase of relations and wants with the means of gratification, we might now acknowledge it to be our duty to study their history more minutely in order to arrive at the secret of their moral worth and social blessings. If our vices are more numerous than theirs, our virtues are not only more various, but are much stronger, better guarded, more fruitful, and more elevated.

There is one trait of character for which the Palaus were remarkable, their fidelity in the engagements of friendship. They carried their ideas of the sacredness of this virtue to a very great extent, and doubted whether it were proper to make a profession of it, in the first degree, to two persons at the same time. On our arrival, the king proposed to us that we should each choose a friend. We answered, that we intended to be the friends of them all, and hoped that they would all be our friends in return. This, however, did not meet the sentiments of the king. He spoke to us of the pleasure, the peace, and the mutual safety which would arise from the kind of confidence required by their laws of particular and inviolable friendship. We complied with his wishes, and the Commodore chose Abba Thulle, each of our officers chose a chief, and the crew made selections from among the people, according to their judgment or their caprice. For myself, it is my prayer always to find as faithful a friend as he was whom I chose at Palau, and never could I pray for a better. He was always watching for opportunities to do me service, anticipating my wants, and giving me information of every danger.

Should it be thought by any reader that the terms of friendship, as here described, must have rendered it mercenary, because the reciprocity led each of the parties to expect a reward for every office of kindness, I would answer that such an objection carried with it its own refutation. The very idea of a perfect reciprocity removes the motive of selfishness, and makes the good which results from united efforts, a social possession. But besides this, the fact deserves a place in my narrative, that when I was about to leave the Palau Islands for the last time, and forever, I found it difficult to persuade the friend whom I had chosen to accept of the presents which I had purchased for him during my absence, and which I knew were particularly agreeable to his taste. My fellow officers found the same disinterestedness in their intercourse with the individuals among the chiefs whom they had chosen for friends.

Marriage was esteemed among these natives as a relation of great importance and responsibility. It was solemnized in presence of the king, or of some chief, whom he had clothed with authority to make the contract binding. Previous to marriage, there seemed to be little restraint imposed upon the sexes by public sentiment, as it regards their conduct towards each other. It was considered an honour for any woman, married or unmarried, to be in a state of pregnancy, and if she were unmarried, it recommended her to a husband. After a marriage, however remarkable as it may seem to us, the women were eminently faithful to their vows.

IN 1806, I SAW TWO MEN at the Sandwich Islands (*Hawaii*) who had been at Palau about the year 1804. I had known them for many years and had confidence in their information. One told me that many revolutions had happened among the inhabitants of the islands since I visited them; that there had been six or eight kings since the death of Abba Thulle; and that the stock which we had carried there was generally doing very well. The sheep, however, had been nearly destroyed. He neither saw nor heard anything of the nutmeg or clove which McClure had taken so much pains to introduce and cultivate. I had a renewed testimony from my two acquaintances that the fire arms and ammunition which we had left with the Palaus had done them incalculable injury. They had divided into parties, and were frequently at war with each other. They were still friendly to the white people, but had lost the spirit of confidence among themselves, and were the victims of alternate stupidity and the violence of contest. It makes me melancholy whenever I think of the unhappy alteration in the character and conduct of this people since they became acquainted with the Europeans. It is a wise provision of nature, that savages should be limited to few and simple weapons of warfare till they have acquired the habits, and have entered into the pursuits, of civilized society, by which their passions shall be checked and regulated. This system of things ought not to be violated by us, as it is when we give them our instruments of mutual destruction, without giving them at the same time the arts, the institutions, and the employments which are necessary to render the instruments a safe possession, and to convert them into the means of lawful defence and supply.

Departure from Palau; New Guinea and Adjacent Islands; Animals and Birds; Passage to Buru and Ceram, Islands in the Moluccas; Attack; To Timor

CHAPTER IV

O N THE 27TH of June, 1791, we took our departure for New Guinea. The winds were from the south and west quarter, and while we continued our course southward, they were light, and interrupted with calms till the 15th of July when we found ourselves on the equator, and in sight of St. Stephen's Island. The northern extreme of this is in latitude 0° 32' south, and in longitude 136° 58' east.

On one of the many islands on our passage we saw a small river which afforded good water, and which was convenient for us to take in wood. We were, however, visited by a gang of natives from New Guinea, or from some of the large islands in the neighborhood, who appeared hostile in their manners. While the last two boats were taking in wood and water, the Commodore made a signal for his men to come on board, and was observed at the same time to be getting under way with the two vessels.

I happened to be the officer on shore with the boats, and immediately sent off one of them which was laden with wood. The other was taking in water up the river. After loading her with water in bulk, we attempted to go out of the river over a bar, where there was something of a swell. The boat hit bottom, and was overturned. The muskets and the ammunition which we had in her were thoroughly wet, and could do us no service if we were attacked.

The natives watched us the whole time we were at work on shore, and now drew near with signs of hostility. They brandished their spears, made motions preparatory to throwing them at us, strung their bows, presented their arrows, and stood a moment to observe the effect of this, and to ascertain what advantage they might expect from our condition. I looked toward the vessels, and saw them going from us quite fast. For the first time I felt a sensation of danger from natives. I fortunately drew the inference from their delay in making the attack, that they did not know the effect of water upon the use of fire arms and powder. We instantly applied the hint to practice, caught up our cartouch boxes, buckled them on though full of water, fixed our bayonets, and shouldered our dripping muskets.

With this parade of courage and defence, we gained time to get the boat upright and off the bar, and steered for our vessels. The natives followed us in their canoes, came within forty or fifty yards of us, and were constantly on the watch for a moment when we should be off our guard, or under some new embarrassment, of which they could take advantage. We arrived safe on board, with an armed and ferocious band of savages pressing close upon our rear and thirsting for our blood.

We knew from the journals of several English Indiamen that the natives in this region were hostile to all white people. The natives of New Guinea and of the adjacent islands are negroes,[5] or woolly headed, and are well known to hate white people so much as to reward an individual by making him a chief when he will bring them a white man's head. If he will bring three, they will make him a chief of the first rank. The causes of this hatred are, in a great measure, traceable to our own misconduct toward them.

When Europeans first visited New Guinea, the natives manifested no spirit of enmity. But the Europeans seized and carried them away as slaves, in a most treacherous manner. It was common for them to hook the yard tackles of a ship to a canoe, hoist her on deck with all the crew in her, transport them and sell them for slaves. The natives have heard also of the cruelties practised toward the inhabitants of other islands, and even of the enormities committed by white people against each other. It is not therefore a matter of surprise that the natives should encourage and transmit this hatred toward Europeans. The white people have too often, and to their everlasting disgrace, used their arts and force, as members of civilized society, to betray, to kidnap, or to seize openly and violently, the natives for the most selfish and inhuman purposes. Happy will it be, when the time shall arrive, that we ourselves furnish no longer the chief obstacles to the civilization and moral improvement of the natives, according to the laws and religion of christian countries.

NEW GUINEA, ON THE SOUTHEAST, is often called Papua. There is an immense body of land, stretching many degrees south and east, and seeming to be thickly peopled. From the little intercourse which we had with the natives, we had reason to suppose that the country was furnished with many of the comforts of life. There were hogs, barn door fowls, many kinds of quadrupeds, and innumerable birds with beautiful plumage. We purchased of the natives four kinds of the bird of paradise;[6] and I have been told since, that there are in New Guinea four other kinds. One of the species is entirely white, but very rare.

Another species is sixteen inches long, and is partly sea green, and partly a steel blue. The crested kind is sometimes eighteen inches; and there is said to be a species, in the islands of the Indian Ocean, twenty-eight inches.

We also purchased of the natives two species of the lory, a great many of which are found in New Guinea. They belong to the family of parrots, have a great variety of the richest colours, are extremely beautiful, and are unrivalled in the power of imitating articulate sounds. They are nine or ten inches long; climb up by the bill; erect their feathers when angry; feed upon nuts, acorns, and seeds; and live to a great age.

We saw a species of the crested pheasant, a handsome, proud and courageous bird. The cassowary also abounded there. This is a very large bird, sometimes measuring seven feet from the bill to the toes, of which it has three, like the ostrich of South America.[7] I have known a cassowary to weigh sixty or seventy pounds. The fore part of the breast is without feathers; the thighs and legs have scales; the wings are remarkably small; the feathers are thinly scattered, and terminate in bristles, giving a very unfinished and strange appearance to this bird. It is strong, runs with great speed, and devours any thing without apparent preference in its taste. When pursued by a dog over small loose stones, it will throw them backward with so much force as often to prevent the continuance of the chase. The ultimate mode of defence adopted by the cassowary is worthy of notice. The bird throws itself upon its back; with its large strong leg and hard foot strikes a dog, or even a man, with prodigious force; and has been known to break a limb of the assailant by a blow. Caution and skill are requisite to gain the victory without a material injury.

The feathers worn on the heads of the natives satisfied us that the ostrich was to be found on the island. Pigeons were there in the greatest abundance. We were often within gun-shot of immense flocks. We killed many of them, and admired their various and beautiful plumage. We shot also a number of a species of the duck, which is probably the same with the Chinese duck, having a pendent crest, and a great diversity of handsome colours.

At New Guinea we again saw multitudes of those bats which we had seen at the Palau Islands, and which have been already mentioned under the name of the flying fox. I have since learned that this animal is also called the flying macauco and that it is not considered by all persons as a bat. Its wings are not absolutely naked like those of the bat, but bear some resemblance to those of the flying squirrel. It has the colour of the red fox, is as large, and bites with great severity and courage, when it is wounded. I have seen the air darkened with these macaucos as they flew over our vessel when we were lying in the straits. The islands abound with gold dust, grains of gold as large as shot; with pearls; and with the long nutmeg. We saw none of the oval nutmeg and clove, but have no reason to doubt that they grow there in plenty.

The sago tree, a species of the palm, particularly attracted my attention. Its trunk is from fifteen to twenty-five feet high, and is very thick. The branches are short, and the leaves are enormous, measuring from three to six feet. The fruit is shaped like a plum, is of a reddish yellow, and contains a brown nut whose meat tastes like a chestnut. The trunk of the tree is filled with a pith as white as snow, and the wood about it is not more than two inches in thickness. When the natives make sago, a species of starch, from it, they fell the tree, cut it into lengths of six feet, split them, put the pith into troughs with water, work it with sticks till it is soft and easily molded into any shape, pour it into holes made in wood about the size of our bricks, and dry it hard. We purchased twenty-five hogsheads of it from the natives, as a substitute for bread, paying not more than twenty-five dollars for it in trinkets. We found it very palatable and nourishing when made into puddings, or porridge, seasoned with spice. When sago is prepared for the European or American market, it is reduced to grains by being passed through a copper, or tin riddle, and dried in the sun. The wood of this tree is tough and elastic, and is used by the natives for bows and other weapons of war.

THERE WAS A SMALL SETTLEMENT OF MALAYS on the south east side of the western entrance of the straits, called Savage Town. They cultivated rice, yams, and sweet potatoes in small quantities. This was the only place on the island where we ventured to land. And even here we should not have taken the hazard of doing it had it not been that while we were lying off before the town, two or three of the Malays came on board with some articles for sale. We inquired of them if there was any danger to prevent us from going ashore. Having Malays with us, we could converse with them very well. They said that they did not wish us to land. So many disputes had arisen between white people and the natives concerning their women that they were afraid similar difficulties would occur, and our crew would then be treated with great barbarity.

We pledged ourselves that no improprieties of this nature, or of any other, should be committed by us, and satisfied them that our objects were those only of gaining information and gratifying a laudable curiosity. The Malays returned from the ship, the coast appeared to be clear of New Guineans, and we determined to hazard a landing. The surgeon, a lieutenant, and myself, with half a dozen men, went on shore. The women immediately left their houses, taking their children with them, and ran into the woods.

We walked into the village, were treated civilly by the

MALAY PROWS AND CANOES.
(FROM THE COLLECTIONS OF THE LIBRARY OF CONGRESS)

men, and were conducted into their habitations. These were built upon piles six or eight feet above the ground, and were thus raised, not only to be in part removed from the damps of the low ground where they lived, but to avoid the intrusion of reptiles.

The houses were one story and handsomely constructed. The materials used for covering them was bamboo split, and the roofs were thatched with the leaves of the cocoa-nut tree, the sago tree, or other leaves found on the island in great variety.

These Malays had not been long in Savage Town. They had come from Ceram to New Guinea, had been attacked, as they told us, several times by the natives, and still lived in some degree of fear. Their object in making an exchange of islands was the increase of their trade. The Malay prows (*small sailing vessels*) visited them from Ceram and the other islands, and bought of them gold dust, pearls, birds of paradise, and many other articles. They were not prompt to expose any thing for sale to us, from a suspicion, as we thought, that we would be unjust, and perhaps violent, using the force of our armed vessels against their town if we should find any occasion for a quarrel. The Europeans and others have not conducted themselves with sufficient integrity and disinterestedness to remove all apology for this suspicion.

The largest pork I ever saw was brought us at this island. It was of the wild hog, the hair burnt off, and the skin made as black as a hat. The meat was fat, but sweet. We also purchased a great plenty of good fish. The soil was good, as far as we could judge from the produce. Much of the land lies low and must be frequently inundated. The climate cannot be very safe for Europeans, although the natives were healthy, robust and numerous.

Their transportation of all heavy articles is done by canoes which can pass under the houses. The piles are driven about six feet into the bottom, and are ten feet above it. The mode of driving them is ingenious for savages without the mechanical advantages of civilized life. A canoe, loaded with stones of the amount of two or three tons, is lashed to the pile, one on each side at high water, and as the tide ebbs, a heavy stick of timber is made to fall successively upon the top of it, which, acting with the immense weight of the canoes, forces the pile into the ground rapidly. The few windows which are necessary in so warm a climate are made of the inner transparent part of the pearl oyster shell, as in China. I have seen a town on this coast, thus built, covering more than a mile square.

The New Guineans have some iron tools, which they have procured of the Malays. But they still use some which are made of oyster shells, and some of flint. They have an extremely ingenious mode of lashing a short piece of wood to the end of a long one for a handle, at an acute angle with it on the inside, and then fasten the shell or the flint to the short piece, like an adz, with which they work very well. They grind the flint to a perfect edge with other stones.

While we were at anchor, we obtained plenty of good wood at a small island. We dug more than a dozen wells, ten or twelve feet deep, and got brackish water, which from the colour of the clay where it was found, was as white as milk. On most parts of the coast, it is very difficult to procure water because of the dangers from the natives. For a month, the thermometer stood between 80° and 83°.

We put to sea on the 9th of September from the southwest cape of Revenge Straits. On the 19th we anchored in Cajeli Bay in the island of Buru, latitude 3° 23' south, longitude 127° 27' east. The fort saluted us with seventeen guns. The resident chief came on board, and we gave him an English national salute.

This settlement belongs to the Dutch East India Company. They keep a garrison of twenty-five Europeans here, and a great number of Malays. Their business is to cut down and destroy the nutmeg and clove tree; to collect black, white, yellow, red, and still other kinds of ebony, for the European market; and to prepare various sorts of beautiful wood besides for cabinet work. A part of the cargoes of two ships in a season usually consists of these varieties of valuable wood. The chief told me that he had destroyed more than thirty thousand nutmeg trees that season, and a vast number of the clove. The islands of Ambon and Banda are the only two of the Spice Islands (*the Moluccas*) on which the Dutch cultivate nutmegs and cloves. These fruits are destroyed by an order from the government in all the others.

Cattle, deer, serpents, and crocodiles in the rivers, are found in abundance in Buru. Deer were sent to us gratis, and we were allowed to hunt them at pleasure. The Malays drove them by us, a thousand in a herd, and we shot as many as we wished. Among the species we saw were multitudes of those which are spotted with white upon a red brown, and which are very handsome. They are a little smaller than the common deer, but leap remarkably well.

The serpents of Buru are most remarkable. The Resident, or Governor, told us that some of them had swallowed a buffalo, a story which we should hardly have believed, notwithstanding the reasons he gave us to obtain our confidence, were it not that so many testimonies to the same effect are multiplied among men of information and veracity. The boa is known to be often about forty feet long, and is said, in books, as I am told, to be much more.

The climate is good, the air pure, the soil rich, and the productions various. The Resident was extremely attentive to us, supplied all our wants without solicitation, and was in every respect a model of hospitality. When we arrived in Canton afterwards, we procured a handsome silver urn with an inscription upon it, testifying our sense of his kindness and worth, which we sent to him by a Dutch supercargo.

LEARNING THAT WE SHOULD BE well treated at Amboyna (*Ambon*), we got underway the 24th of September to visit that island. Commodore McClure was particularly desirous to go there, in consequence of the notoriety which it had obtained for the massacre of the English by the Dutch, and because no English vessel had been to the island, as it was reported, for more than seventy years.

When we arrived on the 28th, we anchored off Fort Victoria, and saluted the castle with nine guns, which were immediately returned. We received friendly and polite treatment, and found Ambon a truly agreeable residence. A general invitation to dine with the governor was given us soon after our arrival.

We became acquainted here with Dr. Hoffman, an eminent chemist and botanist. He was professionally employed in extracting volatile oils from the principal trees and plants of Ambon — the nutmeg, clove, cinnamon, culibaban, cajuput, and many others. His laboratory was large and convenient, built of brick, and contained a row of copper stills which were all heated by one fire. The distilled oils, accompanied by water, were received into white China pots. The oils, of different beautiful colours, appeared at the top, and made a fine show in the numerous white vessels. We bought a considerable quantity, particularly of the culibaban and the cajuput, which we sold for a good profit at Bencoolen (*Bengkulu, Sumatra*).

The nutmeg tree grows from twenty to thirty feet high, is from nine to fifteen feet in diameter at the lower part of the trunk, and the first limbs are eight to ten feet from the ground. The top of the tree is a regular cone. The common or female nutmeg is oval, and is covered by a husk which is cured, and is the mace of commerce. The husk grows round the fruit in a spiral form. The shell, containing the nut, which is loose in it, is not thicker than that of a hen's egg. The shell must be kept on the fruit in order to have it cured. Without this, it will always spoil. We made trials of it while we were at New Guinea. All the green nutmegs which were brought to us, we lost by taking off the shell. We learned afterwards to keep the shell on, to throw them into lime water, and dry them till they would rattle. Then we could break the shell, and not lose the fruit. The long, or male, nutmeg has a different husk from the other, which makes an excellent pickle. The husk, mace, nut, and shell, afford very good preserves.

The clove resembles the red cherry tree, is not quite as

large or as high as the nutmeg, and grows without the same regularity. The fruit grows in what is called the mother of the clove, which opens at the proper season, and the cloves are shaken out upon a sheet spread under the tree. The mother of clove is sometimes used for a preserve.

The inhabitants of Ambon have attended much to the cultivation of their gardens. They have introduced almost all the varieties of beans, peas, potatoes, turnips, beets, carrots, and other vegetables. The sugar cane grows abundantly in all the eastern island. The people do fine work in silver and gold, and are eminent in cabinet manufacture. Many of the Chinese are among them, and are noted for their industry and ingenuity.

THE FASHIONABLE PHRASE FOR calling a party together at this island is to *smoke a pipe.* They meet at six o'clock in the evening. The gentlemen take a room by themselves till ten, smoking and drinking gin and beer, which are both from Holland. They are then joined by their wives and daughters, and have a hot supper, served up in an elegant style. Their furniture is various and handsome. I have often seen three beautiful chandeliers, white, blue, and red, hanging in a line in one room, over a table, and giving a splendid effect upon the china, the glass and the plate. The evenings are sometimes spent in dancing, and the first people always have a band of music of their own. The slaves, who are chiefly Malays, with a few negroes from New Guinea, are taught to play admirably well on various instruments.

We were invited to smoke a pipe every evening we were there. In return we gave a ball, to which we invited all the best class of people. The entertainment was sumptuous, and the party in excellent spirits. The ladies particularly seemed to enjoy the evening with their whole hearts. So great was the exhilaration on their part, and so entirely did we give our own minds and efforts to the objects of the occasion, that we found ourselves in some danger of producing a counteraction in the spirits of the Dutch gentlemen. My fellow officers were intelligent and agreeable men; their manners were easy, simple, and cordial; they were fond of society, and capable of enjoying it to a very high degree.

The ladies flattered us by saying that we had contrived to make our party more delightful than any which they formed themselves for the season. They jocularly asked us why we could not stay with them at Ambon, or take them with us to England. Our answer was of course prompt and courteous, that we were at their command, and should be delighted to have them for companions on shore, or in our wanderings upon the ocean. They would make us forget, with their songs and their smiles, the anger of the storm and the roar of the billows. Many remarks followed; much successful repartee was interchanged; arrangements for the execution of the project were pleasantly detailed; allusion was made to the amusements of the English metropolis, and the interest of a tour for the ladies of Ambon through the towns and villages of Britain. This led to a comparison between the advantages of society in Ambon and in England; and we discovered that the ladies had spoken of the latter in terms too flattering for the peace of our Dutch friends. They remembered the hostility which had been transmitted between the English and the Dutch in consequence of their old controversy in the island, and actually took the whim into their heads that we had laid a plan to carry off some of the ladies at the close of the party, not only for our own gratification, but by way of revenge for the former massacre of the English.

While we labored to return the courtesy we received, and to praise the place where we were, still we discovered great uneasiness in the remarks of the Ambon gentlemen, which the ladies appeared to be quite willing, for the sake of variety and frolic, to excite, rather than to allay. At last we became a little alarmed ourselves, and by a happy effort, which all seemed of understand without consultation, we succeeded in turning the attention and sympathies of the whole party to other subjects and new modes of amusement, and in restoring a safer kind of mirth.

WE HAD ORDERS TO SEARCH FOR a strait through the southern part of the island of New Guinea, according to the suggestion which had been made by Captain Cook. We therefore sailed for the island again the 10th of October, and made the coast on the 15th in latitude 2° 21' south. We anchored in six fathoms water off against a large village, built upon piles, according to the common custom of all the islands which the Malays have visited, and over which they have had an influence.

The 26th was a day of adventures. Our object was to go up what has ever since been called McClure's Inlet.[8] I had the morning watch, and asked White, the second lieutenant, to assist me in taking the bearings of the land. A small breeze springing up from the northwest, the Commodore ordered the vessels to be got under way. At eight the anchors were stowed, and we sailed eastward up the bay, along the side of a sand bank on the north shore, which lies full a mile from the land. This bank is dry at low water. As we began to heave at the capstan, we saw several canoes filled with natives coming round a point westward of us at a distance of four or five miles. We discovered with the glass that there were three large canoes with about thirty men in each, and eight small ones with each about ten men.

They came to the bank, near to which we had been lying at anchor, and there got out of their canoes and hauled them over the shoal. They approached us with flags of various colours flying, red, white, and blue, which were of different forms, and fancifully disposed. They made signs of friendship, waving a white cloth, and pouring water upon their heads with their hands. This is a universal practice, and one of great significance among the eastern islands. Treachery is peculiarly base when it is preceded by this token of peace and confidence. We answered all their signals of friendship and showed ourselves ready for a harmonious and pacific intercourse. They dropped down across our stern, and pulled up for the *Panther*, the *Endeavor* being just ahead. The canoes came very near to us, and the people held up birds of paradise in their hands, and wore them on their heads.

Dr. Nicholson, who was on the quarter deck, prepared to get into the long boat, which was towed astern, for the purpose of trade. When the motion was made to haul the boat up, the natives appeared to be a little alarmed, and some of them bent their bows to shoot their arrows. But as soon as they saw the doctor get into the boat, with signs of good will, they resumed their attitude of peace. He held some calico in his hand which he gave them, and the Commodore threw a piece of white cloth to him to be given to them also. This was done to inspire them with confidence in us, as we thought that they might thus be prevented from committing any act of hostility, and save bloodshed for both parties.

One of the canoes was holding fast to the stern of the long boat, and a native manifested a desire that the doctor should enter it. He imprudently complied, and two of the natives conducted him to the middle of the canoe where he sat down, while several of them stood round him, one dancing, and all exulting. This excited a little suspicion in my mind relative to their designs. A large canoe came near to the long boat, and one of the natives jumped into her. The boat keeper, a favourite Dane with the crew, was standing on the bow, and the native walked up to him, put his arms about his neck, and tried to throw him overboard. But the Dane with one hand held on to the rope which was made fast to the vessel, and with the other drew a jack-knife out of this pocket, opened it with his teeth, and was struggling to get an opportunity to use it, when the native suddenly slid into the water to avoid the danger, and laid hold of the side of the boat for support.

Our men were generally below at breakfast, but I was standing on the arm chest upon the quarter deck, anxiously observing these transactions.

We always kept two wall-pieces mounted on the tafferel, which the Commodore had ordered to be cleaned and loaded, after the canoes came in sight. They had however been poorly cleaned, and one only was loaded, and slightly lashed by the breech. While I was unlashing it with as little motion as possible so as not to excite suspicion, I received an arrow in my breast which was shot with such force, that although it hit directly upon the bone, it stuck fast. I immediately drew it out with my hand, and looked for vengeance upon these false savages from the grape shot and balls with which I knew the wall-piece was loaded. The natives were only twenty yards distant, but in attempting to fire among them, the powder flashed in the pan without effect, and to my great disappointment and vexation, I had only shown my disposition to hostility, and had killed nobody. A cloud of arrows flew at every part of our vessel, at the men in the tops, at those going up, and at all who were upon deck. The sails and the rigging bristled with weapons of the natives.

Our people immediately mustered from below, and with the muskets in the tops and on deck, opened a brisk fire upon the canoes, while the *Endeavor* luffed from under our bow, and brought her broadside to bear directly against them. This they could not stand, and very quickly dropped astern. Before we began the fight on our part, we saw the negroes shoot several arrows into Nicholson, and hew him down with a large instrument like a butcher's cleaver. He must have expired almost instantly. We continued our fire upon the canoes, with good execution, till we drifted too far to reach them.

During this unexpected and totally irregular action, where every man did what he thought proper, the boatswain, whose conduct heretofore has been mentioned to his disgrace, was as active, brave and useful as any man in the crew. He was prompt to get into service the six pound brass piece on the forecastle, and assisted me constantly and ably in loading and discharging her against the enemy. Had the wind and tide permitted, we should have pursued the savages and cut them all off. But as it was, we have good reason to suppose that we killed forty or fifty of them, besides ruining a number of their canoes, and destroying the out-riggers of several others. It is remarkable that they wounded but four of us, notwithstanding they were expert in the use of the bow and arrow. The cause of this must have been the confusion into which they were thrown by our fire arms, and by the unexpected manner in which we met their treachery. They had previously, in other parts of the island, brought arrow heads to sell to us, and probably thought that we should fight them with weapons similar to their own. I cannot otherwise account for their miserable conduct in the close of this affair, when they commenced it so artfully and bravely.

Our wounds were dressed, order was restored, and we were ready to proceed on our survey at half past eleven the same morning. We had a consultation on the subject of trying to get the body of Nicholson, but it was unanimously

The *Thames*, an English East Indiaman, or ship of the East India Company. (From the collections of the Library of Congress)

thought to be inexpedient to make the attempt.

During the action, the quartermaster at helm received an arrow in his hip which could not be immediately extracted, and which was too long to allow him to continue his duty with it in that state. I broke it off, leaving a fragment of six inches in him, and he stayed at the helm till the engagement was ended. The fragment was then pushed forward, till the point and barbs appeared on the other side of the hip, and was drawn out with pliers. Much true courage and fortitude were exhibited by the quartermaster.

A circumstance of a quite different kind happened while we were fighting, which forced a little mirth upon the boatswain and myself in the midst of our danger. We had made the gun at the forecastle so hot by continually firing her, that she broke all the breeching which we could supply.

The cartridges were too large, but we could not then stop to make them less. With one very heavy charge, she flew backward into a large pen of pigs on deck, broke the legs of two or three, set the whole sty squealing in a tremendous concert, and quite drowned the cries of the women, a considerable number of whom were on board, and who had been shrieking in the cabin over the murder of poor Nicholson. The noises and some of the associations of the scene before us were so completely ludicrous, that we were obliged to relieve our sides by joining, though with laughter, in the common roar.

The arrows of the New Guineans are about four feet long, and half an inch in diameter. The shaft is a reed, and the head is of wood, bone, or stone. The sago tree is most generally used, when the head is of wood; but the shin bone furnished the greatest number. Many of these were offered to us in trade. The bone is put into the hollow end of the reed, is closely lashed with cord, and then glued. A single arrow will often have from fifteen to twenty barbs, each of which may be an inch in length.

The town near which we had the battle covered a mile square, and was the largest we had seen. The population may be estimated at twenty or thirty thousand. It was at this place that the *Queen Indiaman* lost three boats at once with all the crews, cut off by the natives. She was on this coast making her eastern passage to China, and was in great want of water. The people, when they discovered this town, appear not to have known or suspected how savage the New Guineans are. The second and third officers were sent with two boats on shore. But they saw so many proofs of hostility among the natives, that they thought it proper to return without water to the ship. The chief officer made some severe remarks upon this conduct and said he would go himself and get water. The command was of course given to him by the captain. The second officer requested that he might be of the party, and three boats were fitted out with the three mates and more than twenty men. When they landed at the town, the natives told them that there was fresh water a little distance from the shore. Most of the party went in pursuit of it, and the savages sought a favourable opportunity and massacred all but two of them. One was a lad whom they treated with no great cruelty. The other was a man whose hands they tied behind him and fastened him to a stake driven into the ground so that he could not stand upon his feet. They kept him in this position till morning, and afterwards liberated him with the privilege of life. He and the boy were sold to the Malays, who came from Ceram. They were carried on board an English India-man, and satisfactory payment was made for them to the Malays. One or both of them arrived in England.

WE CONTINUED OUR COURSE EASTWARD till the 3rd of November, exploring the bay till we found it so narrow as scarcely to leave us room to turn our vessels around. Although this was not the place where we were ordered to seek a strait through New Guinea, yet we hoped to find one. The bay was filled with shoals, and we could not advance without sending boats to sound the channels. At length the bay narrowed to a river, and the water was deep enough for a ship of any size. After we entered the river we had natives about us constantly. We plainly perceived that they only waited for a good oppor-tunity to take some advantage of us. On account of their sav-age disposition, we called this Cut-throat Creek. We went nearly to its source and found that our vessels could go no fur-ther. We stopped and made an attempt to get a supply of wa-ter, of which we were very much in want. The natives told us that we could procure it by going up a small stream, where only a boat could pass.

The Commodore said we must have water at all events, if possible. The natives were as thick as bees about us, and crowded our decks. Hearing the Commodore's declaration, we looked at each other with great significance, waiting to learn on whom the order to go out for water was to fall. At length White was selected, a man not more than twenty-two years of age, although we used to call him old White. I could plainly see his colour fade, and his features fall. I confess that I felt myself relieved when the command of this excursion was given to another. The launch was manned with eight Europeans, and White set off, with a chief and two of the natives for guides to show him the watering place. About forty canoes, full of natives, followed them up the creek. I felt that I should never see old White again. We kept hostages however on board from among the savages to secure his safe return.

White told us later that when he was out of sight, the chief pulled a large kind of knife out of his basket, drew the edge of it across his own throat, counted his fingers, and pointed to his neck, to show how many heads he had cut off with his knife, and then he rubbed it across White's throat to prove how convenient the instrument was for the purpose of beheading a man. With amusements of this nature, they passed the time in search of water. At the head of the creek, the natives took White a third of a mile into the woods and there showed him a very small spring where he might fill a joint of bamboo, which would hold a gallon. In this scanty measure, it must be carried to the boat, and then taken to the vessel. The project of obtaining it in this manner was of course given up.

White, after all this variety of intercourse with the chief and the natives, returned to us as pale as a shirt. And indeed his danger was great, notwithstanding the hostages whom we had kept on board. These might have thrown themselves into the water, as they sometimes have done, and taken the risk of getting ashore. Commodore McClure was too easy, not to say careless a man, to take the precautions which I should think necessary to secure them by chains.

The natives continued round us all night. Those who were on board were ordered to quit the vessels. We heard them paddling softly along the shore till near morning. We were lying under a high land which hung almost over the vessels. On this hill they kindled about a dozen fires from which they might have thrown brands on board. Fearing this, we began to discharge our muskets at them, and soon drove them away. We heard several screams and I suppose that we wounded and killed some of them.

We had much difficulty to prevent our vessels from getting aground here. The flats were extensive and muddy. We had to use warps from the shore, while at anchor, and when moving, we had to keep boats ahead to tow us. This put us on the watch constantly. The whole navigation of Cutthroat Creek was filled with alarms and sufferings.

In this vicinity, some natives brought us an abundance of the long nutmeg and a small quantity of gold dust. We were not in a situation to pay much attention to the productions of the soil. We left the river and sailed down the gulf more towards its south side than we did when going up. We saw White Island and steered for Fresh-water Bay, described by Dampier. His description of the bay is so excellent that we found it without the least difficulty. Indeed we have never discovered any thing but truth in Dampier's accounts. He made difficult things plain, and simple things useful.[9]

The anchoring place in the bay was in latitude 2° 56' south, and longitude 132° 25' east. The watering place was north 34° west, half a mile distant. There we procured plenty of wood as well as water. There were no natives about the place, and the shores are easy of access.

The 17th of November we moved slowly south and east, and satisfied ourselves that there was no strait through New Guinea at the place where we were directed to seek for one; so we altered our course and endeavoured to go north and west, but the winds blew into this deep bay from that quarter, and made it necessary for us to go further from land.

The natives on every part of the coast of New Guinea we visited were negroes, hostile and treacherous. The only persons whom we saw who were not of this description were the Malays of Savage Town. In Cut-throat Creek, the alligators were so numerous that I have seen twenty of them at once, some lying on the shore, some in the edge of the water, and some swimming in the river. They were of various lengths, the largest about twelve feet. They seemed to be indifferent to us except when we shot at them, as we often did, and then I have seen them jump their whole length clear of the ground, always toward the water. Their mouths are extremely large; they can run fast in a straight line, but turn with difficulty; and they appeared to us to be stupid. There are immense numbers of snakes on the island, and black scorpions which are the most venomous.

The articles brought here for trade should consist of all kinds of coarse cutlery, calico, India cottons, beads, small looking glasses, tin ware, crockery of different colours, and all sorts of trinkets. Every thing should be coarse and cheap, and the colours should be gay. In return the trader may receive gold dust, pearls, turtle shells, mother of pearl, sago, birds of paradise, nutmegs, honey, bees-wax, the edible birds nests, sandal wood, various kinds of beautiful wood for cabinet furniture, and a great abundance of the beach-le-mar, a kind of slug found everywhere on the shores of these islands and which the Asiatic epicures consider as a great luxury. A ship in this trade must be well armed, and a good sailer in order to keep clear of the Dutch settlements.

It is not advisable to work against the monsoon much at any time. Not regarding this, we were twice very near to a loss of our vessels on this coast. The first instance was after we had passed Revenge Straits. We stretched out westward the 9th and 10th of September while the south east monsoon, in which direction we were bound, was blowing strong. We were kept at close haul in the wind, and obliged to carry such a press of sail that we could do little else than attend to the vessel and the sails. We were not sufficiently faithful to the lead and the line, and we did not keep a good look-out. Suddenly we came on a shoal as we were standing off from land and were considering ourselves, on that account, as safe. This obliged us to come to anchor without having time to take in our sails. We rode there till we could ride no longer; got our anchor, I can hardly tell how, ran back from the shoal, fell to leeward in a chain of small islands, and among sand banks, and had as much as we could do to get clear.

The second instance was when we were working north and west out of the last gulf we explored. The wind continued strong from the north west and compelled us to make long boards or tacks off shore at night. We were outside a long sand-bank, within which we had passed when we pursued our course south. On the 20th, at two o'clock in the morning, as we were making our board on shore, having been sounding in twenty-two fathoms water, and on muddy bottom for some time, we suddenly found the water at nine fathoms on sand. The officer who had the watch on deck, stepped into the cabin to inform the Commodore, who had fortunately heard the quartermaster sing the soundings. He sprang from his bed, put his head out of the quarter gallery window, and called to the man at the wheel to hard to weather the helm, and wear ship. The helm was instantly put to the weather; the ship wore in only four fathoms water, and the breakers were within fifty yards of us. We concluded we should never be able to make the passage in the north west monsoon, which would last as long on this coast as the north east monsoon blows in the China Sea, till the 1st of May.

WE LEFT THE COAST OF NEW GUINEA in latitude 5° 40' south, and longitude 137° 52' east. Crossing over to the coast of Australia and passing westward of Endeavor Straits, we never had less than twelve, nor more than forty fathoms water. The bottom was generally muddy. We were apprehensive that we should not be able to go to the west of the gulf of Carpentaria, a gulf much dreaded by seamen because the wind makes so strong a draught inward, and it is so difficult to get out. But the wind favored us some, and the current did not set to the leeward much. We got the advantage of the coast of Australia and the winds then were south and east, which had blown strong from the north west at New Guinea.

The natives whom we saw on the coast appeared to be naked, were tall and stout, but we could not obtain an interview with them. We showed them cloth and other articles at a distance, and made signs of friendship, but they were timid, and ran from their houses, taking the coverings with them, which were mats, or basket work. I presume that all the north side of that coast is peopled, and have no doubt that the lands are generally rich and fertile, judging from what we could see. The wood is abundant.

When we landed at Timor we found the same generous hospitality which Lieutenant Bligh and Captain Edwards did. The latter had not been gone long when we arrived. We were met at our landing by a number of the best people of the town who conducted us to the governor's house, a house never yet occupied, and which had been built at the public expense for Governor Vanjon, which he very politely offered to us for a residence during our stay in the island. We gratefully accepted the offer, and found the house spacious, surrounded by a handsome yard and high trees growing in a square on each side of it. Some of these trees had been transplanted when they were nearly a foot in diameter.

Commodore McClure made it his custom to take a house for the convenience of himself and his officers in every port he visited, when he expected to spend any length of time. As he considered me the most acquainted with commercial affairs and the details of business, and having no regular purser on board, I was commissioned to purchase whatever was wanted for both vessels. This duty I performed, after we left Macau, till I quit the service. He was satisfied with my conduct, and thus gave me a greater opportunity to be on shore than any other officer in the expedition enjoyed. The Dutch ladies and gentlemen called me Mr. Secretary, a title which they usually conferred on the purser of a ship.

In every Dutch place which we visited, we were treated with the same unreserved hospitality that we had experienced at Buru and Ambon. As we had been pretty severely tried in various dangers and hardships at New Guinea and the other islands, we considered ourselves as the fourth set of Englishmen who had arrived at Timor in want and distress. The Dutch said that they believed all our vessels which were unfortunate paid them a visit. Lieutenant Bligh, after the mutiny against him in the *Bounty* by Fletcher Christian, was the first. The second was a boat's crew, which had sailed from Botany Bay, and traversed more than three thousand miles of ocean in an open boat, on a very dangerous coast. The third was Captain Edwards who lost the *Pandora*, and who found the boat and crew from Botany Bay on his arrival.

When all the circumstances of the boat and its crew from Botany Bay are considered, they will be thought as wonderful as those of Bligh or Edwards. According to Barrington's history, a man named Bryant with his wife and two children, taking with him seven other convicts, escaped from New South Wales on the night of the 28th of March 1791, in a boat. The master of a Dutch snow furnished them with a chart and compass, and with these they hoped to reach Timor, as they actually did, but after many sufferings. When they landed on the island, they represented that they had been cast away on a reef southeast of it, and that all the ship's crew had perished except those in the boat. Bryant called himself captain, and said that his name was Martin. The only officer saved besides himself was the boatswain. The Dutch gave full credit to their story and advanced money for their use, taking bills drawn on the English government. Bryant lived at more expense, it seems, and with less care, than his situation and story required. In a period of irritation, and as some say of intoxication, the boatswain, in order to get revenge upon the captain for some insult, disclosed the whole history of their escape. The Dutch immediately confined them all in close jail. This confinement commenced not many days before Edwards arrived with his boats. They were delivered to him, and he carried them to England for trial.

I have since understood that Bryant, the boatswain, and most of the other convicts were transported again to Botany Bay, and that some of them were executed. The woman, having but six months of her exile to serve from the time of her escape, and having suffered very severely in the voyage in the boat, was allowed to stay in England, and complete the term of service there. All the boats but one, in which these different parties of distressed persons came to Timor, were left there as a curiosity, and we saw them.

At Timor, the soil is rich, of a dark colour of a bituminous appearance, and is productive. The climate is excellent like that of Trinidad in the West Indies, the one being nearly in the same latitude south in which the other is north. The air is good, and the thermometer stands at 85°, seldom varying more than four or five degrees from this point. It affords the necessaries of life in great abundance, rice, wheat, Indian corn, garden roots and vegetables, and all the tropical fruits. Cattle, buffaloes, deer, goats, horses, hogs, sheep and several kinds of poultry are in plenty on the island.

There are many kinds of valuable wood for cabinet furniture, and among them is the sandal wood of a very excellent quality. There is a great quantity of bees-wax, and of honey which has the most agreeable aromatic flavor. It is far more delicious than any honey in our country. The bees are so numerous that they have been said sometimes to take possession of a vessel near the shore, swarming up the rigging and making the crew leave the deck. Their sting is more venomous than that of the bees with us. Fish of a fine flavor are found about the island. On the beach immense quantities of ambergris are found. It was confidently asserted that masses of this had been picked up weighing eighty or ninety pounds. I have since read a history of ambergris which asserts that a piece was thrown ashore on the island of Tidore weighing 182 pounds and measuring 5' 2" in length.

There are various opinions concerning the origin of this singular substance, but that to which I have been led by my own observation, and which seems to be most generally adopted in modern books, is that it is generated in the bowels of the spermaceti whale. Whether it be the effect, or the cause of disease, I know not, but I have seen a considerable number of whales opened and never found ambergris in those which appeared to be healthy.

THE FORT AT COUPANG (*KUPANG*) which is designed to protect it, could not hold out long against two or three frigates. A beautiful river runs through the town, coming down from the country, and passing over picturesque falls. A short distance from the mouth of the river is one of these falls, where we used to resort in the afternoon to bathe. The parties on these occasions were very pleasant. Ladies and gentlemen were collected; male and female servants prepared the tea, the smoking apparatus, bottles and glasses, and the bathing clothes; and thus we all set out for the place of the bath, while some of the servants played on instruments of music, and others sang. They were Malays, and played and sang extremely well. The walk was usually half to three-quarters of a mile. The bank of the river was covered with beautiful rows of fragrant trees, under which small houses were placed to afford convenient shelter for throwing off, or putting on clothes.

The Dutch people wore a Malay garment into the bath, and we adopted the same style. This garment is a sort of petticoat which comes up as high as the arms, but always leaves them free. The ladies, as well as the gentlemen, tie them below the arms, although they make them so as to cover the bosom. Some of these bathing robes were extremely fine and beautiful. When prepared, the ladies and gentlemen go into the stream together, sitting, or standing with their backs to the current, and letting the water, in its natural course, rush over their heads, or flow around them. A place between two rocks, with a stone in front against which to support the feet, was a favorite spot where one might sit securely and enjoy the current without being disturbed by it. Half an hour, or three quarters, we often spent in the water in this manner. After dressing in the small house, the company assembled at tables which were spread under the trees, with a charming prospect before them.

The river was twenty yards wide; the water foamed over the rocks with a most graceful motion in some places, and with a sublime violence in others; and below, it spread itself out like a calm and transparent lake reflecting delicious scenery from its bosom. In such a climate, nothing could be more delightful. The tables were furnished with fruits and liquors of exquisite flavor.

But we paid too dearly for this pleasure of fresh water bathing. We took it so frequently, and stayed in the stream so long, that we brought on intermittent fevers, and several of our officers died. All would have died, had we not left off this indulgence. Europeans must be always cautious how they bathe in fresh water in hot countries.[10]

Besides this amusement of bathing, we had parties for dancing, and often to smoke a pipe, as at Ambon. Adrian Van Este, who was governor of the island when Bligh was there, was now dead; but his widow was living, and paid us the most flattering attentions. Among other civilities, she sent her band of music, which was remarkably fine, to serenade us every morning at the earliest dawn. The musicians took their stand under the large trees about our house, and while they gave the sweetest tones to the ear, they also furnished a charming scene to the eye, as the day advanced, and showed their handsome liveries amidst the green foliage.

(*To account for these luxurious receptions, Delano offers the following explanation.*) It must be remembered that the expedition of Commodore McClure was a public enterprise, under the direction of the English government; that it possessed a general interest, especially for the inhabitants of all the eastern islands, who were pleased to have the attention of the world called to their importance, and thus to enlarge their intercourse; that the officers of the expedition were capable of appreciating hospitality and of increasing the pleasure of those who bestowed it; and that the manners and temper of McClure himself were remarkably adapted to conciliate affection, and invite confidence, wherever he went.

The natives of Timor are Malays, whose origin is not clearly ascertained, but who are scattered over an immense portion of the islands and coasts of the east. They are Mahometans. They had a rajah or prince at their head who resided seven or eight miles from Kupang, to whom the Dutch paid but little regard. We had some curiosity to see him, and made him a visit. We carried a number of presents with us of small value, which he graciously received. He returned our visit, and brought with him as a compliment to our Commodore a young male buffalo which had been recently taken, and was perfectly wild. The Malays led and governed him by a number of their strongest vines which were fastened above his horns, and which were held by different parties of eight or ten, both before and behind. In this manner they kept him from attacking them, although he was exceedingly restive under their management. After he was led into a yard, his head was brought close to the trunk of a tree, and there confined. Our people made a bowline knot, or noose, in the end of a rope, threw it down by his feet, and pricked him till he stepped into it. But the force and activity of his legs were so great, that he kicked himself loose from the rope fifty times in succession, and we almost despaired of gaining the victory over his heels. And when at length we succeeded in making the noose fast upon his legs, and drew them behind him so as to force him to lie flat upon his side, yet the moment a man approached with a knife to cut his throat, as the present was designed for the table, he made such efforts with his wild unconquerable strength, that it required considerable courage to give him his death wound, with the deliberation necessary to prevent a repetition of the stroke and cruel continuance of the pain by mangling his neck. He had the most vigorous muscle, untameable spirit, and made the most obstinate resistance of any animal I ever saw. Indeed I confess that his native courage, his wild proud spirit, his scorn of his numerous foes and their arts, his persevering reliance upon his own strength, and the fear he inspired even when he was subdued, surrounded him with such associations of magnanimity and fortitude under unjust sufferings, that I found myself more interested in him than in any of the human forms in the circle, and instinctively gave him for the moment a higher rank. Our pride on such an occasion receives but a poor homage from art, which is offered at the expense of natural strength and courage, when so many men are required to vanquish a single champion from the forest.

If the wildness of nature, and the boldness of courage in a savage state, excite our admiration, the blessings and enjoyments of civilized life, when these animals are tamed, will interest our benevolence. The buffalo may be perfectly domesticated, and is then eminently useful to society, while he is equally happy for himself under the kind treatment of a good master, in all the variety of employments to which oxen and cows are appropriated. Two of the males are considered as strong as four horses in the labors of the cart or plough; while the females furnish families with milk, butter, and cheese for their tables. The beef also is nourishing and good, though not of so high a flavor as that of the ox.

*Personal Encounters Touching the Mutiny on
the Ship* Bounty; *The Fate of the Mutineers;
The Settlement on Pitcairn Island;
Captain Mayhew Folger Tells of his Discovery
of the Lost Colony; Other Accounts*

CHAPTER V

I HAVE NOW arrived at a point in my narrative where it is more proper for me, than at any other place, to introduce a subject which has excited much interest in the public mind, and which is calculated to afford many valuable reflections upon human character. This subject is the singular family which has been discovered on Pitcairn Island, and which sprung from the mutineers of the English ship *Bounty* and the Otaheitan (*Tahitian*) women whom they carried with them.

The reason which I have for interweaving this story with my narrative will I trust be thought sufficient. At Timor I found in the possession of Governor Vanjon, a manuscript history of the cruise of the *Pandora*, written by Captain Edwards himself, who was sent out by the English government in search of the *Bounty* and the mutineers. This manuscript I copied, and shall present the substance of it to the reader.[11]

I have also lived a considerable time with Captain Folger, the first person who visited the family upon Pitcairn Island, and from whom most of the information concerning the state of it has been derived. He very often conversed with me upon this subject, and gave me a number of details which have not been before printed. The most interesting facts, recorded in other books, will be summarized in this chapter, and to these some additions will be made from the information which it has been in my power to obtain.

It is well known that Lieutenant William Bligh was selected by the English government in 1787 to command an expedition to Otaheite (*Tahiti, in the Society Islands*) to obtain the bread-fruit tree for the West Indies. His commission was dated the 16th of August. The vessel purchased and fitted out for this object was named the *Bounty*, with a reference to the nature of the enterprise. A very convenient arrangement was made in it for a garden of pots with the bread-fruit plants. The crew consisted of forty-six persons, of whom twenty-one were officers, twenty-three were seamen, and two were gardeners.

The *Bounty* sailed from Spithead on Sunday the 23rd of December, 1787. She attempted first to make her passage by the way of Cape Horn, and was in sight of Tierra del Fuego March 11th, 1788. But in consequence of the difficulty of the navigation in this course, Lieutenant Bligh determined, with advice, to go by the way of the Cape of Good Hope, and changed his direction accordingly. He stayed thirty-eight days in False Bay, and sailed again the 1st of July. He discovered, the 19th of September, a cluster of small rocky islands in latitude 47° 44' south and in longitude, 179° 7' east, thirteen in number, and a hundred and forty-five leagues east of the Traps, which are near to the south end of New Zealand. These he named after the ship, the Bounty Isles. The 25th of October, at six in the evening, he saw Tahiti. At anchor, a great number of canoes came immediately around him. The natives inquired if the people in the ship were "tyos," friends, and if they were from "Pretanie," Britain, or from Lima. As soon as they were satisfied, they crowded the decks of the *Bounty*, without regarding the efforts which were made to prevent them.

Lieutenant Bligh stayed at Tahiti twenty-three weeks. During this time, he and his crew became intimately acquainted with the natives, and were treated with the greatest hospitality. They interchanged civilities in the ship and on shore, and lived in the exercise of mutual good will. No appearances of discontent on the part of the crew were discovered. At some time indeed three seamen deserted, but they surrendered themselves afterwards, and were received. The 6th of February, 1789, all the bread-fruit plants, amounting to 1015, were taken on board in a healthy state. Besides these, the *Bounty* had a number of other plants.

The 4th of April Lieut. Bligh stood out to sea from Toahroah harbour, having visited several islands in the course of the month, then steered westward to go south of Tofoa, and gave orders for this direction to be followed during the night. The master had the first watch, the gunner the middle watch, and Mr. Christian the morning watch. Thus far the voyage had been peaceful and prosperous. After this the scene changed.

The following is part of an account given of the mutiny by Lieutenant Bligh himself.[12] "Tuesday, the 28th of April 1789, just before sun rising, while I was yet asleep, Mr. Christian, with the master at arms, gunner's mate, and Thomas Burkitt, seaman, came into my cabin, and seizing me, tied my hands with a cord behind my back, threatening me with instant death if I spoke or made the least noise. I however called as loud as I could in hopes of assistance; but they had already secured the officers, who were not of their party, by placing sentinels at their doors. There were three men at my cabin door, besides the four within. Christian had only a cutlass in his hand; the others had muskets and bayonets. I was hauled out of bed, and forced on deck in my shirt, suffering great pain from the tightness from which they had tied my hands. I demanded the reason of such violence, but received no other answer than abuse for not holding my tongue. The master, the gunner, the surgeon, Mr. Elphinston, master's mate, and Nelson, were kept confined below; and the fore hatchway was guarded by sentinels. The boatswain and carpenter, and also the clerk, Mr. Samuel, were allowed to come upon deck, where they saw me standing abaft the mizenmast with my hands tied behind my back, under a guard, with Christian at their head. The boatswain was ordered to hoist the launch out, with a threat, if he did not do it instantly, 'to take care of himself.'

"When the boat was out, Mr. Haywood and Mr. Hallet, two of the midshipmen, and Mr. Samuel, were ordered into it. I demanded what their intention was in giving this order, and endeavored to persuade the people near me not to persist in such acts of violence; but it was to no effect. 'Hold your tongue, Sir, or you are dead this instant,' was constantly repeated to me.

"The master by this time had sent to request that he might come on deck, which was permitted; but he was soon ordered back again to his cabin.

"I continued my endeavors to turn the tide of affairs, when Christian changed the cutlass, which he had in his hand, for a bayonet that was brought to him, and holding me with a strong grip by the cord that tied my hands, he with many oaths threatened to kill me immediately, if I would not be quiet. The villains round me had their pieces cocked, and bayonets fixed. Particular people were called on to go into the boat, and were hurried over the side; whence I concluded that with these people I was to be set adrift. I therefore made another effort to bring about a change, but with no other effect than to be threatened with having my brains blown out.

"The boatswain and seamen, who were to go in the

boat, were allowed to collect twine, canvass, lines, sails, cordage, an eight and twenty gallon cask of water, and Mr. Samuel got a hundred and fifty pounds of bread, with a small quantity of rum and wine, also a quadrant and compass; but he was forbidden on pain of death to touch either map, ephemeris, book of astronomical observations, sextant, time keeper, or any of my surveys or drawings.

"The mutineers having forced those of the seamen, whom they meant to get rid of, into the boat, Christian directed a dram to be served to each of his own crew. I then unhappily saw that nothing could be done to effect the recovery of the ship. There was no one to assist me, and every endeavor on my part was answered with threats of death.

"The officers were next called upon deck, and forced over the side into the boat, whilst I was kept apart from any one, abaft the mizen-mast, Christian, armed with a bayonet, holding me by the bandage that secured my hands. The guard round me had their pieces cocked, but on my daring the ungrateful wretches to fire, they uncocked them.

"Isaac Martin, one of the guards over me, I saw, had an inclination to assist me, and as he fed me with shaddock, my lips being quite parched, we explained our wishes to each other by our looks; but this being observed, Martin was removed from me. He then attempted to leave the ship, for which purpose he got into the boat; but with many threats they obliged him to return.

"The armourer, Joseph Coleman, and two of the carpenters, McIntosh and Norman, were also kept contrary to their inclination; and they begged of me, after I was astern in the boat, to remember that they declared they had no hand in the transaction. Michael Byrne, I am told, likewise wanted to leave the ship.

"It is of no moment for me to recount my endeavors to

bring back the offenders to a sense of their duty. All I could do was by speaking to them in general, but it was to no purpose, for I was kept securely bound, and no one except the guard suffered to come near me.

"To Mr. Samuel I am indebted for securing my journals and commission, with some material ship papers. Without these I had nothing to certify what I had done, and my honour and character might have been suspected, without my possessing a proper document to have defended them. All this he did with great resolution, though guarded and strictly watched. He attempted to save the time keeper and a box with my surveys, drawings and remarks for fifteen years past, which were numerous, when he was hurried away with 'Damn your eyes, you are well off to get what you have.'

"It appeared to me that Christian was sometime in doubt whether he should keep the carpenter, or his mates: at length he determined on the latter, and the carpenter was ordered into the boat. He was permitted, but not without some opposition, to take his tool chest.

"Much altercation took place among the mutinous crew during the whole business. Some swore, 'I'll be damned if he does not find his way home, if he gets any thing with him,' meaning me. And when the carpenter's chest was carried away, 'Damn my eyes, he will have a vessel built in a month.' While others laughed at the helpless situation of the boat, being very deep, and so little room for those who were with her. As for Christian, he seemed as if meditating destruction on himself and every one else.

"I asked for arms, but they laughed at me, and said I was well acquainted with the people among whom I was going, and therefore did not want them. Four cutlasses however were thrown into the boat after we were veered astern.

"The officers and men being in the boat, they only

waited for me, of which the master at arms informed Christian; who then said, 'Come, captain Bligh, your officers and men are now in the boat, and you must go with them. If you attempt to make the least resistance, you will instantly be put to death:' and without ceremony, with a tribe of armed ruffians about me, I was forced over the side, where they untied my hands. A few pieces of pork were thrown to us, and some clothes, also the cutlasses I have already mentioned; and it was then that the armourer and carpenters called out to me to remember that they had no hand in the transaction. After having undergone a great deal of ridicule, and been kept some time to make sport for these unfeeling wretches, we were at length cast adrift in the open ocean.

"I had with me in the boat 18 men. There remained on board the *Bounty* 25 hands, the most able men of the ship's company.

"Having little or no wind, we rowed pretty fast toward Tofoa, which bore north east about ten leagues from us. While the ship was in sight, she steered to the west north west, but I considered this only as a feint; for when we were sent away, 'Huzza for Otaheite' was frequently heard among the mutineers.

"Christian, the chief of mutineers, is of a respectable family in the north of England. This was the third voyage he had made with me; and as I found it necessary to keep my ship's company at three watches, I had given him an order to take charge of the third, his abilities being thoroughly equal to the task.

"Haywood is also of a respectable family in the north of England, and a young man of abilities, as well as Christian. These two had been objects of my particular regard and attention, and I had taken great pains to instruct them, having entertained hopes that as professional men they would have be-

A MODEL OF A KETCH, *ELIZA*, BUILT IN SALEM, MASSACHUSETTS,
IN 1794 BY ENOS BRIGGS FOR ELIAS HASKET DERBY.
(COURTESY OF THE PEABODY ESSEX MUSEUM)

come a credit to their country.

"It will very naturally be asked, what could be the reason for such a revolt; in answer to which I can only conjecture that the mutineers had flattered themselves with the hopes of a more happy life among the Tahitians than they could possibly enjoy in England, and this joined to some female connections most probably occasioned the whole transaction.

"The women at Tahiti are handsome, mild and cheerful in their manners and conversation, possessed of great sensibility, and have sufficient delicacy to make them admired and beloved. The chiefs were so much attached to our people, that they rather encouraged their stay among them than otherwise, and even made them promise of large possessions. Under these, and many other attendant circumstances, equally desirable, it is now perhaps not so much to be wondered at, though scarcely possible to have been foreseen, that a set of sailors, most of them void of connections, would be led away; especially when in addition to such strong inducements they imagined it in their power to fix themselves in the midst of plenty, on one of the finest islands in the world, where they need not labour, and where the allurements of dissipation are beyond any thing that can be conceived."

Such is the account which Lieut. Bligh has given of this mutiny. The boat into which so many persons were forced was twenty-three feet long, six feet and nine inches wide, and two feet nine inches deep. In this they passed many islands, ran along the coast of New Holland (*Australia*), and on the 14th of June, forty-seven days from the mutiny, landed at Timor. Their sufferings and dangers were extreme.

"Our bodies were nothing but skin and bones, our limbs were full of sores, and we were clothed in rags. In this condition, with the tears of joy and gratitude flowing down our cheeks, the people of Timor beheld us with a mixture of horror, surprise, and pity.

"The governor, Mr. William Adrian Van Este, notwithstanding extreme ill health, became so anxious about us, that I saw him before the appointed time. He received me with great affection, and gave me the fullest proofs that he was possessed of every feeling of a humane and good man."

From Timor, Lieut. Bligh went to Jakarta, and from thence he sailed to England, where he landed at Portsmouth, the 14th of March, 1790. Out of the nineteen who were forced into the launch, twelve survived the hardships of the voyage and revisited their native country.

THE 7TH OF NOVEMBER THE SAME YEAR, Capt. Edward Edwards sailed from England on the ship *Pandora* to search for the *Bounty* and the mutineers. He went round Cape Horn to Tahiti where he arrived the 23rd March, 1791, having touched at Teneriffe and Rio de Janeiro. (*The substance of Capt. Edward's account is taken by Delano from the* Quarterly Review, *July 1815.*)

"After we entered Matavia bay at Tahiti, Joseph Coleman, one of the mutineers, and several natives came on board. In the course of the day, Peter Haywood, George Stewart, and Richard Skinner, also of the *Bounty's* crew, came on board. From them we learned that the *Bounty* had been twice at Tahiti since she had been in possession of the pirates; that she sailed from thence on the 21st of September, 1790, with Fletcher Christian and eight other crew members, including Alexander Smith and Isaac Martin, and several male and female natives of the island; that Joseph Coleman, Thomas McIntosh, Charles Norman, Michael Byrne, and twelve others were left at Tahiti by their own desire; and that some of them had sailed from Matavia bay on the very morning before our arrival for Papara, a distant part of the island where some other of the pirates lived. They went in a schooner which they had built for themselves. In consequence of this intelligence, we sent two boats in pursuit of them the same evening, but the pirates saw the boats, and put to sea immediately in their schooner. The boats chased her, but the wind blowing fresh, she outsailed them, and they returned to the ship. The schooner had very little water or provisions on board, and could not continue long at sea. Persons were employed to look out for her and give information, should she return to the island.

"The 25th of March, Michael Byrne came on board the *Pandora* and delivered himself up. In the morning of the 27th, intelligence was received that the schooner had returned to Papara, and the pirates were gone into the mountains to conceal and defend themselves. Mr. Corner, the second lieutenant, was sent in the launch with twenty-six men to take them; and Mr. Hayward, the third lieutenant, was sent in the pinnace with a party to join the launch. In the evening of the 28th the launch brought to the ship James Morrison, Charles Norman, and Thomas Ellison, three of the pirates taken at Papara. The schooner was captured the 1st of April. On the 7th, Corner and Hayward marched with a party round the island on the opposite side from Papara and succeeded in taking all the pirates. They had left the mountains and were near the shore when they were discovered. They surrendered themselves on being commanded to lay down their arms.

"It was reported to us that Charles Churchill, *Bounty* master at arms, had been killed by Matthew Thompson, able seaman, several months previous to our arrival, and that Thompson was afterwards killed by the natives, and offered as a sacrifice for the murder of Churchill, whom they had made a chief.

"We learned that Christian, after he had turned Lieu-

tenant Bligh adrift, went with the *Bounty* to the island Too-
bouai (*Tubuai, one of the Austral Islands*), and intended to settle
there. But being in want of many things necessary for this
purpose, he returned to Tahiti to procure them. He told the
natives that Lieutenant Bligh was left at an island, which he
had discovered, and where he designed to make a settlement.
The natives believed the story and gave a supply of every
thing which they had — hogs, goats, bread fruit trees, other
plants, and various seeds. Christian then returned to Tubuai,
taking with him several women. He and his companions had
nearly finished a fort at this place, when they agreed to abandon it because of quarrels among themselves, and wars with
the natives which they had brought on by their depredations.
They determined by a majority of votes to go to Tahiti, and
there leave as many as desired it. Accordingly, sixteen men
were left, while the others went away with the ship. Most of
their spare masts, yards, and booms were lost at Tubuai. The
small arms, powder, canvass, and stores were divided equally
among them all.

"The only intelligence which we could obtain after this
period was that the *Bounty* was seen to the north west on the
morning after she sailed; that Christian had been heard to say
that he would seek an uninhabited island in which there was
no harbour for ships; and that he would run the *Bounty* ashore,
break her up, and get from her whatever would be useful to
him in his intended settlement. Provided as he was with live
stock, plants and seeds, and having women with his men, this
plan was highly probable.

"The pirate schooner was equipped as a tender; two
petty officers and seven of our men were put on board her. We
visited most of the islands in the neighborhood and proceeded
to Whylootacke and Palmerston. On the latter we found a
yard marked 'Bounty's driver yard.' We could not however

discover the track of the *Bounty* or her people. In searching for information around this island, we lost a midshipman and four seamen in a cutter. We supposed the yard had drifted hither from Tubuai.

"Hilbrant, one of our prisoners, told us that Christian had declared to him he would go to an island near to Danger Island and, if he found it suited to his purpose, he would stay there. In consequence of this, we visited that island, and some others in the neighborhood, but found no traces of the ship or the mutineers.

"The 23rd of June, we lost sight of the tender off the island of Oahtooah, and never saw her again. After cruising two days about this place, we made the best of our way to Rotterdam, one of the Friendly Islands (*Tonga Islands*). We had agreed in case of separation to rendezvous there. We visited Navigator's Islands, saw several not delineated in any chart, and returned to Rotterdam. We sailed thence the 2nd of August with the intention to go to England by the Endeavour Straits. On the 25th, we fell in with a reef and with islands which we supposed were connected with it on the east side of New South Wales (*which then included Queensland*). Along this reef[13] we sailed south to the east, searching for an opening in it, which we found on the morning of the 28th. We sent an officer in a boat to examine the opening, and were informed by signal that it had water enough to permit the ship to run through. Signal was made for the boat to come on board, but it was night before she reached us, and we lost sight of her.

"By discharging guns and burning fires we made known our situations to each other. About half past seven in the evening we got soundings in fifty fathoms water. At the same moment, the boat was seen close to our stern. We thought the water was discoloured, and hauled our tacks on board; but before the sails could be trimmed, and just as the boat got along side, the ship struck upon the reef. We hoisted out the boats to carry off an anchor, but before this could be accomplished, the ship made so much water that it became necessary to employ every body at the pumps and in bailing. We had more than eight feet of water in the hold. Soon after this the ship beat over the reef. We let go an anchor, and brought her up in fifteen fathoms. The water gained upon us only in a small degree, and we flattered ourselves for some time, that by the assistance of a thrummed topsail, which we were preparing, and intended to haul under the ship's bottom, we should be able to free her from water.

"This flattering hope did not continue long. As she settled in the water, the leak increased so fast that there was reason to apprehend she would sink before daylight. But with great exertion at the pumps and in bailing, we put off this event till we saw the sun rise, and had an opportunity to ascertain our situation and its danger.

"We kept our boats astern, and put into them a small quantity of provisions and other necessary articles. We made rafts, and unlashed the booms and every thing else upon deck. At half past six, the hold was full; water was between decks; it washed in at the upper deck ports; we began to leap overboard and take to the boats; but all could not get out of her before she actually sank. The boats continued astern, in the direction of the tide from the ship, and picked up the people who had laid hold of rafts and other floating articles which had been cast loose for this purpose. We loaded two of the boats with people and sent them to an island about four miles distant. Boats were immediately dispatched again to look about the wreck and the reef for those who were missing, but returned without finding an individual.

"Being mustered, we found that eighty-nine of the

ship's company, and ten of the pirates who were prisoners on board, were saved; and that thirty-one of the ship's company, with four of the pirates, were lost.[14]

"We hauled up the boats to fit them for our intended run to Timor; we took an account of provisions and other articles saved, and spread them out to dry. We put ourselves on the following allowance: three ounces of bread, which was occasionally reduced to two; half an ounce of portable soup; half an ounce of essence of malt; one glass of wine; and two glasses of water. The soup and malt were not issued till after we left the island.

"In the afternoon of the 30th, we sent a boat to the wreck to see if any thing could be procured. She returned with the head of the top gallant mast, a little of the top gallant rigging, and part of the lightening chain, but without a single article of provision. A boat was sent to fish, but returned with the loss of a grapnel, and without a fish.

"The boats were completed and launched the 31st; we put every thing we had saved on board; and at half after ten in the forenoon we embarked. The island, or key, that we left was only thirty-two yards across at high water, and a little more than double the distance in length. It produced not a tree, nor a shrub or a blade of grass. It had no water, and the only useful article which we procured there was a few shell fish.

"We steered north west by west. We soon discovered that the water in two of our largest vessels was so bad as to be rejected even by people in our situation, and that we had not twenty gallons fit to be drunk. We saw land the 1st of September, probably New South Wales, and sent the yawl ashore. Water was found, and two kegs were filled. We ran into a bay of what Lieutenant Bligh calls Mountainous Island, and there saw Indians on the beach. They waded off to us, we made them small presents, and gave them to understand that we wanted water. They filled a vessel for us and returned to fill it again. They made signs for us to land, but we declined. Just as a native was stepping from the shore to bring us a second vessel of water, an arrow was shot at us, and stuck in the quarter of the boat. We fired a volley of muskets, and they fled. We had previously seen that they were collecting bows and arrows, and were upon our guard.

"We afterwards landed at what we named Plum Island, from a species of plum we found upon it; but we obtained there no water. We steered our course in the evening for the Prince of Wales Islands, and at 11 o'clock at night came to a grapnel in the sound near one of them. The next morning we landed, and by digging, found good water. We filled all our vessels, and two canvass bags besides, which we had made for this purpose. But with all this, we had only a gallon of water for each man. We sent our kettles on shore, made tea and portable soup, picked a few oysters off the rocks, and had the best meal we had made since the day before the wreck.

"The 2nd of September, we saw the northern extremity of New South Wales (*Queensland*), which forms the south side of Endeavour Straits. From this we took our departure and sailed westward. The allowance of bread, three ounces, the people could not eat, because of excessive heat and thirst. Indeed we suffered more from those two causes than from hunger. The 13th of September, at 7 o'clock in the morning, we saw Timor. Land was never beheld with greater pleasure. We gave him, who first discovered the island, two glasses of water, and to the others one. The yawl and the launch hauled in for the land, and we were soon separated from them. Thinking we saw the mouth of a river, we stood for it; a party swam ashore in search of water; but the supposed river was only the tide of the sea amid islets of mangrove trees. We saw fires on a beach to the south and west; two of our people swam ashore but saw no person, and found no water. We continued our run, and at half past six in the morning of the 14th, we heard a cock crow. We went on shore, found good water, bought some fish of a party of Indians, were joined by the launch, rowed out to a clear reef, and then stood to the west till we entered the straits of Semau in the afternoon of the 15th. On the 16th, we hailed the fort at Kupang, and informed the people who we were. A boat was sent for us. Lieutenant Hayward and myself landed, and were received by Governor Vanjon with his characteristic humanity and courtesy. Refreshments were immediately prepared for us; the people ordered to land, and provisions supplied; and all dined at the Governor's own house. He gave orders for us afterwards to be received on board the *Bamberg*, a ship of the Dutch East India Company, to be carried to Jakarta."

Such is the substance of the account of Captain Edwards given in a brief way in the *Quarterly Review* for July 1815, in the article "Porter's Cruise," where it is also added that of the ten prisoners who were taken to England for trial before a court martial, six were condemned to suffer death, and four were acquitted. Those condemned were Haywood, Morrison, Ellison, Burkitt, Millward, and Muspratt. "To the two first of these his Majesty's royal mercy was extended at the earnest recommendation of the court, and the last was respited, and afterwards pardoned." Those acquitted were Norman, Coleman, McIntosh, and Byrne.

AFTER MENTIONING CHRISTIAN'S DEPARTURE from Tahiti, as it has already been given in the account by Edwards, the *Quarterly Review* proceeds as follows: "From this period, no information respecting Christian or his companions reached England for twenty years; when about the beginning of the year 1809, Sir Sidney Smith, then commander in chief on the Brazil station, transmitted to the Admiralty a paper which he had received from Lieutenant Fitzmaurice, purporting to be an extract from the log book of Captain Folger, of the American ship *Topaz*, and dated Valparaíso 10th of October, 1808.

"About the commencement of the present year (*1815*), Rear Admiral Hotham, when cruising off New London, received a letter addressed to the Lords of the Admiralty, of which the following is a copy, together with the azimuth compass to which it refers."

March 1st, 1813

"My Lords,

"The remarkable circumstance which took place on my last voyage to the Pacific Ocean, will, I trust, plead my apology for addressing your lordships at this time. In February, 1808, I touched at Pitcairn's Island, in latitude 25° 5' south, longitude 130° west from Greenwich. My principal object was to procure seal skins for the China market; and from the account given of the island in Capt. Carteret's voyage, I supposed it was uninhabited; but on approaching the shore in my boat, I was met by three young men in a double canoe, with a present consisting of some fruit and a hog. They spoke to me in the English language, and informed me that they were born on the island, and their father was an Englishman who had sailed with Capt. Bligh. After discoursing with them a short time, I landed with them, and found an Englishman, of the name of Alexander Smith, who informed me he was one of the *Bounty's* crew, and that after putting Capt. Bligh in the boat, with half the ship's company, they returned to Tahiti where part of the crew chose to tarry; but Mr. Christian, with eight others, including himself, preferred going to a more remote place, and after making a short stay at Tahiti where they took wives, and six men servants, proceeded to Pitcairn's Island, where they destroyed the ship, after taking every thing out of her which they thought would be useful to them. About six years after they landed at this place, their servants attacked and killed all the English, excepting the informant, and he was severely wounded. The same night the Tahitian widows arose and murdered all their countrymen, leaving Smith with the widows and children, where he had resided ever since without being resisted. I remained but a short time on the island, and on leaving it Smith presented me with a time-piece, and an azimuth compass, which he told me belonged to the *Bounty*. The time-keeper was taken from me by the governor of the island of Juan Fernández, after I had it in my possession about six weeks. The compass I put in repair on board my ship, and made use of it on my homeward passage, since which a new card has been put to it by an instrument maker in Boston. I now forward it to your Lordships, thinking there will be a kind of satisfaction in receiving it merely from the extraordinary circumstance attending it.

(*signed*) Mayhew Folger"

"NEARLY ABOUT THE SAME TIME a further account of these interesting people was received from Vice Admiral Dixon, in a letter addressed to him by Sir Thomas Staines, of his Majesty's ship *Briton*, of which the following is a copy."

Briton, Valparaíso, October 18th, 1814
"Sir,

"I have the honour to inform you, that on my passage from the Marquesas Islands to this port, on the morning of the 17th September, I fell in with an island where none is laid down in the Admiralty or other charts, according to the several chronometers of the *Briton* and *Tagus*.

"I therefore hove to until daylight, and then closed to ascertain whether it was inhabited, which I soon discovered it to be, and to my great astonishment, found that every individual on the island, forty in number, spoke very good English. They prove to be the descendants of the deluded crew of the *Bounty*, which from Tahiti, proceeded to the above mentioned island, where the ship was burnt. Christian appeared to have been the leader and sole cause of the mutiny in that ship. A venerable old man, named John Adams, — there is no such name among the *Bounty*'s crew; he assumed it only to conceal his real name, Alexander Smith — is the only surviving Englishman of those who last quitted Tahiti in her, and whose exemplary conduct and fatherly care of the whole of the little colony, could not but command admiration. The pious manner in which all those born on the island have been reared, and the correct sense of religion which has been instilled into their young minds by this old man, has given him the pre-eminence over the whole of them, to whom they look up as the father of the whole and one family. A son of Christian's was the first born on the island, now about twenty-five years of age, named Thursday October Christian; the elder Christian fell a sacrifice to the jealousy of a Tahitian man, within three or four years after their arrival on the island. They were accompanied thither by six Tahitian men, and twelve women; the former were all swept away by desperate contentions between them and the Englishmen, and five of the latter have died at different periods, leaving at present only one man and seven women of the original settlers. The island must undoubtedly be that called Pitcairn's. It is abundant in yams, plantains, hogs, goats, and fowls, but affords no shelter for a ship or vessel of any description; neither could a ship water there without great difficulty. I cannot however refrain from offering my opinion that it is well worthy the attention of the laudable religious societies, particularly that for propagating the christian religion; the whole of the inhabitants speaking the Tahitian tongue as well as English. During the whole of the time they have been on the island, only one ship has ever communicated with them, which took place about six years since, by an American ship called the *Topaz*, of Boston, Mayhew Folger master. The island is completely iron bound, with rocky shores, and landing in boats at all times difficult, although safe to approach within a short distance in a ship.

(signed) T. Staines"

"WE HAVE BEEN FAVOURED WITH some further particulars on this singular society. As the real position of the island was ascertained to be so far distant from that in which it is usually laid down in the charts, those aboard the *Briton* and the *Tagus* were not a little surprised on approaching its shores to behold plantations regularly laid out, and huts or houses more neatly constructed than those on the Marquesas Islands.

"When about two miles from the shore, some natives were observed bringing down their canoes on their shoulders, dashing through a heavy surf, and paddling off to the ships; but their astonishment was unbounded, on hearing one of them approaching the ship, call out in the English language, 'won't you heave us a rope now?' The first man who got on board the *Briton* soon proved who they were; his name he said was Thursday October Christian, the first born on the island.

"He was then about five and twenty years of age, and is described as a fine young man about six feet high; his hair deep black; his countenance open and interesting, of a brownish cast, but free from that mixture of a reddish tint which prevails on the Pacific Islands; his only dress was a piece of cloth round his loins, and a straw hat ornamented with the black feathers of the domestic fowl. 'With a great share of good humour,' says Captain Pipon, 'we were glad to trace in his benevolent countenance all the features of an honest English face.' 'I must confess,' he continues, 'I could not survey this interesting person without feelings of tenderness and compassion.' His companion was named George Young, a fine youth of seventeen or eighteen years of age. If the astonishment of captains Staines and Pipon was great on hearing their first salutation in English, their surprise and interest were not a little increased on Sir Thomas Staines taking the youths below and setting before them something to eat, when one of them rose up, and placing his hands together in a posture of devotion, distinctly repeated, in a pleasing tone and manner, 'for what we are going to receive, the Lord make us truly thankful.' They expressed great surprise on seeing a cow on board the *Briton*, and were in doubt whether she was a great goat, or a horned sow. The two captains of his Majesty's ships accompanied these young men on shore. With some difficulty and a good wetting, and with the assistance of their conductors, they accomplished a landing through the surf, and were soon after met by John Adams, a man between fifty and sixty years of age, who conducted them to his house. His wife accompanied him, a very old lady blind with age. He was at first alarmed lest the visit was to apprehend him; but on being told that they were perfectly ignorant of his existence, he was relieved from his anxiety. Being once assured that this visit was of a peaceable nature, it is impossible to describe the joy these poor people manifested on seeing those whom they were pleased to consider their countrymen. Yams, cocoa-nuts, and other fruits, with fine fresh eggs, were laid before them;

and the old man would have killed and dressed a hog for his visitors, but time would not allow them to partake of his intended feast. This interesting new colony, it seemed now consisted of about forty-six persons, mostly grown up young people besides a number of infants.

"The young men all born on the island were very athletic, and of the finest forms, their countenances open and pleasing, indicating much benevolence and goodness of heart; but the young women were objects of particular admiration, tall, robust, and beautifully formed, their faces beaming with smiles and unruffled good humour, but wearing a degree of modesty and bashfulness that would do honour to the most virtuous nation on earth; their teeth like ivory, were regular and beautiful, without a single exception; and all of them, both male and female, had the most marked English features. The clothing of the young females, consisted of a piece of linen reaching from the waist to the knees, and generally a sort of mantle thrown over the shoulders, and hanging as low as the ankles, but this covering appeared to be intended chiefly as a protection against the sun and the weather, as it was frequently laid aside, and then the upper part of the body was entirely exposed, and it is not possible to conceive more beautiful forms than they exhibited. They sometimes wreath caps or bonnets for the head in the most tasteful manner, to protect the face from the rays of the sun; and though as Captain Pipon observes, they have only had the instruction of their Tahitian mothers, 'our dress makers in London would be delighted with the simplicity and yet elegant taste of these untaught females.' Their native modesty assisted by a proper sense of religion and morality instilled into their youthful minds by John Adams, has hitherto preserved these interesting people perfectly chaste and free from all kinds of debauchery. Adams assured the visitors that since Christian's death there had not been a single instance of any young woman proving unchaste, nor any attempt at seduction on the part of the men. They all labour while young in the cultivation of the ground, and when possessed of sufficient quantity of cleared land and of stock to maintain family, they are allowed to marry, but always with the consent of Adams, who unites them by a sort of marriage ceremony of his own. The greatest harmony prevailed in this little society; their only quarrels, and these rarely happened, being according to their own expression, 'quarrels of the mouth.' They are honest in their dealings, which consist of bartering different articles for mutual accommodation. Their habitations are extremely neat. The little village of Pitcairn forms a pretty square, the houses at the upper end of which are occupied by the patriarch John Adams and his family, his blind wife, three daughters from fifteen to eighteen years of age, and a boy of eleven; also a daughter of his wife by a former husband, and a son-in-law.

"On the opposite side of the village is the dwelling of Thursday October Christian; and in the centre is a smooth verdant lawn on which the poultry are let loose, fenced in so as to prevent the intrusion of the domestic quadrupeds. All that was done was obviously undertaken on a settled plan, unlike any thing to be met with on the other islands. In their houses, too, they had a good deal of decent furniture, consisting of beds laid upon bedsteads, with neat coverings; they had also tables and large chests to contain their valuables and clothing, which is made from the bark of a certain tree, prepared chiefly by the elder Tahitian females. Adam's house consisted of two rooms, and the windows had shutters to pull to at night. Under the direction of their common father Adams, the young people cultivate cocoa-nuts, bananas, the bread fruit tree, yams, sweet potatoes, and turnips. They have also plenty of hogs and goats; and the woods abound with a species of wild hog, and the coasts of the island with several kinds of good fish.

"The agricultural implements are made by themselves from the iron supplied by the *Bounty*, which with great labour they beat out into spades, hatchets, crows, etc. This was not all: The good old man kept a journal in which was entered the nature and quantity of work performed by each family, what each had received, and what was due on each account. Besides private property, there was a general stock out of which articles were issued on account to the several members of the community, and for mutual accommodation, exchanges of one kind of provision for another were very frequent, as salt for fresh provisions, vegetables and fruit for poultry or fish, and also when the stores of one family were low, or expended, a fresh supply was raised from another, or out of the general stock, to be repaid when circumstances were more favourable; all of which was carefully noted down in John Adam's journal.

"But what was most gratifying of all to the visitors, was the simple and unaffected manner in which they returned thanks to the Almighty for the many blessings they enjoyed. They never failed to say grace before and after meals, and to pray every morning at sun-rise. 'It was truly pleasing,' says Captain Pipon, 'to see these poor people so well disposed to listen so attentively to moral instruction, to believe in the attributes of God, and to place their reliance on divine goodness.' The day on which the two captains landed was Saturday the 17th of September 1814, but by John Adam's account it was Sunday the 18th, and they were keeping the Sabbath by making it a day of rest and prayer.

"This discrepancy was occasioned by the *Bounty* having proceeded thither by the eastern route, and our frigates having gone to the westward; the *Topaz* found them right according to this reckoning, she having also approached the island from the eastward. Every ship from Europe proceeding to Pitcairn's Island round the Cape of Good Hope will find them a day later, — as those who approach them round Cape Horn, a day in advance, as was the case with Captain Folger and the Captains Sir T. Staines and Pipon. The visit of the *Topaz* is, of course, as a notable circumstance, marked down in John Adam's journal. The first ship that appeared off the island was on the 27th December, 1795; but as she did not approach the land, they could not make out to what nation she belonged. A second appeared some time after, but did not attempt to communicate with them. A third came sufficiently near to see the natives and their habitations, but did not attempt to send a boat on shore, which is the less surprising, considering the uniform ruggedness of the coast, the total want of shelter, and the almost constant and violent breaking of the sea against the cliffs. The good old man was anxious to know what was going on in the world, and they had the means of gratifying his curiosity by supplying him with some magazines and modern publications. His library consisted of the books that belonged to Admiral Bligh, but the visitors had not time to inspect them.

"They inquired particularly after Fletcher Christian. This ill-fated young man, it seems, was never happy after the rash and inconsiderate step which he had taken; he became sullen and morose, and practised the very same kind of conduct toward his companions in guilt which he and they so loudly complained against in their late commander. Disappointed in his expedition to Tahiti and the Tonga Islands and most probably dreading a discovery, this deluded youth committed himself and his remaining confederates to the mere chance of being cast upon some desert island, and chance threw them on that of Pitcairn's. Finding no anchorage near it, he ran the ship upon the rocks, cleared her of the live stock and other articles which they had been supplied with at Tahiti, when he set her on fire, that no trace of inhabitants might be visible, and all hopes of escape cut off from himself and his wretched followers. He soon however disgusted both his countrymen and the Tahitians by his oppressive and tyrannical conduct; they divided into parties, and disputes, affrays, and murders, were the consequence. His Tahitian wife died within a twelve month from their landing, after which he carried off one that belonged to a Tahitian man, who watched for an opportunity of taking his revenge, and shot him dead while digging in his own field. Thus terminated the miserable existence of this deluded young man who was neither deficient in talent nor energy, nor in connections, and who might have risen in the service and become an ornament to his profession.

"John Adams declared, as it was natural enough he should do, his abhorrence of the crime in which he was implicated, and said he was sick at the time in his hammock. This we understand is not true, though he was not particularly active in the mutiny; he expressed the utmost willingness to surrender himself and be taken to England; indeed he rather seemed to have an inclination to revisit his native country, but the young men and women flocked round him, and with tears and intreaties begged that their father and protector might not be taken from them, for without him they must all perish. It would have been an act of the greatest inhumanity to remove him from the island; and it is hardly necessary to add that Sir Thomas Staines lent a willing ear to their entreaties, thinking no doubt, as we feel strongly disposed to think, that if he were even among the most guilty, his care and success in instilling religious and moral principles into the minds of this young and interesting society, have in a great degree redeemed his former crimes.

"This island is about six miles long by three broad, covered with wood, and the soil of course very rich: situated under the parallel of 25° south latitude, and in the midst of such a wide expanse of ocean, the climate must be fine and admirably adapted for the reception of all the vegetable productions of every part of the habitable globe. Small therefore as Pitcairn's Island may appear, there can be little doubt that it is capable of supporting many inhabitants; and the present stock being of so good a description, we trust they will not be neglected.

"In the course of time the patriarch must go hence; and we (*the* Quarterly Review) think it would be exceedingly desirable that the British nation would provide for such an event, by sending out, not an ignorant and idle evangelical missionary, but some zealous and intelligent instructor, together with a few persons capable of teaching the useful trades or professions.

"On Pitcairn's Island there are better materials to work upon than missionaries have yet been so fortunate as to meet with, and the best results may reasonably be expected.

"Something we are bound to do for these blameless and interesting people. The articles recommended by Captain Pipon appear to be highly proper; cooking utensils, implements of agriculture, maize, or the Indian corn, the orange tree from Valparaíso, a most grateful fruit in a warm climate, and not known in the Pacific Islands, and that root of plenty — not of poverty as a wretched scribbler has called it — the potatoe, bibles, prayer books, and a proper selection of other books, with paper, and other implements of writing. The visitors supplied them with some tools, kettles, and other articles, such as the high surf would permit them to land, but to no great extent; many things are still wanting for their ease and comfort. The descendants of these people by keeping up the Tahitian language, which the present race speak fluently, might be the means of civilizing the multitudes of fine people scattered over the innumerable islands of the great Pacific.

"We have only to add, that Pitcairn's Island seems to be fortified by nature as to oppose an invincible barrier to an invading enemy; there is no spot apparently where a boat can land with safety, and perhaps not more than one where it can land at all; an everlasting swell of the ocean rolls in on every side, and breaks foam against its rocky and iron bound shores."

To this information may be added the following extracts from the 5th number of the *Quarterly Review*, February 1810, pages 23 and 24. "About four years after their arrival on Pitcairn's Island, a great jealousy existing, the Tahitians secretly revolted and killed every Englishman except Smith whom they severely wounded in the neck with a pistol ball. The same night the widows of the deceased Englishmen arose and put to death the whole of the Tahitians, leaving Smith the only man alive upon the island, with eight or nine women, and several small children.

"The second mate of the *Topaz* asserts that Christian, the ringleader, became insane shortly after their arrival on the island, and threw himself off the rocks into the sea. Another died of a fever before the massacre of the remaining five took place."

SOME REMARKS WILL HEREAFTER BE MADE upon the difference between this account of the mode of Christian's death, and that already quoted from the *Quarterly Review*, July 1815.

Before I record the further information which I obtained from Captain Folger in conversation, I shall introduce an extract from a letter of his to me, bearing a very recent date, and written in the state of Ohio, where he now resides. Although most of the facts contained in it have been related already, yet there are some new circumstances mentioned which make it worthy of a place in this volume.

Kendal, June 2nd, 1816

"Respected Friend,

"The *Bounty* it seems sailed from England in 1787, and after the mutiny took place, the particulars of which are so well known, the mutineers returned with her to Tahiti. After many delays on the coast, a part of the crew under the command of Christian went in search of a group of islands, which you may remember to have seen on the chart, placed under the head of Spanish discoveries. They crossed the situation of those imaginary isles, and satisfied themselves that no such existed. They then steered for Pitcairn's Isle, discovered by Capt. Carteret, where they arrived and took every thing useful out of the ship, ran her on shore, and broke her up. In February, 1808, on my passage across the Pacific ocean, I touched at Pitcairn's Island, thinking it was uninhabited; but to my astonishment I found Alexander Smith, the only remaining Englishman who came to that place in the *Bounty*, his companions having been massacred some years before. He had with him thirty-four women and children. The youngest did not appear to be more than one week old. I stayed with him five or six hours, gave him an account of some things that had happened in the world since he left it, particularly their great naval victories, at which he seemed very much elated, and cried out, 'Old England forever!' In turn he gave me an account of the mutiny and death of his companions, a circumstantial detail of which could I suppose be of little service to you in the work in which you are at present engaged.

"I should be pleased to see your work when it is finished. I think it must be interesting.

> I remain, with esteem,
> Your assured friend,
> (*signed*) Mayhew Folger"

WITH THIS GENTLEMAN I BECAME acquainted in the year 1800, at the island of Más Afuera, Chile. We were then on voyages for seals, and had an opportunity to be together for many months. His company was particularly agreeable to me, and we were often relating to each other our adventures. Among the topics of conversation, the fate of the *Bounty* was several times introduced. I showed him the copy of the journal of Edwards, which I had taken at Timor, and we were both interested to know what ultimately became of Christian, his ship, and his party. It is not easy for landsmen, who have never had personal experience of the sufferings of sailors at sea, and on savage coasts or desolate islands, to enter into their feelings with any thing like adequate sympathy. We had both suffered many varieties of hardship and privation, and our feelings were perfectly alive to the anxieties and distresses of a mind under the circumstances of Christian, going from all he had known and loved, and seeking as his last refuge a spot unknown and uninhabited. The spirit of crime is only temporary in the human soul, but the spirit of sympathy is eternal. Repentance and virtue succeed to passion and misconduct, and while the public may continue to censure and frown, our hearts in secret plead for the returning and unhappy transgressor. It was with such a state of mind that Folger and myself used to speak of the prospects before the mutineers of the *Bounty*, when she was last seen steering to the northwest from Tahiti on the open ocean, not to seek friends and home, but a solitary region, where no human face, besides the few now associated in exile, should ever meet their eyes.

After several years had elapsed, and we had navigated various seas, we fortunately lived to meet each other again in Boston, when it was in his power to renew our old conversation about the *Bounty*, and to gratify the curiosity and interest which we had so long cherished in common.

The *Topaz* in which he sailed was fitted and owned in this place by James and Thomas H. Perkins, Esquires, and crossed the south Pacific Ocean in search of islands for seals. Being in the region of Pitcairn's Island, according to Carteret's account, Folger determined to visit it, hoping that it might furnish him with the animals which were the objects of his voyage. As he approached the island, he was surprised to see smoke ascending from it, as Carteret had said it was uninhabited. With increased curiosity he lowered a boat into the water, and embarked in it for the shore.

He was very soon met by a double canoe, made in the manner of the Tahitians, and carrying several young men who hailed him in English at a distance. They seemed to be willing to come near to him till they had ascertained who he was. He answered, and told them he was an American from Boston. This they did not immediately understand. With great earnestness they said, "You are an American; you come from America; where is America? Is it in Ireland?"

Captain Folger thinking that he should soonest make himself intelligible to them by finding out their origin and country, as they spoke English, inquired, "Who are you?" "We are Englishmen." "Where were you born?" "On that island which you see." "How then are you Englishmen, if you were born on that island which England does not own, and never possessed?" "We are Englishmen because our father was an Englishman." "Who is your father?" With a very interesting simplicity they answered, "Aleck." "Who is Aleck?" "Don't you know Aleck?" "How should I know Aleck?" "Well then, did you know Captain Bligh of the *Bounty*?" At this question, Folger told me that the whole story immediately burst upon his mind, and produced a shock of mingled feelings, surprise, wonder, and pleasure, not to be described. His curiosity which had been already excited so much on this subject was revived, and he made as many inquiries of them as the situation would permit. They informed him that Aleck was the only one of the *Bounty*'s crew who remained alive on the island; they made him acquainted with some of the most important points in their history; and with every sentence increased still more his desire to visit the establishment and learn the whole.

Not knowing whether it would be proper and safe to land without giving notice, as the fears of the surviving mutineer might be awakened in regard to the object of the visit, he requested the young men to go and tell Aleck that the master of the ship desired very much to see him, and would supply him with any thing which he had on board. The canoe carried the message, but returned without Aleck, bringing an apology for his not appearing and an invitation for Captain Folger to come on shore. The invitation was not immediately accepted, but the young men were sent again for Aleck, to desire him to come on board the ship, and to give him assurances of the friendly and honest intentions of the master. They returned however again without Aleck, saying that the women were fearful for his safety and would not allow him to expose himself or them by leaving their beloved island. The young men pledged themselves to Captain Folger that he had nothing to apprehend if he should land, that the islanders wanted extremely to see him, and that they would furnish him with any supplies which their village afforded.

After this negotiation Folger determined to go on

shore, and as he landed he was met by Aleck and all his family, and was welcomed with every demonstration of joy and good will. They escorted him from the shore to the house of their patriarch where every luxury they had was set before him, and offered with the most affectionate courtesy.

He, whom the youth in the canoe, with such juvenile and characteristic simplicity, had called Aleck, and who was Alexander Smith, now began the narrative, the most important parts of which have already been detailed. It will be sufficient for me to introduce here such particulars only as have not been mentioned. Smith said, and upon this point Captain Folger was very explicit in his inquiry at the time as well as in his account of it to me, that they lived under Christian's government several years after they landed; that during the whole period they enjoyed tolerable harmony; that Christian became sick and died a *natural death*, and that it was after this the Tahitian men joined in a conspiracy and killed the English husbands of the Tahitian women, and were by the widows killed in turn on the following night. Smith was thus the only man left upon the island. The account by Lieut. Fitzmaurice, as he professed to receive it from the second mate of the *Topaz* is that Christian became insane, and threw himself from the rocks into the sea. The Quarterly Reviewers say that he was shot dead while digging in the field, by a Tahitian man, whose wife he had seized for his own use.

Neither of these accounts is true, as we are at liberty to affirm from the authority of Captain Folger, whose information must be much more direct and worthy of confidence than that of the second mate of Fitzmaurice, or of the *Quarterly Review*. The last are evidently desirous of throwing as much shade as possible upon the character of Christian.

Smith had taken great pains to educate the inhabitants of the island in the faith and principles of christianity. They were in the uniform habit of morning and evening prayer, and were regularly assembled on Sunday for religious instruction and worship. It is probable also that Smith composed prayers and discourses particularly adapted to their circumstances. He had improved himself very much by reading, and by the efforts he was obliged to make to instruct those under his care. He wrote and conversed extremely well, of which he gave many proofs in his records and in his narrative. The girls and boys were made to read and write before Captain Folger, to show him the degree of their improvement. They did themselves great credit in both, particularly the girls. The stationery of the *Bounty* was an important addition to the books, and was so abundant that the islanders were not yet in want of any thing in this department for the progress of their school. The journal of Smith was so handsomely kept as to attract particular attention and excite great regret that there was not time to copy it. The books upon the island must have created and preserved among the inhabitants an interest in the characters and concerns of the rest of mankind. This idea will explain much of their intercourse with Captain Folger, and the difference between them and the other South Sea islanders in this respect.

When Smith was asked if he had ever heard of any of the great battles between the English and French fleets in the late wars, he answered, "How could I, unless the birds of the air had been the heralds?" He was told of the victories of Lord Howe, Earl St. Vincent, Lord Duncan, and Lord Nelson. He listened with attention till the narrative was finished, and then rose from his seat, took off his hat, swung it three times round his head with three cheers, threw it on the ground sailor-like, and cried out "Old England forever!" The young people around him appeared to be almost as much exhilarated as himself, and must have looked on with no small surprise, having never seen their patriarchal chief so excited before.

Smith was asked if he should like to see his native country again, and particularly London, his native town. He answered that he should, if he could return soon to his island and his colony; but he had not the least desire to leave his present situation forever. Patriotism had evidently preserved its power over his mind, but a stronger influence was generated by his new circumstances.

The houses of this village were uncommonly neat. They were built after the manner of those at Tahiti. Small trees are felled and cut into suitable lengths; they are driven into the earth, and are interwoven with bamboo; they are thatched with the leaves of the plantain and cocoa-nut; and they have mats on the ground. My impression is that Folger told me some of them were built of stone.

The young men laboured in the fields and gardens, and were employed in the several kinds of manufactures required by their situation. They made canoes, household furniture of a simple kind, implements of agriculture, and the apparatus for catching fish. The girls made cloth from the cloth tree, and attended to their domestic concerns.

They had several amusements, dancing, jumping, hopping, running, and various feats of activity. They were as cheerful as industrious, and as healthy and beautiful as they were temperate and simple. Having no ploughs and cattle, they were obliged to cultivate their land by the spade, the hoe, and other instruments for manual labour.

The provision set before Captain Folger consisted of fowls, pork, and vegetables, cooked with great neatness and uncommonly well. The fruits also were excellent.

The apron and shawl worn by the girls were made of the bark of the cloth tree. This is taken off the trunk, not longitudinally, but round, like the bark of the birch. It is beaten till it is thin and soft, and fit for use. The natural colour is buff, but it is dyed variously red, blue, and black, and is covered with the figures of animals, birds, and fish.

The inquiry was made of Smith very particularly in regard to the conduct of the sexes toward each other, and the answer was given in such a manner as entirely to satisfy Captain Folger that the purest morals had thus far prevailed among them. Whatever might be the liberties allowed by the few original Tahitian women remaining, the young people were remarkably obedient to the laws of continence which had been taught them by their common instructor and guide.

Smith is said, by later visitors, to have changed his name, and taken that of John Adams. This probably arose from a political conversation between him and Captain Folger, and from the account then given him of the *Pandora* under the command of Captain Edwards who was sent out in pursuit of the *Bounty* and the mutineers. The fears of Smith were somewhat excited by this last article of intelligence. As the federal constitution of the United States of America had gone into operation since the mutiny; as Captain Folger had given Smith an animating and patriotic account of the administration of the new government and its effects upon the prosperity of the country; and as the name of President Adams had been mentioned, not only with respect as an able statesman and a faithful advocate of civil liberty, but as an inhabitant of the commonwealth in particular where Folger lived; it is thought to be probable enough that this is the circumstance which suggested the name that Smith afterward adopted.

When Folger was about the leave the island, the people pressed round him with the warmest affection and courtesy. The chronometer which was given him, although made of gold, was so black with smoke and dust that the metal could not be discovered. The girls brought some presents of cloth which they had made with their own hands, and which they had dyed with beautiful colours. Their unaffected and amiable manners, and their earnest prayers for his welfare made a deep impression upon his mind, and are still cherished in his memory. He wished to decline taking all that was brought him in the overflow of friendship, but Smith told him it would hurt the feelings of the donors, and the gifts could well be spared from the island. He made as suitable a return of presents as his ship afforded, and left this most interesting community with the keenest sensations of regret. It reminded him of paradise, as he said, more than any effort of poetry or imagination.[15]

The conversations between me and Captain Folger upon this subject were all previous to the dates of the several printed accounts to which I have referred in this chapter. There are a few points only in which the articles in the *Quarterly Review* differ from the impressions upon my mind at the time when I read them. In the volume for 1810, as well as in that for 1815, the Reviewers appear to have gone out of their way, and to have taken very unworthy pains to connect slanders against my countrymen with their remarks upon Pitcairn's Island. Perhaps in the next chapter, which is to contain some reflections upon the whole subject, this topic may be taken up.

Regarding the extent of the population of the island, Captain Folger says there were thirty-four in 1808. Sir Thomas Staines mentions forty in 1814. The *Quarterly Review* afterwards says there were about forty-six besides a number of infants. As every one of the forty whom Sir Thomas Staines saw spoke good English, and as this cannot be applied to the very young children, there must have been a larger number on the island at that time. The population now (*c. 1816*) must be, at the lowest estimate, not less than sixty.

Reflections on the History of the Bounty and the Pitcairn Island Colony

THE MUTINY which happened in the *Bounty* invites some reflections. This subject was often discussed between Commodore McClure, his officers, and the Dutch gentlemen at Timor who saw Lieutenant Bligh and his companions on their arrival at that island, and who were acquainted both with him and with them during their stay there. The manner in which his officers spoke of him, and the kind of treatment which they observed in regard to him are still distinctly remembered at Timor. The mutineers are not so much excluded from sympathy among the gentlemen at that place as they possibly may be among those in England who have only read the story of one of their parties. My mind was prevented from falling into rash conclusions and censures by the conversations in which I then joined; and it has been placed in a still more impartial state by the information which Captain Folger gave me as he received it from Alexander Smith.

Extreme depravity rarely belongs to persons educated as Christian and his adherents were, and who have manifested so many virtues on other occasions. Acts of a desperate character are not likely to have been performed by such men without considerable provocation. Lieutenant Bligh, I suppose, is still living, and it seems that he has become an admiral. It is proper to speak of him with respect, although we may ascribe to him the ordinary failings of our nature. Anecdotes have been told to me concerning his conduct at Copenhagen with

Lord Nelson which naturally prevent me from viewing him as beyond these weaknesses and defects which most of us are so often obliged to acknowledge. The Quarterly Reviewers are unwise, if they wish to be considered as the friends of Admiral Bligh, to provoke an examination of this subject by an officious and unnecessary bitterness in their condemnation of the leader of the mutineers. The zeal which leads them to record, without any correcting remarks, two contradictory modes of death for Christian, as they do in February 1810 and in July 1815; and the anxiety which they show to have crimes which are incompatible with each other, laid to his charge, cannot be well fitted to engage the reader's confidence or to conciliate his partiality. Perhaps the fling against my countrymen in the volume for 1810, and particularly against so well known and excellent a man as Captain Folger, and the series of abusive attacks upon the inhabitants of the United States at large in the article from 1815, may have rendered my perceptions more ready to detect this unworthy spirit in the representations given against Christian.

I have a great horror of the crime of mutiny, and feel as every master of a vessel naturally will upon this subject. Crews and subordinate officers ought to suffer very extensively before violent measures against the master of a vessel can be vindicated. Indeed I should find it difficult to point out a case in real life where a mutiny was necessary or justifiable. I have known more than twenty instances where crews have attempted to do themselves justice by violent measures against their commanders, and in every one of them, the departures from subordination and obedience uniformly increased the evil, and led to the most unhappy consequences. Probably it is best without a single exception for the sufferers to wait till they are on shore, and can have a regular trial by proper authorities, before they attempt to seek a remedy in any other way than by mild and respectful expostulations.

However much commanders may be tempted by sloth, ignorance, selfishness, or passion to neglect or violate the laws of justice and humanity in regard to the rights and duties of their crews, yet mutiny and piracy are not the means to remedy the evil. The alternative is no doubt often grievous and sometimes hardly to be allowed, either to persuade a commander by mild and respectful representations to be just and humane, or to submit in silence and patience, during a long cruise, to his passions, his caprices, his follies and his oppressions. But this alternative is always found to be less dreadful than that of mutiny and violence. A resort to the last opens a train of evils which seems never to have an end till all the subjects are in the grave, and even their children and relatives continue to suffer. Vengeance will not always sleep, but wakes to pursue and overtake them.

Masters and commanders ought to have been regularly educated on shipboard at least so far as to have an experimental acquaintance with the feelings of the sailor as well as with those of the officer. Mere theory can never give to the mind the knowledge of those sympathies, or those alienations and emotions of hostility, which are developed in the actual intercourse between a crew and their commander. No man's nature is so perfect that he can dispense with the necessity of a personal experience in the operations of feeling and passion on the part of inferiors if he would fully understand the wants, the dangers, and the duties which are attendant upon the exercise of authority over them.

Not only an education on ship-board is required to make an accomplished commander, but he must also be thoroughly qualified to judge of the powers, obligations, and rights of every class in his crew, and of every department in the services which they are to render. While he respects himself, and exacts what is his due, he must also respect them and be as careful to observe the law of gradation in their favour as in his own.

He must never countermand his own orders without very good reasons, and generally such as are obvious. Considerable loss had better be borne than to permit the idea of indecision on his part to be established in the minds of the crew. Rules which he had made for the ship he must regard as punctiliously himself. He will never permit them to volunteer in giving him advice upon his duty, but he will often find benefit in asking it for deliberation, and allowing it to have due weight in his determinations. He will lean toward the system of encouragement much more than toward that of censure and punishment. Understanding the value of praise, he will employ it freely as well as judiciously, and will reward merit twice where he punishes faults once. He will convince his men that their rights and interests are safe when left with him, and that it is not necessary for them to exercise a jealous vigilance over their own claims. The only way in which this conviction can be produced is never to consider justice as a light thing, or as that which may be regarded or not, according to convenience and whim.

How far these principles were reduced in practice by the commander of the *Bounty* must be known to the parties concerned. Probably every reader of Lieutenant Bligh's book has found a disposition remaining with him to ask if there were not other causes for the mutiny besides those which the author has assigned. The character of Christian, notwithstanding the mutiny which deserves severe condemnation, appears not to have been remarkable for wickedness, but rather distinguished for intelligence, the general love of justice and magnanimity. Not malice and hatred, but a sense of injury united with a spirit of forbearance, we discover in the language, "come Captain Bligh, your officers and men are now in the boat, and you must go with them." The expression which follows, "if you attempt to make the least resistance, you will instantly be put to death," is harsh, and painful to the reader, but it was probably well understood to be particularly adapted to the governing motives of the individual to whom it was addressed. It was designed to save bloodshed, as it probably did.

Let the conduct of Christian receive the censure of all good men, but let it also not be condemned beyond its turpitude, or beyond the purposes of good policy in regard to its use as a warning to others. The testimony of Smith in his favor is worthy of our attention. This man has devoted himself so faithfully and successfully to the cause of virtue and piety among his children and subjects, and has given so many proofs of his benevolence and love of duty, that his representations ought not lightly to be set aside, even on the subject of the mutiny. Christian consulted the wishes of those who stayed at Tahiti; he divided the property equally among them all; and he governed with so much wisdom and equity as to produce harmony and peace for a series of years in the island of their refuge.

ATTENTION MAY NOW BE GIVEN to the conduct and virtues of Smith with reference to another subject. This mutineer, with a number of pagan women from Tahiti, has succeeded, according to all the accounts, in training up a community of males and females in perfect chastity, sincerity and honesty. Their hearts appear to be filled with benevolence and their quarrels are only "the quarrels of the mouth." Their moral worth and their practical virtues have stood the test of many years. If they lose their present character, it will probably be through an intercourse with crews from Europe and other commercial countries, claiming the privileges of a more enlightened system of ethics and religion than theirs.

Notwithstanding the variety of licentious scenes which he had witnessed and the numerous transactions in which he had shared, all tending to blunt, if not to destroy his moral feelings, he still manifested to Folger the most benevolent solicitude for the preservation of the innocence and purity of the young men and women under his care. His perception of the beauty of truth, his sense of the value and dignity of innocence, and his sentiments of piety, appear to have been as lively and powerful as though he had never been guilty of the crime of mutiny, nor had made himself liable to a disgraceful death by the laws of his country.

The power of education, when no circumstances in the state of society counteract its effects, is happily illustrated in the innocence, simplicity, and worth of the community of Pitcairn. Intercourse with the world had not corrupted them; artificial laws and institutions had not furnished temptations to their own violation; and their natural interests had not been made to clash with their duties. A mild and paternal system of instruction and government had been left to produce its legitimate effects upon their characters and actions. As to the state of society now, one part of the system too often defeats another. What we teach in one school, in one family, or in one church, another contradicts; and minds which are yet unformed are not infrequently more at a loss in the pursuit of truth than if they had been left to themselves and the gradual development of their faculties in a course of nature.

In the business of education, let a good temper, a habit of benevolence and disinterestedness, and love of justice and truth, and a liberal acquiescence in the diversities of character, be much more an object than any compend of particular views and principles which might be found in the dogmas of sects. In all countries, and under all institutions, it is of far more importance to give efficacy to common sense, and to our best natural affections, than it is to control our philosophical speculations and to establish the faith of our children in the articles of a predominant creed.

It is painful to look forward to the time when the interesting family of Pitcairn shall lose their present innocence and loveliness by the frequent visits, which they must be expected to receive from ships, that will hereafter be attracted to their retreat by the fame of their beauty, the affection of their hearts, and the softness of their climate. Captain Folger is to be envied the pleasure of witnessing the operations of their minds, when they first beheld the inhabitants of other lands before any portion of their freshness and simplicity was removed.

To send missionaries among them, according to the proposal of some good people, would be an unfortunate experiment upon their peace and virtue, unless the individuals selected should be much more enlightened and liberal than any of that class of persons with whom I have been fortunate enough to be acquainted. No mode of destroying their harmony would probably be more successful than the preaching of a man who should declaim to this innocent and uncorrupted community against their natural hearts, and insist upon their being re-fashioned after a model prepared and sent out from the work-shop of the sect. When they should be made anew, under the direction of such an artist, and should learn to decry all that is natural in their affections and manners, as though it were carnal and wicked, they would indeed have their eyes opened to see that no virtue and no happiness are any longer to be found while they are in the body, and that they must suffer until the grave shall release them. Religionists of this cast too often make their doctrines true by the effects which they produce in society when they are believed and followed. The world becomes, as they say it is, quite worthless; the people find themselves without merit by which to claim happiness; and even the saints, according to their own confession, have much more sin than holiness.

Let it be our fervent prayer that neither canting and hypocritical emissaries from schools of artificial theology on the one hand, nor sensual and licentious crews and adventurers on the other, may ever enter the charming village of Pitcairn to give disease to the minds or the bodies of the unsuspecting inhabitants.[16]

Storms; Getting Rid of Vermin; Sumatra; Jakarta

MARCH 24TH, 1792, we left Timor and sailed westward for the Straits of Sunda. On the 2nd of April we made Christmas Island. We sailed entirely round it, within a mile of the shore, and discovered no dangers. Landing upon it appeared to be difficult. We ran northward till the 7th, when we made Java Head.

We saw a Dutch snow, a sloop, and a prow rigged after the manner of the Malays. The snow had the governor of Padang on board, and the other two vessels belonged to him. He was bound to Jakarta with his family and effects, having retired from business and office. He had lost his way, getting east of the Straits of Sunda, and was beating his course on the south side of Java, seeking for the Straits. The captain of the snow had died at Padang and this event left him without a proper navigator. As the *Panther* touched at his port on her outward passage, our commodore and his officer were acquainted with him. The meeting was therefore pleasant. We were gratified to have it in our power to render him a service by setting him right. After this he bore away for Java Head. The wind had been blowing south east, but it shifted to the north west, and soon rose to a gale. The unfortunate Dutchman was driven to the eastward; his snow lost her masts; and it was six months before he arrived at Jakarta. When we met him there, he told us that the prow was never heard of after the gale, that the sloop was lost on the eastern shore of Java, and that the sufferings of himself and family were extreme. The loss of nearly all his property, the defeat of his plans for a life of ease and retirement, and the consequent anxiety and distress, made his story and condition very painful to us and to all who knew him.

We also were driven a number of degrees eastward; both our masts were sprung; and we sustained considerable damage in other respects. The gale continued for fifteen days, and blew as strong at times as I ever saw it off Cape Horn. At length the wind returned to the southeast and permitted us to steer again northwest.

THE 28TH OF APRIL, we anchored in Pulo-Bay, near to Bencoolen (*Bengkulu*) in the island of Sumatra, thoroughly weather-beaten. As our officers had been here before, we met with a friendly reception.

We obtained here the supplies which we wanted; we procured new masts and rigging; and we had nearly completed the task of putting the *Panther* and the *Endeavor* in good repair, when our men began to be sick, and to die, in a most extraordinary manner. Sometimes death followed the sickness of but a single day. The first symptom of the disease was dizziness in the head; then a violent fever; sometimes the bowels swelled; a lethargy succeeded; and the patient died without a groan. We lost nearly twenty men in half the number of days. We were obliged to go out of Pulo-Bay with only one topmast on end in each vessel.

This is one of the finest harbours in the world, but it cannot be occupied on account of its unhealthiness. The English Indiamen are forbidden to go into it. The land next to the sea is low, swampy, and full of stagnant water which exhales a very unpleasant effluvium. This was probably the cause of the mortality among our people.

Getting Rid of Vermin

WE WERE IN THE BAY ABOUT SIX WEEKS, after which we hurried out of it and anchored in Bengkulu Roads, westward of the town. This is a healthy place, but it is dangerous for vessels to lie long at anchor in it as there is no shelter for them against the south and west winds, or the sea. We did not remain many days, but moved to Rat-Island-Basin, where we found a pure air and tolerably good riding. This island, which is no more than a sand-key, lies about six miles southward of the town in the open ocean, and is very small. A reef of coral rock extends a mile or more on the southwest, west and north parts of it, furnishing a safe place in which four or five ships of a thousand tons may ride with safety. Heavy anchors and chains are found in this basin belonging to the English East India Company for the convenience of their ships. With leave of the governor, any vessels may use them. The chains which are fastened to the anchor sometimes lie upon the bottom, several fathoms under water. It is necessary for some one to dive with rope in his hand which he is to tie to the loose end of the chain, that it may be drawn up and attached to the cable.

This service I was one day performing in water of five fathoms depth when, just as I reached the bottom, I saw a large shark coming close to me, with his eye fixed upon mine. I was not a little alarmed at this, and hardly knew in what manner to attempt an escape. To seek the surface of the water was as hopeless as to remain where I was. I had presence of mind enough to fasten the rope to the chain. I then twitched it and was drawn up by the men who held it on deck. The shark followed me while my eye was kept full upon his, and I expected every moment that he would spring upon me. He did not, however, and I got safely on board, wondering at my deliverance. But my surprise was soon abated when I learned that this was a perfectly harmless species of the shark, never biting a man, and that people daily swim among them without fear. A person indeed may dive toward them and make them run away. Some are very large and long, measuring more than twenty feet in length. The violence and voracity of the shark generally are proverbial, but this particular kind is mild and tame, and of a beautiful gold color.

WE SANK THE *ENDEAVOR* AT THIS PLACE for the purpose of destroying the vermin and insects with which she was overrun. They consisted of centipedes, scorpions, innumerable black ants, some rats, millions of cockroaches, and some small snakes. The usual mode in which they get into a ship is by the wood which is brought on board. Wherever white ants in particular are found, it is a rule never to take in wood. There are two kinds of ants much dreaded by masters of vessels; the black whose bite is extremely painful, and the white, which will eat the timbers of a ship so as to ruin it in a few months. In half a year they have succeeded in making the beams fall out of their places, not being able to bear their own weight.

In sinking the *Endeavor*, we scuttled her between wind and water, where she was empty at low tide, and might be easily raised again by stopping the scuttle. The expedient freed her from the swarms of immigrants with which she was colonized.

BENGKULU IS THE PRINCIPAL ENGLISH settlement on the island of Sumatra. The circumference of it is about two miles. The climate is unhealthy, although not to the same degree with some other places on the island. Fishing supports some of the inhabitants, and others gain a living by cultivating pepper trees and rice. It is dependent on the Presidency of Bengal from which it receives its governor and laws. The great article of trade is pepper which is in the hands of the

English East India Company. Salt is also a considerable object of commerce. The houses of this place are built of wood, generally one story, without glass windows, but have blinds, and are variously furnished. The amusements of the English people consist in parties for dancing, music, cards, and riding. Their horses, of which they are extremely fond, are very fine. They are principally the Japan breed from Jakarta, and are handsome, fleet and hardy. Riding on horseback is a favorite amusement. A chair for two persons, drawn by one horse, is also much used in their parties for pleasure. This vehicle is called a *buggie*; the top is of open work, standing upon legs, and is literally a chair. It is light and airy, and may be driven safely with great speed.

The fort is called Marlborough. It stands upon a hill of moderate elevation, and has a delightful prospect. The English keep twelve or fifteen hundred men here. The soil about it is a mixture of clay and loam, and is quite slippery when wet.

The island of Sumatra is large, rich, and stored with a very great variety of productions. There are well cultivated plains among the mountains. The inhabitants choose these as the best places for residence. The temperature of the air is pleasant, the mercury ranging from 82° to 85° Fahrenheit in the hottest part of the day. The large lakes afford many facilities for intercourse between the inhabitants. The native Sumatrans are pagans, but many of them become Mahometans. Cock fighting is one of their amusements. The pheasant of this island is said to be very beautiful. The storks and the cocks are uncommonly large. Parrots are abundant. Alligators are numerous in the rivers, and often destroy the inhabitants when they are bathing. Goats, deer, and hogs which run wild in the mountains, besides bullocks and the hog-deer, are frequent in Sumatra. The royal tiger is abundantly found in the island and is the most perfect of his kind. Buffaloes and many other sorts of quadrupeds are numerous. There are lizards, flying lizards, serpents, and cameleons. The bread fruit tree, indigo, coffee, cotton, ebony, sandalwood, manchineel, and the banyan tree are the productions of this island. The benzoin, or benjamin, is gathered in great quantities and is of excellent quality. It is obtained from a species of the laurus by incisions in the bark through which the gum exudes. It is used for perfumes, cosmetics, incense, and varnish. Camphor trees grow in great plenty, and afford this article for commerce of the best kind. Iron, copper, gold, sulphur, tin, lead, arsenic, and salt-petre are found here. Goiters were seen in the necks of some of the inhabitants of Bengkulu, and were said to be considerably prevalent in the interior. The natives are Malays, and notoriously treacherous.

WE SAILED ON THE 17TH OF AUGUST, having many upon our sick list, and proceeded eastward, through the Straits of Sunda, and arrived at Jakarta on the 16th of September.

This city is the capital of the Dutch settlements in India. (*Delano refers to the entire region of Dutch enterprise throughout Indonesia.*) It stands on the river Jacatra which is about a hundred and seventy feet wide within the town. The harbour is filled with islands which break the force of the winds, and a thousand ships may ride in it with safety. On one of the islands, Onroost, there are excellent dockyards, and all the conveniences for building and repairing ships.

The houses of Jakarta are generally of one story, and very high walls. But the governor's house, the hotel, and the dwellings of some few rich men, are of two stories. There are several bridges in the town. The abutments are built of stone, the covering is of wood, and the braces above and below are iron. These bars are four-sided, and each side is about three inches broad, an enormous size for a bar of iron. The timber is an extremely hard wood, of which standards are made above the bridge, and to them the iron bars are fastened. The river which runs through Jakarta feeds fifteen canals which are all faced with stone. The mouth of the river is often cleared of mud by the labours of a great number of slaves. The Chinese and the natives of the island chiefly inhabit the suburbs. The city is surrounded with land which is low and boggy, and the cause of extreme unhealthiness. There is a citadel, besides many forts and redoubts, for the protection of the place. It was however taken by the English without much loss. The number of inhabitants, as far as I could ascertain it, was about 200,000.[17] Malays probably make half of the whole. They are servants and laborers. A fourth part consists of Chinese, some merchants, some mechanics, and some laborers. Europeans and natives from different countries of India constitute another fourth part. Negroes and Japanese are counted among the Malays.

Fruits and vegetables are extremely cheap in this city. I have purchased a hundred pine apples for a dollar. Still, living is expensive in Jakarta. Whoever would support the character of a gentleman on shore must keep a coach. This and a variety of other causes make it impossible for a captain or supercargo of a vessel to spend time economically in this place.

The productions of Jakarta, and of the island at large, are numerous and abundant. They consist of rice, coffee, sugar cane, all kinds of bread corn, and every species of tropical fruit. The bohan upas, or poison tree, which has been so famous in the stories about Java, and which has been reported to destroy life at the distance of several miles, I have seen and touched. It is no more dangerous than an apple tree, unless the bark be broken and the juice of it be received upon the flesh. As far as I can judge, I should think it to be the same as the manchineel tree of the West Indies.

Canals are cut in Jakarta, and some of them run a considerable distance into the country. I have been fourteen or fifteen miles from the city in several directions, and found the highest cultivation, the most elegant country seats for the gentlemen of fortune, and every thing that could gratify the eye. But the unhealthiness of the place has forced many of the proprietors of the country seats to desert them after having spent immense sums upon them.

Alligators are very numerous and troublesome. They are in all the creeks and canals. I was standing at noon in the door of the principal hotel, in the middle of the city, on one side of the canal, seventy or eighty yards from the spot, and saw an alligator take a child from the steps the opposite side at the edge of the water, and eat it. The mouth of the canal, where the boats of ships enter, in going on shore, is full of them. Sharks throng the roads where ships ride.

Before I leave Jakarta, a few observations upon the mosques of the Malays. I have frequently visited them in the different eastern islands, and seen their worship. A mosque is a shed seven or eight feet high; the sides are open between the upright timbers; the roof is sharp and thatched with the large leaves of the country; it is sixty feet long and forty wide. Around it there is an inclosure two hundred feet square, made of stone or of large pieces of clay three feet long and one foot on each side, baked in the sun. Near the mosque there is a great hollow log which the natives call a *tom-tom*, and which is an enormous drum. The largest hollow tree that can be found is selected; the trunk is cut at the length of twenty or thirty feet; it is often from four to six feet in diameter; the inside is entirely cut out and made smooth. It is laid horizontally on cross stakes at about the height of a man's neck, and both ends are covered with a dried skin drawn tight. The sticks with which the priest, at a given time in the worship, plays upon the tom-tom, are four or five feet long, and are made like drumsticks with a knob at the end. The priest comes out from the mosque in a solemn march, sometimes followed by the whole congregation, and plays with great zeal upon the tom-tom for several minutes, after which prayers are offered, and the priest and the people then return into the mosque.

I was not able to discover the precise import of this part of the worship, but it probably answers in some degree to the praise which we offer to God upon the organ, and with other instruments of music. The Malays carry little tom-toms with them, slung upon the shoulder like a drum, and always play upon them in their engagements with an enemy, and in all dangers. It seems to be martial as well as devotional music, and is used as one mode of imploring divine protection, and securing the advantages of piety in their enterprises and contests.

When I first saw this part of the worship of the Malays, I was disposed to think it ridiculous and absurd, but it appears sufficiently rational upon examination, and changes all its associations when its object is understood. The substance and object of faith are so much alike in all countries, that a thorough knowledge of them is pretty certain to give a catholic spirit to every reflecting traveller.

Borneo; Philippine Islands; Sulu Seas; Drugs

WE SAILED from Jakarta the 2nd of October, 1792, for the Palau Islands. On the south and east coasts of Billiton (*Belitung Island, Indonesia*), we saw but few dangers. But it seems we passed within several dangerous shoals without discovering them. They were just out of sight of land. In a voyage afterward, I was near being lost on them, as I was coming from Canton. I was running in the night, and felt perfectly safe, because I had surveyed this passage on the Belitung side of it, when I suddenly found the water becoming shallow, from twenty-seven fathoms mud to fifteen and fourteen fathoms coral rock. I altered my course, the water was deeper, then shallower, and I was obliged to anchor. In the morning, we perceived that we were very near a long reef, or sand key, extending nearly four miles. We got under way, steered southward, and passed two or three more reefs with rocks on them as large as hay-cocks.

Borneo was said to be the largest island in the world before the discovery of Australia.[18] It is 780 miles long and 720 broad. The air is very good upon the high lands, but very bad upon the low. Mountains are pretty numerous and some of them lofty. The soil of Borneo is very fertile. It produces in abundance all varieties of tropical fruits. The pepper is well known for its superior quality. This plant is a vine like a grape, as large as a pipe-stem, and supported by a stake, or a small tree. The fields of pepper which I have seen are from half an acre to an acre. The clusters are like grapes, and some-times a single plant bears seventy or more of them.

There are some very rare fruits on this island. The ma-dang is one which looks like a large apple, and the balono is another which resembles a mango, has the shape of a kidney, and is of a yellowish colour. Cassia, camphor, benzoin, and wax are also among the productions.

Diamonds are plenty and are sometimes collected from the rivers. Gold-dust, iron, copper, tin, and tutenag abound. The last metal is often called the white copper of China, but zinc is the prevailing ingredient.

Previously I have spoken of the beach-le-mar, often called the swalloo. This is also found in Borneo. (*Delano quotes the following from the* Edinburgh Encyclopaedia.) "There is a species of sea-snail which is esteemed a great luxury and is a pretty lucrative article in their commerce with the Chinese. It is fished by the Biadjoos, the original inhabitants, in seven or eight fathoms depth of water. When the water is clear they perceive the swalloo at the bottom, and strike it with an iron instrument having four points. Swalloos are likewise procured by diving, the best always found in the deepest water. The black swalloo is much preferable to the white; but there is a kind more esteemed than either, of a clear colour, and found only in deep water. Swalloos of this kind are sometimes so large as to weigh half a pound."

At the Palau Islands, swalloos were found in basins of water not more than knee deep, at low tide, on the reefs. The black often weighed a pound. It is about a foot long, as large as a man's wrist, without any perceivable mouth, and with a thick skin. The outer part of the skin is taken off by scalding, and the swalloo is then pickled and dried in the sun, after which it is fit for sale, or use. When it is cut open it looks like the hard meat of a sea clam.

In addition, the island of Borneo also trades in pearls and ivory. Goods to be brought here for sale should include coarse cutlery, coarse chintz and cotton stuffs, and opium which they smoke and chew.

The river Borneo is on the northwest side of the island, and a town of the same name stands upon it, several miles from its mouth. It is built upon piles in the river, on a large shoal, with water enough on each side of it for a vessel of considerable size to pass. It is spacious and contains a vast number of inhabitants. The Portuguese, the Spaniards, the Dutch, and the English have all attempted, at different times, to make settlements upon this island; and have all in turn suffered from the treachery and cruelty of the inhabitants. The character of these people is particularly bad. I have seen several Europeans who have been in slavery in Borneo, and from whom I have learned that the treatment which they received was far worse than the severities of Algerine (*Algerian*) captivity. Those who have read the narrative of Captain David Woodward of Boston will be able to judge, in some degree, how much men are sometimes compelled to suffer from the inhumanity of these savages.

The natives are Mahometans and Gentoos (*Hindus*). A mixed language is spoken. The Arabic in some degree spreads with the extension of the religion of the Koran, but Malay is the general language of the island. The Hindus, or disciples of Brahma, are very numerous and believe in a Supreme Being, in various orders of moral and intelligent creatures, in the obligations of virtue and piety upon mankind, in the immortality of the soul, in the transmigration of it through different bodies, and in rewards and punishments according to character and conduct.

THE PHILIPPINE ISLANDS LIE north of Borneo. Mindanao

is the most southern and Luzon the largest. The islands are under the influence of the Spaniards who have settlements on several of them. Their capital, Manila, is two or three miles in circumference, and has an irregular form, narrow at the ends and wide in the middle. The streets are broad, the houses are well built, and the churches are elegant. There are many convents in it, and the population of christians amounts to about 12,000. The Chinese and Japanese live without the walls, and constitute a much larger population than the christians. The Chinese particularly are the most active and successful merchants and mechanics. The Spaniards are indolent, and have long been in the habit of relying upon the returns of the vessels which they annually send to Acapulco. They formerly employed two in this service, but now five or six. The merchants of all nations at Manila get some share in the trade with South America. Immense quantities of India and China goods are found in this city, and many thousands of dollars find their way to it from Europe and the United States, in addition to those which come in the Spanish galleons. A great article of trade is sugar, of which a very large amount is made in the neighborhood of Manila. Indigo also is manufactured there of the first quality.

I have seen most of the Philippine Islands, have landed on several of them, and have some knowledge of the inhabitants. They resemble the Tartars, who make a part of the population of China. There is a class of people among them who have sprung from Europeans and the natives, and who are said to be peculiarly savage. A large portion of them are of Spanish blood, and are well known as Manila-men. The English will not insure a ship if she has as many as five or six of these people on board. Many sufferings and losses have been experienced from them, and they are often associated with the Malays in piratical attacks upon ships. I have seen many of them gibbeted at Bombay and other English ports. They have murdered several of the Chinese at Macau since my acquaintance with them.

The Malays are known to chew and smoke a kind of plant, by which they are intoxicated, called *bangue* (*bhang or hashish*). This is a most powerful and active stimulant. It begins to operate very soon upon the system; produces an ungovernable frenzy in two or three hours; and gives great vigour to the muscles, while it takes away all discretion from the mind. Our own people, and some of our midshipmen, after being ashore while we were among the Philippines, came on board, and were for a time incapable of being restrained from acts of violence, except by a very superior force, in consequence of having joined with the natives in smoking or chewing the bangue. When they are excited by this, they draw their cresses, which are steel daggers waved at the point, and run ferociously about, stabbing all they meet, whether friend or foe. They do not frequently take the bangue to this extent, but use it sufficiently to produce that degree of intoxication which drowns their cares, and multiplies their joys. A Malay will not voluntarily use this plant in order to run mad, or *run the muck*, as it is termed, unless he is very much oppressed, and has no other way to get revenge upon society for his wrongs. Whenever he does this the Dutch offer a reward, it is said, to any one who will kill him.

The land about Manila is extremely fertile. The Islands produce every variety of fruit, and abound in cattle, deer, buffaloes, sheep, goats, hogs, and monkeys. Gold, iron, and tin are found upon them. Perpetual verdure clothes the trees, and ripe fruits hang upon them through the year.

On the uninhabited island of Balembangan where the ships anchored to procure wood and good water, there are monkeys of every kind. They love fish and we often saw them come down to the shore to collect this sort of food. They hate water, and shake their paws like a cat when they are wet. They catch small fish in basins of water where there is no escape, and draw the shell fish out which are near the shore. Their chattering, grimace, and mimicry, make them irresistibly ludicrous. We shot among them several times. They were frightened, ran a little way, and turned round to look at us with an amusing mixture of the fearful and the farcical in their faces.

Sailing southward and eastward from Cagayan Sulu Island, we soon got into seventy and eighty fathoms water, and then found no bottom with a line of a hundred and forty fathoms. Going eastward towards Sulu (*Jolo*) proper, the sea is clear of shoals. There are no soundings, but the rippling of the currents which run south and east is strong. We fell in with the island Towee-Towee (*Tawi Tawi*) in the Sulu Sea. It is very bold, and on the north side, two leagues from shore, a line of a hundred and forty fathoms did not reach bottom. Sailing eastward we found a chain of islands, lying in great numbers from Tawi Tawi, all the way to Jolo. They are not dangerous. A few leagues east of Tawi Tawi, and three or four miles from the chain of small islands, we found bottom at forty fathoms. Sailing round the south west point of Jolo, we saw an island looking like a small lump, north of the main island. A ship may pass within, or without it. Eastward of this are several islands, like hillocks, some low and some high, which form the north side of the road or harbour of Jolo.[19]

Jolo; Edible Bird-Nests; A Night of Adventure; A Visit to the Seraglio

JOLO ISLAND is from 25 to 35 miles long from east to west and from 15 to 25 miles from north to south. The island is capable of cultivation in every part. The houses of the principal town stand upon piles, and many of them are over the water, according to the custom of the Malays. They are miserably built, with sides of bamboo, and a roof thatched with leaves and long grass. The people are Malays, Chinese, and a few Moors. They speak some Spanish and some Moorish, but no English. The Moors were introduced amongst them as follows:

In 1766, the King of Jolo resigned to the English the island of Balembangan. In 1772 they began a settlement at the north east harbour, which is much better than the south west, and admits vessels of any size. The Malays of Jolo assisted the English in building the houses and the fort, and returned to their own island. Not long afterwards, when the houses were inhabited and the fort had a few guns mounted, the Malays manned a number of prows at Jolo, came to Balembangan in the night, and early in the morning took the fort by surprise. They turned the guns upon the town and managed them with so much promptitude as to make the English fly in utter consternation to the boats and vessels in the harbour for safety. Many were killed, some taken prisoners, and the whole settlement destroyed. A gentleman who was sitting in the house of the governor that morning told me that a cannon ball from the fort entered the walls of the room where the family were, struck a chest of dollars, and made them rattle round the apartment like a storm of hail.

A considerable number of Moors had been employed by the English who were taken prisoners by the Malays, and carried to Jolo. This is one of the sources of the Moorish population and language on that island.

The island of Jolo gives laws to most of the other islands in the group. It has a sultan and several kinds of officers found in Mahometan communities. The trade is in sago and many other articles, but chiefly in pearls. These are procured in great numbers about the islands. A good judgment is required to deal in them. They are of different sizes, shapes, qualities, and degrees of clearness. Their value is not determined by the size alone, and considerable experience is necessary to judge of their worth as they are offered by the natives in the market.

The eatable birds-nests, which are esteemed so great a luxury in China, are found at Jolo. These are the nests of a species of swallow[20] which very much resembles the bank-swallow — so called from making holes in the bank near the sea for nests. The swallow which furnishes the eatable nests is small, between two and three inches long, with a white breast, and a white spot on each feather of the tail. It collects a white glutinous substance from the foam of the sea and from the beach, and makes nests of it in the caverns and crevices of rocks in inaccessible places. Persons seeking for nests are often obliged to dive into the water to enter the mouths of the caverns where the swallows have chosen their residence. I have myself, when we were at Timor, gone down fifty feet by a rope into a chasm between the rocks and caught the swallows upon the nests, and plucked the nests with the eggs. These are four, and perfectly white. The nest is attached closely to the rock, the surface of which makes a part of its side. When taken from the rock, the nest has about the capacity of a quarter of an orange peel of the largest size. It is white like isinglass, and is packed like tea cups, one within another, in bunches of two or three pounds. A single nest weighs about an ounce. I have often eaten the soups which are made of them and have found them possessing a very agreeable aromatic flavour.

This is a good place for ships, which have guns, to procure all kinds of provisions. The cattle are fine and very cheap, an excellent bullock being sold for two or three dollars in articles of trade. Goats are plenty, and one was sold to us for a knife. Vegetables and fruits are in all varieties; and rice in any quantity. Fish of an excellent quality are sold for trifles and toys. Large and good green turtles, weighing from four to five hundred pounds, may be purchased for a song.[21]

It is proper also to make the sultan a visit and carry presents. Otherwise there will be difficulty in persuading the people to trade. Europeans must be always on their guard; must never put themselves in the power of the Malays; and never expose themselves to the chance of having their ship cut off. Fourteen guns and musketry in proportion, are the least force which every vessel should have in holding any intercourse with these people. There are guns at this place by which vessels might be annoyed if the inhabitants were provoked.

Wood is procured with difficulty at Jolo. It is scarce. It must be brought with considerable labour from the hills to the shore, and is then carried by the natives in canoes to the vessels which want it. It is never given, but must be purchased at a pretty good price. Water may be obtained at the town, or about a mile to the eastward of it, where it can be had with more convenience. This watering place is under a large tree, near to a point of rocks, and cannot be easily mistaken.

A Night of Adventure

AS THERE HAD BEEN VERY LITTLE intercourse between the English and the people of Jolo since the attack upon Balembangan in 1772, we did not think it safe for us to go on shore. The natives, however, came to us on board in great numbers without showing the least mark of fear. Some of their most respectable persons, and females of the first rank, were among them.

The daughters of the sultan came and were much gratified with the attention which was paid them, and with the indulgence of their curiosity in every part of our vessels. They conducted themselves with great dignity and propriety, and seemed to have an habitual sense of the value of modesty.

Among our visitors, there was an old Moor who had been a captain in the English service from the taking of Manila to the time when it was given up to the Spaniards. He was a *subahdar* in the sultan's guards at Jolo, and had married there. He seemed to be very much pleased with our company, and I was able to converse with him a little in the Moorish language, to which I had paid some attention. I asked him if I could not go on shore with safety, and if I should not find something for amusement or instruction there.

He answered, yes; and said that he could have me carried in a canoe if I would disguise myself by putting on a Malay turban and a robe which they call a *clout*. I was to sit still, drawing the robe over my head. The canoe could take me within ten yards of his house, and I should be able to enter his dwelling without being discovered. I consulted with the Commodore on the subject, who had, as I knew, a strong desire to obtain more knowledge of the island. He said that the project was extremely dangerous; that I might be taken and considered as a spy; that I might be murdered through jealousy; that the general enmity which they bore to Europeans might induce the inhabitants to take my life; that the clothes I had on might be thought valuable enough to be the occasion of a quarrel to gain them; and that the treachery of the Malays must always be feared, and exposure to it avoided.

After much deliberation, however, he consented that I should go, saying that I was in the habit of working my way well through difficulties, that he hoped some good would grow out of the enterprise, and that he wanted very much to establish a friendly intercourse with the people. We agreed that if I should be detected, both of us should say it was an affair of gallantry, and nobody responsible for it but myself. The Moor knew nothing of the understanding between the Commodore and me.

Between daylight and dark, the son-in-law of the old subahdar came under the bow of the *Panther* and handed in the Malay dress at one of the ports. I put it on over my clothes and descended through the same port into the canoe. I observed the orders given me and sat perfectly still and covered, while my guide paddled between hundreds of canoes to the mouth of a small river which we ascended nearly a quarter of a mile. On one side of it stood a part of the town built upon piles. We went up to the house of the subahdar in the midst of a multitude of people. None of them discovered me till I was going into the house. Then it was perceived by some, from my walk, or manner, that I was a foreigner, but as the good old subahdar came out to meet and conduct me into his house, there seemed to be no offence or hostility manifested by the inhabitants, and my anxiety was allayed.

I was introduced to the old man's wife and to his daughter who was the wife of my guide. They treated me as well as I could wish, offering me whatever they had or could obtain. There was soon a collection about the house. The subahdar went to the people and told them that he had an old friend with him whom he had known for many years, and

that he wished not to be disturbed. If he were, the sultan
would call them to an account. They were silent for a time,
but still wanted very much to come in. Two or three females
only were admitted.

We spent the hours agreeably till midnight, when the
subahdar went out to attend upon his guards, as it was his
duty. I was then the only man in the house.

Fifteen Malays entered, each with a cress, and came
into the chamber where I was. They formed a circle round me
and viewed me with scrutinizing eyes. I was not able to speak
to them in the Malay language, and was entirely silent, while
they looked at me for more than half an hour. My feelings
were those of a man just about to be executed, but I endeavored to suppress them. At length the old Moor arrived. I
asked him what all this meant. He told me, after speaking
with them for some time, that I must not be alarmed, but try
to make myself agreeable to them, and they would soon leave
me. I obeyed him as far as possible, still complaining however
to him aside at their continuance in the house. He spoke to
them a second time, and they made me a salam, or bow, and
took their leave.

The subahdar then told me that these men were his
friends, and would protect me against all violence; that they
belonged to the sultan's guards; and that they came in to
gratify their curiosity, having heard that he had a friend from
the vessel in the harbour to see him. He said, "Were I in England at your house and among your friends, would they not
want to come in and gaze upon me?" I answered, yes. But
having some suspicion that this might be treachery, I told
him that all which I had brought on shore, except the dress
necessary to me, I should leave with him; that if he were to
permit me to be killed, he would not gain any thing by it;
and that as he saw how much the Commodore regarded me,

my death would be avenged. At this he seemed hurt, and accused me of an unreasonable jealousy. Our feelings were reconciled, and our confidence increased by an interchange of our sentiments. We smoked a *hubble-bubble* of tobacco and opium, and were friends.

The old Moor then took another walk through the guards, locking the door as he went out, and taking the key with him. He had not been gone long before the house was surrounded by a multitude who made a great noise and beat upon all sides of it. The wife of the subahdar came up stairs to me and made me understand that the people would pull down the house if a woman who was with us was not immediately delivered up to them. The friends had come after her. I asked why she did not let the woman go out. She said that her husband had locked the door and carried away the key.

This news gave me no pleasure. I felt myself in a bad situation, locked in a strange house, surrounded by an enraged mob of savages, and exposed every moment to be drawn to their vengeance. By signs, and some words, I made my anxiety known respecting what was to be done. She had no advice to give and her mind was in a state of confusion. But the woman who was the object of the search knew well what was to be done. She told me to help her out of one of the chamber windows. This I did, and handed her to the arms of the people below. They were thus appeased; made me a handsome salam, and left the house in perfect quietness. My fears were removed and I felt myself as safe as I should at home. It was evident that no harm was meant me. When the subahdar returned, I told him the story and the circumstances. He enjoyed a hearty laugh; we smoked another hubble-bubble together, and things wore a brighter aspect.

The subahdar said that he believed the sultan knew I was on shore; that he was not displeased; that he was willing to settle terms of a friendly intercourse with us. I became more and more gratified with my visit and my hope was increased that relations of amity might be formed between us and the sultan, according to the wishes of our Commodore. Before I left them, the friends of the old Moor came to see me without any uneasiness on my part, or jealous curiosity on theirs. At daylight I divided all my stock of goods between the females, a stock consisting of scissors, pen-knives, combs, beads and other articles. The Commodore had told me to be generous in bestowing them that the people might have strong impressions in favour of our liberality. After this I bade them farewell, returned to the ship and was cordially welcomed by the Commodore and his officers. Thus finished a night of adventures.

AT NINE IN THE MORNING, the subahdar came on board and gave a general invitation to the Commodore and his officers to make the sultan a visit to his palace. We prepared ourselves for the enterprise, and six of the officers, besides the boat's crew, went on shore. We were received with great respect and conducted to the palace of the sultan. He showed us the most flattering attentions, was very communicative; displayed his jewels and precious stones, and laboured to interest and entertain us. One of his pearls was as large as a pigeon's egg, and he had several which he valued at thirty thousand dollars each. The common calculation is that pearls are worth in Europe double their value in India. The diamonds were large, but in a rough state. The gold ornaments were of immense value. His palace was by no means spacious or elegant. It was a handsome house for the place, but far inferior to a multitude of common gentlemen's country houses in other parts of the world. It was near the centre of the town, upon the river, two stories high, upright posts filled in with bamboo, covered with tiles, and distinguished by handsome walks, trees, and verandahs.

The sultan proposed to take us to his seraglio, a proposition which surprised us, but which was well adapted to gratify our curiosity. He saw that our inquiries were frequently directed toward that part of the establishment, and was willing to admit us into it while he was our guide. He sent word to the seraglio that the women should be dressed as usual as on one of his great visits of state, and that they should make their appearance in the same manner. We entered the court through a strong gate covered with copper and furnished with a number of bolts. The court was surrounded by a wall of those large bricks, pieces of clay three or four feet long, and a foot on each side, baked in the sun. We proceeded along a pleasant walk about thirty feet wide, and between two or three hundred feet in length with rows of houses on each side. Passing back and forth in this walk, we saw streets at right angles with it, on which were the dwellings of the sultan's women. They came out when they saw us, dressed very richly in the Malay style — long and loose robes of various colours, and the finest cotton of India. They wore smiles upon their faces, and were disposed to as much intercourse with us as the sultan would permit. They were evidently gratified with the attentions which we paid to them, and perfectly understood the language of the eyes. The attendants were principally eunuchs, a race of inanimate and contemptible beings who had a degree of authority over the subjects of their charge. We were informed that the sultan's women were between two and three hundred. They are not all young nor very handsome. Youth and beauty however shone in perfection in the countenances and forms of a few. As the sultan was near sixty years of age, he might not have been so particular in the selection of his wives as at an earlier period of life.

A Visit to the Seraglio

What a sacrifice of the rights and interests of one sex to the caprice and tyranny of the other does a seraglio present! How fatal an enemy to the character, improvement and happiness of woman is this system of polygamy! And how grateful ought we to be to a code of ethics, laws, and religion by which it is forbidden and prevented!

In the court of the seraglio was a delightful stream of water, fancifully disposed, and trees were arranged in a pleasing order and variety. To a stranger's eye, the place was enchanting. But it must have been tame and oppressive to those who were condemned to be imprisoned within it. We gave to the women a number of presents with which we had provided ourselves from the vessels, and which they accepted with graceful motions and grateful looks. At our return to the palace, we were treated with all the delicacies of the table which the island afforded.

After this the sultan sent some of his officers to show us the town and fort. The town was, I should think, about three miles in circumference, and thickly inhabited, perhaps 30,000 people. Those houses which did not stand over the water were generally two stories high, the lower story being left open.

The fort is on the east side of the river on which the land projects further into the harbour than on the west side. It is on high ground, so surrounded with houses that it cannot be seen from shipboard. We went into it and over it all. It had a kind of ditch about it, with pickets, but the whole was in the rudest style and in a state of decay. Nearly thirty pieces of ordnance, of different calibre, were there, some of them Spanish, and as large guns as I ever saw, not less than forty-two pounders. All were poorly mounted. The fort could not stand the attack of one sloop of war. There were no men in the fort. They did a little by way of preparation when our vessels first appeared in the harbour, but this was soon abandoned. We walked over the town in any direction, within and without the walls. We took water from the river and from the watering place east of it. We procured all kinds of refreshment that our vessels could take on board; and we supplied ourselves with live stock for the Palau Islands. Among the cattle we selected bulls and cows, and we took sheep, goats, several kinds of deer, and a variety of fowls. The good understanding between the people of Jolo and ourselves continued till our departure.

These people are Mahometans, and their mosques are such as we have already described. We attended their worship and were gratified with many things in it.

My remarks imply that we had full means of intercourse with the natives. This is true. We had with us persons from so many nations and islands that we could speak fluently more than twelve languages. The Commodore and four of his officers could speak Moorish very well and were able to hold easy and full conversation with the old subahdar. We had Malay interpreters for our intercourse with the sultan and with the chiefs of the place. We had New Guineans on board, whom we had bought of the savages, who offered them to us, and by whom we could have communication with several other islands.

In regard to the question of trade, it is my opinion that a very profitable voyage could be made to Jolo and the other islands in the neighborhood, with a ship of three or four hundred tons, properly armed, and under the command of a man qualified to transact business. Take a suitable portion of European or American manufactures for an eastern voyage. Such a voyage should never be undertaken but by a man who has been well acquainted with Malay customs and manners, and is familiar with their mode of doing business. No voyage requires better abilities and higher qualifications in the commander. It can be made successful only by perseverance, enterprise, and promptitude. Canton should be taken in the route and considered as a place to finish the sales and purchases. Many articles would find a better market there than in Europe or America, especially pearls and the mother of pearl. With the last, a ship might be loaded in any one of the islands.

Palau Revisited; A Final Word on Abba Thulle; Outrigger Canoes; Palau's Children; Palau Hymns

CHAPTER X

(Delano sketches the sail from Jolo through the sea of Celebes, among various islands, on their return to the Palaus. He details the crew's careful selection of passages along the way, the shoals and currents, and the never-ending search for landings to procure fresh water.)

SAILING EASTWARD one is subject to calms and squally weather. We had a very strong easterly current all the time, till we were as far as 3° north latitude, after which we had a strong north easterly current and steady winds at north east in December and January. In 5° north latitude we had a current setting north west at the rate of forty or fifty miles a day. After passing that latitude to the northward, we had a westerly current nearly as strong. By this, and the strong northerly winds, we were obliged to go southward again in order to get more easting that we might make the Palau Islands. We then stood to the northward, in the latitude of these islands, having strong winds from the north east all the time, with squally and rainy weather.

We arrived at the Palau Islands the 20th of January 1793. We were pained, and the disappointment of our expectations mortified us, when we found the confusion and the sufferings which the misconduct of the successor of Abba Thulle had brought upon the people. Those of our old friends who had survived the civil dissensions consequent upon the death of the good king whom we had left there in 1791, met us with friendship and cordiality.

We had distinct information that Raa Kook, who was on the throne in 1793, was a usurper, and had deposed the lawful successor, and eldest son, of Abba Thulle.

It may be remarked that Abba Thulle is properly a name of office, although I have heretofore used it in this narrative as the name of an individual person, in which sense it is also used by other writers, and was so employed constantly in our conversation, as well as by the Palaus themselves. In regard to Abba Thulle, whom we first knew in 1791, and who deserves to be called great, it may be said in addition that he was not only an eminent warrior, statesman, and sage, but was a most sportive and delightful companion. He was as distinguished for his pleasantry in the hours of relaxation in his house, among his friends, as he was terrible in the field, able in council, and sagacious in morals. The women of his court wore a species of apron, called a *cray*, which was made of the husk of the cocoa-nut. They had also ornaments upon their wrists, necks, ankles, and in their hair. With any and all of his people, our officers and myself have often seen him, in the flow of feeling and good nature, make amusement for himself, the women, and us, without the least offence to any individual. We became so much acquainted with the language that we could enter into the spirit of his wit and humour, and were able to find new sources of admiration for his character in his moments of greatest levity.

When we sailed in 1791 from the Palau Islands for New Guinea, we left two boys with Abba Thulle, who was to be a father to them and teach them whatever was to be learned in regard to their language, manners, customs, arts, religion, and laws. Their names were Ross and Terence. They were born at Bombay of European parents, and were active, intelligent, and interesting. The king and the natives were extremely fond of them, and treated them like young princes. They had every facility for improvement and happiness which such a state of society afforded; and they promised to be of great service to the Commodore in the project which he had formed of extending the blessings of civilization, agriculture, and christianity among the Palau islanders.

The design in leaving them, however, was not accomplished, partly because of the civil dissentions which followed the death of Abba Thulle, and partly because McClure abandoned the enterprise, which probably extended at one time in his mind to the idea of becoming the king of the islands. This idea was not in fact so extravagant as it would at first appear, nor was it at all connected with a purpose of usurpation by violence or injustice. McClure was always, and everywhere, a great favourite with the natives, and particularly at the Palau Islands. In consequence of his design, and the efforts which he used to introduce among them the domestic animals and the arts of agriculture, he was voluntarily made equal to the king in the administration of the government, and in the direction of all their affairs. Everything was managed according to his wishes. At his age therefore, about thirty, it is not surprising that he should have cherished the idea of becoming sovereign in this dominion, and of forming a people and their institutions after a model of his own.

Although I have said that there is not sufficient evidence of the design which has been ascribed to him — spending his whole life at Palau, and abandoning England forever — yet it is highly probably that he intended to execute some great project which would have required many years to be brought to maturity. The decision on this question cannot now be known, since he died not long afterwards at an early age.

On our return we found the boys had been separated,

Ross remaining at Palau, while Terence was taken to Artingal. This separation was not the effect of any hostility to the boys, but of the policy and self interest of the contending parties. Each wished to have some pledge of their attachment to the English, and of the care they had bestowed, during our absence, upon the wards left behind. Hence it was that Terence was carried away to Artingal. We did not see him while we were at Palau, but he was afterwards delivered to the Commodore, and brought away in the *Panther*. Ross we took on board with us when we went to Macau.

At this visit we parted our vessels for a time, and I went on board the *Endeavour* while the *Panther* stayed at Palau. The *Endeavour* remained about a month at the islands, and the *Panther* about two, but McClure continued there with the *Panther*'s launch for a number of months.

A circumstance on our arrival from the Moluccas will show the wonderful activity of the natives of Palau in managing their canoes, and the rapidity with which they can sail. As we approached the town, a canoe, having a sail and an outrigger, with ten or twelve men, came off to meet us. We were going at the rate of seven or eight miles an hour. We threw out a rope for them which they caught while in the centre of the canoe, not knowing the effect of it upon themselves. The canoe was immediately turned over and over, and they let go the rope. They were, as they always are, excellent swimmers. They got their canoe upright at once, bailed out the water, arranged the sail, and with the wind and their paddles overtook us at the distance of a mile.

Their canoes always have one outrigger. Some of those for war are thirty and forty feet long, from two and a half to three feet deep, and eighteen inches wide. They can go equally well with either end first, and always keep the outrigger to the windward in sailing. The mast is in the centre, with a lateen sail, the yard shifting at pleasure from one end of the canoe to the other. The outrigger preserves the balance, and the narrowness of the canoe permits it to be propelled very fast through the water. Sails and paddles are both used when great speed is wanted. The canoes are beautifully ornamented with inlaid work of mother of pearl, or any other oyster shell, or shells which are white. The outside is always painted red, and the white figures are very conspicuous by contrast. The decorations are in imitation of birds, fishes, flying foxes, and men. The paddles often are adorned in a similar manner, especially those of the king and the chiefs. They have each but one blade. In some of the eastern islands there is a blade at each end, the hands are in the centre, and the paddle is used alternately upon the sides of the canoe.

Children of the Palau Islanders are all taught to swim very early, the girls as well as the boys. I have seen the mothers throw them into the water twenty times in succession when they were not more than two or three years old, and catch them up again after they had paddled awhile with their hands and feet, and were about to sink. In this manner the art of swimming is acquired incredibly early, and affords them complete protection against drowning since they can all swim like dolphins.

They are remarkably sharp sighted, although they dive a great deal in salt water after oysters and other shell fish, a practice which is said to injure the eyes. The mothers are in the habit of squeezing green lime-juice into the eyes of their children, when they are a week old, and afterwards. I have seen this done often even to adults. At first, it produces exquisite pain and makes the children writhe in agony. But after a time, the painful effect ceases.

The taro root is the same as our dragon root. It has, if I remember right, a yellow flower; it grows in low marshy land; is cultivated with as much care as we bestow upon Indian corn; is collected by the women, who are sometimes drawn out of the bog, where it grows, with a rope; and is often cut into thin slices and dried like apples. It cannot be kept in its green state longer than a week without turning sour; and just before it is spoiled it becomes glutinous. It must be boiled much or it will take the skin off the tongue and mouth. It has the shape of a beet with annular ridges at the top and half of the length, and is as thick as a man's arm. It is propagated by cutting off the root and putting the part which remains into the earth.

The swalloo I found in much greater abundance on the shores and reefs of the Palau Islands than in any other place I ever visited. Among themselves they have a system of barter in fishing lines and tackle; in cocoa-nut oil for the hair and body; in fish; in cocoa-nut shells beautifully wrought and inlaid; in *kypattles*, or hatchets, formerly made of flint, oyster shell and bone, but now of iron or steel which they procure by intercourse with Europeans and others; in bows, arrows, spears, swords and all the implements of war; and in ornaments for the ears, wrists, body, and hair. These we were able to purchase for trifles, to any amount we wished.

At this writing (c. 1816), my brother Samuel tells me that while he was at Macau in the latter part of 1807, he saw a vessel which had just arrived there from the Palau Islands with a very valuable cargo of swalloos, oysters and tortoise shells, cocoa-nut oil, and a variety of valuable kinds of wood for cabinet work. The cargo was sold for a large amount and the profits of the voyage were very great. The islands seem to be in a better condition; trade more important; and the stock of animals much increased. Some Europeans have settled there, taking wives, according to custom, from among the natives and raising a population of mulattoes.

ADDING TO MY EARLIER ACCOUNT of religion among the Palau peoples, I several times heard the singing of pious hymns, and often saw the men and women sitting together after sunset, particularly on moonlight evenings, and heard the women chant their prayers and praises, while the men would listen and at intervals join in the chorus. The meaning of the words was not always the same, but always included a prayer for Abba Thulle. I remember one instance in which the impression made upon my mind by their devotion was deep and interesting. It would not be in my power to give an adequate translation of the hymn, but it began with thanksgiving for the serene and beautiful evening; for the peace which they enjoyed under Abba Thulle; for health and prosperity; and then it offered a prayer for his continuance in life, for his success in war and his wisdom in government; for their parents, children, and friends; for good seasons, abundant fruit, and tranquil days for their enterprises on the water and the collection of fish and food; for the deliverance from civil war and domestic contentions; and for the fruitfulness of the women.

The *Panther* had just come from Palau at the time when I first became acquainted with Commodore McClure at Macau. The ship had brought two Palau women, and Cockawocky, the Palau man. One of the women was a daughter of Abba Thulle, who had formed a desire to visit China under the protection of the Commodore. While we were lying in the harbour at Macau, and on our passage back to the Palau Islands, it was a custom with these women and Cockawocky, as it was afterwards with the women whom we carried with us to New Guinea, to take their seats together in some retired part of the deck and sing a religious hymn in a peculiarly plaintive and touching manner. We were often listening to them while appearing to be engaged only about our own concerns. We could plainly distinguish many of the sentiments which they sang, and heard prayers to the Deity, that he would protect their families, and that he would allow themselves to return to their native lands in safety; that he would send them fruit, and give them peace.

A circumstance of considerable interest happened when we were returning to Palau from Artingal, after the treaty of peace with those who had revolted, the sixty female hostages with us. Abba Thulle and Wedgeborough, my friend and fellow officer, were behind the launch and the greatest part of the canoes employed in the expedition. We were desirous of stopping at some place till they should come up. It was a delightful evening at twilight when we saw in passing one of the islands, a beautiful cove where we might have a charming place to lie at rest till the king and his party should overtake us. During this period, the chiefs were pleased to unite in a song of thanksgiving for the advantages which they had received from the English in the success of the present expedition. They offered praise to God for the assistance of the brave Englishmen, just, generous, greater than others, and equal to gods, expressed their gratitude for a victory and a peace without the shedding of blood; hoped they should never have war with the English; said they would rather be their servants than their enemies; wished them prosperity in their expedition; and prayed that they might return to their friends in health and safety.

All this was done with some ceremony and with great solemnity. The natives stood upon the benches of their canoes and kept time with their feet as well as with their hands. The sound which they produce by striking the flat hand upon the hollow part of the thigh is wonderful. It is loud and clear when an individual does it alone, but when it was done by this multitude together, the report, and the echo from the forest through the stillness of the night and over the unruffled surface of the cove, were deep, and awful beyond description.

This song continued about twenty minutes. It is the common practice on such occasions for one to name the song and the few short and simple sentences which are to be sung. The sentences are always direct and brief, easily remembered and repeated, and many of them handed down by tradition, are learned early, and can by habit, be called up to the mind at pleasure. They have persons among them who can make with facility such alterations and additions as any new combination of circumstance may require.

Leaving these islands, we sailed for China through the straits of Formosa (*Taiwan Strait*). We had severe gales, thick and stormy weather, a remarkable high cross sea, and found the passage uncomfortable, as it usually is in the north east monsoon. Off the south end of Formosa (*Taiwan*), there are many dangers which it was difficult to avoid entirely, especially as the commander of the *Endeavour* was quite young and seemed not to be thoroughly acquainted with navigating this sea. Fifteen leagues east of Grand Lama we got soundings in a thick, dark, stormy night. With much difficulty we made the Asses-Ears, two peaks on the China shore, about a mile distant, bearing north east, three leagues from Grand Lama. We were then in nine fathoms water. The Ears were a guide by which we entered Canton bay. After this we found no difficulty till anchoring in the Typa.

From Macau to Mauritius; Captured; An Atmosphere of Revolution; The "Golden Dream"; Comments on Privateering

ON OUR arrival at Macau I found that most of the European and American vessels had sailed from Canton. One remained, the ship *Eliza* from New York, commanded by Captain William R. Stewart who had come from the island of Más Afuera, Chile, with seal skins. Captain Stewart wished to find a market for his skins, and after I became acquainted with him, we concluded to go to Canton together, leaving the *Eliza* in the harbour. I had come to Macau for the purpose of getting a passage to America and thought the *Eliza* would afford me one.

It was March 1793 when we were in Canton. A scene very different from what we expected presented itself to Captain Stewart. The Chinese government, finding that he had come to Canton without his ship, leaving her out of reach of the laws of the empire, caused the house where he was to be surrounded by a great number of soldiers, and charged him with the breach of an established and indispensable usage in coming to Canton to learn the state of the market and take advantage of the information, while his ship was not liable to pay the common perquisites for a place of anchorage, measurement, and other privileges. Compensation was demanded in money. After much difficulty and anxiety, it was settled by the agency of our friend, the chief Dutch supercargo, that Stewart should be released for $500. He thought himself fortunate to escape with so little injury from the storm which he had raised.

The price of seal skins was very low at this time and Stewart was not able to raise funds enough to load his ship on his own account, although she was small. He therefore took a freight of sugar for Ostend in Flanders.

It was now time for me to bring my accounts to a close with the English government for my service in the expedition under Commodore McClure. The chief supercargo of the English at Canton paid me two dollars a day for two years. This was not the whole time during which I had been employed by them. But the Commodore had always granted me many privileges and good opportunities to gain a profit in various parts of the expedition, and I felt no disposition to complain of my wages.

The *Panther* and the *Endeavour* sailed from Bombay in August 1790. I have their journals complete from that date to July 1793, when they returned. These journals have been useful in constructing this narrative.

Having agreed for a freight, Captain Stewart ordered his ship to Canton. He sold his cargo of 38,000 seal skins, for only $16,000, so reduced was the price for this article. The Dutch gentleman, Mr. Van Braam, who freighted the ship, knew that Captain Stewart was not a regularly bred seaman, and wished that I could go in her to Ostend. For a small consideration, as I desired very much to get home, I took the command of her by agreement with Stewart. We had the sugar put on board, and on the 10th of April, we sailed for Ostend. As we were to pass Macau, we took provisions on board for the *Panther* and *Endeavour*, having purchased them at Canton. For this service I received $200.

I soon discovered that the *Eliza* was a very leaky ship and extremely dull in sailing. We were late in the north east monsoon when we left Canton, and at latitude 8° 30' north, we met the south west monsoon. After this we had head winds, calms, and flattering weather which carried us to the Straits of Sunda. The sea is interspersed with sandy islands, small and low. We landed on several of them and seldom failed to procure plenty of fine green turtles. Saddle Island is a good place for them.

The passage by the straits of Banca (*Bangka, east of Sumatra*) is most frequented, but in my opinion it is not as good as the passage eastward of it. Its navigation is intricate, and you are liable to be attacked by the Malay pirates who haunt the straits. A small ship must not encounter this danger if it can be conveniently avoided. I once saw a fleet of prows come out of a small bay and pass across our fore-foot at the distance of a mile and a half sailing in a line, one ahead of another with the wind directly after them. As soon as they passed our bow, they hauled under our lee and formed nearly a semi-circle round us. This manoeuvre did not please me, and I ordered two pound guns to be fired with round shot at the foremost prows. This was done, and repeated a few times, when the Malays altered their course, and left us free. I have no doubt they had bad intentions toward us.

I have long been convinced that a ship not strongly armed should never let a Malay fleet of prows approach very near. It is different with Europeans or Americans. With them it would be a mark of ignorance, or fear, to waste ammunition as soon as there should be the least chance of hitting a vessel of the enemy; but with the Malays, fire as soon as you can reach them, even if you are not near enough to do them any injury.

After beating in the China Seas for two months, we got through the islands and as far as the Straits of Sunda. Filling up our water and supplying ourselves with wood, we pro-

ceeded to the Isle of France, called Mauritius by the Dutch
who discovered it. We arrived the 10th of July, worn down
with fatigue in working at the pumps. In all my life at sea, I
never knew a ship to leak at such a rate as ours did during
that whole passage. The two pumps sometimes gave fourteen
hundred strokes an hour, and seldom less than a thousand.
Our sugar was wet, and a large part of it dissolved and
mingled with the water which was pumped out of the hold.
From this, or some other cause, we were surrounded with an
immense multitude of fish of all varieties, from the largest
whale down to the smallest sprat, the whole distance from the
Straits of Sunda. We caught many of them with the hook,
with grains, and with the harpoon. We ate some of them, and
the greater part of the crew was poisoned. Which of the fish
was the cause, we did not know, but we supposed it to be the
bonito.

WE TOOK A PILOT off Quoin de Mer. After he had got us
from under the fire of the guns of four frigates which were lying outside of the buoys, he told us that Louis XVI was beheaded; that France had declared herself a republic; that she
had made war with England, Spain, and Holland; that there
was then an embargo in Mauritius; and that the people of the
island had fitted out fourteen privateers which were then at
sea, some as large as forty-gun ships. This information struck
us dumb. But we had hardly time for reflection when the
frigates sent their boats on board of us, and took possession.
Our ship was warped (*hauled by rope or line*) into the basin.

I went on shore and found a number of Americans in
the same situation with myself, embargoed, and without any
certain prospect of an immediate release. We were indignant
at this conduct, as we considered our nation on terms of particular friendship with France, perhaps the only friendly

Captured

THE HARBOR AT PORT LOUIS, MAURITIUS, 1831.
(FROM THE COLLECTIONS OF THE LIBRARY OF CONGRESS)

power she then had. Nearly all the supplies of Mauritius came from us, and yet the government did not treat us with respect or justice. It was mortifying to see very low men, without talents or integrity, in power, and using it for the worst purposes, under the name of liberty. I soon discovered that what they meant by this word was to do as they pleased, while others should be bound to conform, or die. Those who declaim the most vehemently in favour of the levelling system are, as far as my experience has extended, among the greatest tyrants when they get the power. Liberty and law are excellent when they are properly mixed. The one cannot make men happy without the other. The attempt to establish perfect liberty must of course fail, for it is not in the nature of man to prevent the strong and violent from overcoming the weak and timid, except by the forms of civilized society.

It is idle to look for an equality of talents, accomplishments, influence or property. In regard to all the causes by which we rise to power and gain possessions in the social state, nature has made us unequal, and circumstances still more so. There is however a limited sense in which men are equal. Our right to use our talents and lawful advantages for our own happiness in connection with the happiness of those around us; to have our responsibility measured by our means and opportunities; to seek for knowledge, influence and enjoyment, according to the relations we sustain in a society where a natural and fair competition is allowed to all its members; to be governed by just and equal laws; to be punished no more than our crime demands; to use our invention, skill, and enterprise for our own benefit when we do not interfere with the same right in others; to make the most of our existence as members of the family, the state and the church: our right to these, and to many other things, is equal. Liberty and equality have suffered much from the violence and excesses of their French defenders, and are sounds which now offend the ear. But we are not to go to the opposite extreme, under the idea that whatever is hostile to error, in one of its forms, is of course truth.

We passed our time as well as we could in this place, and that was miserably enough; for we saw our people eating out our cargoes, and the worms eating up our ships. It was not common then for vessels in the merchant service to have the bottom coppered and defended against worms.

The sugar which I had on board belonged to Mr. Van Braam, the Dutch supercargo at Canton. The French were at war with the Dutch, and it became necessary to lose the sugar, or to make it appear that it belonged to me and Captain Stewart. I saw every day that the French were taking from American ships all the property of enemies which they could find. I kept my cargo, and had never shown my bills of lad-ing. My ship's papers the French had obtained at the custom house, and would not let me have them, saying that I had property of their enemies on board. I held no argument with them, and made no parade about the charge, but unloaded my ship as fast as possible in order to repair her bottom. As soon as I could, and without many words, I sold the sugar for what it would bring in the market.

I found the ship so much eaten by the worms that I did not think her worth the cost of repair, and sold her also. Captain Steward and myself had each of us between 12,000 and 15,000 dollars. Mr. Van Braam's property, which we had, amounted to about the same sum. I was repeatedly examined at the custom house in regard to this property, but succeeded at last to secure it to the right owner. After consultation, Stewart and myself agreed to purchase a large prize ship, and return to Canton by Bombay, taking a freight of cotton at that port. Having the benefit of a neutral flag, we thought that we might be able to do something handsome for ourselves and Mr. Van Braam with a large ship. He was a friend to us both, and might greatly assist us in China, as he would be the more induced to do from the efforts we had successfully made to save his property. At an auction of ships, there was one belonging to the Dutch company, the *Hector*, of fourteen hundred tons, pierced for sixty guns, new, and suited to our purpose. We bought her, and had, as we thought, money enough left to fit her for sea. We went to work preparing her, but soon found that the undertaking was too much for us. Our daily expenses were very great, and the colonial assembly laid one embargo after another, stating publicly that such a ship as ours ought not to be permitted to go into an English port in India, where she would be employed as a man of war, and would return to blockade their own harbour. We were detained till all our money was gone, and we had to take up more, at an exhorbitant interest, to be paid at Bombay. All this time, we had between one hundred and twenty and one hundred and seventy men on board, our expenses being 100 dollars a day. The 21st of February, 1794, we got clear, and sailed for Bombay, having nearly twenty English gentlemen on board as passengers, besides a number of ladies, from whom we never received a farthing, as they were all in distress at the time.

WHEN THE INHABITANTS ON MAURITIUS received news of the declaration of war in 1793, they were industriously pursuing their agriculture and commerce, and were as honest and honourable as people usually are in a place of trade. But they soon learned to cry, "Liberty and equality," "the tyrant is dead," "oppression is destroyed," "the rights of man are triumphant." They fitted out privateers and got a number of them at sea, ships mounting from twenty to forty guns. They owned them in shares, commonly having five hundred shares in a ship, and sometimes more. Thus all ranks of men were able to embark in privateering. The effects of this, and the nature of the principle, will make a benevolent man shudder. This system of licensed robbery enables a wicked and mercenary man to insult and injure even neutral friends on the ocean; and when he meets an honest sailor who may have all his earnings on board his ship, but who carries an enemy's flag, he plunders him of every cent.

In honourable warfare, private property is to be respected. The object is not to do injury to the individuals of a nation with which we are in hostility, but to seize or destroy the property of the government, and to kill, or take captive, the troops by which the war is carried on against us. We wish so to distress or affect the rulers of our enemy that they may do us justice, regard our rights, and wish for permanent peace. Privateering is entirely at variance with this first principle of honourable warfare. The distress which it causes is the distress of individuals, and reaches the government but remotely. The benefit of it is also the benefit of individuals, and makes them rich while it adds nothing to the immediate powers of the nation to continue the war. Privateersmen are under the restraints of neither civil nor military life. I would not say that all men engaged in this business are wicked and corrupt, but it is certainly true that few situations could be imagined where a man's conscience, his moral feelings, his sentiments of honour, and his generous ambition, would suffer more.

Privateering is a mode of warfare never to be encouraged, although it is sometimes tolerated by a lawful government. It should be considered as an expedient to which resort must not be had except the circumstances are peculiar, the necessity urgent, and the promise of utility as a national measure very great. It is not easy to prevent the abuses of it unless by abolishing it entirely.[22] When the subjects of Abba Thulle cut down the cocoa-nut trees of an enemy in the spirit of private revenge, he asked them why they acted in opposition to the principles on which they knew he always made and conducted a war. They answered, and let the reason make us humble, "The English do so."

MAURITIUS IS ABOUT 150 MILES in circumference, well watered, and fertile. The air and climate are excellent. Sugar is produced in great abundance. Coffee and indigo are found in smaller quantities. Oranges, citrons, lemons and pine apples are there in great perfection. The island has ebony and dye wood. Indian corn is cultivated with great care and attention. It was introduced into the island by M. de la Bourdonnais, whose administration was remarkable for its patronage of every improvement and useful virtue. By his zeal, aqueducts, bridges and hospitals are said to have been built. Indian corn, which he introduced, furnishes the common bread of the inhabitants. It is not unusual to see the best people eating it from the ear in the market. Women boil it, and carry it about in covered baskets to sell. There are two crops annually, one of wheat and the other of Indian corn. The market is well supplied with poultry, fish, all kinds of meat, and every variety of fruit.

The number of inhabitants in 1790 was about 8,000 white people, and 12,000 black, besides those enrolled for the military service. Twenty-seven years have elapsed since this census was taken, and the number is probably more than doubled.[23]

Hurricanes sometimes do great damage in the island, blowing down houses, destroying fields of corn and cane, prostrating valuable trees, jeopardising life, and wrecking ships.

The situation of Mauritius is remarkably good for the purpose of commerce. It lies in the track of all vessels bound from any part of Asia to Europe, Africa, or America, and of most of the vessels bound eastward. The merchants have in general grown rich very fast. Their character however has the stain upon it of the numerous privateers which they have been in the habit of sending to sea on every occasion. At the period I was there, the people were divided on the subject of the difficulties in France, some wishing to remain quiet, and others burning to enter into the levelling system, and make all that they could from the revolutionary mania. The majority belonged to the corps of *sans culottes*. They obliged the men of property to receive the paper money of the colony, which had lost nine-tenths of its value, and to pay for it in specie, to the amount of one fourth of all they had. They at length became so violent that they would go to a gentleman's house or store where there was flour, beef, pork, wine, or other articles they wanted, break the doors open, and take away whatever they wished, paying the owner in the depreciated money of the colony.

He who was governor while I was there was one of the best of men, and was peculiarly adapted to the time and the place. His name was Malartick. He did all that was in his power to restrain them from doing wrong and from acts of violence.

The form of government was a colonial republic. When the Assembly met to legislate, a self-authorized club would meet and prescribe what they should do. This club consisted of low and unprincipled men who still had great popular influence. When the Assembly was about to pass any law which the club did not like, a clamour would be raised, and threats used to prevent it. On some of these occasions, Malartick would rise and begin to speak in favour of the law in a conciliatory manner. The sans culottes would seize hold of him, threaten him, and shake him violently for a time. He would remonstrate with them, tell them that they ought to hear him, and that they would find him their friend. He would then go on and point out to them the great advantages of having the proposed law, and the immense evils of being without it, until the leaders would find the multitude too much affected to permit them to continue their violence, and the law would be passed. Many of the people would relent; and some of those who attacked him fiercely at first, I have seen go up to him, after the manner of Frenchmen, and embrace, kiss, and caress him like lovers. The good old man died in the place, and a splendid monument has since been erected to his memory on the Champ de Mars where he was buried. It was undoubtedly owing to his practical wisdom and judicious moderation and firmness that thousands were not guillotined on the island. A guillotine was in fact built while I was there, and I saw an inscription on the front of it, in French, "A cure for aristocracy."

Hurricanes; Bombay, and the Collapse of our "Golden Dream"; Commerce at Bombay; Life and Customs; Snakes; Caves of Elephanta and Salsette Islands

FROM MAURITIUS we proceeded towards Bombay. On the fourth day out, we had a tremendous gale of wind. It blew violently for eight hours between east and west, at all points of the south half of the compass. We lost three topsails, which were chewed up in the first part of the gale, and as we hoped that it would not be any thing more than a squall, we did not hand them (*roll them up securely*) till the wind became so hard, I dared not send my men aloft, fearing every moment the masts would go over the side. Our fore yard broke in the slings quite into halves. The masts played in the upper deck nearly a foot during the gale. The lower rigging of a ship, especially of a large one, should be over the common size, rather than run the least risk by its being under it, and should have a wide spread. When it is new, it should be set up well before going to sea, and as often afterwards as it is found to be stretched. Otherwise, should there be a period of warm and rainy weather, your masts may take their leave of you — a circumstance not very congenial to the feelings of a good seaman.

The hurricane differs from other gales of wind in several respects. It commonly comes on with a squall, blows for a few moments with astonishing violence, then is nearly calm for the same length of time, and afterwards returns with full force in a direction perhaps four points different from what it at first pursued. Thus it may take a ship off from the wind, or perhaps aback if there be any sail set, either of which would be an evil when lying to, but when scudding, the sudden and shifting gusts would be still worse. Add to this the cross sea which is produced and which all seamen dread.

Repairing our damages, we proceeded to our course, and in fifteen days after leaving port, we struck soundings on Mahé Island, in the Seychelles bank in the night, in latitude 5° 10' south, and longitude 56° east. At one o'clock a.m. we anchored until sunrise. We ran into irregular soundings, from five to seven miles an hour, on different courses, between north and east, nearly the whole day, before we got clear of the bank. The water was so clear that we sometimes saw the large coral rocks at the bottom, and expected the ship would strike upon them. The sun shone brightly all day and enabled us to distinguish the colours of the rocks, which were red, white, and black. No land was in sight at any time. We frequently saw a Portuguese snow on the banks, which had come out of Port St. Louis with us from Mauritius. We thought she was aground, and she thought the same of us. The soundings were so extremely irregular that we were both anxious to get into better water, and often tried to meet for inquiry, but did not, and escaped without injury.

Immense numbers of sharks were on this bank. They followed the lead whenever it was thrown, and appeared to be much inclined to play with it as a novelty. They were from three to ten feet long, of a beautiful gold colour, and were not fierce or voracious. We put out hooks and lines which were well baited, but we could not tempt them to touch the bait. They were of the same species as those I saw in Rat-Island Basin.

After getting clear of this dangerous bank, we sailed northward with light winds, interrupted by calms all through the month of March and into April till we fell in with the east coast of Africa. We passed between Cape Gwardafuy and the island Socatara (*Socotra*) and came to the coast of Arabia Felix in the gulf of Babelmandel. We sailed near to the place where the *Commerce* was wrecked, a ship commanded by Captain Johnson, and owned by merchants of Boston. Captain Johnson was standing northward in the early part of the night and at twelve o'clock came upon soundings of thirty-five fathoms. He thought he was on the coast of Malabar, near Bombay, and gave orders to haul the ship to the westward to find sea room. After this, he did not throw the lead once to ascertain the soundings till four o'clock p.m. when his ship struck and was lost five or six miles from the shore. It was a strange mistake indeed in Captain Johnson to suppose the coast of Arabia Felix was that of Malabar, and especially as he was sailing northward. The crew, getting ashore in boats, was attacked by the Arabs, and afterwards many of them died in the sands of the interior as they were making their way to Muskat (*Muscat or Masqat, Oman*). To this place the survivors arrived by the aid of some of the roving tribes of the country, after having suffered incredible hardships. Johnson came home from Calcutta in the ship *Three Brothers*. On board this ship, he did duty as chief officer under captain Brown, and I was a passenger. I had therefore an opportunity of hearing the story of the loss of the *Commerce* frequently, and was never satisfied with the apology of Captain Johnson for his mistake and its calamitous consequences. He afterwards became a kind of preacher in our country in some of the migratory companies of religionists.

AT BOMBAY WE MET OUR OLD FRIENDS with joy and experienced the most perfect hospitality. The members of the government passed warm encomiums upon our characters and conduct for what we had done in favour of the English and others in Mauritius, and for giving passage to so many of them in our ship. They allowed our former ship's papers to give us the privileges of an American flag, and a neutral power.

The news, however, of which we were the bearers did not assist our purposes of business, particularly that part which showed that American ships were not respected by the French, according to the treaty with Louis XVI. These circumstances discouraged all persons from putting property into our ship as freight in this port. After lying here several months, and finding the season gone for doing any thing toward a voyage to China, we turned our thoughts to Calcutta.

We had now to pay the debt which we had been obliged to contract in Mauritius. This gave us great difficulty, for it had accumulated to nearly 20,000 dollars. At length we found a gentleman by the name of Dunlap, who wished to go to America, and would advance the money for us upon a respondentia, if we would give him a bottomry bond on the ship, and would allow him an exorbitant profit. He would wait for us to get a freight, and then go with us. The state of the times prevented our selling the ship, if we wished to do it. We were very unwilling to relinquish our high hopes of making a fortune by our large ship and our neutral flag. But we were ultimately compelled to accept Dunlap's proposal, and to yield the golden dream.

The soil of Bombay may not be called fertile, but is considerably productive, and every part of it is cultivated. The climate is mild and the island enjoys a refreshing sea breeze. It produces rice, cocoa-nuts, all kinds of garden vegetables, and a small variety of the eastern fruits. Cattle, sheep, goats, horses and buffaloes are found upon it. The population of the island is more than 150,000.[24] It is the great mart of the western coast of India. The best cables and anchors should be provided for ships going to Bombay. The English Indiamen commonly procure a good kayar-cable, which is found by experience to be much better than one of hemp. The kayarcable is made from the husk of the cocoa-nut, and is far more elastic than the common cables. It will hold a ship riding at sea as long again as one of hemp will. A thousand ships may lie in the harbour at once.

The people of Bombay have many large ships of their own. The largest merchant ships in the world are built there, and belong to the commercial capitalists of the town. The ship builders are all natives, and are pre-eminent in their profession. They build many ships of teak wood which they call the king of the oaks. It is as large as our largest oaks, the timber very straight, free from knots, and excellent for planks. I have seen it grow fifty feet before a limb shoots from the trunk. Some of them are three feet in diameter. There is another kind of tree which is called there sissoo-wood, and which is the best in the world for the crooked timber required in ships. It is extremely hard and durable.

Thirty or forty of these large ships are loaded with cotton at Bombay in a season for China. Other articles are also sent to that market from this place — sharks-fins for soup, sandal wood, and sometimes a cargo of rice free from all duties. The yellow cotton for all the nankin (*nankeen, a kind of cotton cloth*) is sent from Bombay, and never receives any dye after it is taken from the tree. The traffic of the island is very great.

There is an extraordinary octagon building at Bombay, 150 feet in diameter, for pressing cotton. There are in it twelve sets of wooden screws, and one set of iron. The wooden screws are like those which we use in cider-mills. A very strong frame is made of planks into which the cotton is put, with a gunny bag at the bottom and at the top for a part of the covering. The cotton is pressed by the wooden screws from six feet to less than three, as far as the screws can carry the pressure. The bolts are then taken off and they fall away from the cotton, which is made into a bale to be pressed again under the screws of iron. These are so arranged that sixty men can work at the levers, and apply a force which would raise a thousand tons. Four bales are here pressed at once into a size of fourteen inches each. In this manner, the bulk of the cotton is so reduced that a ship may be loaded with it and cross the ocean safely with very little ballast.

Bombay has walls and is well fortified. As many cannon were said to be mounted on the ramparts as there are days in the year. I have been over every part of it, and should think it impossible to take it by sea or land. There are seldom less than 12,000 or 15,000 good troops stationed there.

The island is four or five miles distant from the mainland where there is an abundance of all kinds of provision. By the rules of their religion, the natives live on fish, vegetables, and rice. They have a dish, called cudgeree (*kedgeree*) which is made of dhal and ghee or butter. The dhal is a kind of pea as large as duck-shot. This is boiled with rice till they are completely mixed, and not more wet than damp coarse meal. The ghee is then put on it, and it is considered as a great treat with fish. Ghee is butter made from the milk of buffaloes as well as cows, and is boiled or skimmed when it is new. After this it never becomes hard, and it continues sweet much longer in hot climates than butter in the common state can. They drink no kind of ardent spirit, and are very healthy.

The appearance of Bombay is that of an old, dirty, weather beaten place. The buildings and walls are of stone, brick, and clay. The windows of the English are glass, but of the rest they are thin shells in wooden frames. The apartments of such houses are dark.

Crows are extremely abundant, are never killed, and are permitted to act as scavengers of the city. They fly in thousands wherever they please. They are perfectly tame, come in at the windows, fly round the room where you are at dinner, and I have seen them pick the bread off from the table when they were not watched and driven away by the servants. They sometimes drop their excrements upon you in the streets, and often upon the window seats of the houses, or even the dining table.

The people of India do not bury their dead, and hence a great quantity of putrid flesh is exposed to the open air. Some of the castes among the natives carry out the dead, lay them on high scaffolds, and watch to see which eye the vultures will take out first. This they consider as ominous, according to the principles of their superstition, and draw an inference from it in regard to the future condition of the souls of the departed.

A complaint of the liver is prevalent among the diseases. The liver becomes inflamed, an abscess is formed, and an incision is made in the side of the patient for relief. Sometimes he dies, but more frequently recovers.

There are the first Arabian horses in Bombay that I ever saw. Riding is a great amusement, both on the saddle and in the carriage. The horses are broken in the following manner. A man takes a young horse out upon the Apollo-Green, a place of parade without walls. A rope of thirty feet in length is tied to the horse's head or neck, and fastened to a swivel in a large rock. The man then whips the horse to make him go round at the rope's length. The animal is very obstinate, kicks with the greatest rage when he is whipped, and often attempts to bite. After one horse is thus broken till he is obedient, two are put together, and the same process pursued. When both become obedient, a drag is fastened to them by a strong harness, and they are whipped till they draw it uniformly and kindly. They are black and dark bay, particularly vicious, and also proud. They have been known several times to throw their riders, and stamp them to death. I often had, during my stay there, the horses of Mr. Tate, an eminent merchant, and a gentleman of fortune. They went in a coach at my service whenever I wished to take a ride out upon the island. The coachmen used to adorn their heads with artificial flowers, green, yellow, blue, and red, and they were so disposed that the horses could see them upon each other as they were in the harness. Their bodies were covered with silken nets, ornamented with tassels and fringes. They were as vain of their dress as a beau or a belle, and would show it in their motions and spirits.

Many of the coaches were made in the English style. Those in the fashion of the country were contrived with a bed or mattress at the bottom, covered with scarlet silk on which the passenger might repose. A top shields him from the sun. A place is arranged in which one's shoes or slippers are put, and the comfort of the vehicle is as great as that of a palanquin.

On this coast there are two kinds of snakes which are very poisonous, numerous, and troublesome. One is the cobra-di-capello, and the other is the cobra-manilla. The former is the hooded snake. I have often seen the cobra-di-capello carried about in a basket for a show. When he is approached, he raises nearly one-third of his length from the ground, bends his neck like a goose, sometimes hisses, then spreads his neck perfectly flat from the head for three inches, makes it form almost a circle, and at length raises the fold higher than his head, giving it the appearance of a hood. It has some resemblance to the shape of a heart, and is not peculiarly disagreeable. The person who carried the snake about, played on a pipe or reed, which either pleased or vexed the reptile so as to make it always raise its neck in this form of a hood.

The cobra-manilla is not much larger than a pipe stem, has a greenish colour, is not thick for its length, is found about old houses and old wood, and climbs trees. The bite of it is mortal, and will produce death in half an hour. The poison is more rapid in its operation that of the cobra-di-capello. In the house where I lived at Bombay, I opened a window shutter and brushed one off the window seat without thinking. The snake ran under the house before I could kill it. This reptile is very much dreaded by every body. The natives are often prevented from climbing trees for fear they may put their hands on one of them among the limbs. The legs of the bedsteads in Bombay all stand in large vessels with water to keep centipedes, scorpions, and the cobras from creeping into bed at night when they are wandering about. The cameleon is often found here. I have frequently seen them upon the guns, then on the carriages, on green grass, and afterwards upon bricks, continually changing as nearly as their nature allows to the colour of the substance on which they rest.

On the subject of the trade of Bombay, a remark may be made upon the country near it, and especially upon Surat. All this region is filled with the manufactures of the east. Surat is an immense factory, producing in the greatest abundance all the varieties of chintz, and sending at the same time nearly all the cotton to Bombay, which is shipped from there to China. It is one of the first places where Europeans were allowed to settle, and to establish manufactories. It now contains more than 300,000 inhabitants, and is a place of the first importance in the circle of the useful arts, and in the traffic of the east.

Before I leave Bombay, I cannot omit to speak of the

celebrated antiquities in the islands of Elephanta and Salsette. I visited them and think that they surpass all the curiosities which I have ever seen. The caves had so much water in them when I went to see the wonders which they contain, that I could not go into them, a disappointment which I bore with no small impatience. I learned from my companions whatever was most interesting in the interior of the excavations. The cave on Elephanta is the largest. The island is high and has two summits which are covered with wood. It is five miles in circumference, and the cave is less than a mile from the beach. The elephant, from which the name of the island is derived, is the size of life, cut out of rock, and is black. It stands near the mouth of the cave which is formed in the solid rock, 135 feet in length and breadth. A great number and variety of figures in high relief are found in it. The whole is supposed to be of Hindu origin, although the common people are told that it was made by the gods. The exhibition of the benevolent as well as of the terrific principle in the religion of the sculptors must have mingled with their design and with the choice of figures.

It has been thought that the caves of Elephanta and Salsette are proofs not only of great perfection in the arts at a very remote period of antiquity in Asia, but of a much earlier and higher degree of perfection than in Egypt. The priests of the Nile are supposed to have gone to the Ganges, not to carry, but to acquire knowledge and improvement. The characters of some ancient language are found inscribed on the pillars of the caves which no one living has been able to interpret.[25]

From Bombay South Along the Malabar
Coast; Sri Lanka; Madras and Calcutta;
Storms; A Bore of the Tide; Financial Disaster

CHAPTER XIII

WE FINISHED our business at Bombay and attempted to go to sea, but before we could get out of the harbour with the ebb tide, the flood met us, and we were obliged to anchor. We rode sixteen hours with a violent wind and sea, after which we were able to leave the harbour and steer down the coast of Malabar.

Our course was in water from 25 to 30 fathoms, soft and muddy bottom. We might have sailed in less depth, had it not been for the numerous large stakes, or trunks of trees which are put down along the coast for the use of the fishermen in the management of their nets. Some of these stakes have a diameter of thirty inches. They are left round, are sharpened at the small end of the trunk, and are driven much in the same manner as the piles on which the New Guineans build their houses. The vessels which are used for this purpose on the coast of Malabar, instead of being canoes, are sometimes twenty tons burthen, two of which are lashed with cables to a single pile, and force it into the earth as the tide ebbs, and as motion is added by the wind and the sea. In this manner the stakes are so firmly fixed in the bottom that they sometimes break in the bows of a ship and compel her to seek a port immediately for safety. They are from 20 to 200 and 300 feet apart; from 10 to 20 feet above water; from 3 to 6 miles distant from the shore; and in 8, 10 and 12 fathoms water.

The term Malabar is supposed to have the same meaning with our word mountaineer, and to refer to the mountains
of Hindustan from which the people of the coast came. Pepper is a very important article of trade in all this country; also
the areca nut, the wild cinnamon, and various kinds of cotton
goods.

At Goa, the principle place of the Portuguese on this
coast, my friend and fellow officer Wedgeborough sustained
the office of master attendant, and died in 1805 or 1806. His
wife died at the same place with him, and on the same day,
both of the fever of the country. He was a man of excellent
character in all respects; his head was as good as his heart. The
news of his death was particularly painful to me when I heard
of it, and united with other circumstances to awaken recollections which filled my mind with melancholy and regret. He
was distinguished by the attachment of all the crew in our
eastern expedition with McClure, and was always judicious
and self-governed when many of us were tempted to rashness
and excess by the vicissitudes which we met among the islands. It was well for him, although it unfortunately ended in
his death, that the English had gained such an influence over
the Portuguese government as to have him appointed master
attendant of the port of Goa. This office is important and lucrative. He who fills it has the care of all the vessels in the
port. They must all report to him; no one can be moved, or go
away, without his permission; and if any quarrel arises upon
this subject between the owners of vessels, it must be referred
to him, and his decision is obligatory and final.

This place was conquered for the Portuguese by the famous Admiral Afonso de Albuquerque, who ultimately took
Goa, in 1510, and other important places along the coast of
Malabar. He left the Portuguese possessions in Hindustan in
the most prosperous condition. He was an equally great gen-

eral and statesman; was proverbially temperate, just, generous, and exemplary in private life.

BEFORE I PASS FROM THE COAST of Malabar to that of Coromandel (*southeast India*), the important and interesting island of Ceylon (*Sri Lanka*) demands some attention. A reef of sand and shells from the island to the continent is called Adam's Bridge, in consequence of a tradition that Adam, after the fall, passed upon it from the island which was paradise, to the continent. The Portuguese discovered, and for many years possessed Sri Lanka. The Dutch took it from them, and the English took it from the Dutch. They all in turn entered into wars with the king of Candy (*Kandy*), the sovereign of the native Ceylonese, and whose capital is in the interior, surrounded by woods and mountains.

The conduct of the Europeans of all parties in this island has been marked by a disposition to make conquests and to monopolise trade. It is painful to every benevolent and impartial observer, as he visits the Asiatic coasts, or the oriental islands, to be obliged to acknowledge that the natives find numerous apologies for their treachery and cruelty toward Europeans, in the treachery and cruelty of the Europeans toward them. The king of Kandy was extremely grateful to the Dutch for assisting him to drive out the Portuguese, but it was found to be only an exchange of one selfish and mercenary power for another. The Dutch used the gratitude of the Kandians to fortify themselves, to prepare the means to gain the entire control of the country, and to appropriate its commerce exclusively to their own benefit. The English too invaded the territories of the sovereign of Kandy, and retribution accompanied them, cutting them off in a cruel manner, in the very heart of the enemy's empire.

The prospect presented to the eye at sea by the hills,

valleys, and the fields of Sri Lanka, is eminently beautiful, and perhaps unrivalled. Groves of cocoa-nut trees are growing in great luxuriance upon the high lands, and rice in the valleys, while various kinds of cultivation, with useful and ornamental fruits and flowers, unite to produce the most agreeable impression upon the imagination. To the mind of a traveller from Massachusetts nothing can be more enchanting than a country which appears to realize what is known only in our poetry — a perpetual spring.

Among the mountains of Sri Lanka is one called Adam's Peak where there is a flat stone on which is an impression of a man's foot, twenty-four inches in length, which some say, is that of our first ancestor, and others, the print left by the god Buddha when he ascended to heaven to be an intercessor with the supreme God for his followers. It is very remarkable that the following language from the *Edinburgh Encyclopaedia* should be so much like that to which we are accustomed in the books of our own religion. The Ceylonese "acknowledge the existence of one Supreme Being, the creator and governor of the world, but they have also a number of inferior deities and evil demons. Of the former, the most exalted is Buddha, whom some represent as originally a divine person, and others, as the spirit of a good man crowned with divine honours. He is said to have appeared in the world in the form of a man, and after having performed a vast number of virtuous actions, and been transformed into a great variety of shapes, he ascended again into heaven, where he acts as a mediator with the Supreme Being, and procures the pardon of his worshippers."

The same authority, the *Edinburgh Encyclopaedia*, shows how painful and unnatural the profession of a pearl diver is. It must be followed from infancy in order to acquire the power of suspending respiration long enough for success in the fishery. The pearl divers usually continue under water two minutes, but it is said by some that they have extended the time to five, and that a Kaffir boy has remained seven; but from abundant experience I am led to believe that no man ever remained under water voluntarily more than two minutes and a half. Blood frequently issues from the nose and ears as they rise to the surface of the water.

The Ceylonese chew the betel nut, a habit prevailing over all the eastern islands. This nut produces in the mouth a crimson liquor which looks like blood when it is thrown out. When it is mixed with other substances, as it often is, it leaves the mouth and teeth black, an effect which the natives consider as a beauty, and think that white teeth should be the privilege only of brute animals. At the Palau Islands, it is allowed to leave the teeth a dark red. It is a stimulant and an opiate, and is used as a luxury and a sensual indulgence. I have myself chewed it, till it has produced a considerable degree of intoxication.

The population of Sri Lanka is loosely stated to be 1,500,000.[26]

AT ALL PLACES ON THE COROMANDEL COAST where I have had an opportunity to make observations, I have found the power of the priests to be very great over the consciences of the natives. The following test of the innocence or guilt of an individual charged with a crime, I have frequently seen applied, and never knew it fail of success. The accused is called before a priest who gives him a handful of rice, and tells him to chew and swallow it. If he is innocent, it will do him no harm; if he is guilty, his present life will be embittered with evils and remorse, and his future life will be spent under the wrath of God, who will continue to increase the intensity of his punishment. The guilty person rarely has hardihood enough to swallow the rice, at least the whole of it. The effort is often commenced boldly, but generally conscience gets the victory before the whole is swallowed.

I saw two women tried. One of them chewed and swallowed the rice very quickly. The other chewed it slowly and heavily. Some of the rice was falling out of the corners of her mouth, and after some time was spent in a state of internal agitation and indecision, she threw down the remainder which was in her hand and made a full confession. This ordeal has had more effect on the conscience than any that I ever knew. The deliberation with which the unboiled rice is to be chewed and swallowed gives the criminal time for much reflection and repentance, and is found by experiment to be irresistible upon the superstitious mind. Some good at least is thus done by a prejudice which appears sufficiently gross in our eyes.

Madras is a town standing quite upon the margin of the sea, and in a place so dry and sandy that water is brought from a considerable distance, except what is caught in cisterns during the rains. The land is perfectly barren, producing nothing spontaneously, and meagerly rewarding the labours of the cultivator.

The climate is excessively hot, but is relieved by sea breezes. There is no port for the town, and boats are used to load and unload all vessels employed in trade with this place. These boats are made very differently from ours and are well adapted to the purposes for which they are designed. They are flat bottomed, constructed without metal, and sewed together with twine made of hemp or rattan which is split into very small threads. They are considerably flexible and can bear without injury the shocks of the surf where one of our boats would be dashed to pieces. Their seams are filled with *chinnam*, a kind of cement made of shell-lime, wood oil, and

A BRIG, *ELIZA*, BUILT IN PROVIDENCE, RHODE ISLAND, IN 1800.
(COURTESY OF THE PEABODY ESSEX MUSEUM)

sometimes white of eggs and sugar. This plaster is very adhesive, utterly impervious to water, and allows some motion without breaking. The bottoms of all the ships built in India are covered with it before the copper is put on. It is used also for the tops of the houses, which are flat, and is a perfect security against rain. It may be made smooth like polished marble. The houses often have an awning above the roof, and thus furnish an agreeable place upon the top for conversation and enjoyment of the sea air. They are usually built of brick and have one story. A few have two stories, and many are raised one story from the ground for coolness and security.

The whole population of the town is estimated at 300,000.[27] They consist of Hindus, Mahometans, and Christians. One part of Madras is called White Town, and the other Black Town. White Town is also denominated Fort St. George and is inhabited by the English. One of the suburbs is occupied by the black watermen who live in thatched cottages. The town is well fortified and has two hundred pieces of cannon mounted.

We took a pilot in the Balasore Road, off Calcutta, crossed the western brace, or sea reef, off the mouth of the Hooghly River, and were compelled to anchor at night as the weather became bad and it was not considered safe to run. At ten a.m. we parted our small bower cable by which we were riding, called the pilot and all hands; let go the best bower, gave out seventy-five fathoms; attempted to bring up the ship, but she would not look toward it; parted the cable in the hawse before she came head to the wind, and let go the sheet anchor; gave out one hundred and ten fathoms and were thus held till morning.

At midnight whilst we were riding by the sheet, the ship sheered, the cable crossed our forefoot, and parted two bobstays out of three. The helm was put the other way and the ship was sheered so as to keep the cable on the other bow. We soon found that the bowsprit was sprung, made great exertions and got runners and tackles on it and down to the parts of the bobstays which were left in the stem, and got everything off from the foremast.

After daylight we found by signal, that the pilot snow, which according to custom accompanied us, had parted her cables also. The pilot who was one of the best men in his calling remarked that if we should lie there another night we should lose all our masts; and as the weather then was very bad he did not like to run; but it was the only alternative, for in drifting in the night we had got within a mile of the breakers on the eastern brace.

We made signal to the pilot snow to get under way and began to heave at the anchor when the cable came short, the pawls of the capstan gave way, the bars flew round and knocked down, or threw against the guns and other articles, sixty men, breaking some heads, some legs and arms, and producing other shocking effects. The ship was held by a short part of the cable; the pawls of the capstan were fixed again; the people who were able returned to work. Finally, after further difficulties, we made sail and followed the pilot vessel which had got under way long before us. She ran for the first buoy, then made a signal for the second buoy. This had also shifted greatly in the storm, so we made for the third buoy.

Before we got up to Calcutta, we let go the spare anchor; but a *bore of the tide*, a peculiar swell of water in this bay, took the ship, after all sail was set in order to get under way, and we were obliged to cut our last anchor to avoid a still greater misfortune. Thus we lost four anchors, averaging 4500 pounds each; parted and cut four cables, the smallest nineteen inches and a half; sprung our bowsprit; and experienced other damages, the whole of which could not be repaired in Calcutta for less than 10,000 dollars. This was indeed a disastrous current in the sea of our fortunes.

What is called a bore of the tides is a large wave with a white head which is seen and heard at a considerable distance. There are three of them. The first, as a general fact, comes at about two hours of the flood tide; then two hours calm, and the second comes; again two hours calm, when the third comes. The longer it keeps off, the more violent is its approach, and the more destructive its course. It is greatly to be dreaded by seamen who are not well prepared to sustain the shock which it gives.

The face of our affairs was now gloomy and oppressive. On our arrival at Calcutta, we waited upon Benjamin Joy, Esq., American consul at the time, to whom we had written from Bombay in the hope that he would be able to procure us a freight for our ship. But he had a ship of his own at Calcutta, and soon expected another. To this was added a general stagnation of business, and it was out of his power to do anything for us. He however treated us with every mark of respect and gave us his friendly offices in a sincere and generous manner.

Dunlap, who had advanced the money for us at Bombay, held out allurements to us whenever he supposed Mr. Joy would do anything in our favour, and thus determined to keep a claim upon the ship. Our prospects continued in this unsatisfactory state for some time, when news arrived that the United States had laid an embargo for thirty days under President Washington. It was also reported, and believed by many, that England and American were at war.

This crowned our misfortunes, and decided our fate. Dunlap immediately pretended that he wanted his money, or further security, and we were obliged to transfer the ship to him. We gave him a complete bill of sale of her, uniting some consideration for our own interest with the force of his importunity, as we feared that our ship would be seized as American property.

The spirits of my partner and myself were now sufficiently depressed. But we had yet another trial to meet. Dunlap was not contented with the security which we had given him, and insisted upon the payment of the money. The ship would not sell for half the sum which she would bring in the market at a period of active business. He commenced suits against us, one against each, and one against the ship. We were obliged to keep out of his way, and for this purpose went to Serampore, about 18 miles north of Calcutta, which was a Danish settlement, and the usual place of resort from Calcutta for men in our situation.

Under these circumstances, Mr. Joy enlisted himself for

us, and made an arrangement with Dunlap, obliging him to receive the ship at 90,000 rupees, a sum much greater than anybody else would have given at that time. We could have kept the cause in court so long that the ship would have been worth nothing by the time a decision should be obtained. For Mr. Joy's services on this occasion I shall always hold myself under an obligation of sincere gratitude to him, and shall be ever ready to bear public testimony to his generosity. The balance due us for the ship was little more than what was necessary to pay our debts in the country, and thus ended our speculation in Mauritius in the purchase of the *Hector*. It was originally planned for the purpose of saving Mr. Van Braam's property, which the French were about to seize. Our design was to return to Canton and settle with Mr. Van Braam, and then to continue our enterprise for ourselves. But the whole project failed, and proved to be a total loss of all the capital for Van Braam, Stewart, and myself, as will hereafter more fully appear.

Bengal, Description and Customs; Punishments; Wives; Castes; The "Black Hole" of Calcutta; Sailing for Boston; Ship Building; Preservation of Food; Reflections

BENGAL (*east India and Bangladesh*) is the most fertile part of India. It lies in the torrid zone, with the exception of a small portion of the northern side. Europeans find the climate hot and unhealthy. But as they become more temperate in their manner of living, and as the physicians understand the nature of the prevalent diseases better, they enjoy more health and live to a greater age. The fine sand which flies in the air in the dry season, and the effects of putrefying bodies thrown out upon the banks of the rivers by inundations, must be permanent enemies of health.

The season of rain is between June and October. Sometimes the quantity which falls is so excessive as to destroy the crops upon the low lands and to leave an extensive covering of sand upon the soil. Instances are said to be frequent when rice has been reaped in boats. Droughts are also very severe and ruinous at times. In the latter part of the 18th century there was a drought so extreme that a famine followed, thousands of people died, and the air was filled with pestilence from the unburied bodies. So many carcasses were thrown into the rivers that the water and fish became unwholesome, and as much mortality was from such food as from starvation.

To alleviate the evils of drought, immense reservoirs of water are prepared, some of which occupy an acre of land.

These are called *tanks*, which are filled by the inundation, and emptied according to the wants of the husbandmen. Dykes are made along the banks of the rivers to prevent indiscriminate overflow of the land in the rainy season. These are often too feeble to resist the swell of water; are frequently broken away, and the crops are ruined in the track of the torrent. The periodical floods of the Ganges and its tributary streams, notwithstanding the sand which they sometimes leave upon the soil, generally enrich it, and render it extremely fertile. The soil is a mixture of clay, sand, and decayed vegetation, and is thus a loam of great fertility, ranging in depth from a few feet to twenty or thirty. It is said that sand, the remains of wood, and shells are found below the soil, and are sufficient evidence that the present is not the ancient surface, but is secondary, and comparatively modern.

Rice is the principal object of cultivation. Wheat and barley of a small kind are produced. Maize, peas, beans, and other sorts of pulse are cultivated. Different crops are seen surrounding one another, ripening at different periods, and are gathered in such a manner as to do great injury to those which come to maturity last. The husbandry is bad, the fields are not inclosed, the best kinds of grain are not selected, and the arts of agriculture are but imperfectly understood. Were the same pains and skill applied to farming as in some parts of Europe, Bengal would be able to feed an addition to its present population of twenty fold. The land is generally level and surrounded by mountains. The woods are called *sunderbunds*, and many of them on the frontiers of the province are left for defence against foreign invasion. The variety of beautiful trees is very great.

The number of wild animals is large, and among them the royal tiger is remarkable. He is said to be sometimes five or six feet high, able to carry off a bullock, and possessed of the power to leap a hundred feet. An animal between a bull and a buffalo is called a *gyal* (*gayal, a kind of ox*). The horses are Persian and Arabian. The birds are astonishingly tame and familiar. Crows, sparrows, and kites fly about the people in the manner described at Bombay. A species of stork is called the *adjutant* because of its martial strut. It eats toads, lizards, serpents and insects.

The carriage by land is effected by oxen, horses, and in a few instances by buffaloes. Water carriage is so easy, however, and reaches so generally to all places, that it must be the common mode of transportation forever. It is said that 30,000 boatmen are employed in Bengal and its dependencies.

The population of the presidency of Bengal is stated at 30,000,000,[28] and half within Bengal proper. Four fifths are Hindus, and the others are Moguls, who are all Mahometans. The English, Dutch and Danes have settlements in Bengal.

CALCUTTA IS THE CAPITAL of this district, and of all the English possessions in India. It stands upon the river Hooghly, extends along the river three miles, and about a hundred from the sea. The river is navigable for the largest ships as far as Calcutta, and for small vessels still further. The English dwell in houses which are extremely elegant, and resemble palaces. They are built of brick, and are covered with the plaster called *chinnam*, a cement that admits of a fine polish, and looks remarkably well. The apartments are spacious; verandahs are generally a necessary appendage of a convenient house. Nothing is admitted into the domestic economy which shall obstruct the circulation of the air and the attainment of comfort.

The part of the town where the natives live is directly the reverse of this. The streets are narrow and crooked; the houses low, small, and ill contrived; they have commonly but one story; and many are built of bamboo and covered with thatch.

The citadel of Fort William was begun by Lord Clive in 1757, and is an extraordinary fortress, exciting great attention from strangers, and affording the best protection to the town. The barracks are bomb-proof and can accommodate 10,000 men. The work could mount six hundred pieces of cannon. The fort is built upon a plain, not many feet above the water level. It is reported to be near two miles in circumference, and is a star fort. The ditch, I think, is thirty feet wide and twelve feet deep, paved with brick on the bottom, and guarded with brick at the sides. The trenches were kept so clean, and were so cool, that it was common for gentlemen to walk in them in the morning. In case of need, the ditch could be filled with water from the river, eight feet deep. Inner trenches run to a sharp angle at the bottom, and are adapted to wedge the bodies fast which should fall into them. The parapet is fifteen feet above the plain, and twelve feet thick. Trenches were dug fifteen behind the platforms for carriages with bridges across them. The fort was deemed a perfect security for the town from which it stands a quarter of a mile. The land between the fort and the city is appropriated to exercise, relaxation, riding, or any other mode of enjoyment in the open air. It is a resort for all classes of people, and in the evening the most elegant and costly equipages are displayed there.

On one side of this plain is the government house, founded since I was first there, by the Marquis of Wellesly. It cannot be adequately described, either within or without. It must be seen before it can be justly appreciated. The marble hall is a wonderful exhibition of beauty and grandeur in architecture. The specimens of sculpture, which adorn the avenues to it, are appropriate and impressive.

The tank of Calcutta is an object which soon arrests a stranger's attention. It supplies the wants of the inhabitants in the dry season. It covers twenty-five acres, is dug fifteen or twenty feet deep, and has a great many springs at the bottom. It is shaped as a parallelogram, and is surrounded by a rail. No persons are allowed to wash in it, though all may take as much water as they want. Those inhabitants who can afford it, have water brought to their houses on the backs of men who use animal skins for bags. The skins are dressed whole, and when filled with water have the shapes of the limbs of the animals from which they were taken. The head is downward upon the back of the man who carries it, the legs projecting out. A tap is fixed into one of them, and the water is easily discharged from it. The tank is kept particularly clean.

The adjutant stork walks on the parade at Fort William as familiarly as the officers do, and appears to feel as much pride as a beau in full dress. It has a white breast and thighs with dark coloured back and wings. Two or three of these storks will pull a man out of the river if he is floating near the shore. The jackall abounds here, and helps to remove filth. It sometimes makes a noise exceedingly like the human voice. In the night these animals set up their cries, and you would think that there were multitudes of girls and boys alternately screaming and laughing together.

There are 700,000 inhabitants in Calcutta,[29] consisting of Europeans, and of all the nations of the east. Most of the laboring people are Bengalees, or Lascars, industrious, peaceable, and harmless. Though not athletic, they are active. They are well protected by the English laws, and may embrace any religion which they choose. They are commonly bare footed and bare legged. They have loose drawers made of white cotton, a white frock or jacket, and wear turbans. The females are handsome, wear short gowns and petticoats, with short chemises, and the hair done up with ornamental combs.

It is common opinion among natives that the water of the Ganges and its branches washes away sins. They throw the bodies of their deceased friends upon the river, and even put them into the water to die when the physicians have despaired of effecting a cure. I have often seen them bring their fathers, brothers, and sons, when they were about dying, to the river on their backs; plaster the mouth, nose, eyes, and ears with mud, and leave them to be carried away by the tide. I have stayed at the bank to watch the conduct of the victims afterwards, and have seen them blow the mud from their mouths and noses; lie still till the water began to rise upon them; turn over upon their faces; crawl upon their hands and knees to the market place; lie down again upon their backs, and cry out for alms or assistance. They were shunned, their cries disregarded, and they were considered as losing their caste for having refused the blessing of dying in the Ganges according to the custom and faith of their religion. The power of the clergy over the popular faith is so great that it is extremely difficult to regain one's standing in a caste after it is lost.

Outcasts are often punished in the following manner: two hooks are put into the back; these are fastened to the end of a pole which is suspended in the middle about fifteen feet high. A rope is attached to the other end of the pole. Drawing this rope raises the victim, who has a basket of flowers in his hands. He is obliged to scatter the flowers upon the heads of the people below as he is carried round upon the end of the pole, which is fixed upon a pivot and makes a full circle. Some prescribed service is chanted during the punishment. It would be gratifying to us if no tortures in the persecutions carried on by Christians could be found to compare with this in cruelty. But while the excesses of the Dominicans, the bar-

barities of the Inquisition, and the mutual destruction too often effected between opposing sects of Protestants make us ashamed of many nominal Christians, we still remember the purity and benevolence of the religion whose laws are violated whenever its disciples indulge such passions and cruelties.

I HAVE SEEN ONE WOMAN BURNT with her deceased husband. This practice, which is constantly diminishing, seems to have arisen from several causes. The most natural one is that of attachment to the husband, and of the grief at the loss which may easily seem at first to be inconsolable. Another reason is the assurance given by their religion that the wife who proves her fidelity by this extreme suffering, shall live with her husband in paradise forever. It is also an idea, handed down by tradition, that as the ashes of the parties are mingled when their bodies are burned together, so their souls shall be united in affection and happiness for eternity.

Wives in India, and under the laws and religion of the Hindus, are considered as entirely at the command of their husbands, and as included in them in the same manner that the term mankind includes all women as well as all men. On this principle, the wife is to die when the husband does. Some have supposed that the jealously of the husband extends beyond the grave, and that the wife is to be burnt to gratify this passion. But such a reason is not consistent with the general character of the Hindus, and is too vile to be admitted without far stronger evidence.

When the husband dies it is common to inquire of the oldest wife if she wishes to burn herself with his body. If she refuses, the next is asked, and so through the whole number. Whatever might once be thought of a refusal, it is not now considered as a crime, although to make the sacrifice is an honour and a great distinction. The laws of both Christians and Mahometans have tended powerfully to diminish the custom, and a premium must be paid in order to gain permission to be burnt. This premium is high, and often cannot be paid.

When a widow is about to offer herself with the body of her deceased husband, the funeral pile is prepared. The wood is split very fine, and I believe is wet with spirits of some kind to make it burn easily and rapidly. A bed of this is raised six feet square and two feet thick. The corpse is brought and laid upon it; a priest leads the widow who steps upon the pile and lays herself down by her husband, putting her arms about his neck, and his arms are laid so as to embrace her. Two bamboo poles are then fastened into the ground, and are bent over the bodies, crossing each other, the ends being held by two priests. The pile is kindled in several places at once. It burns rapidly and the poles are pressed down upon the bodies till the widow is suffocated and ceases to move. During this ceremony the priests chant hymns and prayers, and sometimes the voice of the victim is heard for a moment mingling its tones of faith and triumph with the notes of the priests. The bodies are burnt to ashes, and these are preserved — a preservation however which must be temporary, and which is every year of less and less importance.

THE CASTE OF BRAHMANS ONCE consisted of the most harmless beings in the world. According to their ancient rules, they take the life of no creature; they eat no animal food; they are very superstitious; they worship idols, and particularly some kinds of cattle; a white cow is perfectly sacred in their eyes. A brahman will brush the earth before he sits down and pray that as he has been merciful to the ant, the Deity may be merciful to him.

The Hindus have always been divided into four castes which never intermarry. The *sudra* is the lowest caste and includes menial servants. The next is the *byse* (*vaisya*), consisting of the merchants of all ranks. The third is the *ketri* (*kshatriya*), or the military tribe. The kings and rulers belong to this caste. The last and highest is the cast of the brahmans. The sudras are from the feet; the vaisyas from the belly; the kshatriyas from the heart; and the brahmans from the head of Brahma. Notwithstanding the ancient purity and benevolence of the brahmans, they are often immoral, ignorant, and cruel. Many of them do honour to their caste, but like all other classes of privileged men, there are many also extremely corrupt. The learning of India is confined to them, and they have the same divisions and theories on subjects of literature and science which prevail among Europeans. I have been told by learned men that the Greeks borrowed much of their philosophy from the brahmans.

The castes regard their laws so much that it is difficult to get them to do anything out of their order. No man will do any kind of labour which does not belong to his caste. A military man considers himself disgraced by any other employment. When the sepoys, who are of the military caste, were with us on the coast of New Guinea, I could not get a musket from them, although on any other occasion they would have trembled at my frown, and would have done anything sooner than disobey a regular order. I have seen one seized and flogged at the gangway for stealing a ball of twine from the sail maker, and when he was asked what he had to say in his own defence, he said with a boast that he was of the thief-caste.

The river Hooghly is of the first importance to this country, although its navigation is considerably difficult and dangerous. A pilot must be obtained soon after you pass Point Palmyras. At the junction of the Hooghly and the Ganges there are dangerous banks, and ships are lost upon them. For-

THE ENGLISH FORT IN CALCUTTA, IN 1810.
(FROM THE COLLECTIONS OF THE LIBRARY OF CONGRESS)

merly there was no quay at Calcutta for the use of ships in loading or unloading their cargoes, but now one is built, and a great extension of it is designed. Ships of all nations lie in the harbour.

Calcutta stands upon low, marshy and unhealthy land. It was fatal to European constitutions, but now the tanks or ponds in and near the city are filled up; many woods are cleared away; and many of the causes of disease are removed.

The market is good; vegetables are exceedingly cheap. Cowries are the only kind of coin used, and they are very convenient. There is here a kind of hemp called *jute*, eight or ten feet long after it is dressed. It is excellent in all respects, but will not bear tar, and therefore is not suitable for the use of ships.

The famous "black hole" of Calcutta which was held sacred for a long time, and was so in 1794, is now converted into a warehouse, or what is called in the east a *go-down*. In

1756, Surajah Dowlah, the adopted son of the old Soubah of
Bengal, formed a design to drive the English from the country. He summoned his forces and attacked Calcutta, of which
Mr. Drake was then governor. The governor was alarmed, pretended to be a Quaker, and fled for refuge, with some of the
principal persons of the city, to ships which were lying in the
river, and escaped. Mr. Holwell then took command of the
fort in which the English force was stationed. He had but 250
effective men. After a brave resistance, which was unavailing,
Mr. Holwell hung out a flag of truce. A negotiation with
Surajah Dowlah was terminated by a promise from the
Soubah that no injury should be done to Holwell and his
party if they would surrender themselves. The promise was
treacherous and Holwell with 146 persons was driven into a
dungeon, called the Black Hole, a cubical apartment 18 feet
on each side.

The night was hot even for the climate, and there were
but two windows with iron bars, and both on the same side of
the cell, for the admission of air. Heat, thirst, and suffocation
subjected them to the most excruciating misery. Their perpetual cry was water and air. A message was sent to the
Soubah for relief, but he was asleep and no one dared to wake
him. The prisoners sucked their clothes to obtain the water
furnished by their own perspiration. In three hours one-third
of the whole number perished. At length the Soubah waked,
and after inquiry, as he thought that Holwell could tell where
a treasure in money was concealed, he let them out of their
confinement. Of the 146, twenty-three survived and were released, but with a putrid fever.

The Soubah laid Calcutta in ruins. But the following
year, the town was retaken by the English, vengeance was inflicted, and the Soubah was put to death. His successor paid
a large sum to the English Company for this outrage, and as

a pledge of future tranquillity. A monument is erected near the spot to perpetuate the infamy of this transaction, the treachery and cowardice of Drake, and the fortitude and bravery of Holwell and his associates.

Serampore is the only possession of the Danes in Bengal. It is a small town on the Hooghly, about three leagues above Calcutta, on the opposite side of the river. One ship of the Danish East India Company annually visits it and takes a cargo. The trade is of very little consequence to any other persons. It is a place of resort for all those in this part of the world who are not Danes, and who are afraid of the laws of other European powers in India. The means of living are cheap, and the society not very good.

The wealth of the English in India is immense; the trade of the country is regulated nearly as they please. Bombay and Calcutta are famous for the fine ships which they build. At Calcutta there are many European ship builders who send out as good vessels as any in the world. It is the exclusive privilege of the East India Company to send vessels this side of the Cape of Good Hope.

I LEFT CALCUTTA WITH A FRIEND, Jeremiah Stimson, who owned the ship *Three Brothers*, and was about to sail for Philadelphia. He was so kind as to offer me a passage with him gratis, an offer which I accepted, leaving the country with but one gold moore. My high hopes were thus disappointed and my mind wounded and mortified. Stimson was friendly and generous toward me, and labored to cheer my spirits, but my accumulated losses, and especially the loss of Mr. Van Braam's property, preyed upon me constantly. My motives were perfectly pure and honest, I knew, in making the purchase of the *Hector* in Mauritius, but on reflection, the attempt to manage so large an enterprise with so small a capital was unwise, and now caused me much self reproach. Those who know all the circumstances said that if we had arrived at Calcutta six months sooner, or six later than we did, we should have made a fortune. But hazards of this kind always exist, and we went beyond our depth, and suffered the unhappy consequences. I took great pains to inform Van Braam of everything respecting this business; and he at last let me know, through the medium of friends, that the whole affair was settled at the insurance office.

The spirit with which I met my friends in my native country, after so long an absence, was far different from what it would have been had I not been the sport of so many disappointments. The smile upon my countenance was mingled with mortification, and my observation was alive to every symptom of neglect or affected pity which might appear in the conduct or salutations of my acquaintances on shore. My experience has taught me how different is the reception which a sailor meets after a prosperous voyage from that which he finds when his hands are empty, his dress threadbare, and nothing but his wants abundant. It must be acknowledged that I never saw my native country with so little pleasure as on my return to it after a disastrous termination of my enterprises and my hopes.

To complain, however, was useless. I went to work with what skill and strength I had, and with what spirits I could revive within me. After a time they returned to their former elasticity; I transacted a good deal of business; I took the head of a shipyard as master builder; and found the benefit of employment in the restoration of my cheerfulness.

My brother and myself built a small ship of two hundred tons and more, with the plan that I should take a voyage in her to the Pacific Ocean. She was launched and fitted; the company for the voyage was formed; and she was manned and armed for the South Pacific, and for the north west coast of America. A suitable cargo for this coast was put aboard; eleven six pound guns were mounted; a crew of thirty men was shipped; and everything was prepared for a double voyage.

The common expression, "I believe she will perform the voyage 'well enough'" is a disgrace to the judgment and feelings of him who uses it; it shows a feeble, inefficient mind, and a spirit of self-defeating economy. The fair conclusion should be "I know that she will perform the voyage, if any ship can." She should be at least two hundred tons, and never four hundred, as so large a ship is never required. She should always be coppered, and the metal should be fresh. Except when whales or seals are the objects of the voyage, and the ship is to return immediately to America, she should be armed, and that according to the tenor of the voyage. If she goes to China with what is necessary for that market, she should have from six to ten guns, some of them long to reach objects at long shots.

Let every article of the rigging be good. Put the bread in new casks, or in those which have been filled with brandy, and are well dried — any other liquor tending to give the bread a bad taste. They must be air tight, or the bread will surely spoil. Butter, lard, and pickles should be put into double casks, the outside one filled with salt or brine. The beef and pork for such a voyage ought to be packed with particular care, and the cheap kind as it comes into the market should not be purchased. I have had beef put up by Samuel Greggs which I have carried round the world in a three years' voyage, half the time between the tropics, and out of nearly a hundred barrels, I never opened one in which the beef was not as sweet and good as when it was first put up. I brought some of it home to Boston again, which was cooked, and considered as corned beef.

As a contrast to this, I have known "put up" beef to spoil in six months and be thrown over board. This is no small or unimportant difference, and it is an article demanding much more attention than it commonly receives. There should be a large stock of beans, peas, dried apples and whortleberries (*related to the blueberry*), pickled cabbage, pigs and cattles' feet and ears, tripe, and other pickles. Take plenty of livestock and a great abundance of water. To crown the whole, keep the stores in the best order. Let the hold, and all parts of the ship, be thoroughly and constantly aired; keep the hatches off in good weather; employ wind sails freely to force the air below; and remember the necessity of this to preserve the provisions of a perishable cargo. Have frequent examinations or overhaulings. See if the casks are out of order; inspect the powder; and have it turned over once every two months. Mark one side of the barrels with an X; stow that side up; and in two months put it down. One half of the powder in the casks will be spoiled without this precaution.

In voyages for seals you must have men who understand the business, and not raw hands who will certainly make it a losing enterprise. Out of twenty, which should be the least number for a crew, the captain and six others at least ought to be able to teach the rest their business with skill. Such a set of men will do more and better than twice the number of those who are untaught.

Let every man depend on his share of the seals for the voyage. In no other way will the men do well. Including what has been previously received, half the voyage may be computed and paid at Canton, as a fair principle. The shares to prime seamen, or sealers, should be one percent, or a hundredth part of the voyage where there are thirty men belonging to the ship including the captain and officers. The money is to be divided after the expense of the boats for carrying the skins to Canton from the ship is deducted. No other expenses are to come from the skins. The perquisite of the captain should be ten percent on all that can be realized from the cargo on the return of the ship.

I now come to the close of a chapter which is also the close of a series of voyages in foreign countries, some fortunate and happy, and others disastrous and afflictive. My recollections of the time spent with Commodore McClure and his officers are full of interest and pleasure, mingled with regret that such feelings as I then enjoyed should not be longer in continuance. At that period my mind was elastic and ready to draw agreeable emotion from every companion, every object and every event. But the trials and depressions which I have since met and endured have taken away this elasticity, and have left me with that kind of tranquillity which always succeeds the permanent disappointment of high hopes, and which is some compensation for their loss. Chastised expectations, a sort of contentment with ordinary comforts, diminished activity, and the small, still pleasures of a life of peace without much responsibility remain.

In the voyage of survey and discovery among the oriental islands, I had an opportunity to learn much of the human character in various circumstances, and under various institutions. Virtue and vice, happiness and misery, are much more equally distributed among nations than is supposed by those who have never been from home, and who believe, like the Chinese, that their residence is in the center of the world, of light, of privilege, and of enjoyment.

National prejudices, to a certain extent, may be very useful, and possibly necessary; but they are always attended by considerable evils in the narrow and intolerant spirit which they perpetuate, and in the contentions which they produce. The more enlarged a mind becomes in its views of men and the world, the less it will be disposed to denounce the varieties of opinion and pursuit, and the more it will enjoy the benevolent results to which wisdom and philosophy point.[30]

VOYAGE OF 1799–1802

From Boston around Cape Horn; Falkland Islands; Wildlife; Tierra Del Fuego

ON THE 10th of November, 1799, we took our departure in the ship *Perseverance* from Boston light, and made our way towards Cape Horn. We had very disagreeable weather after we passed below the latitude of 12° north, with constant rains, a hot sultry air and calms till the sails mildewed whilst hoisted, and every thing on board ship was covered with a blue mold. In this place we began to feel the southeast trade winds which cleared the air, and the rain ceased.

On the 23rd of December, at two p.m., we saw three small islands bearing west by south, two or three leagues distant. We bore away and at three, were abreast of them. We hoisted the small boat out, went on shore, and found them to be nothing more than a cluster of craggy rocks with no sort of vegetation upon them. These rocks are five in number; only two of any considerable magnitude. They nearly connect with each other and form a kind of harbour on the northwest side. Here we made shift to land, but obtained nothing except a number of boobies. It seemed the most dreary spot I ever saw, the sea roaring and surging on all sides.

We caught plenty of fish in the harbour, and at six p.m., returned on board. Sharks were numerous about the ship, and our people, in attempting to take them, lost a number of hooks and lines, and broke several pair of grains (*fish spear or harpoon*). We sounded within two miles of the islands, but found no ground with a line of eighty fathoms. At eight p.m. we made sail, and had pleasant weather during the night.

These rocks are called in the chart, St. Paul's Islands (*St. Peter and St. Paul Rocks*), and are very erroneously laid down. We observed their latitude to be 0° 55' north, and longitude 30° 15' west. They may be seen at the distance of three or four leagues, and always make like three sails when first seen. They are very dangerous if fallen in with at night. The islands which are above the reach of the surf are covered with birds' feces. They were hatching their young when we were there. The month of November would be the season to procure eggs at this place in abundance. They are not very sweet, all oceanick birds' eggs being fishy.

We continued our course till the 25th when we saw the island of Fernando de Noronha, and passed to the westward of it. This island lies in latitude 3° 56' south, and longitude 32° 32' west. From this we had a free wind round Cape St. Augustine. Fernando de Noronha is very remarkable for a peak upon it which is called the pyramid. It looks at a distance like an immensely high steeple or tower, and I should suppose was several thousand feet high.

It is necessary here to mention that the longitude laid down by me in this voyage is from Greenwich by a series of lunar observations, taken with good instruments, and may be considered in general correct.

WE CONTINUED OUR COURSE southward with fine breezes and pleasant weather, running along the Brazil coast until the 26th of January 1800, when we anchored in North West Harbour in one of the Falkland Islands, where we found the *Diana* of London, commanded by Captain John Lock. She was an English whaler that came last from Botany Bay round Cape Horn. Two sailors deserted from her and came on board my ship, unknown to me. Their names were George Giles, an extraordinarily faithful and confidential man, and James Blake, a man of an opposite character.

West Point Harbour affords plenty of fresh water. The most convenient place for obtaining it is near the head of the cove on the south side. There is no wood to be got here, except it be some drift wood. There are great numbers of geese at this place, but they are very fishy. Wild hogs may be hunted on the island that forms the west side of the harbour.

The Spaniards have a settlement on the easterly end of the Grand Maloon. They are chiefly convicts from the west coast of South America, River of Plate (*Rio de la Plata*), etc. They cultivate the common necessaries of life; but these islands are a very barren group, affording no tree, bush, or shrub, that grows spontaneously. We saw no quadrupeds except one fox, which we shot, and some wild hogs on the small island to the westward of the Grand Maloon, but I have since been informed that on some of the islands foxes are numerous. There are a few seals, both of the fur and hair kinds;[31] but they have been principally destroyed, and the few that remain are so shy that it is very difficult to get near enough to kill them. Very large sea elephants are likewise found here. Six or eight barrels of oil are sometimes made from one of them. They resemble the seal, but have no hind flippers like them, and their tail is more like that of a particular kind of fish.

Several kinds of salt water birds are found here. Some of them are good to eat. One that is called the upland goose is a very sweet tender bird, and nearly as large as our tame geese. It is of a reddish grey, and is always found on the upland near fresh brooks or ponds. The ducks are similar to the wild ducks of this country, and are good eating. Teal is likewise found here. All the others are not palatable, being so strong and fishy that most people would refuse them when they could get salt provisions.

There are three kinds of penguins found here: the king, the macaroni, and jackass. The king penguin is as large as a goose, walks erect, its legs projecting directly out behind; it stands upright, and at a distance resembles a man. The breast is white, head and back nearly black, mandibles tapering and sharp at the points, long strips of red feathers, resembling eyebrows, over each eye, running down two inches on the neck, giving the bird a very handsome appearance.

The macaroni penguin is not more than two-thirds as large as the former. It is like them except the colour, which differs a little, being more white about its throat; and instead of the red feathers over the eyes, it has a number of long fibers or feathers, resembling the long hairs round the mouth of a cat, giving it a macaroni look, from which it takes its name. These two kinds lay their eggs on the ground in rookeries as will be described hereafter.

The jackass penguin is so called from the noise it makes, which very nearly resembles that animal's bray. It does not differ much in size or colour from the macaroni, but is smaller if anything. It goes upland to make its nest, digging holes under tussucks in any ground clear of stones, commonly choosing the side of a hill. They go on shore at night, male and female, and after dark set up the most disagreeable noise or braying that can be imagined.

The next remarkable bird here is the albatross.[32] It is the largest bird that I know of which gets its living out of the sea. There are two or three kinds of them; the largest is of a greyish colour, and shaped exactly like our sea gulls, having a remarkably large head and beak, and will bite very hard. They have monstrously large feet, one of which would nearly cover the bottom of a water pail, and their wings are fourteen feet from tip to tip. They lay their eggs in rookeries. There is a

smaller kind, of a white colour on the breast, and black on the
back of its wings and head. They lay their eggs like our field
birds, making their nests on the sand promiscuously.

When they commence a rookery, they choose a piece of
ground that is level and as clear of stones as possible, near water, and lay out the land in squares, the lines running through
at right angles, as true as they could be drawn by a surveyor,
leaving the squares just large enough for nests, with room for
alleys between them. They carry away all the stones which
they can find or root out of the ground, and lay them outside
of the outer walk which would commonly be ten or twelve
feet wide, running round on three sides of it; leaving the
fourth side next the water open. The outer walk round the
rookery was made as level, regular and smooth as the side-
walks in any of our cities. They would many times occupy
from three to four acres, but some are much smaller. After
they prepare the rookery, each pair takes possession of one
square for a nest. All the different kinds of birds that lay in
the rookeries, except the albatross, make their nests as one
family, and are governed by one law. They never leave their
nests for a moment until their young are sufficiently large to
take care of themselves. The male stands beside the nest when
the female is on it, and when she is about to get off, he slips
on as soon as she has made room for him — for were they to
let their eggs be seen, their neighbors would steal them. The
king penguin was foremost in thefts of this nature, and never
neglected an opportunity to rob those near him. It sometimes
so happened that when they hatched out their young, there
would be three or four kinds of young birds in one nest.

It appeared to me that something handsome might be
made of these islands, were due attention to be paid to them.
The soil is very good and clear of rocks, and capable of easy
tillage. There are plenty of good fish to be caught amongst

them, and what is called the right-whale. It is now an excellent place for a ship to refresh at. The climate is very healthy, but the weather is dreary and misty the greatest part of the time.

THE COAST OF PATAGONIA from the latitude of 44° south to the Straits of Magellan is a rough ragged coast, indented with deep bays and coves, and most parts lined with rocks and dangers. The straits are very difficult to pass when bound to the westward. They are filled with shoals, and have such deep water in many places that a ship could not find anchorage. The prevailing westerly winds which blow a great part of the time between the two high lands render it very difficult for a ship to make a passage. I have not known a ship to pass through them for many years, and all that ever did, experienced much more difficulty than had they made the passage round Cape Horn.

There was once a settlement formed in these straits by the Spaniards. They sent three or four hundred people and left them at a pleasant place, for that climate, which has since been named Port Famine. They were all left to famish and die, not having any supplies sent to them. The place has since been visited by several English commanders who report that they found traces of what those people did in cultivating the land. There were many garden spots, some trees, etc., but before anything came to maturity sufficient for their subsistence, the poor creatures starved to death.

An extract from the journal of Captain Wallis's voyage round the world in command of his Britannick Majesty's ship *Dolphin* says: "At this place, the Spaniards, in the year 1581, built a town which they called Phillippeville, and left in it a colony consisting of 400 persons. When our celebrated navigator, Cavendish, arrived here in 1587, he found one of these

unhappy wretches, the only one that remained, upon the beach: they had all perished for want of subsistence, except twenty-four; twenty-three of these set out for the River Plata, and were never afterwards heard of. This man, whose name was Hernando, was brought to England by Cavendish, who called the place where he had taken him up, Port Famine."
— *Hawksworth's Coll. vol. 1, p. 411.*

The island Tierra del Fuego takes its name from its formerly having been very noted for volcanoes, and I believe they burn on some part of it at this time. It is inhabited by a race of poor half-starved miserable beings, who are very little removed from the brute condition. They live on fish and seal's flesh, when they can get them. They eat the seals raw and nearly rotten. Their numbers are but small. The land is very mountainous, generally clothed with wood to the summit. Some parts of the island appear pleasant, especially on low, or moderately elevated points, and in valleys, which have been burned, and by some means cleared, and over which the grass has grown.

A certain kind of green tussuck grows on some of these islands and likewise at the Falkland Islands. It grows up as large as a half barrel tub, and some are four times that size. It has a covering which appears like beautiful green velvet. I do not know of what substance they are under the covering, but they emit a clear transparent white balsam, which comes out on the surface in large bunches, and is considered by some to be of an extraordinarily healing nature.

Sailing toward Cape Horn, we passed Strait Le Maire on February 8th, with a northwest wind. Our course was south, and south by east, against a violent head sea which made the ship labour the most of any sea I ever experienced. We continued working off Cape Horn from the 9th of February till the 12th of March, before we considered ourselves fairly round. The winds blew for the most part from the westerly quarter, between west northwest and west southwest — strong gales, not allowing us in general to carry more sail than a reefed foresail and storm staysail, which made us very uncomfortable, as our ship was deep waisted, and kept half filled with water a great part of the time.

The sea was tremendous during the gales, rolling in mountains from the westward; but the weather was not worse than I have seen in other high latitudes in many places.

There are innumerable swarms of birds on the islands round Tierra del Fuego of the same species we saw on the Falkland Islands. Several kinds of excellent fish may be caught on these coasts, and in the harbours. Whales are plenty round all the shores. Plenty of fowls which are good to eat may be shot with very little trouble — such as geese of various kinds, seven or eight kinds of ducks and teal, plover, curlews, snipes, partridges, quails, etc. There are many kinds of birds of a beautiful plumage found here and several kinds of animals on the main island, such as foxes, hares, and rabbits.

Coast of Chile; Trading; Whales; Captain George Howe's Story; Indians and Spaniards

ON THE 12th of March, 1800, we considered ourselves far enough to the westward of the cape to stand to the northward with safety. It is very difficult to obtain observations for longitude in making a passage round Cape Horn on account of thick weather. All ships find a strong current setting constantly to the eastward; winds blow chiefly from the south west after getting northward of latitude 50° south.

On the 26th, we saw the island of Juan Fernández, and on the 31st, arrived and landed at Más Afuera Island. (*Delano gives a general description of the islands and settlements along this coast.*) The Spaniards have settled the island of Chiloe (*Ilsa Grande de Chiloé*). Its northern extreme lies in latitude 41° 40' south. It is a great place for catching and curing fish. I have had several hundred weight of them. They exactly resemble the cod which is caught in the bay of St. Loire, and are a very delicate table fish. It also abounds with excellent timber, suitable for ships and buildings and common cabinet work.

The country in the kingdom of Chile is remarkable for its mountains; in Chile, called the Andes, and those in Peru the Cordilleras. They lie nearly parallel to the shore, from fifty to a hundred and fifty miles inland. They appear magnificent beyond description when viewed from a ship's deck eight or ten miles off shore, particularly when the sun is near setting and the atmosphere clear. It then shines on their westerly side next the sea, in some places beautifully shaded where one mountain stands a little in front of another, making the most interesting and splendid appearance that can be conceived of.

The next remarkable objects of this country are the mines of gold and silver which have spread their fame over the four quarters of the world. In the kingdoms, as they are called, of Chile and Peru, there are great numbers of them, though but few that are profitable. I have seen a great quantity of copper at the port of Coquimbo.

I was informed by the Spaniards at Concepción that there were rich mines to the southward in Chile which they do not work because the natives are so formidable in their vicinity and are their enemies. I had it from undoubted authority that there are natives in the southern interior of Chile whom the Spaniards have never conquered, and to whom they are obliged to pay tribute to keep peace with them; and that they had followed them over some parts of the Andes where it was so cold that some of their men and horses were frozen to death in crossing the mountain.

The port of Talcaquana (*Talcahuano*) is nine miles from the city of Concepción in a northwest direction, through a fine level plain. The road then, for about three miles, runs parallel with and near the shore where there is a beautiful beach on one of the branches of the harbour. It is defended by two batteries, one lying on the easterly side of the port on low ground. The guns are not more than fifteen or twenty feet above the level of the sea. The other is to the north west on the side of a hill between one and two hundred feet above the level of the water, and has seven or eight heavy guns in it, twenty-four or thirty-two pounders. They have a very commanding situation; the two forts can cross each other's fires when playing on a ship in the harbour.

There is a great trade carried on between Talcahuano

and Lima. Many ships are employed in carrying wheat from here. This country abounds with it for many degrees north and south. They also carry boards, spars, and timber; some wine, raisins, and other dried fruits; and considerable of the herb of Paraguay, which the inhabitants call *matte*. It is the tea of the country, and very much drunk by all classes of people on the coasts of Chile and Peru. The country here, like the other ports of Chile, is well cultivated, and abounds with the best of provisions. They make great quantities of very good wine.

Animals are plentiful and may be purchased at very low rates: for a good bullock, four dollars; a good horse, twenty, and common ones from four to eight dollars; a sheep for half a dollar. Foreigners are charged more for what they purchase.

The feathered race of animals far exceed anything of the kind I ever saw, particularly for those good to eat. The Spaniards here are not allowed to use fire arms in common, and as they have no Indians who hunt them, birds are very plenty and tame. I have often gone out by permission on horse back, and shot a horse load in three hours, killing seven different kinds of ducks and teal with various other sorts of fowls. They have the finest fish, and in the greatest variety, of any place I ever visited.

The ladies vie with any I ever saw in point of beauty. They are modest, mild, and very agreeable. Their dress is a little singular, as they wear the old fashioned hoop round the waist, of an extraordinary size. They are rather partial to the Americans and to Englishmen. I never can think it a crime to reciprocate their sentiments. The Spanish gentlemen are the noblest spirited men I ever was acquainted with. The idea that is entertained of their being a very jealous people is not true. I never saw gentlemen more free from it. In the city and port of Concepción and its vicinity, there are about fifteen or twenty thousand inhabitants of all descriptions.[33]

At Valparaíso there are more fruit and vegetables in the markets than at Concepción, such as peaches, apricots, oranges, lemons, melons, onions, and pumpkins. It is the port town of the capital of Chile, which is called St. James, or St. Jago (*Santiago*), and has more trade than any port on this coast. There is considerable land commerce between the Rio de la Plata and this port. They march slaves over land, from Buenos Aires, to avoid carrying them round Cape Horn, and ship them again for the coast of Peru. There is one pass only that crosses the Andes to go and come by. They transport from one coast to the other many articles of merchandize across this pass on the backs of horses or mules, and considerable quantities of gold and silver are carried in the same manner to be shipped for Spain. They have a mint at Santiago where they coin two or three millions of dollars in gold and silver in a year.

In the harbour of Valparaíso there are great numbers of the humped-backed and right-whale. Spermaceti (*sperm whales*) are caught off this coast, but it is said they never come on soundings, the truth of which I have reason to doubt, as I have known them taken near this coast; and the squid, which they feed upon, is frequently found in this harbour. I often caught squid here which were three or four feet long.

I HAD FREQUENT OPPORTUNITIES of being acquainted with many captains who are employed in the whale fishery on this coast. These men are possessed of a great share of courage and intrepidity in the pursuit of their business; but are in the habit of boasting of their superiority when in company, and of exaggerating their exploits.

While lying in the harbour of Valparaíso, Captain

Whales

George Howe was on board my ship. One calm and very pleasant day we discovered a large whale asleep within twenty rods of some of the ships. We thought this a good opportunity to try our skill in killing whales. We fitted out a whaleboat belonging to Captain Howe, which was properly manned, and my boatswain, who had been in the business before, was to steer and direct the expedition. We prepared and rigged a lance, which was made for the purpose of killing sea elephants, having an iron shank about two feet long, with a pole to it, six or eight feet in length, and a small line attached to it, with the other end fastened to the stem of the boat to prevent it being lost.

Thus equipped we rowed up softly within twenty feet of the whale, when I threw the lance into her, a little abaft the fore fin, which entered more than the length of the iron part. The whale, on feeling the hurt, raised its tail fifteen feet in the air, and brought it down with such force, within six feet of the boat, that it was half filled with water, and produced a most violent agitation for a great distance around us. It may be considered a fortunate circumstance that we escaped injury, for had it hit the boat it would have been staved to atoms, and probably some of us been killed.

Her head lay towards the shore, and she started in that direction, brought her head out of water, making the most terrible bellowing that can be imagined, turned herself round and went out of the bay, spouting blood till out of sight. Thus ended our first and last enterprise in killing whales. The experiment convinced us that it was a difficult and dangerous business, and ought never to be attempted by any except those who have been bred up to and perfectly skilled in the art. The method we adopted was correct, excepting the first instrument thrown should have been a harpoon with barbs to it, to prevent it from drawing out. To this should be a line or warp attached, three or four hundred fathoms in length, by which means we could have held on to the whale, and pulled the boat up so as to throw the lance with the most sure effect. The shank of a lance whalemen use is four feet in length, with a pole fixed to it like the one we used. I have since had frequent opportunities of seeing whales killed by those who understood it, and was perfectly satisfied that it required courage and judgment.

HAVING MENTIONED Captain George Howe, I shall give some account of him, particulars of which are probably known to no one but myself. He was born in Stonington, Connecticut, and sailed out of the port of New London in command of the schooner *Oneco*, on a sealing voyage. He arrived at Más Afuera in 1800, and was compelled by misfortunes to go into Valparaíso and sell his vessel. Being disappointed in not receiving payment according to contract, he was obliged to go to Santiago, the capital, before he could obtain justice. He got his money and returned to Valparaíso, and deposited upwards of twenty-two hundred dollars in the hands of a Spaniard, at whose house he resided, and was taken sick soon after. When I was at Valparaíso, in 1805, I made inquiry and found the house in which he lay sick.

I was not a little surprised at finding him, and at the strange conduct of the people belonging to the house, as I had dined there several times since my arrival, yet they had neglected telling me of his being at the same time in the house; especially as it was well known to them we were friends, and had been particularly intimate when in this port on a preceding voyage.

I found him in a back room, no better than a hovel, in a most deplorable situation. He was lying on a miserable bed, or couch, in a very languishing state, his flesh wasted, till he was almost a skeleton; and no one near to afford him assistance, or friend to offer him a word of comfort. There was a well of water in the room adjoining, not more than twelve feet from his bed, from which was drawn all the water used by the family, with a door opening into his room, which was kept open most of the time. He had lain in this situation for five or six months. My feelings on the occasion can be better imagined than described.

We had spent many happy hours together, and I could not help contrasting those times with what I now saw. I endeavoured to raise his spirits, and told him that I would take him on board my ship, and bring him home. I procured a barber and had him shaved, his clothes shifted, and dressed him in a decent manner, putting on his handsome Spanish cloak, and led him into the parlour, with an intention of giving him an airing. But the poor man was so reduced that he fainted and was obliged to be placed on a sofa, and soon after carried back to his room, from which he never again was removed till a corpse. I visited him daily while I lay in this port, and each day sent him a kettle of soup, but I found he was too weak to be removed on board the ship. He died about ten days after I left Valparaíso. He was a man of a noble mind, sincere in his friendships, honest and honourable in his dealings, and a remarkably pleasant companion; but his misfortunes broke his spirits.

The following particulars concerning Captain Howe, which took place after I left him, I had from Captain Bacon, whom I took with me when I left Lima, and who was with him most of the time after I sailed till he died. He informed me that a short time before Captain Howe died, the bishop who was then at the port, had baptized him, and that he had received the sacrament; thus he died a Roman Catholic. This is made an important point with the priests of that religion.

Just as he was dying, the man who kept the house, and with whom he had deposited his money, undertook to make a settlement with him. He brought forward his books and made Howe acknowledge the different charges which he had prepared, when he was so far gone as to be just able to articulate, yes — without probably knowing what he said; thus defrauding him of his money, besides bringing him in debt.

This transaction very much displeased the Spaniards here; and a remarkable accident happening about eight days after Captain Howe died, caused them to make many remarks upon the landlord's conduct, and say that it was a visitation of the judgment of God. There was a very high bank that was directly back of his house, which in consequence of a great rain, gave way, and fell on the very part where Howe had lain, and buried it under more than a hundred tons of earth.

THE INHABITANTS OF THE COAST of Chile are but a very small part Europeans, who are principally Spaniards. They hold themselves much higher than the Chilean born, who have mixed their blood with the aborigines so much that the European Spaniards undervalue them.

The native Indians of South America are better featured than those of the northern part of the continent. They are treated in the south in the same manner as they have been in the north. The Spaniards have made war upon, harassed, and distressed them, till they have pretty much thinned them off near the sea coast. Some are made slaves by being taken prisoners in time of war, or by purchasing them from their enemies. I have been struck with horror to hear a Spanish priest call them brutes; telling me at the same time they were not Christians, and no better than cattle; when that same arrogant man's countrymen had robbed and despoiled the unfortunate Indian of all that was dear to him. Thus, "thinks I to myself," goes the world: one man robs another of his country, his wealth, and his liberty; and then says he is a brute, and not a Christian. In such cases as these, I will say with the meritorious physician to whom Bonaparte made the proposition to poison his soldiers at Joppa: "If those be the requisites necessary to form a great man, I thank my God I do not possess them."

In horsemanship these people excel any men I have ever seen. Whether mounted on a well-broken, or an untutored horse, they ride in the best manner, and show great skill in the management of their steeds. It is seldom that the most vicious animal unhorses his rider. They tutor their horses to start with astonishing quickness, and to stop suddenly. I have seen them ride with the greatest speed well within six feet of the side of a house, and there stop as suddenly as if the animal had fallen dead on the spot. Sometimes I have seen them attempt to stop the horse in full career, and he would throw all his feet forward and slide perhaps more than four yards. Frequently the hinder feet would slip from under him, and seat him on his backside, in the position we sometimes see a dog.

The ladies also are fond of this exercise, and most of them ride extremely well. The better sort ride sidewise, like the women of this country. Their manner of mounting a horse was singular, and sufficiently ludicrous in the eyes of a stranger. At first I was unable to comprehend how the feat was performed. I soon, however, had an opportunity of receiving a lesson at a house where several ladies were assembled for the purpose of amusing themselves with a ride. When the horses were brought and all things ready, they prepared to mount. As a sailor is generally foremost when a lady is present, I offered my assistance, and the offer being accepted, one of them said, "Help me first." "O, yes," said I with all the gallantry I possessed. She went to the side of a horse, held by a servant, and leaning her breast against his side, threw her arms over the saddle across his back, and stood in that posture, saying, "Help me." I stood awkwardly enough, not seeing any part that delicacy would allow me to take hold of in order to aid her ascent. The servant perceiving my embarrassment, left his post, and taking one of her ankles in each hand, she gave a jump, and he lifted her with all his strength, till she was high enough to be seated. She then turned herself in the air, aided by the man, who crossing his wrists, brought her into her seat, with the utmost grace and dexterity.

Houses are mostly made of clay and have either tile or brick floors. The tile or brick being always laid on the ground make these dwellings very unhealthy, more especially for women, on account of the dampness. The first class of people commonly build their houses of wood, with good wooden floorings, and are much more healthy. On one side of the sitting room the floor is raised about a foot, a little inclined from the wall, and about eight feet wide. This is covered with a carpet and mats, and next the wall are a number of small benches, elegantly covered with cushions of crimson silk velvet or satin. This elevated place was the usual seat of the ladies. Their mode of sitting is cross-legged, in the Turkish fashion, or like a tailor on his shop-board. I was frequently in their parties and found this a most agreeable resting place, especially when the ladies sat near me. Their prattle was innocent and lively, and they had a disposition to render the visits of their guests entertaining. Most of them sang well, accompanying the voice with guitar, their favourite instrument. A customary compliment is for a gentleman to hand one of these instruments to a lady, who is ever ready to gratify him with her performance. The instruments most in use are guitars, which nearly all the ladies play, accompanying them with their voices which are very melodious. They likewise have harps, spinnets, harpsichords, and piano-fortes, which are very common, and on which they perform extremely well. The gentlemen play on flutes and clarinets. They dance with the most majesty and grace of any people I ever knew. Their dances are minuets, long dances, cotillions, and a very singular kind of dance, called fan-dango, which is common in old Spain. This graceful dance is usually performed by two persons, commonly a lady and gentleman, sometimes by two ladies.

Gentlemen and ladies meet in parties at a friend's house at times, and the gentlemen form a party round a large table for cards. The game they generally play is similar to our game of loo. It is called banco, a game that is common in other nations. The ladies never join the party at table, but sit on their platform by themselves, playing on their guitars, and singing to amuse those engaged in play. Any gentleman who prefers their company to cards has liberty to take a seat with them. Parties formed to ride, both male and female, are very fond of concluding their diversion by going on board ships, or indeed of any excursion by water.

The employment of the men, other than amusements, is in laying out and planning their buildings, vineyards and gardens, and transacting their mercantile affairs. A large proportion of them are employed in offices of government, either in a military or civil capacity. A great many are employed riding about the country transporting money, bullion, and all kinds of merchandise, most commonly conducted by convoys of horses and mules. These convoys sometimes consist of two or three hundred, laden with some kind of traffic. Many of these cross the Andes to and from the Rio de la Plata.

Some of the men are employed as mariners in the ships that are owned in the country. There are few good mechanics; medical men are likewise scarce. The ladies' employment is nothing more than sewing, or making their own clothes, some trifling embroidering and lace work, and in superintending their household affairs; they commonly, however, live pretty free from labour.

I have been at almost all the ports on the coast of Chile repeatedly, and have often transported Spaniards who had been prisoners of war, or otherwise distressed. I have taken them off the Gallipagos (*Galapagos*) Islands after they have run away from English ships, thus preventing them from being carried to England. I have also prevailed on several English captains to deliver some of their prisoners to me, whom I afterwards delivered to their friends in safety. On the other hand I have taken out of different Spanish prisons on the coasts of Chile and Peru, more than one hundred and fifty Englishmen at several times, and put them on board other ships, or kept them on board my own, until I arrived at some friendly port, or returned to America. Both the English and Spaniards in the Pacific Ocean have in general treated their prisoners with cruelty, but the conduct of the Spaniards has been most severe.

The bay of Coquimbo is one of the finest harbours that nature ever formed. It is a good place for a ship to lie at whilst the people are procuring seals off the islands in the Pacific; and it is a good place, in the proper season, for a ship to fill up with right-whale oil, as the whales come into this bay in great numbers.

The Bird Islands lie about six or seven leagues from the mainland, 29° 36' south, and I believe have no dangers near them. I think there might be four or five thousand seals taken off those islands in the course of two or three months; they are of both kinds, fur and hair. It is probable also that there would be some further chance of success to the northward; for in sailing in that direction, will be seen several more islands about the same distance from the coast as the Bird Islands, and all appear to have seals about them. My business, however, was of such a nature at that time, that I could not stop to take them. They are mostly of the hair kind.

Sealing Among the Chilean Islands, and Methods of Work; Delano's Version of the "Robinson Crusoe" Story and of Alexander Selkirk's Island Refuge; A Near Disaster on a Seal Hunt

CHAPTER XVII

MÁS AFUERA lies in latitude 33° 48' south, and in longitude 80° 34' west, is nearly circular, and about twenty five miles in circumference. It is clear of any kind of danger, keeping two miles from the land all around it; but on the southeast lies a shoal that breaks half a mile distant in bad weather. When within half a mile of land there will be found from twenty to fifty fathoms water. I should advise any vessel exceeding one hundred tons burthen, never to attempt to anchor, except from some unavoidable necessity. All the fresh provisions it affords are goats, plenty of good fish, and seals, of which we sometimes ate a part.

Water can be got in many places, but the best or easiest to be found is on the south east side at the place called the landing. It may be known by a rock which lies on the southerly part of the island and looks like a sail when seen at a distance. Water must be rafted off in casks, as boats cannot land to take it in. In the rainy season all the gullies to the north east afford water, but it is more troublesome to take it from them, on account of the many large rocks which lie about the shores and off in the surf. This difficulty extends all round the island. Wood can be procured in abundance, but with some labour. It is best to go on the mountains to cut it and tumble it down. In that case it can be cut into small pieces without much trouble, as it commonly breaks and splits in the fall.

That picked up on the beach will be found hard and almost impossible to be cut or split.

The island of Más Afuera has been much injured by volcanoes, but where there is any soil, it is pretty well clothed with wood, and the land is fertile. Whilst there were from ten to twenty ships sealing there from the year 1800 to 1804, they cultivated almost all kinds of vegetables. Hogs, sheep, and goats, and most kinds of domestic fowls were also bred here. All the wild birds we saw were a kind of hawk, which we called rooks, and two or three kinds of sparrows. To this place resort those celebrated birds called "mother Cary's chickens," for the purpose of laying and hatching their eggs on the shore, and also the kind of bird called noddy. They make holes under the rocks to secure themselves from falling prey to the rooks.

WHEN THE AMERICANS CAME to this place, about the year 1797, and began to make a business of killing seals, there is no doubt but there were two or three millions of them on the island. I have made an estimate of more than three millions that have been carried to Canton from thence in the space of seven years. I have carried more than one hundred thousand myself, and have been at the place when there were the people of fourteen ships on the island at one time, killing seals. The first ship that came to this place for the purpose of procuring seals for the Chinese market was the *Eliza*, of Captain Stewart, which I took the command of on her arrival at Canton, in the year 1793, which has been before stated.

The method practised to take them was to get between them and the water, and make a lane of men, two abreast, forming three or four couples, and then drive the seal through this lane. Each man was furnished with a club, between five and six feet long, and as they passed, he knocked down such of the seals as he chose, which are commonly the half grown, or what are called young seals. This is easily done, as a very small blow on the nose effects it. When stunned, knives are taken to cut or rip them down on the breast, from the under jaw to the tail, giving a stab in the breast that will kill them. After this all hands go to skinning.

I have seen men, one of whom would skin sixty in an hour. They take off all the fat, and some of the lean with the skin, as the more weight there is to the skin the easier it will beam. This is performed in the same manner in which curriers flesh their skins, after which it is stretched and pegged on the ground to dry. It is necessary to keep it two days in pegs, in fair weather, to make it keep its shape. After this they are taken out of pegs, and stacked in the manner of salted dried cod fish. They will sweat whilst in the pile, so it is necessary to open them and give them air two or three times. After which they may be stacked on shore, or put into a ship's hold, and will keep for years and take no hurt, if kept dry.

After being conveyed on board the ship, they are carried to Canton for a market, where they are sold. They have been sold there as high as three or four dollars a skin, and as low as thirty-five cents, but the most common price which they have brought has been about one dollar. Three-fourths of the payment for them is generally made in teas.

Seals in the southern latitudes go on shore in the months of November or December for the purpose of bringing forth their young. Males and females remain near or on the shore from that time till August or September, when they go off to sea, all together. When they come on shore they creep up sometimes one or two hundred rods from the water. They bring forth their young and nurse them in the same manner as the canine species do, and for several weeks after the young are as helpless as young pups. They are perfectly ignorant of swimming until five or six weeks old, when the dam drags them to the water by the neck and teaches them to swim.

Fur seals feed upon squid, the same as the spermaceti whales eat. The hair kind feed upon all kinds of small fish. They copulate on shore. The females go eleven months with young, according to the best calculation we were able to make. They seldom have more than one, and never more than two pups. Their young never come on shore during the first year after they are carried off to sea.

JUAN FERNÁNDEZ ISLAND LIES in latitude 33° 40' south and thirty four or five leagues eastward of Más Afuera.[34] From its south side, Goat Island will be seen, lying to the west of the main island, at a distance of about one or two miles. The harbour, or bay, is on the north side. This is the celebrated place of the exile of Robinson Crusoe, or more properly, of Alexander Selkirk, who was left here by Captain Straddling, from on board the ship *Cinque Ports.*

Some time about the year 1705, the English ship *Cinque Ports* touched at the island Juan Fernández.[35] During their stay there, on account of some difference between Captain Straddling and Mr. Alexander Selkirk, one of the mates, the captain put the latter on shore with only his chest, clothes, bedding, mathematical instruments, books, and stationery, a gun, one pound of powder and balls, or shot adequate to it, and went off and left him there. He resided on the island about four years when the *Duke* and *Duchess,* two English privateer ships from Bristol, commanded by Captain Woods Rogers, touched there. They observed smoke on the island, but when they first went on shore, they could not find the inhabitant that had occasioned it. They searched for the person, but could not discover who it was for a long time, as

Selkirk had secreted himself, being apprehensive they might be Spaniards, of whom he stood in great fear. At last he satisfied himself concerning the newcomers, came forward and gave an account of himself. Captain Rogers took him on board.

On his return to England, Mr. Selkirk went to a person of some literature, who had a taste for such kind of narratives, and showed him his journal which he had kept during the whole of his stay at Juan Fernández. He asked him if anything could be made from it for publication, which would be advantageous to him, as he was in extremely necessitous circumstances and had been reduced so low by his extraordinary exile that he did not feel able to endure the labour necessary to obtain a livelihood. An amanuensis privately took minutes from Selkirk's journal and returned the book, telling him that he could not make any thing of it. Shortly after, this same person had the injustice to avail himself of the hard earned labours of Selkirk by the publication of his journal under the title of the "History of Robinson Crusoe" — the poor man being thus robbed of the only advantage he hoped to reap from his sufferings, and at a period of his life when he was so much in need.[36]

I HAD THE MISFORTUNE TO VISIT the same Juan Fernández island for the second time in the year 1805. My first visit was in 1800, when I only landed on the west side of the island, opposite to the bay, or settlement. The island had been settled for a number of years, and is now a place to which convicts are transported from Chile and Peru, and who are guarded by a few troops. It was on my second visit that I met with misfortunes.

Early in the morning I left my ship from four to six miles off the north west end of the island, and steered for

Goat Island. My object was to catch seals; if no seals could be found, to land at the settlement on the north east side. I gave notice of my intentions accordingly and ordered the ship to keep near enough to see the boat, and observe my signals. But these orders were neglected.

After I left the ship, the wind continued to the westward, and freshened. As I could not land on Goat Island, owing to the surf being so high, I made signal to the ship to follow to leeward, but, from some cause, it did not. I continued my course, watching the shores for seals, and sometimes lying by to see if the ship would follow. The wind increased every moment and about five o'clock, I reached the bay.

I was met on the pier by the governor. He was an Irishman by the name of Thomas Higgins, and was nephew to the great and worthy Ambrozio Higgins, who was president of Chile, and afterwards viceroy of Lima.

Don Thomas asked me who I was, and what I came there for. I handed him my ship's papers; he read them, and then informed me I could not have anything from the land. I told him I had been a long time at sea, the last port being on the south coast of Australia, and that I had a number of men sick on board my ship, with what I supposed was the sea scurvy. This statement was bona fide true. I informed him that all I wanted was some vegetables and fruit, with which the place abounded, so that I could be well supplied without putting them to any inconvenience.

He observed to me that the last governor, whose name was St. Maria, and who owned the island which bore his name, had been removed from his post on account of his lenity to the Americans, and was, in consequence, then under arrest at the city of Concepción. He did not intend that the same fault should be found with him, and accordingly assured me in the fullest terms that I could not have any thing.

I expressed my regret that his orders should be so strict as not to allow him the liberty of affording some little refreshment for my sick people. I told him that I had the pleasure of being acquainted with Captain St. Maria, and that I presumed he could find some opening in his instructions through which a basket of fruit might be drawn for my necessities. As I found he needed much persuasion, although it seemed to produce but little effect, I went on to remind him that I had rendered services to the Spanish people at different times sufficient to deserve so small a favour as I had solicited. I asked him if he had not heard of several Spanish prisoners on board English ships whose release I took pains to procure, and who, but for my interference and exertions, would have been sent to England. I informed him that I had received the thanks of two or three governors on the coast of Chile for similar deeds. He shrugged his shoulders, and said he did not remember much about it.

I then begged him the favour to allow me to stay on shore till the next morning, as my ship was so far to windward that I could not reach her that night, and as it then blew almost a gale of wind from the north west.

He told me I must not stay on the island, and had no business to separate from my ship. I told him it was as much as my life was worth to leave the land and look for my ship at that time. He said he could not help it, and I must go. I then observed that I never had begged my life, but thought what I had already said amounted to the same, and asked him to allow me to take a stone or two from the little pier, which he refused me. I took out a handful of dollars, and desired him to take as many as he chose for a stone. As he knew that there was no place on the island at which a boat could land on such a night, and that with the assistance of a stone or two, I might possibly weather the gale, he allowed me — with a *len-*

ity which, I hope, did not deprive him of his post! — to take two stones without pay. These stones, without doubt, were the means of saving our lives.

We then shoved off, and just as the sun set, it being thick and overcast, we discovered the ship on the horizon, about as big as a man's thumb, directly to windward. We pulled at the oars, but could not make much headway as the winds blew so strong and there was so much sea. I had the advantage of a good whale boat and an excellent crew. We rowed till about ten o'clock when, with a musket which was not so wet but it could flash powder, I made false fires for two or three hours, till at length it became too wet to be used at all. The wind came on to blow so fresh, and there was such a cross sea, that we shipped water very fast. Sometimes it would be half way up to the boat's thwarts before it could be bailed out. By hard exertion, we got so much offing as to insure us sea room till morning, if we did not row any longer; and moreover it became so rough that we had to be very accurate in calculation to prevent the boat filling with water.

I consulted my crew, which was not very usual with me, who, with the exception only of an outlawed Botany Bay convict, did not seem to have very good courage. He said it was not a worse night than he had experienced in crossing Banks' Straits in the king's boat, which they had stolen when they ran away from the Derwent River, in Tasmania.

Well, thought I, if a convict, or anyone else, has survived equal distress, we shall yet surmount our difficulties. I then ordered the people to take all their oars and lash them together, and make a span, or bridle, with a piece of rope fast to each end of them, leaving it slack, so that one of the stones which we had so much trouble to obtain from Don Thomas Higgins, might be made fast to the middle. Then, by making the boat's painter fast in another span to each end of the oars, putting them and the stones overboard, they would sink partly under water, which would not only break the sea, but keep the boat's head to windward. This was done, and had the desired effect. The boat made much better weather after, although the wind and sea increased.

Thus we continued through the night, suffering hardships in the extreme. For myself, my sufferings were greatly increased by the thinness of my dress. Before I had left the ship I shifted my thick clothes and put on nankin pantaloons which were very tight upon me; and my waistcoat and sleeved jacket were of thin white cotton cloth, and likewise very tight. After we got our drag overboard, it became necessary for all to sit, or lie, low in the boat. I stretched myself down in the bottom of her, and lay more than six hours with the water washing over me all the time, which with the tightness of my clothes, gave me a cramp with which I suffered very much.

At length daylight appeared; but no ship nor land were in sight. The sea and atmosphere looked as horrid as can be imagined. As we had no quadrant or compass in the boat, and neither provisions nor water, the prospect before us was far from agreeable. We lay with our oars as before till ten o'clock in the forenoon, when the atmosphere became more clear, and the land appeared at about five leagues distance. At noon the weather was perfectly clear, but no ship could be seen.

We began to pull for the shore, and had not proceeded far before we saw the ship coming down before the wind. At half past two o'clock they took us on board. I was as unable to stand as if I had no legs. On inquiry, we found the ship had been brought to close reefed main topsail and courses, during the gale, and had been compelled to hand the fore and mizen topsails. After taking some refreshment, shifting my clothes, and enjoying a few hours rest, I recovered my strength.

A Near Disaster on a Seal Hunt

WE THEN BORE AWAY for the island of Santa Maria, near Concepción, in latitude 37° 2' south, longitude 72° 36' west. It has been well stocked with black cattle, with most kinds of quadrupeds, and has had a family living on it for many years. There are now some of the vestiges of fruit and of gardens, apple trees, two or three kinds of other trees, and several kinds of garden herbs — balm, sage, saffron, and all kinds of mint, together with rose, currant and gooseberry bushes. There were some cabbages and pumpkins, but they have been largely destroyed by the hogs which remained the longest on the island of any of the stock. These were so much hunted by the different people who visited this place, that they were all killed off. There were appearances of corn hills which convinced me that Indian corn or maize had been a product of the island.

The south head is a great place for shags, and is as white as a snow bank with their ordure on a clear day when the sun shines so as to dry it. They go off to sea in the middle of the day to catch fish, and at night come on shore to roost. I have seen more of them here in one flock than would load a large ship. They sometimes come into the bay, flying and diving after the shoals of fish in such numbers as to make it as dark as on a thick cloudy day.

In the proper season, gulls' eggs abound. They are sweet and very good eating. The method we adopted to get fresh eggs was to go at night and pick up all that were to be found; by doing this, we were certain that what we found the next day would be good. There are other kinds of birds here during the season for them, such as ducks and teal, eagles, hawks, turkey buzzards, and curlews of two or three kinds, and several kinds of sand birds. Good fish may be caught with seines in the bay. Whales are plenty here some part of the season — so much so that ships might load here with right-whale oil very conveniently.

It is a great place of rendezvous for the English and American ships, as they can get water and wood with little trouble; and on such long voyages it is very convenient to exchange civilities. It is not uncommon to see ten or fifteen American and English ships at anchor here in this road. They come in from off whaling ground, from sealing islands, or any pursuit that may call them into these seas; and here they can enjoy themselves very well.

Santa Maria has sometimes been made a residence for people who have got out of Spanish prisons; and likewise for those who come from Más Afuera with a view to procure themselves a passage in ships that may be bound for home, or other shores.

I have seen the glowworm here and in Concepción. It is an extraordinary insect. I have picked them up on a dark night out of the mud, being discovered by their effulgence which was brighter than anything I recollect seeing in nature except fire. They are about an inch long, the fore body something in the form of a lobster, with four or six very short legs. The after body, which was the part that reflected such splendor, was also shaped something like that of the lobster, except the under part, which was like a caterpillar. I have carried them into houses, washed them clean, and put them in a dark place to see with what beauty they would appear. But as soon as they were dry, or dead, the brightness was no more to be discovered.

Capture of the Spanish Ship Tryal at Santa Maria Island, Chile

(This chapter records a striking incident occurring in the course of Delano's third voyage. As Delano himself notes, he made little attempt to separate events chronologically from his second and third voyages where the action is in the western Pacific Ocean off the coasts of Peru and Chile. The dates of the Tryal incident are given in several official documents which follow this chapter: February 20 through April, 1805. At the time of the Tryal encounter, Delano, on the Perseverance, and his brother Samuel, captain of the schooner Pilgrim, had already spent many unsuccessful months hunting seals off Australia and Tasmania, and had then sailed across the South Pacific to continue their business in South American waters.)[37]

W E WERE in a worse situation to effect any important enterprise than I had been in during the voyage (*1803–1807*). We had been from home a year and a half, and not made enough to amount to twenty dollars for each of my people, who were all on shares, and our future prospects were not very flattering.

To make our situation worse, I had found after leaving Australia, on mustering my crew, that I had seventeen additional men, most of whom had been convicts at Botany Bay. They had secreted themselves on board without my knowledge. This was a larger number than had been inveigled away from me at the same place by people who had been convicts, and were then employed at places we visited. The men whom we lost were all of them extraordinarily good men. This exchange materially altered the quality of the crew. Three of the Botany Bay men were outlawed convicts; they had been shot at many times, and several times wounded. After making this bad exchange, my crew were refractory; the convicts were ever unfaithful, and took all the advantage that opportunity gave them.

But sometimes exercising very strict discipline, and giving them good wholesome floggings, and at other times treating them with the best I had, or could get, according as their deeds deserved, I managed them without much difficulty during the passage across the South Pacific Ocean, and all the time I had been on the coast of Chile. I had lately been at the islands of St. Ambrosio and St. Felix, and left there fifteen of my best men, with the view of procuring seals, and left in the company of my consort the *Pilgrim*. We appointed Más Afuera as our place of rendezvous, and if we did not meet there, again to rendezvous at Santa Maria.

I proceeded to the first place appointed; the *Pilgrim* had not arrived. I then determined to take a look at Juan Fernández to see if we could find any seals, as some persons had informed me they were to be found on some part of the island. I thence went to Santa Maria, arriving the 13th of February. We found there the ship *Mars* of Nantucket, commanded by Captain Jonathan Barney. The day we arrived, three of my Botany Bay men ran from the boat when on shore. The next day, I was informed by Captain Barney that some of my convict men had planned to run away with one of my boats, and go over to the mainland.

I examined into the affair and was satisfied as to the truth of it; set five more of the above description of men on shore, making eight in all I had gotten clear of in two days. Captain Barney sailed about the 17th, leaving me quite alone. I continued in that unpleasant situation till the 20th, never at any time daring to let my whale boat be in the water fifteen minutes unless I was in her myself, from a fear that some of my people would run away with her. I always hoisted her on deck the moment I came along side, by which means I had the advantage, for should they run away with any other boat belonging to the ship, I could overtake them with the whale boat. During this time I had no fear from them, except of their running away.

Under these disadvantages the Spanish ship *Tryal* made her appearance on the morning of the 20th, and I had in the course of the day the satisfaction of seeing the great utility of good discipline. In every part of the business of the *Tryal*, not one disaffected word was spoken by the men, but all flew to obey the commands they received; and to their credit, it should be recorded that no men ever behaved better than they, under such circumstances.

On the afternoon of the 19th, before night, I sent the boatswain with the large boat and seine to try if he could catch some fish. He returned with but few, observing that the morning would be better, if he went early. I wished him to go as early as he thought proper, and he accordingly went at four o'clock.

At sunrise, or about that time, the officer who commanded the deck, came down to me while I was in my cot with information that a sail was just opening round the south point, or head of the island. I immediately rose, went on deck, and observed that she was too near the land, on account of a reef that lay off the head; and at the same time remarked to my people that she must be a stranger, and I did not well understand what she was about. Some of them observed that they did not know who she was, or what she was doing, but that they were accustomed to see vessels show their colours, when coming into a port.

I ordered the whale boat to be hoisted out and manned. Presuming the vessel was from sea, and had been many days out without perhaps fresh provisions, we put the fish which had been caught the night before into the boat, to be presented if necessary.

Everything being soon ready, as I thought the strange ship was in danger, we made all the haste in our power to get on board, that we might prevent her getting on the reefs. But before we came near her, the wind headed her off, and she was doing well.

I went along side and saw the decks were filled with slaves. As soon as I got on deck, the captain, mate, crew and slaves, crowded around me to relate their stories, and to make known their grievances, which could not but impress me with feelings of pity for their sufferings. They told me they had no water. After promising to relieve all the wants they had mentioned, I ordered the fish to be put on board, and sent the whale boat to our ship with orders that the large boat, as soon as she returned from fishing, should take a set of gang casks to the watering place, fill them, and bring them for relief as soon as possible. I also ordered the small boat to take what fish the large one had caught, and what soft bread they had baked, some pumpkins, some sugar, and bottled cider, and return to me without delay.

The boat left me on board the Spanish ship, executed my orders, and returned to me about eleven o'clock. At noon the large boat came with the water which I was obliged to serve out to them myself, to keep them from drinking so much as to do themselves injury. I gave them at first one gill each, an hour after, half a pint, and the third hour, a pint. Afterward, I permitted them to drink as they pleased.

They all looked up to me as a benefactor; and as I was deceived in them, I did them every possible kindness. Had it been otherwise there is no doubt I should have fallen a victim to their power.

The Spanish captain, Don Bonito Cereno, had evidently lost much of his authority over the slaves, whom he appeared to fear, and whom he was unwilling in any case to oppose. An instance of this occurred in the conduct of the four cabin boys. They were eating with the slave boys on the main deck, when — as I was afterwards informed — the Spanish boys, feeling some hopes of release, and not having prudence sufficient to keep silent, some words dropped respecting their expectations, which were understood by the slave boys. One of them gave a stroke with a knife on the head of one of the Spanish boys, which penetrated to the bone, a cut four inches in length. I saw this and inquired what it meant. The Captain replied that it was merely the sport of the boys, who had fallen out. I told him it appeared to me to be rather serious sport, as the wound had caused the boy to lose about a quart of blood.

Several similar instances of unruly conduct which, to my manner of thinking, demanded immediate resistance and punishment, were thus easily winked at, and passed over. I felt willing however to make some allowance even for conduct so gross when I considered them to have been broken down with fatigue and long suffering.

The act of the negro, who kept constantly at the elbows of Don Bonito and myself, I should, at any other time, have immediately resented; and although it excited my wonder that his commander should allow this extraordinary liberty, I did not remonstrate against it until it became troublesome to myself. I wished to have some private conversation with the captain alone, and the negro as usual following us into the cabin, I requested the captain to send him on deck. I spoke in Spanish and the negro understood me. The captain assured me that his remaining with us would be of no disservice, that he had made him his confidant and companion since he had lost so many of his officers and men. He had introduced him to me before as captain of the slaves, and told me he kept them in good order.

I was alone with them, on board by myself, for three or four hours during the absence of my boat, at which time the ship drifted out with the current three leagues from my own, when the breeze sprang up from the southeast. It was nearly four o'clock in the afternoon. We ran the ship as near to the *Perseverance* as we could without either ship's swinging afoul the other. After the Spanish ship was anchored, I invited the captain to go on board my ship and take tea or coffee with me. His answer was short and seemingly reserved, and his air very different from that with which he had received my assistance.

I was at a loss to account for this change in his demeanour, and knew he had seen nothing in my conduct to justify it, and as I felt certain that he treated me with intentional neglect, in return I became less sociable, and said little to him.

After I had ordered my boat to be hauled up and manned, and as I was going to the side of the vessel in order to get into her, Don Bonito came to me, gave my hand a hearty squeeze, and, as I thought, seemed to feel the weight of the cool treatment with which I had retaliated. He continued to hold my hand fast till I stepped off the gunwale down the side, when he let it go, and stood making me compliments. When I had seated myself in the boat, and ordered her to be shoved off, the people having their oars up on end, she fell off at a sufficient distance to leave room for the oars to drop. After they were down, the Spanish captain, to my great astonishment, leaped from the gunwale of the ship into the middle of our boat.

As soon as he had recovered a little, he called out in so alarming a manner that I could not understand him; and the Spanish sailors were then seen jumping overboard and making for our boat. These proceedings excited the wonder of us all. At this moment, one of my Portuguese sailors in the boat spoke to me and gave me to understand what Don Bonito had said. I desired the captain to come aft and sit by my side, and in a calm deliberate manner relate the whole affair.

In the meantime, the boat was employed in picking up the men who had jumped from the ship. They had picked up three — leaving one in the water till after the boat had put the Spanish captain and myself on board my ship — when my officer observed the cable was cut and the ship was swinging. I hailed the *Perseverance*, ordering the ports got up, and the guns run out as soon as possible. We pulled as fast as we could on board, and then dispatched the boat for the man who was left in the water, whom we succeeded to save alive.

We soon had our guns ready, but the Spanish ship had dropped so far astern that we could bring but one gun to bear on her. This we fired six times without any other effect than cutting away the fore top-mast stay, and some other small ropes which were no hindrance to her going away. She was soon out of reach of our shot, steering out of the bay.

We then had other calculations to make. Our ship was moored with two bower anchors, which were all the cables or anchors of that description we had. To slip and leave them would be to break our policy of insurance by a deviation against which I would caution the masters of all vessels; for should any accident subsequently occur whereby a loss might accrue to the underwriters, they will be found ready enough to avail themselves of the opportunity to be released from responsibility, and the damage must necessarily be sustained by the owners. This is perfectly right. The law has wisely restrained the powers of the insured, that the insurer should not be subject to imposition, or abuse.

At length, without much loss of time, I determined to pursue, and to take the ship with my two boats. On inquiring of the captain what fire arms they had on board the *Tryal*, he said they had none which they could use; that he had put the few they had out of order so they could make no defence with them; and furthermore, that they did not understand their use, if they were in order. He observed at the same time that if I attempted to take her with boats we should all be killed, for the negros were such bravos and so desperate, that there would be no such thing as conquering them. I saw the man in the situation that I have seen others, frightened at his own shadow. After the boats were armed, I ordered the men to get into them, and they obeyed with cheerfulness. I was going myself, but Don Bonito took hold of my hand and forbade me, saying, you have saved my life, and now you are going to throw away your own. Some of my confidential officers asked me if it would be prudent for me to go, and leave the *Perseverance* in such an unguarded state, and also, if anything should happen to me, what would be the consequence of the voyage. Every man on board, they observed, would willingly go, if it were my pleasure. I gave their remonstrances a moment's consideration, and felt their weight.

I then ordered into the boats my chief officer, Mr. Low, who commanded the party; and under him Mr. Brown, my second officer; my brother William; Mr. George Russell, son to major Benjamin Russell of Boston; and Mr. Nathaniel Luther, midshipman; William Clark, boatswain; Charles Spence, gunner; and thirteen seamen. By way of encouragement I told them that Don Bonito considered the ship and what was in her as lost; that the value was more than one hundred thousand dollars; that if we would take her, it should be all our own; and that if we should afterwards be disposed to give him up one half, it would be considered as a present. I likewise reminded them of the suffering condition of the poor Spaniards remaining on board, whom I then saw with my spy-glass as high aloft as they could get on the top-gallant-masts, knowing that death must be their fate if they came down. I told them, never to see my face again, if they did not take her; and these were all of them pretty powerful stimulants. I wished God to prosper them in the discharge of their arduous duty, and they shoved off.

They pulled after and came up with the *Tryal*, took their station upon each quarter, and commenced a brisk fire of musketry, directing it as much at the man at the helm as they could, as that was likewise a place of resort for the negroes. At length they drove the chief mate from it, who had been compelled to steer the ship. He ran up the mizen rigging as high as the cross jack yard, and called out in Spanish, "Don't board!" This induced our people to believe that he favoured the cause of the negroes; they fired at him and two balls took effect. One of them went through his side, but did not go deep enough to be mortal, and the other went through one of his thighs. This brought him down on deck again.

The ship made such headway that the boats could hardly keep up with her, as the breeze was growing stronger. They then called to the Spaniards, who were still as high aloft as they could get, to come down on the yards, and cut away the ropings and earings of the topsails, and let them fall from the yards so that they might not hold any wind. About the same time, the Spaniard who was steering the ship, was killed; so that both these circumstances combined, rendered her unmanageable by the people left on board. She came round to the wind, and both boats boarded, one on each bow, when she was taken by hard fighting. The negroes defended themselves with desperate courage; and after our people had boarded them, they found they had barricaded the deck by making a breast work of the water casks which we had left on board, and sacks of matta, abreast the mainmast from one side of the ship to the other, to the height of six feet. Behind which they defended themselves with all the means in their power to the last, and our people had to force their way over this breast work before they could compel them to surrender.

On going on board the next morning with handcuffs, leg-irons, and shackled bolts to secure the hands and feet of the negroes, the sight which presented itself was truly horrid. We got all the men who were living made fast, hands and feet, to the ring bolts in the deck. Some of them had part of their bowels hanging out, and some with half their backs and thighs shaved off. This was done with our boarding lances which were always kept exceedingly sharp, and as bright as a gentleman's sword. Whilst putting them in irons, I had to exercise as much authority over the Spanish captain and his crew as I had to use over my own men on any other occasion, to prevent them from cutting to pieces and killing these poor unfortunate beings. I observed one of the Spanish sailors had found a razor in the pocket of an old jacket of his, which one of the slaves had on. He opened it and made a cut upon the negro's head; it bled shockingly. As others were about to engage in the same kind of barbarity, I commanded them not to hurt another one of them, on pain of being brought to the gang-way and flogged. The captain also, I noticed, had a dirk, which he had secreted at the time the negroes were massacreing the Spaniards. I did not observe, however, that he intended to use it until one of my people gave me a twitch by the elbow to draw my attention to what was passing, when I saw him in the act of stabbing one of the slaves. I immediately caught hold of him, took away his dirk, and threatened him with the consequences of my displeasure if he attempted to hurt one of them.

After we had put everything in order on board the Spanish ship, and swept for and obtained her anchors which the negroes had cut from her, we sailed on the 23rd, both ships in company, for Concepción, where we anchored on the 26th. After the common forms were passed, we delivered the ship and all that was on board her, to the captain whom we had befriended. We delivered him also a bag of doubloons, containing, I presume, nearly a thousand; several bags of dollars containing a like number; and several baskets of watches, some gold, and some silver — all of which had been brought on board the *Perseverance* for safe keeping. We retained no part of this treasure to reward us for the services we had rendered.

AFTER OUR ARRIVAL AT CONCEPCIÓN, I was mortified and very much hurt at the treatment which I received from Don Bonito Cereno; but had this been the only time that I ever was treated with ingratitude, injustice, or want of compassion, I would not complain. I will name only one act of his towards me at this place. He went to the prison and took the depositions of five of my Botany Bay convicts who had left us at Santa Maria, and were now in prison here. This was done by him with a view to injure my character, so that he might not be obliged to make us any compensation for what we had done for him. I never made any demand of, nor claimed in any way whatever, more than that they should give me justice; and did not ask to be my own judge, but to refer it to government.

Amongst those who swore against me were the three outlawed convicts, who have been mentioned before. I had been the means, undoubtedly, of saving every one of their lives, and had supplied them with clothes. They swore everything against me they could to effect my ruin. Amongst other atrocities, they swore I was a pirate, and made several statements that would operate equally to my disadvantage had they been believed — all of which were brought before the Viceroy of Lima against me.

When we met at that place, the Viceroy was too great and good a man to be misled by these false representations. He told Don Bonito that my conduct towards him proved the injustice of these depositions, taking his own official declaration at Concepción for the proof of it, and that of others at the marine port, and that he never had seen or heard of any man treating another with so much dishonesty and ingratitude as he had treated the American.

The Viceroy had previously issued an order, on his own authority, to Don Bonito, to deliver to me eight thousand dollars as part payment for services rendered him. This order was not given till his Excellency had consulted all the tribunals holding jurisdiction over similar cases, except the twelve royal judges. These judges exercise a supreme authority over all the courts in Peru, and reserve to themselves the right of giving a final decision in all questions of law. Don Bonito had attempted an appeal from the Viceroy's order to the royal judges. The Viceroy sent for me and acquainted me of Don Bonito's attempt; and at the same time recommending to me to accede to it, as the royal judges well understood the nature of the business and would do much better for me than his order would. I then represented that I had been in Lima nearly two months, waiting for different tribunals to satisfy his Excellency what was safe for him, and best to be done for me, short of a course of law, which I was neither able nor willing to enter into; that I had then nearly thirty men on different islands, and on board my tender, which was then somewhere amongst the islands off the coast of Chile; that they had no method that I knew of to help themselves, or receive succour, except from me; and that if I was to defer the time any longer it amounted to a certainty that they must suffer. I therefore must pray that his Excellency's order might be put in force.

Don Bonito, who was owner of the ship and part of the cargo, had been quibbling and using all his endeavours to delay the time of payment, provided the appeal was not allowed, when his Excellency told him to get out of his sight, that he would pay the money himself, and put him — Don Bonito — into a dungeon, where he should not see sun, moon, or stars; and was about to give the order, when a very respectable company of merchants waited on him and pleaded for Don Bonito, praying that his Excellency would favour him on account of his family, who were very rich and respectable. The Viceroy remarked that Don Bonito's character had been such as to disgrace any family that had any pretensions to respectability, but that he should grant their prayer provided there was no more reason for complaint. The last transaction brought me the money in two hours, by which time I was extremely distressed, enough, I believe, to have punished me for a great many of my bad deeds.

When I take a retrospective view of my life, I cannot find in my soul that I ever have done anything to deserve such misery and ingratitude as I have suffered at different periods, and in general, from the very persons to whom I have rendered the greatest services.

Official Documents Relating to the Tryal

(*Additional facts and details of this extraordinary incident in Delano's chronicle are selected from lengthy depositions taken at the official hearings beginning February 24, 1805, at Talcahuano. Amasa Delano and his first officer, Nathaniel Luther, testified in English. Delano notes that the translations to Spanish were, in his judgment, poor. They were translated into English. However, he inserted in his book the official documents, "without alteration."*

The following details relating to the conditions and fate of the Senegalese slaves are of special interest. No mention is made in these documents of Don Benito Cereno's initial prevarications and evasions. In fact, Cereno's testimony bears out all essentials of Delano's own account.

The depositions were given before Doctor Don Juan Martinez de Rozas, Counselor of the Royal Audience of Chile, Jose de Abos, and Padilla, his Majesty's Notary of Royal Revenue and Registers.

Delano also notes "that the difference of two days in the dates of the process at Talcahuano, that of the Spaniards being the 24th February and ours the 26th, was because they dated theirs the day we anchored in the lower harbour, which was one day before we got abreast of the port, at which time we dated ours; and our coming by way of the Cape of Good Hope, made our reckoning of time one day different from theirs.")

DECLARATION OF FIRST WITNESS, DON BENITO CERENO: He said that the 20th of December last he set sail with his ship from the port of Valparaíso, bound to that of Callao, loaded with the produce of the country and seventy-two negroes of both sexes, and of all ages, belonging to Don Alexandro Aranda, inhabitant of the city of Mendosa. The crew of the ship consisted of thirty-six men, besides the persons who went as passengers. The negroes numbered twenty from twelve to sixteen years; one of about eighteen or nineteen years old named Jose who was the man that waited upon his master Don Alexandro and who spoke Spanish well; a mulatto named Francisco, native of the province of Buenos Aires, aged about thirty-five; a smart negro named Joaquin, who had been for many years among the Spaniards, aged twenty-six, and a caulker by trade; twelve full-grown negroes, aged from twenty-five to fifty years, all raw and born on the coast of Senegal — whose names are as follows: Babo, and he was killed; Mure son of Babo; Matinqui, Yola, Yau, Atufal, who was killed; Diamelo, also killed; Lecbe and Natu, both killed; and he does not recollect the names of the others. (*Cereno reported that at least half of the above named were killed in the battle aboard ship.*) There were twenty-eight women of all ages, and nine sucking infants.

All the negroes slept upon deck, as is customary in this navigation, and none wore fetters because the owner, Aranda, told him that they were all tractable. The twenty-seventh of December, at three in the morning — all the Spaniards being asleep except the two officers on watch, the boatswain Juan Robles, and the carpenter Juan Balltista Gayete, and the helmsman and his boy — the negroes revolted suddenly, wounded dangerously the boatswain and the carpenter, and successively killed eighteen

Spaniards of those who were sleeping upon deck, some with sticks and daggers, and others by throwing them alive overboard, after tying them. Of those on deck, they left about seven, alive and tied, to manoeuvre the ship, and three or four more who hid themselves.

The mate and another person attempted to come up through the hatchway, but having been wounded at the onset, they were obliged to return to the cabin. The deponent resolved at break of day to come up the companion-way, where the negro Babo was, being the ring leader, and another who assisted him, and having spoken to them, exhorted them to cease committing such atrocities — asking them at the same time what they wanted and intended to do, offering himself to obey their commands. Cereno said that notwithstanding this, they threw, in his presence, three men, alive and tied, overboard; that they told the deponent to come up, and that they would not kill him. They asked him whether there were in these seas any negro countries where they might be carried, and he answered them, no. Then they told him to carry them to Senegal, or to the neighbouring islands of St. Nicolas. Cereno answered that this was impossible, on account of the great distance, the bad condition of the vessel, the want of provisions, sails and water. They told him he must carry them in any way possible, that they would do and conform themselves to everything the deponent should require as to eating and drinking. After a long conference, Cereno was absolutely compelled to please them, for they threatened to kill them all if they were not at all events carried to Senegal.

He told them that what was most wanting for the voyage was water; that they would go near the coast to take it, and thence they would proceed on their course.

The negroes agreed to it, and the deponent steered towards the intermediate ports, hoping to meet some Spanish or foreign vessel that would save them.

Within ten or eleven days they saw land, and continued their course by it in the vicinity of Nasca. The deponent observed that the negroes were now restless and mutinous because he did not effect the taking in of water. He told them they saw plainly that the coast was steep and the rivers designated in the maps were not to be found, and that the best way would be to go to the island of Santa Maria. The deponent said he did not go to Pisco, nearby, nor make any other port of the coast because the negroes had intimated to him several times that they would kill them all the moment they should perceive any city, town, or settlement on the shores. (*Cereno hoped that either in passage or at the island itself, he might find means of escape.*)

Eight days after parting from the coast of Nasca, the deponent being on the watch a little after daybreak the negro Mure came to him and said that his comrades had determined to kill his master, Don Alexandro Aranda, because they said they could not otherwise obtain their liberty, and that he should call the mate who was sleeping, before they executed it. The deponent prayed and told Mure all that was necessary in such a circumstance to dissuade him from his design, but all was useless. Mure answered that the thing could not be prevented, and that they should all run the risk of being killed if they should attempt to dissuade or obstruct them in the act. The deponent called the mate, and immediately the negro Mure ordered the negro Matinqui, and another, Lecbe, who died later on the island of Santa Maria, to go and commit this murder. The two went to the berth of Don Alexandro and stabbed him in his bed, and dragged him half alive and agonizing to the deck and threw him overboard. The clerk Don Lorenzo Bargas, was sleeping in the opposite berth, and upon awaking at the cries of Aranda, and surprised at the sight of the negroes with bloody daggers in their hands, he threw himself into the sea through a window which was near him and miserably drowned, without its being in the power of the deponent to assist, or to take him up.

Cereno said that a short time after killing Aranda, they got upon deck his german-cousin, Don Francisco Masa; and the other clerk, Don Hermenegildo, a native of Spain; the boatswain, Juan Robles; and several others; all of whom were wounded, and having stabbed them again, they threw them alive into the sea. Juan Robles, who knew how to swim, kept himself the longest above water, making acts of contrition, and in the last words he uttered, charged this deponent to cause mass to be said for his soul, to our Lady of Succour. Mure told him that they had now done all, and that he might pursue his destination, warning him that they would kill all the Spaniards if they saw them speak, or plot anything against them.

Before the last occurrence, they had tied the cook to throw him overboard for something he had said, and finally they spared his life at the request of the deponent. A few days afterwards the deponent agreed to draw up a paper, signed by himself and the sailors who could write, and also by the negroes Babo and Atufal, who could do it in their language, in which he obliged himself to carry them to Senegal — and they agreed not to kill any more, and to return to the Spaniards the ship with the cargo, once the negroes reached safety.

After forty-two days navigation, reckoned from the

time they sailed from Nasca, during which they had only a scanty allowance of water, they at last arrived at the island of Santa Maria on Tuesday the nineteenth instant, at about five o'clock in the afternoon, at which hour they cast anchor very near the American ship *Perseverance*, commanded by the generous Captain Amasa Delano, but at seven in the morning they had already descried the port and the negroes became uneasy as soon as they saw the ship. The deponent, to appease and quiet them, promised to say and do as they directed. They, in turn, warned him that he and his companions would be killed instantly if they should give the least intimation of past occurrences.

About eight in the morning, Captain Amasa Delano came in his boat on board the *Tryal*, and all gladly received him, the deponent acting the part of an owner and a free captain of the ship. He told him he came from Buenos Aires, bound to Lima with that parcel of negroes; that at the cape many had died — all the sea officers and the greatest part of the crew, that the heavy storms off the cape had obliged them to throw overboard the greatest part of the cargo, and the water pipes. He declared that Delano immediately offered them sails, pipes, and whatever he wanted to pursue his voyage to Lima without entering any other port, leaving it to his pleasure to refund him for these supplies at Callao, or pay him if he thought best.

(Cereno's story continues, corroborating events described already by Nathaniel Luther in the ship's log, and by Delano himself, emphasizing that it was not within his power to tell a single word, nor give Delano the least hint that he might know the true state of things, because Mure, a man of capacity and talents, performed the part of an officious servant, with all the appearance of

submission of the humble slave, and did not leave Cereno one mo-
ment. Following the bloody battle aboard ship, Delano left nine
men in charge of the Tryal, *and acompanied her with his own*
Perseverance *to port.*)

The deponent said he had not seen the twenty negroes, from twelve to sixteen years of age, to have any
share in the execution of the murders. Of the twelve or
thirteen negroes, from twenty-five to fifty years of age,
with the leaders of the revolt, five or six of them were
killed in the attack, and the rest remained alive or prisoners. The negresses of age were knowing of the revolt, and
influenced the death of their master, used their influence
to kill the deponent, and that during the acts of murder
and before the battle aboard ship, they began to sing, and
were singing a very melancholy song during the action to
excite the courage of the men. Of the thirty-six men of the
Tryal's crew and passengers, twelve only, including the
mate, remained alive, besides four cabin boys.

(*Benito Cereno signed this declaration, giving his age*
as twenty-nine. Witnesses were Doctor Rozas and Padilla.
The deposition of Amasa Delano and Nathaniel Luther,
midshipman, were witnessed and ratified by the same people,
plus a third, Ambrosio Fernandez.)

SENTENCE

In this city of Concepción, the second day of the month of
March, of one thousand eight hundred and five, his Honour Doctor Don Juan Martinez de Rozas, Deputy Assessor
and learned in the law, of this intendency, having the execution thereof on account of the absence of his Honour,

the principal having seen the proceedings which he has
conducted officially against the negroes of the ship *Tryal*,
in consequence of the insurrection and atrocities which
they have committed on board of her — he declared that
the insurrection and revolt of said negroes, being sufficiently substantiated with premeditated intent, the twenty seventh of December last, at three o'clock in the morning; that taking by surprise the sleeping crew, they killed
eighteen men, some with sticks, and daggers, and others
by throwing them alive overboard; that a few days afterward with the same deliberate intent, they stabbed their
master Don Alexandro Aranda, and threw Don Franciso
Masa, his german-cousin, Hermenegildo, his relation, and
the other wounded persons who were confined in the
berths, overboard alive; that in the island of Santa Maria,
they defended themselves with arms against the Americans, who attempted to subdue them, causing the death of
Don Jose Moraira, the second clerk, as they had done that
of the first, Don Lorenzo Bargas; the whole being considered, and the consequent guilts resulting from those hei-
nous and atrocious actions as an example to others, he
ought, and did condemn the negroes, Mure, Matinqui,
Alazase, Yola, Joaguin, Luis, Yau, Mapenda, and Yambaio,
to the common penalty of death which shall be executed
by taking them out and dragging them from the prison,
at the tail of a beast of burden, as far as the gibbet, where
they shall be hung until they are dead, and to the forfei-
ture of all their property, if they should have any, to be
applied to the Royal Treasury; that the heads of the five
first be cut off after they are dead, and be fixed on a pole
in the square of the port of Talcahuano, and the corpses of
all be burnt to ashes. The negresses and young negroes of
the same gang shall be present at the execution if they

should be in that city at the time thereof; that he ought and did condemn likewise the negro Jose, servant to said Don Alexandro, and Yambaio, Francisco, Rodriguez to ten years confinement in the place of Valdivia, to work chained, on allowance and without pay, in the work of the King, and also to attend the execution of the other criminals; and judging definitively by this sentence thus pronounced and ordered by his Honour, and that the same should be executed notwithstanding the appeal, for which he declared there was no cause, but that an account of it should be previously sent to the Royal Audience of this district for the execution thereof with the costs.

> (*Signed*) by Doctor Rozas
> before Jose De Abos Padilla,
> His Majesty's Notary of the
> Royal Revenue and Register.

OFFICIAL RESOLUTION

The Tribunal has resolved to manifest by this official resolve and pleasure for the exactitude, zeal and promptness which you have discovered in the cause against the revolted negroes of the ship *Tryal*, which process it remits to you, with the approbation of the sentence for the execution thereof, forewarning you that before its completion, you may agree with the most Illustrious Bishop, on the subject of furnishing the spiritual aids to those miserable beings, affording the same to them with all possible dispatch. At the same time this Royal Audience has thought fit in case you should have an opportunity of speaking with the Bostonian captain, Amasa Delano, to charge you to inform him, that they will give an account to his Majesty, of the generous and benevolent conduct which he displayed in the punctual assistance that he afforded the Spanish captain of the aforesaid ship, for the suitable manifestation, publication and noticety of such a memorable event.

> God preserve you many years.
> (*Signed at*) Santiago, March the twenty-second, of one thousand eight hundred and five, by Jose De Santiago Concha, and Doctor Don Juan Martinez De Rozas.

ON MY RETURN TO AMERICA in 1807, I was gratified in receiving a polite letter from the Marquis De Case Yruso, through the medium of Juan Stoughton, Esq., accompanied with a gold medal, having his majesty's likeness on one side, and on the other the inscription, "Reward of Merit." I had been assured by the president of Chile, when I was in that country, and likewise by the viceroy of Lima, that all my conduct, and the treatment I had received, should be faithfully represented to his majesty Charles IV, who most probably would do something more for me. I had reason to expect that I should most likely have received something essentially to my advantage. This probably would have been the case had it not been for the unhappy catastrophe which soon after took place in Spain, by the dethronement of Charles IV, and the distracted state of the Spanish government, which followed that event.

Philadelphia, 8th September 1806

Sir,

His Catholic Majesty the king of Spain, my master, having been informed by the audience of Chile of your noble and generous conduct in rescuing, off the island Santa Maria, the Spanish merchant ship *Tryal*, captain Don Benito Cereno, with the cargo of slaves who had mutinized, and cruelly massacred the greater part of the Spaniards on board; and by humanely supplying them afterwards with water and provisions, which they were in need of, has desired me to express to you, sir, the high sense he entertains of the spirited, humane, and successful effort of yourself and the brave crew of the *Perseverance*, under your command, in saving the lives of his subjects thus exposed, and in token whereof, his majesty has directed me to present to you the golden medal, with his likeness, which will be handed to you by his consul in Boston. At the same time permit me, sir, to assure you I feel particular satisfaction in being the organ of the grateful sentiments of my sovereign, on an occurrence which reflects so much honour on your character.

I have the honour to be, sir,

Your obedient servant,

(*signed*) Marquis De Case Yruso

Captain Amasa Delano, of the American Ship *Perseverance*, Boston.

Easter Island; Discovery of "Pilgrim Island" by Samuel Delano, August 12, 1805

S
T. FELIX, the western island of this group off the coast of Chile, is in latitude 26°14' south, and in longitude 79°25' west. It is the island most visited by those in pursuit of seal skins, and I would recommend it for fish and eggs; but as for fish, they can be caught at any one of the islands in great plenty. St. Ambrosio lies to the east-south-east of the first mentioned island, at about fifteen miles distance.

The center of Easter Island lies in latitude 27° 15' south, and longitude 109° 55' west, by our observations. When we came abreast the place where Captain Cook recommends it as best to anchor, we prepared a boat and made an attempt to land; but on our approach near the shore, we found the surf was so bad, that it was not in our power to effect it. The natives came down in great numbers, and made friendly signs to invite us on shore, holding up sugar-cane, yams, and many other things, which we could not distinguish. There appeared to be two or three hundred people near the place where we were trying to land, and I should suppose we saw five or six hundred inhabitants as we ran along the north side of the island.

We saw a number of statues representing human forms of a very large size. I should suppose them to be upwards of twenty feet high, very large in proportion to their height. Captain Cook says they are made of stone; but he does not mention so many as we saw, nor so many inhabitants. It is my opinion they have populated fast since Captain Cook visited the place, and that they have built many of those statues and other buildings.

We saw a large kind of house near the shore that must have been two hundred feet long, and also many more of different forms. The most common form we saw was like a haycock. Some appeared to be built with stone, and others thatched over.

The greatest part of the island had the appearance of being capable of cultivation, and much of it was cultivated in beautiful plantations. I have no doubt, if the weather was good and the sea smooth, so that a boat could land, plenty of vegetables might be obtained.

HAVING HEARD SEVERAL CAPTAINS of whale ships speak of birds being seen seven or eight degrees to the eastward of Easter Island, and nearly in the same latitude, I was induced to dispatch the *Pilgrim*, under the command of my brother Samuel, to search for this supposed island. My object was to find some place where seals might be procured. I was convinced of the capability of my brother to effect the object of discovering the island, if any such existed. I thought it worthy of our attention, and accordingly on the 19th of July 1805, the *Pilgrim* parted company from the *Perseverance*, on the coast of Peru, in latitude 14° south, and sailed to the south west in pursuit of this object.

Our information had been incorrect as to the longitude of this imaginary island, but by observing the flight of birds every day, at length he found the land on which they went every night to roost.

(*"Pilgrim Island" is in latitude 26° 30' south, and in longitude 104° 50' west. The island is mostly rocks, and Samuel's people could not land.*)

Discovery of "Pilgrim Island" by Samuel Delano

I WILL HERE REMARK, that the olive branch, or a branch of a green tree or bush, is an emblem of peace in nearly every part of the world that I have ever visited. It is in Peru as in Chile; and in New Guinea, Australia, in the Society Islands, as Captain Wallis describes at Tahiti; and in almost all the islands in the Pacific Ocean that I know of, or have read of.

Also I cannot help remarking here, that in all the countries which I have visited, that are styled savage, it is an universal custom, to pay strict attention to the one who is speaking; and if he is in the habit of speaking too long, or too frequent, his superiors gently chide him, after he has finished speaking. Would it not be well for nations more refined to follow the example of the savages, in this as well as in many other respects? It should be remembered, that with gentlemen of fine feelings, there cannot well be offered any thing that is more repugnant to their feelings than to interrupt them, or to pay no attention to what they are saying in public; and on the other hand, the man who is occupying a great proportion of time, without considering that he is intruding on the rights of others, is seldom very wise or amusing to the hearers.

DURING MY FIRST VOYAGE in the ship *Perseverance*, in the years 1799 to 1802, we did not visit the coast of Peru, although we did the Galapagos Islands; but in the second voyage, in 1803 to 1807, we were on the coasts both of Chile and Peru, down as far as the equator. In giving a description of the different places, and the events which took place while at them, I have made no difference whether it was during my first or second voyage, as it could be of no consequence to the reader at what time the information was obtained. During our stay on this coast we were constantly backwards and forwards from the different ports on the coast to the islands which lie off, and from one island to another, in pursuit of the objects of our voyage.

We completed our business on the coast of Chile, and took our departure from Más Afuera on the 18th day of October 1801, and directed our course toward the Galapagos Islands, where we arrived, the second visit, on the 3rd of November following.

Remarks and Observations on the Galapagos Islands from Several Visits; Encounters with Tortoises on Land and Aboard Ship; Dove Hunting with Sticks

THE BEST general account of the Galapagos Islands that I have seen is that of Captain Colnett, which is tolerably correct information, though we found some things different from his statement. The greatest number of these islands received their names from Captain Colnett, who visited them about the year 1792 and 1793, in the ship *Rattler* from London. The *Perseverance* and the *Pilgrim* made the easterly part of Chatham (*Isla San Cristobal*) and Hood's (*Isla Espanola*) islands nearly at the same time, and stood in between them. We traversed all the south west side of Hood's Island, from the most extreme south to the north west end, and tried to land with the boat, but found it all an iron bound shore, until we rounded its northwest point where we found a good landing place.

We went over all parts of the island, and procured plenty of tortoises. We saw many albatrosses with their young, and some sitting on their eggs. There were snakes, and a very large kind of lizard. Plenty of green turtles were to be obtained. We likewise saw marks of former visitors. There were some very large trees which had drifted on shore here, that were much larger than any to be seen growing on either of these islands. They must have drifted from the continent, and most probably from somewhere to the northward of the bay of Panama. They were of the kind of wood commonly called Spanish cedar, which is nearly as handsome as mahogany. It is a convenient place for procuring wood and tortoises, which are all the island afforded.

In our run to James's Island, we passed between Albermarle (*Isla Isabela*), Barrington, Duncan, and Jarvis's (*Isla San Salvador*) Islands, down to James's Bay. We stood into James's Bay where we anchored in seven fathoms, good bottom; and found it to be a good safe harbour, sheltered from all prevailing winds. We likewise found fresh water here, as Captain Colnett mentions, which was very good, and filled eighteen or twenty of our butts. We caught plenty of fish, but they were not very good. We also killed some flamingoes and teals in the salt ponds that lie just within the sands beach, abreast of the anchoring place. We cut a supply of wood between the ponds and the sea and found it to be the best to burn of any I ever saw.

When we arrived in this bay we found two Spanish brigs riding together by another brig which had been sunk. They had all three been cut out of Pisco. They were prizes to the ship *Henry* of London, commanded by Captain William Watson, who arrived on the 23rd of July from a whaling cruise. I had flattered myself that on the arrival of the *Henry*, I should have much pleasure in the company of the captain. As the two Spanish brigs were left with only one man, one boy, and a Spanish negro prisoner, I was confident the *Henry* could not be long absent, but when she arrived I was very much disappointed in my anticipations.

The captain was, in my opinion, the greatest drunkard, and the most low and mean spirited man that ever was put in charge of property. Here was one instance of the abuse of power, given to a villain, who made use of it to rob and plunder on the high seas. He had it in contemplation to plunder me, and I have no doubt he would have attempted it, had his officers and crew been willing to have assisted in such an outrage.

He found me with only ten men on board my ship when he came into the bay. Several of them were sick with the scurvy and other complaints. I had buried one but a few days previous who died of a scorbutic complaint. In this weak and helpless condition, he threatened to take away my men as British subjects. He came on board once and demanded my chief officer. I found that I must either let him take him, or have recourse to some very hostile measures. On my telling him, however, that he should take no advantage of me with impunity, although I was in such a disabled state, he did not seem to be disposed to pursue his designs, especially when he found there was some appearance of opposition in the way.

The *Henry* mounted fourteen six pounders, most of which were too light for actual service, and I found her commander to be not of the fighting cast, but one of the blustering sort of men. They left us on the 30th of July, to our great satisfaction. They left Captain Anderson, late of the *Castor and Pollux* of London, who had been put, with seven of his men, on shore on the weather-head of Albermarle Island to recover from the scurvy, which they all had very badly. During their stay on shore, a Spanish privateer ship, called the *Atlantic*, fell in with and captured his and one more English ship, that was in company. Captain Anderson had no knowledge of his ship, or what had happened to her, at the time he left this bay. He had been left there in charge of one of the *Henry*'s Spanish prizes, called the *St. Bartholomew*. He fitted and rigged her and left, intending to proceed to London by way of Cape Horn.

THE TERRAPIN, OR LAND TORTOISE, that is found here is by far the largest, best, and most numerous of any place I ever visited. Some of the largest weigh three or four hundred pounds; but their common size is between fifty and one hundred pounds. They have a very long neck, which, together with their head, has a very disagreeable appearance, very much resembling a large serpent. I have seen them with necks between two and three feet long, and when they saw anything that was new to them, or met each other, they would raise their heads as high as they could, their necks being nearly vertical, and advance with their mouths wide open, appearing to be the most spiteful of any reptile whatever.

Sometimes two of them would come up to each other in that manner, so near as almost to touch, and stand in that position for several minutes, appearing so angry that their mouths, heads, and necks appeared to quiver with passion; when by the least touch of a stick against their necks or heads, they would shrink back in an instant and draw their necks, heads, and legs into their shells. I was put in the same kind of fear that is felt at the sight or near approach of a snake when I first saw a very large one. I was alone at the time and he stretched himself as high as he could, opened his mouth, and advanced towards me. His body was raised more than a foot from the ground, his head forward in the manner of a snake in the act of biting, and raised two and a half feet above his body. I had a musket in my hand at the time, and when he advanced near enough, I held the muzzle out so that he hit his neck against it, at the touch of which, he dropped himself upon the ground and instantly secured all his limbs within his shell.

They are perfectly harmless, as much so as any animal I know of, notwithstanding their threatening appearance. They have no teeth, and of course they cannot bite very hard. They take their food into their mouths by the assistance of the sharp edge of the upper and under jaw, which shut together one a little within the other, so as to nip grass, flowers, berries, or shrubbery — the only food they eat.

They are very prudent in taking care of themselves and their eggs, and in the manner of securing them in their nests; and I have observed on board my own ship as well as others, that they can easily be taught to go to any place on the deck which may be wished. The method to effect this is by whipping them with a small line when they are out of place, and to take them up and carry them to the place assigned for them; which being repeated a few times will bring them into the practice of going themselves. They can be taught to eat on board a ship as well as a sheep, or a goat, and will live for a long time if there is proper food provided for them. This I always took care to do when in a place where I could procure it. The most suitable to take on board a ship is prickly pear trees, the trunk of which is a soft pithy substance, of a sweetish taste, and full of juice. Sometimes I procured grass for them. Either of these being strewn on the quarter deck, the prickly pear being cut fine, would immediately entice them to come from all parts of the deck to it, and they would eat in their way as well as any domestic animal. I have also known them to live several months without food, but then they grew lighter and lost their fat.

At one time, I carried from James's Island three hundred very good terrapins to the island of Más Afuera, and there landed more than one half of them, after having them sixty days on board my ship. Half of that number died as soon as they took food. This was owning to their stomachs having got so weak and out of tone that they could not digest it. As soon as they ate any grass after landing, they would froth at the mouth, and appeared to be in a state of insanity, and died in the course of a day or two. This satisfied me that they were in some degree like other animals, and only differed in that it takes a longer time to produce an effect upon their system than that of other creatures. Those that survived the shock occasioned by this sudden transition from total abstinence to that of abundance, soon became tranquil and appeared to be as healthy and as contented with the climate as when they were at their native place, and they would probably have lived as long had they not been killed for food.

Their flesh, without exception, is of as sweet and pleasant a flavour as any that I ever ate. It was common to take out of one of them ten or twelve pounds of fat when they were opened, besides what was necessary to cook them with. This was as yellow as our best butter, and of a sweeter flavour than hog's lard.

They are remarkable for their strength; one of them would bear a man's weight on his back and walk with him. I have seen them at one or two other places only. One instance was those brought from Madagascar to Mauritius; but they were far inferior in size, had longer legs, and were much more ugly than those of the Galapagos Islands.

The land iguana is very similar in shape to the lizard or alligator, but about two and a half feet long. Their shape is like a short thick snake with four legs, but it is a very innocent animal. Its colour is like that of burned rocks, or cinder, and its skin looks almost as coarse and rough. They are tolerably good eating and would be made use of for food were there not so many terrapins and sea turtles to be got at this place.

The sea iguana resembles the land iguana, but its back and head go up to a sharp ridge on the top, and a comb runs from near the nose over the top of its head to near the end of its tail, which gives it the most disagreeable appearance of any animal to be found here. The colour of the skin is nearly black and has as rough and coarse an appearance as the land kind. It obtains its living entirely out of the sea.

The largest kind of lizards found here resembles the land iguana in everything but size, being only a little more than half the length. Their colour and coarse appearance are the same with the exception of a bright vermilion red throat, which makes it appear as if bloody. There are also two smaller kinds of lizards. The smallest is not much longer than a man's finger. The other is in between. They are very harmless animals.

The snakes we found here appeared to be harmless, none possessing any venomous qualities that we had any knowledge of. One kind of them is four or five feet long, and not thicker than a person's finger, and is striped. There was a short thick snake which is not more than two and a half feet long. Its colour is clouded with a mixture of dark gray, black, and red.

THE PELICANS OF THIS PLACE are much like those in the West Indies. They have a monstrous large bill, more than a foot long, with a cot, or bag, growing to the under part of the bill. The under jaw is divided in such a manner that it can be spread open similar to a net bow, so as to contain near a peck of grain. They are the most clumsy bird I ever saw. When diving they make the most awkward appearance that can be imagined, which cannot be better described than by comparing it to the manner in which a sailor washes his clothes, by making them fast to the end of a rope and throwing them from the forecastle into the sea. When they strike the water, they spread out, with the trousers in one direction, the shirt in another, and the jacket in a third. The pelican makes a plunge into the water for the purpose of obtaining its food in a similar manner — its wings extended, its mouth open, and its bill expanded, with two enormously large feet spread out behind.

The ring dove is not so large as a turtle dove, and is more of the colour of the quail of our country. It has a ring of feathers round its neck of a light colour, and is a little simple, stupid kind of a bird. They are commonly found on the ground, amongst the groves of trees where there is not much underbrush. They are a very delicate bird, and good eating. The method we practised to take them was by going into the woods and taking with us small sticks, five or six feet long, and start a flock of them, when they would light upon the little bushes. We would then walk up near enough to reach them with our sticks, and with a gentle motion place our stick close to the side of their neck, and while they would sit nodding, and looking stupidly at the stick, give them a sudden blow and break their necks. By these means, three or four of the crew could go into a grove and kill five or six dozen in two hours, which would be sufficient to make our ship's company a good dinner.

There is another remarkable bird found here which has not before been described. It is called the diver (*a gannet, booby family*). They resemble the small kind of booby, and something similar to the kind which is described at the Lobas Islands, called Bonaparte's army, excepting they are of rather a darker colour on the breast and neck, and their beaks and feet are of a Prussian blue. These birds collect together in small flocks for the purpose of diving. They fly round in a circle and continue to rise till they get to the height of from sixty to a hundred yards in the air, when one of them makes a pitch to dive, at which motion every one follows. They fly down with remarkable swiftness till within four or five yards of the surface, and then suddenly clasp their wings together and go into the water with the greatest velocity that can be conceived of, exceeding anything of the kind that I ever witnessed. This bird should be contrasted with the pelican.

I have often stood upon the ship's taffrail, and sometimes have gone into one of the tops, to observe the motions of these birds whilst they were diving. They go into the water with such force as to form a curve of thirty or forty yards in length, before coming to the top again, going to a great depth under water. They glide under water at almost as great a degree of swiftness as when flying in the air. The water was so very transparent where the ship lay, that they could plainly be seen during all their submarine course.

THESE ISLANDS AFFORD SOME SEALS of both the fur and hair kind, and I think a vessel might procure several thousands of the two kinds upon the whole of this cluster of islands, as all of them afford some. Green turtles are found here in the greatest plenty; and they are the easiest procured of any place that I ever visited in any part of the world.

The method we took to fill with water here was to raft our empty casks on shore and haul them onto the shelf of the rock by means of a hauling line, place them beside a basin worn in the rock, and leave a man with them constantly night and day to attend and dip the water as fast as the basin filled. By this means we could sometimes save three hundred gallons in twenty-four hours. We got the casks off to the boat again by means of a hauling line made fast to them. After this they were rolled into a kind of pit which was worn into the rocks by the constant surging of the sea. They were then hauled to and taken into the boat by means of a par-buckle, if the boat was sufficiently large and strong to receive them; otherwise we towed them to the ship.

Were it not for the advantages which these islands afford to the American and English whaling ships in getting a supply of fresh provisions when in these seas, I know not what they would do, especially in time of war, as they then could not possibly obtain any from the Spanish settlements. Without this convenience ships would not be able to keep to sea but a few months before their people would die with the scurvy.

The most extraordinary phenomenon happened while we were riding in James's Bay in the year 1800, that I ever witnessed in my life. I do not remember to have ever heard or read of anything like it either before or since. I will here insert an extract from the ship's journal, described by the officer who had the care of the log book: "As our boat was coming from the watering place on the evening of the 21st of August, between sunset and dark, with a load of water, we saw a large black cloud gathering over the highest mountain on Albermarle Island, which was the same place where one of the men on board our ship had asserted that he had seen a volcano burning in 1797. Soon after the cloud gathered, it formed a spire or piked end similar to that of a cloud when about to meet a water spout. It descended to the top of the mountain with a body of fire following it, apparently of the size of the largest part of the steeple of a meeting house. Its illumination was so great that it attracted the attention of all the people in the boat, although they were at the time rowing with their backs toward it. After the fire had descended to the top of the mountain, it continued some seconds when it broke like a water spout and left a streak where it had passed, which appeared as brilliant as a column of fire, and continued for near half an hour before it wholly disappeared."

To The Hawaiian Islands; "Captain Stewart," the King's Son; Inoculations for Small Pox; A Cultural Shock; Captain Kendrick of Boston; The Shipwrecked Japanese

WE SAILED from the Galapagos Islands for Canton on the 9th of November 1801, and directed our course toward the Hawaiian Islands, where we arrived on the 10th of December.

The highest land of Owhyhee (*the island of Hawaii*) is three large mountains, which are some of the highest in the world. They can be seen forty or fifty leagues at sea in clear weather. The king generally makes his home at Karakakooa Bay, and where he resides a ship is not so much troubled with the natives, and is in no danger of being attacked by them. This island affords plenty of hogs, fowls, some potatoes and yams, but they are very dear, owing to so many vessels stopping here. They may be bought cheaper in almost any part of America.

When visiting any of these islands, it is necessary to be very cautious in keeping the natives out of the ship, and never permit so many to come on board as to be in fear, especially if they have any inclination to be hostile. The white people who are on these islands are very serviceable to ships; for by their assistance the water casks may be filled and brought off without getting the boats out and risking the people on shore. I once went on shore where the king was, and was treated very hospitably, and saw no appearances of any danger from the natives, but I thought it was owing to the king's being with me.

Tomahammaha, the present king, is very well disposed towards the white people who stop here; but should some one of the chiefs be invested with the reins of government on the death of this king, I do not think it would be safe for small vessels to stop. There are many chiefs wicked enough to take any advantages and cut a vessel off whenever they could get an opportunity.

In my visit to the Hawaiian Islands in the year 1806, we ran the voyage in latitude 20° 30' north, with the intention to go to Mowee (*Maui*), but we made Hawaii first. We then hauled further to the northward and made Maui, where we observed several pretty little bays. Some parts of the island were well cultivated. On rounding the northwest end of the island, great numbers of canoes came off to us with fowls, yams, potatoes, cocoa-nuts, and several kinds of fruit. We anchored on the south west side of the island in ten fathoms water, muddy bottom, one quarter of a mile off shore, abreast of a handsome little village. We found this island to be much more fertile and pleasant than Hawaii.

I went on shore at the village repeatedly, and found it to be a delightful spot of low level land, of a very rich soil and exceedingly well cultivated. I was treated very civilly by all descriptions of people, and obtained a considerable stock of vegetables and some hogs; but everything was dearer than it was on my previous voyage. I was informed that the king was at Woahoo (*Oahu*), and I made up my mind to visit that island, it lying to leeward.

Maui did not appear to be much burned with volcanoes. Very recently they had brought here one of the bulls that Capt. Vancouver landed at Hawaii. He made very great destruction amongst their sugar canes and gardens, breaking into them, and tearing them to pieces with his horns and digging them up with his feet. He would run after and frighten the natives, and appeared to have a disposition to do all the mischief he could, so much so that he was a pretty unwelcome guest among them. There was a white man at this village who told me that they had not killed any of the black cattle that Capt. Vancouver brought there, and that they had multiplied very much. Some years later I was told by several captains that they had increased so much that the islanders now frequently kill them for beef.

ON MY ARRIVAL AT OAHU, in 1806, I was received coolly by the king, on account of my not returning a natural son of his, who had sailed with me from Hawaii in 1801. The circumstances were as follows:

When I was at Hawaii in the year 1801, I was upon the best terms of friendship and intimacy with the king. I observed a remarkably likely youth of about twenty-one years of age when I was on shore at Toweyhee Bay. His appearance prepossessed me very much in his favour. His behavior was dignified, comely, and sprightly; his body, limbs, and features, handsome. In his address and conversation he was governed by the strictest propriety, but his speech was accompanied with that native modesty which ever accommodates good sense.

As he seemed remarkably attentive to me, I was induced to inquire who he was, and was informed by George McClay that he was the natural son of the king. I was told that he had taken the name of Alexander Stewart, which was the name of a gentleman then residing on the island, but was more commonly known by the name of captain Stewart. I soon ascertained that the king did not notice him, but I was satisfied that this was owing to a political consideration.

There were others on the island in a similar situation, and should the king notice any one of them more than another, it naturally would create a jealousy. The young man called captain Stewart soon made application to me through the medium of George McClay, to take him away from the island with me. I replied that if the king had no objection I would do it, as I had made up my mind previous to my arrival to take one of their boys, as I once had one, who was a native of these islands, and one of the best boys I ever saw.

George observed that I could take one now, and that he would find out the king's pleasure respecting his son. I very shortly received intelligence that it was congenial to the feelings of the king, and that I had liberty to take anyone that I pleased. It was accordingly settled that captain Stewart should go with me, and I agreed that I would also take a younger boy, provided I saw one that I liked. More than one hundred boys presented themselves in the course of two hours for my approbation, but I did not see one that I liked till I went into a house where the king's wives were. They questioned me who I was going to take with me, and asked if I had found a boy that I liked. Being answered in the negative, one of them asked how I liked that one, pointing to one that was standing behind her, who was employed to fan his mistress with a large tassel of long feathers made fast to a stick to keep the flies from her. After inspecting him for a moment, I answered her that I liked him very well. She then said, "You shall have him," and told him to come to me. He lay down his fan of feathers and took his station at the back of my chair, and did not leave me one minute after, till I went on board.

When we had got the ship under way, it being then nine o'clock in the evening, with the king's son and my boy with me, I observed captain Stewart's mother had taken a station in the main anchor chains, and was making great lamentation for her son. Her cries I never can forget, as they were so expressive and on a subject so tender to a mother's feelings. She said I was going to take away her only son and child, where she should never behold him again; that she could not leave the ship without him. I called to one of the canoes that was not yet out of hearing, and desired them to come along side, which they did, after we had backed the main topsail. I told captain Stewart he must go on shore with his mother, that I could not carry him away and leave her thus distressed. He said he "could not go back, as it would be unmanly, that it would redound very much to his dishonor to have it said that he had relinquished a design of such importance, for no other reason than that his mother cried about it; that she was nothing but a woman and she would forget it by tomorrow and be well enough." This reasoning, however, did not satisfy me. His mother's tears argued more powerfully than words, and operated upon my feelings to such a degree, that I was perplexed to know what to do. Neither the man, nor woman, would leave the ship without my using compulsory measures. After detaining the canoe for more than an hour, we succeeded by entreaties and with presents, to prevail on the mother to go on shore.

After we were fifteen or twenty leagues from land, I discovered that we had three more of the natives on board, who had secreted themselves in the ship without my knowledge. When I arrived in Canton, my first concern for these people was to have them inoculated for the small pox.[38] I had in my previous voyages seen many of these poor creatures die with that loathsome and fatal disorder in that place. I accordingly had them all five inoculated immediately after my arrival. I had found on an earlier voyage that there was a substitute for the small pox by inoculating with the kine pox, which would answer all the purposes as a preventive, and at the same time would be attended with no dangerous consequences to the patient. I procured some of the kine pock matter from an American ship which we passed in the river as we were going up to Canton. I was perfectly convinced from this experiment, as well as from a great number of instances since that time, that it is a complete preventive to the small pox. I should recommend it to all captains who are employed on voyages.

The five who were inoculated against small pox had it very favourably; but during the time they were sick with it, I found it would be very inconvenient as well as expensive to have them with me at Canton, and I was under the necessity to keep them on board the ship at Huangpu, nine miles below the city. I had discharged several of the men on my arrival, one of which was a great favourite with Stewart. This man had shipped himself on board an English Indiaman. He often came aboard the *Perseverance* to see his old ship mates, and persuaded the king's son to leave me and go with him on board the English ship. I think it very probable that Stewart felt that he was alone and neglected in my absence, and was discouraged — he having a noble and generous mind, and very tender feelings.

On being informed of the circumstances, I waited on the captain of the Indiaman. He did not deny having knowledge of the business, but said he had been informed that I had so many of these people on board my ship, that I did not care anything about their leaving me, and that if I wished it, Stewart should be immediately returned. He likewise remarked that as he had left my ship voluntarily and seemed to be very much pleased with his situation, if I would give my consent to let him remain on board his ship, he would treat him in the same manner as if he were his own son; and that on his arrival in England he would take care that he should be noticed in his true character.

I answered that it was contrary to my principles to take the natives of those unfrequented countries away from their homes, and so neglect my duty to them as to let them go unprovided for in a strange country; and that I still felt far greater obligations towards the king's son whom he had got, and the boy who was still with me, than I did for the other three natives who were then on board. I had taken the former from their friends, who would reasonably expect me to take prudent care of them, but the latter came on board my ship against my will, for which reason I felt no obligation towards them farther than common humanity.

After I had considered the whole subject, I made up my mind to let Stewart stay with the English captain, giving him a statement of his true character. The captain renewed his promise of friendship and kindness towards him, which was the last knowledge I had of the king's son, except for a vague report that he was taken notice of on his arrival in England by a gentleman of consequence who took him to his own house with an intention of giving him an education.

To the boy, I gave the name of Bill, and brought him with me to Boston, where his merits were duly appreciated, and he was generally known, together with my treatment towards him. He performed on the Boston stage several times in the tragedy of Captain Cook, and was much admired by the audience and the public in general. He afterwards returned to his native island with me; but not wishing to remain there, he went to Canton in the *Pilgrim*, where he was paid off, and I have heard nothing of him since.

A word about George McClay, aforementioned: He was my carpenter in the ship *Eliza* when I left Canton in 1793, and went to Mauritius with me. He was also carpenter in the large ship *Hector* which was purchased at that place. He went with me to Bombay, after which he had travelled in that part of the world until he found his way to the Hawaiian Islands, where he was noticed by the king on account of his being a good natured, honest fellow, and a very good shipbuilder. He built nearly twenty small vessels and a few as large as forty or fifty tons whilst he was at the islands. He likewise put in a new keel, and nearly new-planked a small ship called the *Lily-burgh*, a ship well known in that quarter of the world for a number of years. All this labour he performed for the king. I made a confidant of George McClay whilst at these islands, in all my negotiations with the king, and others with whom I had intercourse.

As I have before mentioned, the king received me cool-ly on my arrival at Oahu. The women of the highest ranks were very particular in their inquiries of me concerning the youth who had left me in China. They gave me to understand that all classes of people had built their hopes very much on him, and entertained high expectations of his returning with me after acquiring some knowledge of the world, whereby he might be better qualified to make them a good king.

I was informed that as soon as it was known that I was to windward amongst the islands, great preparations were made for my reception at Oahu. They collected hogs and other provisions for me, expecting I had the king's son on board. But when I arrived, and they found that he was not on board, they appeared to show more grief than anger. This op-erated more powerfully on my feelings than any other passion that they could have discovered. I felt the full force of my conduct in having left him at Canton, and considered myself to blame for giving my consent on any account whatever to have him separated from me until returned to his friends at his place of nativity. I was treated very civilly by all, but not with that cordiality that I once had received.

A Cultural Shock

ALL THE CLOTHING WORN by the people of these islands is made of the bark of a remarkable shrub, called the cloth tree, which does not commonly grow larger than a man's wrist. It is peeled from the stem of the tree in the same manner that birch bark is, and is then pounded on a log with a small piece of wood until it is as thin as brown paper. The nature of the bark is such that by being wet and beat, it will expand to any size necessary, as long as there is substance to work upon.

The women commonly wear a square piece wrapped round their waist, which reaches from their hips to the calves of their legs. They sometimes wear a piece over their shoulders, similar to a shawl, but most commonly go without this. The males wear a very narrow strip round their loins, the same as the common class of natives all over India, and in the eastern islands. It is called a land-gouty in India.

They eat pork, which is exclusively the privilege of the men. Dogs, fowls, fish and all kinds of vegetables and fruit are eaten by both sexes. Their most common drink is cocoanut milk, sweetened water, and a kind of ardent spirit which they distill from a disagreeable sickish-tasting root, and from sugar cane. It is unwholesome and unpalatable, and has been the cause of the death of a number of the white men residing there, as well as many of the natives.

The idea of making use of dogs for food is disgusting to the people of our country, but I can assure them that they are very good eating — a satisfactory proof of which I experienced while at these islands: On my arrival at Oahu, I found a gentleman there by the name of Hudson, whom I had known at Más Afuera in the year 1801. He was a man possessed of a large share of natural as well as acquired abilities, and was very enterprising and honourable in all his transactions. Captain Hills was likewise there at the time, who com-

THE BRIG *ATTATANT* OF BOSTON, BUILT IN SALEM IN 1797.
(COURTESY OF THE PEABODY ESSEX MUSEUM)

manded the brig *Lydia* of Boston; and Captain Ebbets commanding the ship *Pearl*, and Captain Jonathan Winship commanding the ship *O'Cain*, both of Boston. We were much of the time together and formed a very pleasant society among ourselves.

Captain Hudson kept his own house while on shore, which the king had built on purpose for him, and had it very well furnished. When on shore, we all breakfasted, dined, and supped at his house, each one contributing something to the mess. We had roasted pigs, fowls roasted or boiled, fresh fish, all kinds of vegetables, fruit, and plenty of the best melons that I ever ate. It happened one day while we were at dinner that the conversation turned upon having a dog cooked and served up with the rest of our good fare. One of the company observed that we had not yet had one. I made reply that I did not desire to have one cooked for our table, as I had a peculiar prejudice against eating these animals; that although I had eaten skunks in America, rats in China, water snakes on the coast of Australia, and a number of other animals, merely to satisfy myself what was proper food for a man to eat, yet I had lived too long and been schooled too much to wish for any further experimental knowledge in that way. I was answered that I should not know the difference between a dog and a pig when it was cooked.

The next day at dinner two pigs, as they called them, were brought to the table — one without a head, which was placed opposite to where I sat. I was very politely asked what I would be helped to. A piece of a pig, I answered. The gentleman who sat near the one which had no head asked if he should help me to a piece of it, which was baked in the country's style, and he said he would recommend it far before the other, which was roasted. Yes, I replied. I was helped, and ate very heartily. The gentleman who had helped me said that there was a plenty more that I could be helped to if I liked. My reply was that I never tasted anything better, and was again helped, and finished my dinner.

In the course of the afternoon there were many jokes passed on the subject of eating dogs, till at last I began to suspect there had been some trick played upon me. After inquiring into the affair, they satisfied me that what I had made so hearty a meal of was a dog. It caused some disagreeable sensation for the moment, and I was a little angry. But on reflection, and seeing my comrades make themselves merry at my expense, I thought it most prudent to turn it off with a laugh. I sincerely believe that eating of the dog has not done me any harm, unless it was that I possibly might have partook a little more largely of the canine spirit.

I SHALL CONCLUDE MY ACCOUNT by stating that the most celebrated circumnavigator that England has produced,

Captain James Cook, died here. He was killed by the natives of Oahu at Karakakooa Bay. Captain John Kendrick of Boston, the first American commander that ever visited the northwest coast of America, and who opened that channel of commerce to this country, also died at this place. His death was occasioned by a salute that was fired by an English commander in honour to him. One of the guns, through accident, was loaded with round and grape shot, which killed Captain Kendrick and two boys while on his quarter deck.

I was intimately acquainted with him in Canton bay in the year 1791. He was a man of extraordinary good natural abilities, and was noted for his enterprising spirit, good judgment, and superior courage. As a seaman and a navigator, he had but few equals. He was very benevolent, and possessed a heart filled with as tender feelings as any man that I ever was acquainted with. I wish to impress it strongly on the minds of every American not to let his rare merits be forgotten, and to cast a veil over his faults, they being but few compared with his amiable qualities.

ON MY ARRIVAL AT OAHU in 1806, I found eight Japanese who had been taken off a wreck at sea by Captain Cornelius Sole of Providence, Rhode Island, who was bound from China across the Pacific Ocean to the coast of America. After he had passed by, considerably to the eastward of the Japan Islands, he fell in with the wreck of a vessel that belonged to those islands. He found eight men on board. This generous captain took the sufferers on board his vessel, the *Tabour*, and being then near the longitude of the Hawaiian Islands, steered for them and landed the men with all their clothing and effects at Oahu, where I found them.

He left them in the care of the king with whom he made an agreement to take care of them and provide for their

THE SHIP *COLUMBIA*, OF CAPTAIN JOHN KENDRICK OF BOSTON.
(COURTESY OF THE PEABODY ESSEX MUSEUM)

support until something should turn up for their relief. He left one of the anchors which was taken off the wreck, forty axes, and some other articles to compensate for their living while on Oahu. He also left a letter with them describing their situation at the time he found and relieved them, and recommending them to the care and assistance of any visitor that might touch at the island. I regret very much my having mislaid the copy of this letter, as it would do the writer much honour to have it published.

On my arrival, I found that the Japanese had pretty much exhausted their welcome. The king informed me that they had lived out more than the worth of what was left by Captain Sole for their support, and if something was not done for them soon, he should turn them out amongst his people to get their own living.

I went to see them, and concluded to take them with

me, either to the place of their nativity, which was the town or city of Osaka, or to Canton. I took them on board and proceeded to sea, after which I maturely considered the danger of going to Osaka in the month of October, on account of its being so late in the season that I should most probably encounter severe gales of wind, on a strange coast, with a ship going on the fourth year of her voyage, and very much run out in sails and rigging, and cables worn out. I therefore continued my course for China, where I arrived in safety in the month of November.

On our arrival at Canton, I was enabled to obtain a tolerably correct narrative of the Japanese who I had with me. I ascertained that they write the same characters as the Chinese, though they pronounce the language so differently that they cannot understand each other. With the assistance of a servant I had in the factory there, a native of China, who understood some Japanese, I asked them questions.

Question: What place did you leave last, previous to your being shipwrecked?

Answer: Osaka on the island of Nippon.

Question: What time did you leave it?

Answer: Some time last February or March — as near as I could understand by comparing their time with ours.

Question: How many men were there of you on board when you left Osaka?

Answer: Twenty-two.

Question: What happened to the other fourteen?

Answer: Some were washed overboard in the gale of wind in which we lost our masts, rudder, and were otherwise materially injured; and a still greater number were killed and eaten for food to save life — all of which died by lot, fairly drawn.

Question: How were you treated by Captain Sole?

Answer: We acknowledge him as our saviour; next to God, we adore him. He not only took us away from that horrid death which stared us in the face, but he gave us victuals, and carried us safe to land; after which he befriended and provided for us.

Many other questions were put to them, all of which they satisfactorily answered. I could discover the greatest number of favourable traits in the character of these people of any that I ever saw. They were remarkably religious, but I could not find out exactly their tenets. They seemed to pay some adoration to the sun, the moon, and some of the stars, but not in so great a degree as I have seen in the Hindus and other natives of India. I observed them at their devotions every night. They kept a religious and constant care over all their actions towards each other, which convinced me that they had lived under a good government, where merit was rewarded and crimes punished. I shall hereafter give an account how these Japanese were disposed of.

Passage to Canton; Japanese Sailors;
Raising a Sunken Vessel off Nagasaki;
Oriental Justice; Return to America

CHAPTER XXII

FTER HAVING taken in a supply of fresh provisions and water, we took our departure from the Hawaiian Islands on the 20th of December, 1801, and steered a course for Canton; and on the 21st of January following, we fell in with and passed through between the Ladrone Islands (*Mariana Islands*).

It is to be remembered that all ships bound to Canton must stop at Macau and report at the Chinese chop, or customhouse, which will give a permit and a pilot for Canton, without which the ship is liable to be seized. After having got a pilot on board, it is always requisite to keep a watch over him and not let him run the ship into shoal water, or into any other danger that a commander has any right to judge of, as the China pilots are in general very ignorant of a ship, or the navigation from Macau to Canton; and if a navigator sees anything doing that is not right, and will tell the pilot modestly that he is going wrong, he will always pay attention to what is said to him and not be angry. I have been on board two different ships when they were run aground through the ignorance of the pilot. One was the *Ganges* of Philadelphia, which was near being lost by this means, the other a vessel from the northwest coast of America — which makes it a matter of consequence to be vigilant.

On arriving at Huangpu, the port of Canton, it is considered best for small ships to pass up the river above Dane's, and anchor abreast French Island, nearest the north shore, on account of a wreck that is sunk on the south side. After the ship is secured, and a passage provided to Canton, the next important concern to those who have no agents, or factors residing there, is to select a security, or what is called in their language, hong merchant. There are twelve of them appointed by government, who become surety for all the ship's duties and the behaviour of persons on board, whether good or bad, that come to the port to trade. As a security must first be provided, the most common method is to make some agreement for the cargo with the merchant to whom you are obligated; otherwise they will refuse taking that responsibility on themselves, it being a hazardous business for them, as they not only become surety for what the commander, or supercargo does at Canton, but for all they might have done prior to their arrival, and after they leave it, whilst any where within the jurisdiction of the China law, such as smuggling, depredations, or misdemeanors of any kind whatever.

After that point is settled, any further trouble is unnecessary, more than to consult the hong merchant on all important occasions. The method of doing business is soon learned, as any European or American who is acquainted there will give a stranger any relative information. England, Holland, France, Spain, Denmark, Sweden, Russia, and the Grand Duke of Tuscany have factories, and keep supercargoes there constantly. The English stand the highest of any, having more than the last twenty years pretty much engrossed that trade to themselves as far as it concerned the European flag. I have found particular satisfaction in the acquaintance and favour of Dutch supercargoes. They have befriended me more than any other Europeans, except the English, in that port.

After our arrival in Canton with the Japanese on board, they were visited by people of all nations who were there, and many questions were asked concerning them. The Chinese seemed to wonder as much as any of the other visitors to find men they could correspond with by writing, and still could not speak one word of their language. After much being said about them, the Dutch supercargoes offered to take charge of them, and send them to their own islands, by way of Jakarta. I accordingly delivered them, and Mr. J.H. Rabinal, then chief of their factory, made me a present of five hundred dollars. They were then sent to Jakarta by a Chinese junk. I saw them afterwards all in good health, on my arrival at that port, which was occasioned by distress of weather. I was particularly noticed by the governor general and others in that government. They made me several valuable presents, amongst which was a Japanese sword, for the kindnesses shown to those distressed islanders. They were afterwards sent to their own country by an American ship called the *Mount Vernon*, with Captain Davison of Philadelphia, and arrived safe, as I have been informed by authority I have no reason to doubt.

I SHALL HERE MAKE a few remarks about the empire of Japan from as good authority as any person could have who has not visited the place. The Dutch are the only Christian people who have been allowed any privilege of trade there for more than a hundred years past.

Their laws are considered by some that I have been acquainted with, and who have spent much time in that empire, to tend more to keep men in order, and make them good members of society than any in the known world. Here is an instance which I had from the gentleman who was my partner in the purchase of the ship *Hector* at Mauritius, already mentioned. He went four times to Japan in command of a ship after he and I were together, and sailed three times from Jakarta in the employ of the Dutch East India Company, and once

CHINESE TRADING AND FISHING VESSELS.
(FROM THE COLLECTIONS OF THE LIBRARY OF CONGRESS)

from Bengal; but he did not succeed in opening a trade while he was under the English flag.

Captain Stewart informed me that he was driven on shore by a gale of wind on a large, rocky ledge at Nangasaqui (*Nagasaki*), in a ship of between seven and eight hundred tons burthen. The rise and fall of the spring tides were sixty feet, and when the water had left her, she heeled so very much, and lying on the side of the ledge, that he feared she would overset, and had her masts cut away. She started at the shock of the falling of them, slid off, and sunk in twelve or fifteen fathoms of water, with more than six hundred tons of Japan copper on board, besides other heavy articles.

After he had time to consider what was best to be done, and finding himself totally destitute of any means of recovering the ship, except with the assistance of the government, he made application to the Emperor through the medium of the Dutch supercargo, and was favoured with the imperial order, granting all the assistance that was in the power of the government to afford. The first men there, in the public service, went to work and expended great sums of money in making efforts and trying different experiments — but could not get a purchase to raise the ship. During the time of these exertions, a fisherman came often to look and see what methods were being pursued, and seemed to be very attentive in his observations. After the government men had exhausted all their faculties and could not make any progress, or even stir the ship, they gave over the attempt and reported to the Emperor that this important task could not be effected.

When all was done that could be by the government, and everybody had quit the undertaking, the fisherman, before mentioned, came to Captain Stewart and offered to raise the ship without any compensation whatever, more than the honour of accomplishing what had proved insurmountable to the Emperor's men. He was answered that if the power of the Emperor could not effect anything, it was not very likely that a fisherman could.

The Captain was invited to the fisherman's house to look at the plan he had drawn of the manner he intended to effect it. Captain Stewart was satisfied it would accomplish the thing desired, and he thought it advisable to let him go to work. This plan was to make fast two large vessels of two hundred tons and upwards, one to the stem, and the other to the stern of the ship, and as many small vessels to each side as he could. The fisherman was wealthy and owned a number of vessels of different sizes, so that he could do all the business without employing any vessels or men but his own.

After he had made everything ready, at low water, he hove all down and made them fast. When the tide began to flow, the cables, lashings, and vessels all began to crack as if everything would part; but after all were fairly brought to bear equal share in the burthen, the ship began to rise from the bottom. She was floated into a convenient cove, and at high water was hauled on shore so far that at low water when small vessels were taken away, the ship was left dry. The cargo was taken out, and necessary repairs made. It was again re-shipped, and everything made ready for sea, free from any expense to the commander.

As soon as the knowledge of what the fisherman had done reached the Emperor, he sent for him to court, conferred the rank of nobility on him, of the first or second order, and gave him two swords, that being the custom of the country for the nobility; a bodyguard of thirty-six pike men, and a competent salary to support the dignity of his rank. This was bestowed upon him in consideration of his having performed more than any man in the Emperor's service could. In this manner they reward merit; and on the other hand, if a man is guilty of a violation of the laws, he is punished according to his crime.

Their laws are very simple and easily understood by all classes of people. A man of superior merit is sure to be rewarded, and a villain is equally sure to be punished for his crimes. There are no tedious delays in obtaining justice; no swarms of professional men to confound and perplex in the due execution of the laws, and create doubts on points that are perfectly plain to any man of common sense.

For the purpose of showing with what dread punishments for violations of the laws in this empire are held, I shall insert an anecdote which was told me by a man of undoubted veracity who was on the spot at the time it happened: a Chinese being at these islands, who was in the commercial line, and having purchased a quantity of pearls that he wished to convey out of the country without paying the duty, which was very high, adopted the following stratagem: He put them into a pumpkin and attempted to pass it into a boat amongst twenty or thirty others of nearly the same shape and size. A mandarin, who was looking after what was going on board, took each pumpkin in his hands and passed it to another to put into the boat. When he came to the one that had the pearls in it, his sagacity was great enough to discover it to be heavier than the rest. He gave it a shake and put it by for examination, and passed the remainder of them through his hands as before. When they were all passed, the mandarin called for a knife and cut one in halves that had the pearls in it. At the instant it was done, the Chinese who was standing by, cut his own throat from ear to ear, and died in less than five minutes on the spot. So much was he in fear of the law. The punishment in such cases, I have never learned, but am satisfied it is capital.

After having disposed of our skins at Canton, and taken in a cargo of teas, sugar, and other articles, we sailed from Huangpu on the 6th day of April 1802, for Boston. We passed the Straits of Sunda, and arrived at Mauritius on the 5th of June, and left there the 23rd of July, doubled the Cape of Good Hope, and arrived in Boston November 1st, after having been absent a few days short of three years.

VOYAGE OF 1803–1807

Voyage to the South Sea by way of Trindade Island, Brazil; The Tristan Da Cunha Island Group, and Cape of Good Hope; Settlements of Australia and Tasmania; Encounters with Porpoises and other Wildlife; The People

FTER MY return to America in November 1802 in the ship *Perseverance*, from a voyage on which I had been three years absent, I set about making preparations for another excursion to the Pacific Ocean. I had a tender of sixty-two tons burthen, built by my brother Samuel with the assistance of my brother William. We rigged her as a schooner, and called her the *Pilgrim*.

I had the *Perseverance* refitted, coppered her and the *Pilgrim*, and put both in the best order possible for sea. The *Perseverance* mounted twelve six pound cannon, and the *Pilgrim* mounted six guns from nine pound carronades to four pound fortified cannon, having all parts of their armament fitted in the best manner to correspond with their number of guns.

Being the principal owner of both vessels, I took special care to have them equipped with everything necessary for a sealing voyage, loading them with provisions and ship stores, and shipped sixty prime men. After a more than ordinary share of difficulty and perplexity, we again set sail on the 25th September 1803, bound to the South Sea by way of the Cape of Good Hope, and the south cape of Australia.

On my leaving America on this voyage, I was placed in a situation that caused me more anxiety than I had ever experienced at the beginning of any enterprise. I had with me my

SAMUEL, A SCHOONER OF BOSTON.
(COURTESY OF THE PEABODY ESSEX MUSEUM)

two brothers, Samuel and William, who were all I had, and a nephew of seven years old, who was an invalid. He had lost the use of his arms, and wanted as much attendance as common children of three years old. I had entered into a contract that had more powerful effect on my feelings than all the other causes put together, and moreover, I found myself less active in body and mind than I was at the age of twenty-five years.

I considered the responsibility I was under when I took from my parents all the sons they had, and one grandson, and from my sisters all their brothers, and of the importance it would be to all should anything happen to our vessels so that they might never return. Almost the whole of our connections whom we left behind had need of our assistance, and it was no more than a reasonable calculation to make, that our absence would not be less than three years. All these important causes came under consideration, together with the extraordinary uncertainty of the issue of the voyage, as we had nothing but our hands to depend upon to obtain a cargo, which could only be done through storms, dangers, and breakers, and taken from barren rocks in distant regions. But after a voyage of four years for one vessel, and five for the other, we all were permitted to return safe home to our friends, and not quite empty-handed.

Many were the perils and dangers we three brothers encountered during this long, extraordinary and tedious voyage. We built both the vessels we were in ourselves and navigated them two and three times round the globe. Each one of the brothers has been master builder, master rigger, and navigator of ships and vessels in all quarters of the world.

Being now about to start on my third and last long voyage, I will state the principles which have actuated me in my pursuit, so far as I have gone through life. The first was an ambition to excel others in achievements, the next was to satisfy my own curiosity in a knowledge of the world, and particularly to know how far myself and others were imposed upon with exaggerated accounts of the world, and false statements of things a great way from home; and lastly, and for many of my latter years by far the greatest, was, honestly and honourably to obtain a competency sufficient to support myself and family through an old age, should I live to see it; to do a benevolent act now and then, and to leave an unblemished character behind me. As a child of misfortune, I have felt for the distress of others, and may these feelings remain with me as long as I have breath to draw.

In preparing for such a long voyage, a man should take great care that his business should be so settled, and agreements made so binding, that on his return home, he could keep clear of being dragged into the law, harassed and wronged out of all his hard earnings, which is peculiarly poignant to the feelings of a man who has earned his money in the hard way that globe beaters generally do theirs. On returning from a voyage of three or four years, to be called upon to pay sums of money that he never owed, and sometimes to people he never saw before to his knowledge, is very disagreeable, and should be guarded against in the beginning of the voyage. Never let an account lie open with friend or foe, although they may say, "let it all lie just as it does till your return"; for in such cases the simple or fair balance seldom or never pays the demand, especially when the sailor has got a little money.

When a man has been absent a great length of time, he sees things quite differently when he returns home. He is vulnerable at all points to either love, friendship, gratitude, or benevolence; and at the same time holds his honour at too high a rate to get along very well with people who do not set so high a value upon theirs.

WE SET THE COURSE OF THE VOYAGE southward; the *Pilgrim* in company, commanded by my brother Samuel. We did not separate until the 4th of January, 1804, in latitude 40° south, and longitude 4° east, when the *Pilgrim* was instructed to make the best of her way to Bass Strait, which are formed by Australia on the north, and Tasmania on the south, and there rendezvous at King Island. We found the *Perseverance* and *Pilgrim* to be very near alike in point of sailing, but the former the best of the two, and the latter one of the best sea boats of her size that ever crossed the ocean. On the 16th of October, we observed the *Pilgrim* astern manoeuvering in a manner I did not understand. We hove the main top-sail to the mast and waited to see what she was doing. She shortly got on her course again, came up and spoke with us, and informed us that they had lost their cook overboard by accident, and that all their exertions to save him had proved ineffectual.

We proceeded on with pleasant weather for most of the time until the 16th of November, when at four o'clock in the morning, the *Pilgrim* brought to the Danish schooner *Experiment* of Copenhagen, commanded by H. Giambery, from the coast of Africa with one hundred and five slaves on board, bound to St. Croix (*in the Virgin Islands*). We requested the favour that she would remain with us until daylight, so we might have opportunity to write by her. The captain very obligingly consented, and all of us who wished to write occupied two hours in endeavouring to inform our friends at home what progress we had made. A little after the sun had risen, we lowered down our stern boat, and after calling along side the *Pilgrim* for letters, I went on board the *Experiment* and delivered to the captain more than a dozen for our different friends. I supplied him with beef, of which he stood in great need, and with potatoes, and in return received a pig, a few fowls, and yams. I make mention of these particulars on account of my hearing that the Danish schooner never arrived at any port, and not one of our letters was ever received.

On the next day we crossed the equator in longitude 30° west, spoke a Spanish frigate from Cadiz bound to Buenos Aires, who was likewise obliging enough to wait two hours for letters to be written, and she took them with others I had on board for her port of destination.

In a voyage to the South Seas, if a ship is very much in want of wood or water, it can be got at Trindade Island, in latitude 20° 28' south, longitude 28° 32' west; or if the crew should have the scurvy, it is an excellent place to restore them, as you can get plenty of greens on the southeast part of the island, such as fine purslane and other kinds. These, together with the fine sweet water, soon revive a crew. What soil there is on the island is on the east side, where there are several sand beaches, above one of which the Portuguese have a settlement, and have done much work in making streets, or roads over the valleys. They have walled in a number of enclosures for the purpose of making fields, at the expense of much labour. Wood may be cut on the mountain just above the first landing place, and can be taken off if you have a small oak boat. The method in which we filled our water was carrying it in kegs and buckets to the place where we floated our casks on shore. All the south side of the island is indented with small bays; but the whole is so iron bound a shore, and such a swell surging against it, that it is almost impossible to land a boat without great danger of staving it. The south part is a very remarkable high square bluff head, and is very large. It has an arch under it that a boat could pass through in clear smooth water, but I should caution against landing on the beach; for just at the lower edge of the beach and amongst the breakers it is full of rocks, which are not seen until amongst them. Where we landed we saw the remains of at least two or three boats which had been knocked to pieces by landing. We found plenty of goats and hogs. The latter were very shy, but we killed some of them, and a number of goats.

We continued our course southerly towards the islands of Tristan da Cunha, fell in with and explored them. We circumnavigated a great part of Inaccessible Island, near to land, but found it to be very difficult of access on all sides. At length, we landed at its south west part, and could not pass along the beach more than one or two hundred yards before we came to a square bulkhead of rocks, projecting into the sea, which stopped us. There did not appear to be anything on or about this island, except a few seals, and it was next to impossible to get them. We caught plenty of fine fish here, in twenty-five or thirty fathoms water.

We did not land on Nightingale Island, or go very near to it, from what I could discover, it differed very little from the other two (*Grand Tristan and Inaccessible islands*). We found no object amongst them worthy of our attention, or that would be profitable, except sea elephants, whales, and a very few seals. The whales were very plenty. All of them were right whale, or the kind that is called black whale. The sea elephants were also very plenty, and I have no doubt but that a large ship might soon load with elephants' oil, if she could get it on board. We saw discoloured water and whales for a great distance to the southward and eastward of the islands.

I should recommend to a navigator to continue eastward in latitude 40° south until getting as far as 140° east; then haul southward to the south cape of Tasmania. (*In this region they explored many shores: King Island, Hunter Islands and others, as well as the coastline of Tasmania, south around the cape, and north again to Cape Barren Island, constantly in search of safe harbors, places from which to send out parties for seals, fresh water, wood and game. Delano makes numerous navigational notes pertaining to currents, winds, location of reefs and shoals. They eventually anchored in Kent's Bay, Cape Barren Island*).

All the islands of any magnitude in Bass Strait afford plenty of many kinds of game, such as kangaroo, badger, porcupine, and many species of water fowls — black swans, geese, several kinds of ducks, teal, and a variety of beautiful birds in the woods and bushes. A lagoon along the Storm Bay passage, in southwestern Tasmania, is one of the pleasantest places nature ever formed; all its shores are lined with beds of oysters, besides frequent patches of them off from land, and in such quantities, that one man may easily load a boat of a ton burthen in two hours. Besides oysters of excellent flavour, its waters abound in many other sorts of fish and great numbers of water fowls.

From Storm Bay we sailed into and explored the Derwent River. We found the ship *Ocean*, commanded by Captain Martha, who had brought out Governor Collins and people from England to make a settlement there. This place, Sullivan Cove, was very judiciously chosen by Governor Collins, as the cove affords all the natural conveniences for a settlement that can possibly be found to unite together in one place. There is a delightful rivulet running through the part they allotted for the settlement. The governor appeared to be a man very well qualified for conducting a new settlement. When I was there, the new settlers had not been able to procure an interview with the natives, although numbers made their appearance every day near them. This was most probably owing to some improper conduct in the people of the first settlement towards them. I understood they had seized a boy of the natives on their first arrival and kept him for some time against his will, but as soon as an opportunity offered, he made his escape. This usage prevented any intercourse with them, at least until I took my leave of the place on the 23rd of April 1804, which was my second and last visit to these settlements. The country on both sides of the river is very even, and rises to a moderate elevation; the soil is extraordinarily rich, and without doubt, the place will in time be as beautiful as any man would wish to reside at. The climate is temperate, the thermometer seldom higher than 80 to 85 degrees in summer, and in winter the frost is seldom severe enough for ice or snow to remain long on the ground.

THE COUNTRY AFFORDS a variety of game. There are three kinds of kangaroo of which the larger is called the forester, sometimes weighing from eighty to a hundred pounds. The second in size is called the wallowby (*wallaby*), and weighs from 15 to 20 pounds; the third kind is called the kangaroo rat, being but very little larger than an ordinary rat.[39] The flesh of all three is very delicate and good eating. There are also badgers of a very large size with meat of a good flavour, porcupines, ant-eaters, and other small animals, besides many kinds of birds of excellent flavour and not difficult to be shot. The river and adjacent waters are exceedingly well stocked with the best fish, which are easily taken with the seine. Oysters and many other kinds of small fish are likewise as plentiful and well flavoured.

A kind of porpoise, remarkable for its variegated black and white colours, frequents this river in large shoals. When one of these shoals make its appearance, a boat has only to row directly for it. The porpoises will then face the boat and play round its bow, so that with harpoons, previously prepared, one may be struck with every iron in the boat. I have often caught five or six out of a shoal before they would leave us.

I once struck a young one, which is generally preferred for eating. As soon as it was struck and hauled under the bow of the boat, the dam, perceiving the danger to her offspring, came immediately to its succor, urging every possible means the poor creature was capable of for its relief, putting her nose to the wound as if trying to extract the harpoon, and then forcing herself between its shank and the boat's bow, where there was scarcely space enough to pass through, and successively raising herself nearly out of the water to pass over the body of her young while it lay on a level with the surface. The affectionate and reiterated exertions of this poor dumb inhabitant of the deep to save its young was in reality a spectacle so uncommon and so pathetic that I soon began to repent of my bargain. But as the evil was not to be remedied, I thought it best to be callous, and kill the mother too, which I accordingly did, though greatly against my inclination. I must acknowledge I never saw an animal, either human or brutal, strive harder to save its relative than this sensible creature did.

The black swan is very numerous all over this coast. It is a handsome bird, about twice as large as our wild geese, and somewhat of a similar shape, but has a much longer and slenderer neck, and a great deal more sagacity. Its appearance is very majestic; it is quick sighted, and has a soft, plaintive note, rather agreeable to the ear. I have had a dozen of them at a time on board my vessel that were caught in the molting time when they had lost their wing feathers, and were an easy prey. They are not difficult to domesticate, for I have known them to go to the tubs and feed along with the pigs the very same day they were caught and brought on board. I have seen them stretch their necks up till their heads would be nearly six feet high.

There are three kinds of swans. The above is only found in Australia and Tasmania and their vicinities, and it is of a jet black. The white swan is very well known in different parts of Europe, and in the southern states of America. It resembles the former in everything but its snow white colour. The third is an inhabitant of the coast of Chile, and is variegated. It has a dark coloured back, a white breast, and a ring of feathers round the root of its neck. The throat and jowls are of a beautiful greenish cast, which makes it by far the handsomest of the three.

To illustrate the sagacity of this bird: some people on a sealing party at the island of Mocha, off the central Chilean coast, having, as usual, built themselves a hut which is their home for a number of months, observed soon after they landed a pair of swans in a fresh pond on the island, but knowing it to be about the time swans lay their eggs, they did not feel disposed to disturb them. These sealers, having frequent occasion to visit the pond, observed them for some time pairing together. After an elapse of several weeks, they perceived one to be always alone which would, on seeing the men advance, make a noise on which the other would soon make its appearance near it, as if from under water. To satisfy their curiosity, they watched closely every time they visited the pond, but could not find the nest in the thick tussucks of coarse grass. They began to despair of success when they observed something slip into the water from under one of the tussucks, and soon after the second swan made its appearance near the first. They waded through to this place, and by close examination found an opening in one side of it, much like the mouth of an oven, just above the surface of the water. The long grass that formed the roof was curiously contrived to hang over and conceal the entrance, rendering it difficult to find if the exact place is not previously known. They found, I think, about nine eggs in this more than ordinary secure covey, and concluded not to disturb them till they were hatched.

Accordingly, they waited till after the young ones were big enough to leave their nest, and then caught five of them which they carried to a small pond in the vicinity of their own habitation, to which the old ones soon followed, and continued to take care of them. I do not know what became of the other four eggs. The two old ones continued to take care of those five until they were nearly grown to full size, keeping the greatest part of the time about the sealers' habitation, who had it in their power to shoot them whenever they thought fit. But at last, I think they let them entice and lead away a part of the young ones, but two or three of them were killed and eaten. One of them when slung over a man's shoulder, its head was as low as his breast, and its feet would be dragging along on the ground.

The last time I took my departure from the Derwent River, I proceeded through Storm Bay passage, landing several times, and found the soil rich throughout and the land beautifully adapted for cultivation. Here there was one of the finest groves of timber that I ever saw, consisting chiefly of a kind the settlers call stringy bark, from the appearance and quality of its rind, which ran in strips of two or three inches wide to the height of twenty and thirty feet up the tree. The wood of this tree is very hard and heavy, but apt to be shelly and not sound at the heart. There are hundreds of these trees in the space of one square mile, that measured about four feet in diameter, six feet above the ground, growing straight as an arrow for more than a hundred feet. There is likewise a quantity of wood called Botany Bay oak, best known in this country as beefwood, and other kinds of hard wood, but not many of them are very suitable for building.

I HAVE MENTIONED BEFORE that when I left the Derwent River on the 23rd of April, the settlers had not yet had any interview with the natives. On the morning of the 26th following, about twenty miles south of Sullivan's Cove in Storm Bay passage, I saw a party of natives on the Tasmanian side going along the shore on the borders of the wood which they were endeavoring to set fire to in a number of places. I observed at the same time that they had three or four small, rudely constructed and ugly shaped canoes with them, with two outriggers each.

I immediately sent my boat on shore, commanded by a prudent officer, with instructions how to obtain an interview with them, and gave directions for one of our men to be left as a hostage if one of them could not be prevailed upon to come on board. I very soon observed our boat returning with a native, who proved to be their chief. He came on board without any hesitation, as one of our men was left in the custody of his tribe during his absence. He showed no signs of fear whatever, was very much inclined to be sociable, and viewed everything with indifference. What most attracted his attention was the vessel's being hollow. After looking down the different hatchways, he would stamp and try to shake the deck, seemingly not satisfied as to the reality of it. He was shown down into the cabin, where he received clothes and presents, but refused the victuals that were offered him. He appeared to be at least seventy years of age, of the negro cast, being without any clothing, more than a kangaroo skin over his shoulders. I could not discover any traits of either good sense, activity of mind, ambition, or much animation in this man, and from what I learnt from those that went in the boat, he was a pretty fair sample of his tribe. They are rather an undersized people in comparison with those of America and Europe, and are destitute of every necessity of life that civilized people are accustomed to. Both men and women go naked and did not seem to have any sense of shame.

When the chief returned on shore dressed as he was, and with presents consisting of some knives, one or two pair of scissors, an old hatchet, a looking glass, and lastly what he seemed most to value, an earthen plate, which was the only thing he asked for, his tribe came round him with the same kind of indifference he had shown on viewing everything on board the vessel. Our man who was hostage for the chief reported that he had been treated well whilst on shore. They did not seem urgent with him about anything except to pull off his clothes that they might satisfy themselves as to his sex, which both sexes seemed anxious to ascertain.

The greater part of birds that are found in the woods here are of the parrot kind. There are several sorts of them; the largest is not much inferior in size to a small hen, and is called the black cockatoo, which is not remarkable for any thing but its ugly looks. The white cockatoo resembles the former in every thing but its colour. Another kind is of a var-iegated colour, green, purple, yellow, and black — a very beautiful bird. There are several kinds of eagles, vultures and crows. The bird of paradise of Australia is the most singular of any of the feathered race in this part of the world. The body is not very remarkable, but its tail is a curiosity that cannot be well described in words. The two feathers most conspicu-ous are long and form two curves that cross each other, so that the lower ends form the exact shape of a heart. These feathers have the nearest resemblance to some rich coloured ribbon I have seen, with several crescent shaped spaces of a rich red and black colour.

I have had many opportunities of acquiring a knowl-edge of the kangaroo. I have frequently had six or eight of them alive at a time on board my ship. They are the most in-nocent animals that I know of. I have seen them eat flowers or berries out of a person's hand on the same day they were caught. The method by which they are taken is by dogs that are taught to hold them fast till the huntsman comes up, when they were secured without sustaining any injury what-ever. Their flesh is the darkest coloured of any animals I have ever seen, and is without any fat, but is very sweet and deli-cate flavoured. Its skin makes the handsomest leather for boots and shoes that can be found, and is very durable.

Competition for Seals in Australia and Tasmania; More Hardships; The Sinking of the Pilgrim's Boat; Across the Pacific Ocean to Peru

CHAPTER XXIV

I T WAS the 20th of February, 1804, when we first arrived at King Island, Australia. We stationed ourselves in Kent's Bay, where the ship *Perseverance* remained moored from the 3rd of March till the 23rd of October. I made two excursions in the schooner *Pilgrim* to the Derwent River and out round the south cape of Tasmania. My brother Samuel made two trips in her to Port Jackson, Botany Bay, and other places in the straits. A greater part of the time we had from four to seven boats exploring the islands in all directions in search of seals, the principal object of our pursuit.

As soon as it was known that our vessels were in the straits, I was visited by six different gangs of men belonging to Port Jackson, who were on the same business as ourselves; all of which were out of provisions. I considered their situation to be similar to people I had been acquainted with on other sealing islands, though I afterwards found that it was not half so bad, owing to the advantages of the different sorts of game that were to be obtained on the surrounding islands.

I supplied all their wants, taking orders on their employers at Sidney (*Sydney*) Cove, every one of which was honoured at sight and accompanied with thanks. But the ungrateful men whom I had supplied and relieved of their wants, did everything in their power to injure me. The leading motive was to prevent me from getting seal. Their ideas were that no foreigner had any right to that privilege near the colony.

These men practised many impositions, such as stealing from me, enticing my men to run away, conspiring to steal my boats, and to cut my vessels adrift. They would sometimes go on to an island where my people were waiting for an opportunity to take seals that were about it, and if not able to take them themselves, do something to frighten them away. They would say and do all in their power to irritate and vex my people. I had to use all my authority to keep my men under subjection, telling them that I would apply to the governor at Port Jackson, and as I had business there unsettled, it would not do for them to undertake to redress their own grievances. My people were certainly under as good discipline as any merchant ship's crew whatever. I kept clear of an open rupture for some months, during which time some of my people left me, as they said, "because they would not be tied down to such close orders as to be obliged to put up with any insults from such villains." At length the time arrived when I was ready to dispatch the *Pilgrim* for Port Jackson. I wrote to the governor general of New South Wales, whose name was Philip Gedney King, the following letter:

Ship *Perseverance*, Cape Barren,
August 4th, 1804

"To His Excellency Governor King:
"Sir,

"The bearer, my brother, who commands the schooner *Pilgrim*, will hand you this. He comes to settle some little business, and if it should meet your Excellency's approbation, to purchase some necessaries for our subsistence on board the ship.

"I came to King Island on false information with the hope of procuring a cargo of seal skins. I was much surprised to find people on that island from Sydney, and very much disappointed at not finding any seals on it of any consequence. I then ran down in to the straits in hopes of finding something there, but was still unsuccessful. We found the *Integrity* cutter, which was lying in the passage, and before we came up with her she made a signal of distress. We anchored near her, went on board, and learnt that she had lost her rudder. The next morning I ordered the *Pilgrim* to take her in tow and assist her in getting into Kent's Bay, where she was brought safe. I then offered any assistance in my power to fit the rudder for her, but the spare irons we had on board the *Pilgrim* were too long. Governor Bowen then agreed with me to carry the passengers and other articles to the Derwent, for the sum of £400 sterling. We unloaded the *Pilgrim*, took the freight and passengers on board, conducted and delivered them safe. He then gave me a draft on your Excellency for the sum, which I hope will meet your approbation. My brother will present it.

"It is with extreme pain that I trouble your Excellency with any complaint whatever; but as it may prevent future misunderstanding, I think I cannot do less than to make your Excellency acquainted with it.

"There is a man in this place by the name of Joseph Morril who has a little vessel belonging to Messrs. Kable and Underwood, and has a gang of men with him. He has taken it into his head that we have no right to procure seals in these straits, and has been trying to drive us out of them. I believe that the man would have accomplished his design if it had not been the winter season, and myself something of an old weather-beaten sailor, who dreaded going out in such extreme blowing weather without the probability of profiting by it on my part. I at first thought the man too insignificant to take notice of, but I was mistaken. He made interest with so many of my people to run away from me, that it has distressed me very much. He has carried six of them out of this bay at one time, notwithstanding I had forbidden him to receive or harbour them in the presence of several respectable witnesses. I took two of them out of his vessel one morning after they had been some weeks absent. He still holds a number of them, and articles that have been stolen from me, or I am very much deceived. There have been so many impositions practiced by this Morril and his accomplices, as persons on board the *Pilgrim* will attest, but I will candidly say that I do not think one of my countrymen out of an hundred would pass over so many insults and injuries as I have done under similar circumstances, on account of his being of another nation. I beg you will have the goodness to order an examination of the persons on board the *Pilgrim*, and favour me with a few lines acquainting me with your Excellency's opinion on the subject. Any civility shown the commander of the *Pilgrim* will be very gratefully acknowledged.

> "By your Excellency's most obedient,
> and very Humble Servant,
> (*signed*) Amasa Delano"

THE ABOVE LETTER WAS DELIVERED by my brother, but as Governor King was out of health, and had recently been put out of temper by some false representations that had been made to him by the same description of men that I was complaining of, respecting some American captains that were in these straits before my arrival, he did not seem disposed to do anything towards giving me satisfaction for the injuries we were daily receiving. But he gave my brother permission to purchase any provisions or necessaries we might want, and in all other respects treated us well, except the grievances as stated in the letter, and forgetting to answer it, although he promised my brother repeatedly that he would. The *Pilgrim* returned, not having effected the object of the visit. I ordered her back with all possible dispatch, my people growing more dissatisfied every day.

In the absence of the schooner this time, an affray took place between our people and those of the convict caste. Some of our men were on a small island ten or twelve miles from the ship, waiting for some seals to be driven up by an easterly wind. The convict people, observing them, contrived to frustrate their plan. A group of the latter went away to the huts where our men usually based. Morril, the head man of the gang, ground his cutlass on our grindstone, and loaded two or three old muskets. He told a lad who was left in charge of the base "that he would make his sweet lips do its duty on the present occasion, kissing his old cutlass repeatedly." When they had got all things prepared, they pulled over to the island, presenting their loaded and cocked muskets to our people, obliging them to abandon their pursuit. There was argument, and when the Port Jackson men shoved their boat in and attempted to step out, they were met by our people armed only with their sealing clubs, and a battle ensued. The other party could not make their guns give fire after snapping them several times at our people, who wrested the muskets out of their hands with their clubs, and the fracas ended by both sides throwing clubs, sticks, stones, and everything they could get hold of.

The result was that Morril and his party got worsted; and they afterwards came to me with a complaint against my men. Four or five of them had their heads, legs, and arms so maimed that they were unable to do their duty. I asked them what they wished me to do. Their answer was that if I should punish my people, and give orders that they should not do the like again, they would be satisfied. I expostulated with them, and tried to reason them into a principle of justice, setting forth the necessity of mankind's treating each other with more propriety. I promised them that my people would use them as well as they were treated themselves. They left me apparently with a disposition to do better in the future; but it lasted only for a short time, as the first opportunity that offered they took the advantage of it to do us injury, and other difficulties took place.

About this time the *Pilgrim* returned the second time from Sydney, and we made preparations to leave the straits. Three or four days previous to our sailing, the people went on shore early in the morning with an intention, I afterwards learnt, to settle some old grievances with the Port Jackson men; but it was without my consent. They landed and took Morril, with two or three of his men who had been foremost in doing them injustice, tied them up to a tree and flogged them, giving them one or two dozen lashes each with a common cat o' nine tails. It must be understood that every one of the people so punished was a convict that had been transported to New South Wales for crimes committed in England. One thing took place that I very much regretted. While they were giving Morril his quota, the convict-caste of men rallied to attack our people, who left him to defend themselves, and drove the assailants off. Morril took advantage of this, and loosed himself from the tree and ran. Our people followed him, and one of my Hawaiian Island men overtook and struck him with a stick on the arm. The blow, falling lengthwise on the part of the arm between the elbow and the wrist, was so heavy as to cause the flesh to burst open.

When I went on shore they again came to me to make their complaints. Morril showed me his arm. I told them I was very sorry they had sustained such injury, but they must bear in mind that when they imposed upon, and insulted any description of men in the manner they had mine, they must expect something would be done in retaliation. I dressed Morril's arm from my own medicine chest, and supplied him with salve and other necessities for dressing it until it should be well.[40]

AFTER MENTIONING one material incident more, I shall take my leave of this country. On the 1st of July, with a piercing wind blowing from the south east, which is a very cold quarter, I undertook to go on shore in a boat belonging to the *Pilgrim* with a number of barrels of fish that our men had caught with the seine and pickled for the purpose of smoking on shore, in a house that we had previously built for that purpose. The men who went with me were two midshipmen, William Delano and Nathaniel Luther, the armourer, and two seamen. The *Perseverance* and *Pilgrim* were moored within one hundred yards of each other, about two-thirds of a mile from the nearest land, to where we were bound with the fish; both having their sails unbent, with their yards and topmasts down.

We set out from the *Pilgrim* in one of her boats. Out of seven that I had belonging to the ship and schooner, six of them were as much as ten miles from us, gone in different directions in pursuit of seals, and of course could not render us any assistance in case any accident should happen to the boat we were then in. About mid-way between the *Pilgrim* and shore, while crossing a horse market — a sailor's phrase for a rough irregular sea, the waves rising all in a heap, occasioned by two tides meeting — the water rushed so rapidly into the boat, that in less than two minutes she sank like a stone to the bottom, leaving us floating on the surface. I soon found that the weight of the fish had immerged our only support too far to render us the least assistance, for I had contrived to keep my stand on the gunwale until she fairly sunk below my depth.

I began to consider the perilous situation we were in, and looking round, saw all my people heading for the shore. I called to them, but the moment was too urgent for my authority to be heeded. My motive in calling them to stop was to consult about getting the oars together, that we might mutually assist each other to weather this more than ordinary calamity. But this proved totally ineffectual, as every individual was too much engrossed in his own imminent danger to think of any means of mutual preservation. I myself began to despair of ever escaping a watery grave, as no succour from either of our vessels could be expected, when it occurred to me that a Mr. Vose had a boat lying a little way up a creek near to where we intended to land, and that his people were building a new one in small cove at some distance off.

I accordingly hallooed and called for help, using all the force of articulation I could muster to give the alarm. No man, perhaps, ever displayed stronger lungs, or made more noise than I did. The people upon whom our salvation depended were at this time eating their breakfast in the hut. They all heard the sound of our distress, but were some time conjecturing what it might arise from, until at last Mr. Vose left the table and ran across a small point to where he had a view of the two vessels and observed them making signals of distress. Seeing no boat, he looked attentively towards the part he heard the cries coming from, and at length discovering our heads above water, he immediately ran toward his boat, giving his men the alarm as he passed the hut, who instantly joined him with hearts and hands. No men perhaps ever exerted themselves more for the relief of their fellow creatures than they did on this occasion. They hauled their old water-soaked boat out of the creek more than one or two hundred yards over the dry sand.

I found myself encumbered by a tight pair of thick

pantaloons, thick heavy boots, and a short tight jacket, without anything in my hands. While treading water, I hit against a bundle of small sticks that had been cut for the purpose of stringing the fish on. I got hold of it and placed it under my breast, which helped prevent me from sinking suddenly between the waves. I was just heading for the land, when looking to the left, I saw one of my faithful sailors, a Swede, named John Fostram, making towards me with all possible exertion. I turned my head from him and used every effort to prevent his reaching me, which I greatly apprehended he would. But the poor fellow finding his attempts fail, relinquished the oar he had grasped in his hand, his head gradually lowering, until his strength being entirely exhausted, he gave up, and sank.

I never until then had experienced any satisfaction at seeing a man die, but so great is the regard we have for ourselves when in danger, that we would sooner see the whole human race perish than die ourselves. I remember but few incidents in the course of my life that were more gratifying to me than that of Fostram's sinking, for I was not only relieved of the dread of his involving me in his own fate, but had likewise the oar he relinquished within my reach, which I immediately seized, and headed again for the land.[41]

Very soon after I observed another of my poor distressed sailors, a native of Nova Scotia, named William Thompson, making towards me on the right hand. I pulled from him, though he did not give me so much uneasiness as the former, as he was at a greater distance. This poor fellow soon met his fate in a similar manner as Fostram. I likewise made shift to procure his oar, placed it under me, and once more headed for land.

I began to feel for the moment a little safer, finding myself considerably supported by the two oars, together with the bundle of sticks, and out of all danger from others, as the remainder of my people were all ahead of me. I recommended my calling for assistance, which I had suspended during my exertions to avoid Fostram. I kept constantly looking for my companions in distress, and saw the remaining three to my great satisfaction, keep their heads pretty steadily above the water. I had the greatest reason to be most concerned about my brother William, as he was but a youth, and born club-footed, as bad as I ever saw with any person, and he was likewise incommoded with a sailor's jacket. I kept my course right before the wind, which blew toward the nearest part of the shore, still hallooing so loud that the people on shore afterwards declared they had never heard a voice so strong or to continue for so long a space of time. At intervals I kept watching my brother William, who was struggling very hard with his lame feet and confined arms.

The time hung very heavy on our hands, as no probability of relief was in view. Whilst jogging on very slowly with the blades of the oars out behind me, a wave forcibly struck them; being off my guard, I was tripped up and hove from my supporters. It was not without some difficulty I replaced them again in their former situation. I had hardly got once more under way when I was again thrown off from my supporters. My strength being by this time very much exhausted, I had to use my utmost exertions to replace myself again, which enfeebled me so much that I was obliged to desist calling and hallooing, and use the greatest precaution not to get misplaced again.

After waiting a while in this situation, I saw the boat that was coming to our relief just turning the point. The sight of her so animated me, that forgetting for a moment my own danger, I exerted my remaining strength to encourage my people, telling them that I saw the boat coming to our succour, and to keep a good heart and all would yet be well. But being off my guard, a sea struck and threw me quite clear of all I had to support me. This last disaster nearly overcame me; it was with the greatest difficulty imaginable I gathered my oars and bundle together, and still greater trouble to replace them again under me. I laid my head to the wind, not daring to look towards the shore for fear the sea would again strike me unawares, as I was well assured I never could recover myself if I had the misfortune to be once more misplaced. In this state of inactivity, I had time for meditation and to observe what my other brother was about on board the *Pilgrim.* By his going from one mast head to the other, with almost the swiftness of an eagle, to learn as much of our situation as possible, his anxiety seemed little short of our own, for it was not in his power to render us the least assistance. I could only judge in imagination of the fate of the brother behind me from the motions of the one before me; just as the female whale when her young is struck stays braving all the harpoons and lances that can be used for her destruction, until her offspring has breathed its last, and not till then does the mother disappear. I then began to reflect on the consequences of my not surviving this disaster, and to those I should leave behind; for them alone I felt. As for myself, I could not perceive that life was of such great importance, as I had already suffered a great many hardships and privations, besides many heartrending scenes of injustice, ingratitude, and disappointments, all of which I must again be liable to experience.

Of my thoughts on futurity on this occasion, I can only say they were that, if I survived, I should hereafter find more favour with God than I had found amongst men, and was not terrified at committing my spirit to him who gave it to me; ever confiding in his infinite goodness. But to say I was not

afraid of dying I cannot, as I considered it a very great preci-
pice to leap down in the dark. In this unpleasant state of sus-
pense, I remained more than half an hour, which seemed the
longest and most irksome I had ever spent in my life. I never
once looked over my shoulder to see if the boat was advanc-
ing, from the time I was last misplaced until the people in her
took hold of me; nor did I hear them making any noise to
give me notice of their approach until a few minutes before
they relieved me from my perilous situation.

When I was taken into the boat, I looked round and
saw my brother William, Mr. Luther, and the armourer lying
in the bottom of the boat, all of them too much exhausted to
keep their heads up. Thus ended our misery for this time, after living upwards of an hour in the cold water and suffering
both in body and mind as much as any human beings possibly could. We were carried on shore to a convenient house
where our wet clothes were taken off, dry ones put on, and a
comfortable fire made, which soon reinstated us in health and
strength.

The bad weather continued for two days before an opportunity came to search for the bodies of the two drowned
men and the boat which had sunk in three fathoms water. A
calm succeeding the storm, two or three of my boats returned
to the ship. As soon as the people heard of the accident which
had taken place during their absence, they came to us immediately and assisted in searching for the boat, which we found
lying on the bottom as steadfast as a rock, with all the barrels
of fish in her, just as she sunk; and near her the body of Fostram was found and taken up by means of a long pole with a
hook at the end of it. But we never got the body of Thompson. The boat was recovered, Fostram decently interred, and
the funeral services read in a more than ordinarily solemn
manner.[42]

MY BROTHERS WILLIAM AND SAMUEL had a similar escape together, the circumstances of which were as follows: I left the *Pilgrim* on the coast of Peru in 1806, fitted for sealing one year longer, the two brothers being left to perform that service. After the time expired, they bent their course towards Canton, and on the 14th of December 1807, in entering the China sea with a stiff gale from north east, a sea struck the vessel and hove her on her beam ends, so that her mast heads were under water. They lost three men overboard and sustained many other damages. After lying in that situation some minutes, the vessel's head swung round before the wind, when she righted again before she filled with water — a circumstance that seldom happens to a ship at sea after being once fairly overset.

IN THE MONTH OF OCTOBER we made preparation for sea, and on the 24th, got under way and sailed out to the eastward through the narrows, shaped our course for the south west cape of New Zealand, found the weather very boisterous, and the wind mostly from the westward.

After we had examined The Snares, small islands off New Zealand, as much as the weather permitted us to do, we proceeded to the eastward with a strong westerly wind, and visited Bounty Islands. These island were discovered by Lieutenant Bligh, commanding his Britannic Majesty's ship *Bounty*, on the 19th September, 1787.

November 7th, 1804. At six a.m. we made the Bounty Islands with an intention of examining them, but it was blowing a strong gale from the westward, with a large sea. We ran down within about one mile of them, but became convinced there was not enough water for our ships. We saw shags and gulls, and a few seals round them, and I believe they are all they afford. It would be very dangerous for a ship

A MID-NINETEENTH-CENTURY PHOTOGRAPH OF
GUANO ON THE CHINCHA ISLANDS.
(FROM THE COLLECTIONS OF THE LIBRARY OF CONGRESS)

to fall in with these islands in the night or in thick weather.

On the 19th of November when in latitude 41° 30' south, and longitude 156° 00' west, we separated from the schooner *Pilgrim*, she being ordered to run in a lower latitude than what was our intention. From the *Pilgrim's* log-book: "In passing the longitude of Pitcairn's Island ten degrees south of it, observed a great number of small birds, which were all the signs of land that we saw till our near approach to Más Afuera, which was the place appointed for our rendezvous with the ship *Perseverance*, and where we found her as soon as we drew near in with the land."

(*Having recorded some observations of his life and work along the South American coasts in earlier chapters, here Delano continues his account of other events, particularly in Peru and along those coasts.*)

The bay of Pisco is large and as clear of all dangers as any I ever saw. The bay is a crescent in the land, and has a number of islands lying before the entrance to the westward which breaks all the sea, or wind. The islands are called the Tinkers (*Chincha Islands*). They have good anchoring under the lee of them, and there are many seals on them.

One day some half Indian sort of men came over the hills from Pisco by a kind of road; and when we first saw them coming down the mountains on horses, at a considerable distance, they appeared like men coming down out of the clouds, as most of the hill they descended was of white sand. There were several small fishermen's huts at the head of the bay in which they occasionally slept and stored their fish, of which the bay affords them a great plenty. The men, after descending the mountain, came on board our ship without hesitation, on my sending a boat for them, and gave us all the information in their power.

In the north part of the bay there is salt to be got at

most seasons of the year. The salt makes in ponds not far from the beach. I believe there are no other inhabitants nearer than Pisco.

The shore or landing place at Pisco is not very good, owing to a bar that lies before the town, but at most times one can land with a good boat, and always procure plenty of refreshment if the governor will give permission. The town is much larger than the other small ports on some parts off the coast, but it is an inconsiderable place. The houses are built after the style of Concepción and Valparaíso. The habits and customs of the people are likewise similar.

The islands to the westward are large and afford nothing but seals, eggs, and birds' manure. The latter is a great article of trade on the coast of Peru. I should estimate the tonnage of vessels employed in that business at seven or eight thousand. They are generally brigs, from one to two hundred tons each. They go off to the Chinchas, and other islands that afford it to load, and then carry it to the best market. It sells for more than one dollar per bushel. I have seen eight or ten vessels loading it at a time, and have been on shore where they were at work. They get it on board by hauling their vessels into any snug cove they can find near the source. They carry it on board in hand barrows and in baskets, taking it from the ground as carefully as if it were corn or grain. I have often seen them dig more than twenty feet before they got to the bottom of the heap, and it lies in that thickness in some places for more than a hundred yards in breadth and a mile in length. It is very much like white lime, but a little different in smell. I have heard it is the best manure for most kinds of soil that ever was used. I was informed whilst on different parts of the coast that they should never be able to make the land produce anything were it not for this manure. The vessels in this employ often make eight or ten thousand dollars

THE GUANO FLEET IN THE CHINCHA ISLANDS.
(FROM THE COLLECTIONS OF THE LIBRARY OF CONGRESS)

in a trip, but the Spanish are not a very industrious people, and do not make such great dispatch as some men would; otherwise they might make money very fast. The quantity of this manure on many of these islands near the coast is beyond belief, and the value of it to the tiller of the land is great. It seems as if every thing turned to good account, and all the bounties of nature fell to the lot of the people of the two kingdoms of Chile and Peru.

There is not any danger in sailing within three miles of land until coming in sight of the city of Lima. The land all round is so low, and the domes and steeples show so high, that the city is very plain to be seen long before the vessel gets so near as to notice the islands that lie off Callao.

Six or eight miles in a south-southeast direction from Lima is a pretty little fishing village where gentlemen and ladies from the city often go on parties of pleasure. It is situated on the southern extremity of the south bay of Lima. It is sufficiently large to hold several hundred ships, but I know nothing of the depth of its water, or the dangers in it.

The Port and City of Lima; Earthquakes; The Viceroy; The Inquisition; The Mint; Church and Society; Prisoners of War; Native Peruvians

THE PORT or citadel of Lima is called Callao. It is very convenient for all kinds of shipping business, and has a very good market for meat, fish and vegetables, and is very convenient for procuring fresh water. There is a great deal of business done in this place separate from Lima.

Old Callao, as it is now called, was destroyed in the great earthquake of 1746. I have been several times with the general of the marine, and the commandant, to view the ruins of Old Callao. The ground on which it stood is not more than twenty feet above the level of the sea, and is now nothing but a coarse, gravely sand beach. When that fatal catastrophe happened which destroyed it, the sea receded so that the ships were left dry at their anchorage. The flood then returned and carried some of them upon the land more than one mile above high water mark. At the return of the water Callao was entirely swept away, and the sea broke over the ground where it stood for several days afterwards. This so entirely destroyed the soil that it has never collected since so as to produce a spire of grass. There are still piles of human bones that lie here. The principal remains or signs of a town were the brick arches and stone cellars. My companions informed me that some of the arches were the ruins of prisons where all the foreigners as well as the lower order of Spanish people were confined. The reason, I was informed, that these arches were filled with human bones was that there were people employed to pick them up as fast as they worked out of the gravel, and to put them into the cellars and arches. Yet we saw many cart loads strewn all over the ground, besides those already picked up and deposited.

I saw two persons in Lima who were living at the time of the fatal event, and were old enough when it took place to remember every circumstance. They were in the city and had several of their nearest kindred buried in the wreck of buildings that were destroyed. One of these survivors was a man, and the other a woman. They were considered persons of veracity, particularly the woman. She told me that there were but few persons saved in Callao at the time, that the tide flowed to within one mile of the gates of Lima, and that there were near 20,000 people at the time in Callao.

New Callao is six miles from the city of Lima, and there is a very handsome road laid out between them, but it is not finished. This road was begun by the celebrated Don Ambrosio Higgins, who died Viceroy of Lima. It was laid out nearly on a straight line from city to port, and was sixty feet wide. The ground over which it passed was level, some parts of it being loose, sandy ground, on which he caused to be placed a covering of large round stones like those used to pave streets. Over these stones it was his intention to have a layer of gravel which would make a smooth road on a solid foundation, but he died before it was completed, and it is now very rough and bad travelling for horses and carriages.

The port, as it is at present, contains eight or ten thousand inhabitants, and has every thing commodious for shipping, except docks and wharves. It is very difficult to erect them on account of the swell that sometimes rolls in. This swell commonly comes in just before and during the shocks of earthquakes, which are very frequent. I have seen the tide rise in ten minutes when they happen — four times the usual swell of a flood tide.

I have been in Lima, Callao, and the ports of Chile, when there have been more than thirty shocks of earthquakes. They are very common at particular seasons of the year, for a week together, and often occur several times in a day. It is always calm when they happen. The noise ever seemed to begin from the north east. The mountains in that direction are not so near as they are to the eastward or southward. These mountains appeared to have a valley between them in which the noise seemed to me to originate. It commenced with a sound like some very distant rushing of water, and as it approached it became louder, and by the time the shock is felt, the noise resembles the rushing of a shoal of fish, or when near the falling of a large body of water over rocks.

The shaking begins moderately, and continues to increase till it seems to pass by, and proceeds to the southward, when the trembling and sound continue to diminish until they cease. I have been in houses during the shocks, at which times all the males run out into the street as soon as they feel it. The females are generally too much frightened to run, and will commonly lay hold of any one who is near them. The first shock I ever felt was at Valparaíso while sitting at dinner at a friend's house. His wife was sitting near me. I observed something was the matter by the behavior of the company. The woman caught fast hold of me, and I could not understand what the matter was until I heard the noise and felt the trembling.

At a gentleman's house at Lima one early evening, my two particular friends, the general of marine and Colmanares the commandant being of the party, we heard the noise which precedes the shock of an earthquake. The company all started up and went out of doors, except Colmanares and myself. After the shock was over they came into the house, when we had some sport with the general and the other gentlemen. We asked them what they had run for. They asked us if we did not hear and feel the earthquake which had just happened! We answered, yes, but we thought that soldiers and sailors never run from any thing. The general said he was looking after his horse, expecting he might be frightened. The general was a very affable, jocular man, and one with whom liberties might be taken without giving an affront. After this, if any thing happened which produced an alarm, we used to rally him by asking if his horse would not be frightened.

The terror into which the people of this part of the world are thrown at the shock of an earthquake is incredible. At the least noise they do not understand the cause of, they are heard calling out "tombelore! tombelore!" This is owing to the calamities which have happened to them at different times when severe shocks cause the houses to tumble down and bury in the ruins all who were in them.

THE CITY OF LIMA, I was informed, is twelve miles in circumference, and contains between seventy to one hundred thousand persons.[43] It lies on an extended plain, from twelve to twenty miles broad. There is a beautiful river that runs through the city which comes down from the mountains through this extensive plain, and empties into the bay or harbour to the north east of the port, about one or two miles distant. They have turned a part of this river so that it runs through Callao, a little back of the town. A part of the stream is sunk under ground, and comes out close to the salt water at a bay where boats can fill with ease.

The city of Lima is laid out in squares. The streets are rather narrow, but as they do not use many carriages or carts, they require less room than otherwise would be necessary. They ride mostly on horseback and carry all their merchan-

dise on the backs of horses, mules, and jack-asses. All the
streets have a drain in the middle of them, the water in which
can be set running at discretion. I never saw a place so well
supplied with water as this city is.

The river above the city is confined into a narrow focus
or aqueduct by which the water is raised in a fountain of
bronze, adorned with an image of the goddess of fame, which
is in the royal square facing the palace. The fountain spouts
the water ten or twelve feet high, so as to fall into a square
reservoir, from which it continually runs through about
twelve copper pipes into a basin of sixteen or eighteen feet diameter, and has a conductor through which the superfluous
water runs off. The rim of this basin is just high enough for
the people to step over and fill their kegs, which vessels are
the most common in use for that purpose. These kegs contain
about eight or ten gallons. Two kegs are placed endwise in a
panel, slung across an ass's back and fastened with straps of
leather. This is the most general method of conveying water
in the city. Besides this fountain there are many canals, or
streams running through different parts of the city, to most of
the houses, and serve in cases of fire and to water their gardens, and other uses.

The royal square is very handsome, and is situated in
the center of the city. On the east side of it is the palace and
other public buildings belonging to it, which are all well
built. The south side consists of a very spacious, rich, and
handsome church; the north and west sides are occupied by
merchants' shops that deal chiefly in dry goods. On these two
sides of the square, the houses are all in one range, and are
built only one story high on account of frequent earthquakes.
They have a gallery projecting from the upper part about
eighteen or twenty feet into the square, supported by pillars
twelve feet high, with regular arches from one to the other,

THE MUNICIPALITY BUILDING, GREAT PLAZA, LIMA, WITH
COVERED WALKWAYS AND MARKET STALLS.
(FROM THE COLLECTIONS OF THE LIBRARY OF CONGRESS)

the entire length of the square. Under this piazza is the side
walk for foot passengers who are at the same time well guarded against the heat of the sun.

The spaces between the pillars of this colonnade are
filled up with stalls or work shops, occupied by different mechanics, such as watch makers, goldsmiths, lace, cord, and
chenille makers, silk and taffeta ribbon weavers, and vendors
of all other kind of small articles, whilst business of greater
importance is carried on in the shops behind them. This
square measures from two to three hundred yards each way,
and serves for a market place in which I have seen the finest
vegetables, meat, poultry, and tropical fruit, and in greater
quantities than I ever saw in any market before, and at
very reasonable prices. Fish is rather scarce, and but very indifferent.

The palace is one of the greatest curiosities in the city.

It is a handsome and spacious building, the interior of which is so singularly constructed, with so many turnings and windings on going to the Viceroy's office, or apartment in which he personally transacts business, that it would be difficult for a stranger to find his way through them without the assistance of a guide. Although I have been more than fifty times to the Viceroy's office, I greatly doubt whether I should now be able to find it without a conductor. One of the structures adjoining the palace, and built within its walls, is called the royal chest, in which the treasures belonging to the crown are deposited, as well as disputable property, either merchandise or money, similar to that of the court of chancery in England.

The streets throughout the city are handsome and are in a straight line. The houses have a very agreeable appearance, with galleries in front, and trees planted round them as shelter against the rays of the sun. Many of the buildings make up in length or depth for the deficiency in height, some being two hundred feet long and proportionately broad, and have ten or twelve large apartments on the ground floor. The roofs are formed chiefly of reeds, which afford sufficient shelter, as there is never any rain of consequence known to fall here. Some of the rich inhabitants have their floors covered with handsome matting and cotton cloths.

The churches and monasteries are extremely rich, and decorated with many images of saints made of solid gold, which are adorned with jewels and trinkets of immense value.

THE FIRST TIME I HAD an interview with the Viceroy, he very politely gave me the privilege of coming to his apartment at any hour between eight o'clock in the morning and nine at night, on any day, holidays not excepted, on account of my business with Don Benito Cereno. His excellency is a man of very dignified and commanding appearance, without any of that stiff formality so peculiar to the higher class of his countrymen; for he possessed too many natural abilities to require any stiffness to assist him in keeping up his consequence. His dress was in general plain and neat, but I saw him one time dressed in the most superb style that I ever witnessed.

One Sunday morning when I had something particular I wished to impart to him, I did not think it a breach of politeness to wait on his excellency at that time. I accordingly entered the palace, and a person attending as doorkeeper conducted me as usual into a room next but one to the Viceroy's office where two of the body guards are always in waiting. I told them my business, and they informed me that his excellency was just going to church; that the carriage was already sent for, and they thought it would not be very well received were they to acquaint him with my request. I felt a little confused, thinking I had trespassed against the rules of good breeding by coming at church hours, and requested them not to mention it to the Viceroy, as I would come again at some more convenient time. His Excellency was walking in the next room, and hearing what I said, came to the door and requested me to walk in. I made as handsome an apology as I was capable of in the Spanish language for coming at such an unseasonable hour, when he graciously desired me not to be the least uneasy on that account, and that he was glad to see me as he had something he wished to communicate.

I was struck with the majesty of his appearance and behavior. He was dressed in a full uniform of blue silk velvet, laced in the most modest and rich manner possible. He walked and conversed with me for nearly an hour, no person present but ourselves; the carriage and his suite were waiting for him all the time.

He was called from the command at the Rio de la Plata

AN AVENUE IN LIMA.
(FROM THE COLLECTIONS OF THE LIBRARY OF CONGRESS)

to the vice royalty of this place. In his former station he was a great military character, and was considered the first disciplinarian in Spanish America. The inhabitants of Lima trembled, as I was told, when they were informed of his coming; but he put off the character of a soldier for that of a civilian, in which capacity he has acted with moderation and wisdom to the universal satisfaction of the inhabitants. The conversation with and the order he gave Don Benito, concerning my business, was almost the only time he had ever been known to show anger during his vice royalty.

The palace is not so elegant as it is spacious. The dress of the body guards makes the most elegant and extraordinary appearance of anything imaginable. I had read a description of them in Bank's *Geography*, but I did not fully believe the account until I saw them myself. On entering the palace the first thing I thought of was to satisfy my curiosity respecting this guard. I saw six of them standing sentinel in different parts as I went through the several turnings leading to His Excellency's rooms; every one of whom was dressed in a superfine blue broadcloth coat, waistcoat, and breeches which were as handsomely laced with gold as a captain's in the navy. They are about sixty in number, and I was informed they never do any duty out of the palace. They have only to attend about His Excellency's person, and ride out with him. The Viceroy most commonly rides in a very elegant coach, drawn by six handsome mules, followed by two other coaches, one for his secretaries and any other person he might wish to be of the party, and the other for his bodyguards, both coaches being drawn by six mules.

THE INQUISITION, a religious tribunal, has been represented as being tyrannical and cruel, and the mere name of it strikes the people of Protestant countries with horror. A court founded upon the principle of trying and punishing people for their religious opinions is inconsistent with reason and the ideas of liberty of conscience entertained at the present time. But it must be recollected that the people of all countries are governed more or less by some species of priestcraft, and as long as society remains in its present state, there can be no doubt but those possessed of power will make use of it as the best means they can adopt to control the bad passions and propensities which a large portion of their subjects possess.

The Spanish people, perhaps, have been kept more under the influence of superstition and bigotry than most others; but I have had an opportunity of knowing something of them, and am ready to confess, from what I have seen, that they enjoy as much liberty of conscience, and converse as freely on religious and other topics as any people with whom I have had intercourse. My feelings and opinions respecting the Inquisition were similar to those of other people who knew nothing of it except what they had received from those who were as ignorant as themselves, and were governed more by prejudice than by facts, and when I arrived in this country my curiosity was very great to learn everything I possibly could concerning it.

I had a very good opportunity during my several visits to Lima to obtain correct information on the subject, and from what I saw and the accounts given by those whom I had the most perfect confidence in, I was convinced that it was not so terrible as has been represented.

A short time previous to my arrival at Lima, the following incident took place involving the Inquisitional courts. A Spanish woman had married a man who did not believe in the Catholic faith, which description of people are called heretics. This man died, and the woman being left a widow, she formed a determination to live up to her husband's faith, let the consequences be what they would. He never had during his life expressed any opinion upon religious subjects, or troubled himself about them. But after his death the woman boldly and openly made her husband's religious sentiments known, and expressed her own belief in them. This was not long in getting to the ears of the clergy.

They paid her a visit, expecting that they should be able to convince her of her error by arguments, and persuade her from the determination she had taken. But they found themselves very much mistaken. She told them that the clergy were impostors; that they were oppressing the people under a false doctrine; that every one was greatly aggrieved by their villainous influence; and called them liars, robbers, and murderers. On which they took her into the court-house, or prison of the Inquisition, and held an ecclesiastical court to try her for heresy.

She was found guilty, and sentenced to be placed astride an ass, with her back towards his head, and clogs fixed to her feet, and conveyed in that manner across the bridge to the common place of execution, which was on the other side of the river, and there to be beheaded, and her body burned; with a provision that if she would repent before crossing the bridge, and make a humble confession of her fault, and ask forgiveness, she should be pardoned.

They placed her on the ass according to the sentence, and proceeded toward the place of execution, making the animal go in a manner to jolt and hurt her as much as they possibly could, with the intention of making her repent of the determination she had formed, and to renounce her principles. They frequently stopped, when the clergy would try to convince her of the consequence of her stubborn and obstinate conduct, in hopes that they could persuade her to repent; but it was all to no purpose, for she continued to abuse them with all the epithets she could make use of to disgrace them and their religion.

When they came to the bridge, they made a long stop, and expostulated, begged, and prayed to her not to "die as a fool dieth." They repeatedly told her that after she had crossed the bridge, all the repentance she could make would avail her nothing. She told them to move on, which they did, after finding their entreaties were of no avail, and she died a true martyr, if any one ever did, if by sticking to her faith can be called martyrdom.

Additional information about the Inquisition comes from the priests who were my friends and confidants, and likewise many other gentlemen of rank and high standing here. They informed me that the house of the Inquisition was a court and a jail-house, and that the ecclesiastical court sat in the same building where the prisoners were confined. The court consisted of priests, and sometimes a high officer or officers of state. It is conducted publicly, the prisoners being permitted to call any evidence they choose in their defence. This court does not meddle with any thing except infringements upon their holy religion. If, say they, these were to be passed over and let go with impunity, the church and state would fall to the ground. As to this part of the business I will not undertake to defend, but from what happened with the woman, leaves it in my power to know pretty well how that case was conducted. I was informed by Americans, Englishmen, and Swedes, as well as the authority quoted above, that the trial of this woman was as fairly and openly conducted as in any court whatsoever; and that the priests interested themselves as much in her behalf as any men could, and show respect for their religion. To attempt to justify this or any other proceedings of courts, I would by no means think of; but I am ready to admit that the Inquisition is a rigid court of justice, established and continued to maintain their religion.

TWO OR THREE GENTLEMEN accompanied me on a visit to the mint. The master or conductor went with us over all parts of it, and showed us all that was worthy of seeing, and explained every thing to my satisfaction. We came to where they were melting and casting gold and silver in iron moulds. The process with the gold which was performed in my presence, was by bruising the ore fine with mauls, and then wetting it with some liquid, and working it over in the same manner as lime mortar is prepared in at home. This is done on the floor of the room which was all paved with smooth stones, or bricks. This labour is done by negroes, who tread it over with their feet and knead it like dough, after which they put quick silver amongst it, which separates the ore from the other metals that are mixed with it. It had the appearance of yellow mortar, or dough. After it was separated, it was cast into ingots or bars. The silver is separated previous to its being brought to the mint, and cast into pigs that weigh from eighty to one hundred and sixty pounds each. Many tons of these I saw piled up like cord wood.

The master set the people to work at coining dollars and doubloons to show me the last process. Two impressions are cut on two pieces of steel, about the size of a blacksmith's sledge hammer, and not very unlike it in shape, the impressions being cut on the face of each. These two pieces are fixed, one in a frame made of wood and iron on the ground, fastened very strongly with screws, with the impression upwards. The other piece is fixed at the lower end of a large screw, five inches in diameter and four feet long, with the impression side down, and placed directly over the one that is fixed on the ground, all parts of the machine being framed together in a remarkably strong manner.

The Mint

An iron tiller, or large bar, is put on the head of the screw in the same manner a boat's tiller is put over the head of the rudder, the hole for the screw being in the middle of the tiller, which is twelve feet long, having each end of it loaded with about fifty weight of lead, and ropes four or five feet long fastened to each end for the men to pull by, who sit down and take hold of the ropes, being from five to seven in number. The man who puts the dollars under the screw has a hole sunk on one side of the work for him to sit in. When the men were all called to their stations and a thousand dollars emptied near the work, the master stepped to the pile and took a handful which he brought to me to inspect, and showed me where the pins were put in to make up the weight, which were very plain to be seen. One man who stands up at one end of the tiller throws it back and raises the screw. A piece of wood is then taken out from between the two impressions that serves to keep them apart, and a dollar is put under in its stead, on which the screw is turned forward with the full strength of the men placed at the tiller, by which it comes down with incredible force on the dollar. The man at the opposite end of the tiller than heaves it back and raises the screw. The dollar is brushed off by means of a piece of iron twelve inches long, and another dollar is put under. They were handed to me to see how fair and deep the impressions were made, and how completely the pins were pressed in, but I could see on some of them where the pin was. This may often be seen in Spanish dollars, if closely inspected. They could easily finish fifteen in a minute, or one in four seconds. The process with doubloons is the same as with dollars.

I asked the master how much money they commonly coined in a year in that mint. He informed me that they coined from six to eight millions of dollars value in gold and silver, and also that the mint in Mexico coined from fifteen to twenty million, and in Santiago, Chile, from one and a half to three million which was all the money that was coined in these three kingdoms. He told me that the bullion I saw belonged to different people, and was brought to be coined in the same manner as corn is carried to a mill to be ground, and that as fast as it was coined it was taken away by the respective owners.

THERE ARE BETWEEN THIRTY AND FORTY churches in Lima, some of which are the richest perhaps of any in the world. They are very large, and were, as I thought, high; but the priests told me they would have been built much higher were it not for fear of earthquakes. The gold and silver about the altars is immense. The pillars in some are of solid silver, six inches in diameter, and ten or twelve feet long. Many of their vases are of gold, and of an extraordinary value. The rich silk furniture, such as curtains, cushions, and tassels are all of crimson damask. The flooring is marble of different colours, placed in a variegated manner in regular diamonds, and has the highest polish imaginable. The yards round them are spacious and paved with large regular shaped flat stones. The stone steps ascending to the door as well as the railings round the yard are all very neat specimens of architecture. The bells in these churches are the largest I ever saw. There are as many as twelve to twenty in each church. The domes are large and splendid; the vanes on some are images of men in reverence to the saint the church is dedicated to. All churches are built of stone or brick, and are bound together with iron ties or braces in the strongest manner they possibly could be made to prevent them from being shaken to pieces by earthquakes.

The clergy here have great power, and bear great sway. This is the case in all Catholic countries, but I could not see that they much abused their power. Some of them are very

THE CHURCH OF SAN FRANCISCO, LIMA.
(FROM THE COLLECTIONS OF THE LIBRARY OF CONGRESS)

good companions, affable, cheerful, obliging, and humane. I should as soon choose a Roman Catholic priest for a companion and friend, as almost any man. It will be hardly necessary to inform the reader that they are the most intolerable beggars, on which subject we did not very well agree. I commonly told them that I had to help support the church in my own country and it was not fair to ask anything of me, and this in general satisfied them.

I will relate an anecdote which took place here with a priest who used to go about begging for St. Maria's church, which caused considerable diversion. He had a little image representing the Virgin Mary, about two feet long, in a box with a glass front, so that the whole of it could be seen, which was dressed and ornamented in a very beautiful manner. He had several times been to my chamber with it. I had often told him that I was not pleased with his coming there with it; but he was very troublesome and importunate, and would frequently insist on my kissing the image through the glass, which was considered as binding the person to give something.

One day he came to my room at a large hotel, and began with his usual kind of impudence, and insisted on my kissing the Virgin. I showed my displeasure, and some of my company told him that he treated me very ill. After strutting about for a while, he set his image down behind something in the room, and went into another part of the hotel. As soon as he was gone, we placed the image in my bed, and covered it over with the clothes so that it could not be easily discovered. The priest soon returned, and missing his virgin, looking diligently about, but could not find her. He was patient for some time, but after he began to think that he had lost her, he showed much distress. He said he should never dare to go back to the church of the Blessed Lady if he could not find her. After thinking him pretty well paid for his impudence, one of us told him that as he had been so urgent for the captain to kiss her, it might possibly be that she had got into his bed. When he had found her, he was in a worse situation than before, if possible, to think and to have it known, that the Blessed Virgin had been in the bed of a heretic. But after many promises that we would not divulge the secret, he went off and was not seen there again. I had some doubts however, whether he might not bring us into trouble, if he had been so disposed.

THERE ARE THREE COLLEGES for male students. These three contained two hundred and eleven individuals. There are also two colleges for females: Dela Caridad, and the college of Santa Cruz for female orphans, containing sixty-six individuals. Also three alms houses, for foundlings, and for poor women, containing one hundred and thirty-nine persons; eleven hospitals, containing about nine hundred and forty-seven persons; and three jails, that of the court, of the city, and of the Inquisition, containing one hundred and eighty-one persons. In this enumeration are included all the officers, attendants, and slaves belonging to the respective institutions.

The amusements of the citizens of Lima are like those of the inhabitants of other great cities. I have seen very elegant performances in the theatres of Lima. The actors had voices resembling the notes of melodious singing birds. In all the languages that I ever heard spoken, there was nothing so musical as the voices I heard on the stages here.

Cock-fighting is a very favourite amusement in Lima. There is a particular building erected for that diversion in the little square of Santa Catalina, near the walls of the city, surrounded by beautiful gardens and extensive prospects. The building itself forms a handsome amphitheatre of a regular shape with ranges of seats and galleries. This amusement is permitted on Sundays and festivals, besides two working days in the week. On particular days cock-fighting draws a great concourse of people of all kinds for the purpose of betting. In doubtful cases the decision is left to an appointed judge, who, with a party of military, is always present to prevent disputes and quarrels.

There are several beautiful walks about Lima which are much frequented, one of which is called the Alameda, and is

A LADY OF LIMA, 1805. (FROM THE COLLECTIONS OF THE LIBRARY OF CONGRESS)

mostly visited on Sundays, new-year days and other holidays. The multitude of coaches of different shapes and colours, and the neatness and elegance of the costumes, particularly those of the ladies, make a pleasant appearance. They have likewise frolicking parties, which commence on St. John's Day, the 24th of June, and at the close of September. These excursions are mostly to the hills near Lima, and they often take several days.

The plains on which Lima stands are rich and fertile. It is beyond belief how many mule loads of grass they bring into the city in a day to supply the cattle in Lima with, as they never make any hay. I was informed by a gentleman of veracity that there were three thousand mule loads each day brought into the capital during the year. I do not vouch for the truth of it, but am satisfied they do not give anything but grass for food to any of their cattle.

As to curious birds, I never saw any here, and believe that there are not many to be found in this part of the world. Reptiles are not very plentiful in this vicinity. It is not so famous for fish as the coast of Chile. Llamas have been so often described by naturalists and travellers that I shall pass over them, and mention only the vicuna, which supplies the vicuna wool. The animal is wild, and hunted down and killed for the sake of its wool by the Indians, who by their frequent havoc amongst these animals will most probably destroy the whole race in Peru in a short time. Many intelligent natives assert that the vicuna can be tamed and domesticated as well as llamas. Flocks gathered of these animals might open a new speculation to the cultivator, and afford a great commercial benefits to the whole community.

AT THE DIFFERENT TIMES I have been at Lima I took out of prison nearly fifty English prisoners, or those that the

Spanish considered Englishmen, which included pretty much all foreigners. Amongst them was an English captain whose ship was taken in the port of Valparaíso, and he was sent to Lima and confined. I got him out of prison on parole by giving my bond for 10,000 dollars for his good behavior, and took him away with me. To let a captain of a ship out of prison and go home on his parole of honour is a thing that seldom or never happened before at Lima; but as I found favour in this city, I made the best use of it I could to relieve the distresses of my fellow creatures. This captain's name was James Bacon, a native of London. He got safe to England and wrote me a letter expressing his sentiments on my conduct, as well as that of the government of Lima.

There was another English captain by the name of Rowe confined there at the same time for whom I was not able to obtain a parole, owing to some ignorance or oversight of a man who pretended to be his friend. He neglected to get a necessary paper made out in season to send in with the petition that was presented, and which obtained the release of Captain Bacon. But the affair was so arranged at the time between the general of the marine and myself, that Captain Rowe was soon after liberated on the same conditions as Captain Bacon was by the friendship and assistance of a Mr. Baxter, whom I left at Lima, and who was supercargo of the ship *Herkimer* at the time I took Captain Bacon away.

On the 17th of November 1805, I received on board the *Perseverance* from the ship *Victor* — a Spanish privateer of twenty-four guns from Lima — five American prisoners who had been taken off the island of Más Afuera by a Spanish ship of war, for trespassing on the Spanish regulations then existing. The Spanish captain happened to be an acquaintance and friend of mine. As soon as I saw the Americans he had on board, I told him that these men belonged to Mr. Joel Root of

New Haven in Connecticut, and that he was a friend of mine, who had together with Captain Moultrop treated me generously at a time when I stood in great need, and to whom I had made a promise that I would recover their men if it were possible for me to effect it. He told me I should have them, and they accordingly were all sent on board my ship. I provided them an opportunity to go home on good wages, where they all arrived safe, as I have since been informed.

Concerning prisoners of war, the Spaniards are ever jealous of foreigners in that part of the world, on account of being robbed by them of their treasures, as well as other advantages taken of them. They are not a very sympathising people, and feel very little for the suffering part of the community and have treated prisoners of war in general unfeelingly by keeping them confined in close, and many times unhealthy prisons; but of late it is not so bad, and I have reason to think what I have said and done in their favour in that part of the country has done some good.

The prisoners that were delivered to me from the city of Lima were taken out of jail with their hands tied behind them, and driven by the dragoons in the same manner that they drive hogs to the port. I have followed the prisoners who have been thus liberated several times, and as soon as they were outside the gate, I have often prevailed with the horsemen — by giving them a trifle — to untie their hands and let them walk at their ease. The provision made for them whilst in confinement was sometimes tolerably good, and at other times very bad; but a person who never saw a place where prisoners of war are confined in foreign countries cannot judge of the hardships attending them. Some have been in a habit of exaggerating, and making it worse than it is, but it may be believed that it is bad enough to be confined within the walls of a prison for years together, and not have the privi-

lege of once breathing the fresh air in the whole course of that
time.

THE INDIANS OF PERU are in general quick of apprehen-
sion, penetrating, and very fond of study; the females exceed
the men in the lighter branches of learning, and are remarkable for their wit and vivacity. The mestizos, or children of
Spaniards and Indian women, chiefly apply themselves to the
liberal arts and sciences, and make great progress both in
painting and sculpture, considering that in the prosecution of
their studies they are deprived of those models which are
deemed so requisite by the European student. The inhabitants
are all lively, sociable, and polite, which along with a good
taste, seem to be the hereditary qualities of every Peruvian.
The Indians are very well skilled in the use of medical herbs
and plants, of which the country abounds, but are very fond of
keeping their science a secret. Many people have left Lima after their physicians had given them over, and were cured by
the Indians in the neighborhood of that city.

The Indians of the mountains are clad differently from
those in and about the city; the first simply wearing a cotton
shirt, reaching to their knees, while the latter add an outer
garment, either of cotton, coarse baize, or a stuff made of flat
straw, interwoven with thread in the shape of a poncho. The
women wear a long cotton gown reaching to their ankles, and
a mantle of baize over their shoulders. On festivals and other
occasions, they dress in imitation of the Spanish. The small
pox makes the greatest havoc of any disease among them. It
has struck so much terror to them that when the slightest
symptoms of it appear, they immediately flee into the mountains, and remain there until they are persuaded the disease
has subsided.

The Habitos Indians are, in general, strangers to ambi-

tion, avarice, theft, and dissensions, but are much addicted to
intemperance. Their diet chiefly consists of wild bears, monkeys, salt fish, plantains, mani, yuccas, and wild fruits. Their
favourite drink is called massato, which is made of boiled yuccas reduced to a paste, and left to ferment for three days, then
pouring water on it, it becomes a strong and intoxicating liquor. They likewise chew the leaves of the coca plant, which
they mix with a kind of chalk or white earth called manbi.
This is very nourishing, and enables them to labour for entire
days without eating or drinking; but when they can no longer
procure it they feel their strength gradually exhausting.[44] It
likewise preserves the teeth and fortifies the stomach. The
Indians constantly bathe before sunrise, with a view to preserving their health, of which they are in some respects very
careful.

The Indians throughout Peru believe in one supreme
being, who, after he had finished the creation of the world,
retired to some very distant place, and does not trouble himself much about them, only sometimes coming to see how
many of them are still alive. They believe the earthquakes to
be occasioned by his walking on the earth. For this reason as
soon as they hear the least noise they cannot account for, they
precipitately run out of their huts jumping and stamping
about, crying as loud as they can, "Here we are! Here we are!"
They likewise believe in a malicious being who lives in the
center of the earth, and is the cause of all afflictions and misfortunes. Many of the most cunning among them, make the
rest believe they are the emissaries of this being, and are consulted on all particular occasions. The missionaries have found
the Indians in general very docile, and by all accounts the
Christian religion is propagating very fast among them.

Peruvians' Boats; On to Canton; Chinese Customs and Manners

ON THE 27th of March 1806 we took our final leave of Lima and steered our course to the northward as far as the Lobos Islands. The southern Lobos Island, which is called by the Spaniards Lobos de Mer (*Lobos de Afuera*), lies in latitude 6° 58' south, longitude 80° 40' west. The northern Lobos, or Isla Lobos de Tierra, is in latitude 6° 30' south, and longitude 80° 48' west from the *Naval Gazetteer*, which I think to be right.

These islands lie about seven or eight leagues from the mainland of Peru, and are always plain to be seen in clear weather. The native Indians go to them from the mainland to catch fish. They go over on what is called a catamaran, which is formed by a number of large logs lashed together. Being of a light kind of wood, it swims very buoyant. The logs are from twenty to forty feet long and from fifteen inches to two feet diameter, and are secured by small spars lashed across, which keeps them a little distance apart. There is a crib work raised in the middle, four feet high, to secure the masts which are stepped in the bottom logs. There is also a short bowsprit rigged out at one end, and a large square sail a little narrow at the head, which is set by means of a yard made fast to it. They are steered by means of large slabs that are put through between the logs, that hold the water like lee boards. In this kind of craft, they beat to windward for many degrees up, sail down the coast, and stretch off from the land sometimes

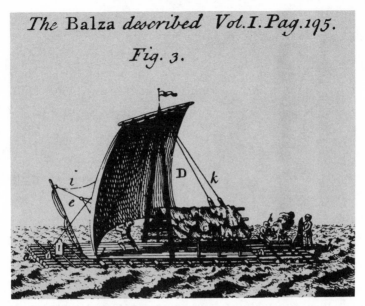

A PERUVIAN CATAMARAN.
(FROM THE COLLECTIONS OF THE LIBRARY OF CONGRESS)

thirty or forty miles. This is the principal craft that the Indians have to transport any thing by water.

They have likewise a skin which they fill with air on which they sometimes go off to catch fish. Two of these skins are fixed by lashing them together, and placing a small board across them, on which they paddle off a mile or two to fish. These are always called bollsys, and the large kind made of logs are sometimes called by the same name.

The Indians go over to the Lobos Islands at particular seasons in great numbers with their bollsys, stay one or two weeks, and always behave with the greatest propriety and civility. They were very kind to me and would often bring vegetables from the main. They were obliged to bring fresh water for their own use, as these islands do not afford any, or any kind of vegetable, all their surface being sand, sun burned rocks, and thousands of ship loads of birds' feces.

There was one kind that I never saw before, which were an excellent eating bird. We called them razor-bills, as their bills resembled that instrument more than anything I could compare them with. They are always in flocks, are shy, and not very plenty. They are as large as one of our teal.

All the coast from Lima down to these islands is more sun-burnt and barren than that nearer the city, affording verdure only in patches, and fresh water is difficult to obtain in most parts of it. It is very thinly inhabited, and wood is likewise extremely scarce. There is enough salt to be found here to load all the ships in the world, which is found in mines to the northward of Lima. It is very convenient loading with it there, as a vessel can go in and get it on board without much labour. They cleave large pieces from the side of the mine which weigh many tons each. It is commonly broken or hewed into square pieces, three feet long and one foot square, for convenience in handling, and to load on the backs of mules. It is sent several hundred miles into the country of Chile.

This is good ground for whaling as it is always pleasant weather, and on almost all parts of the coast whales are very plenty.

(*They arrived on the 27th of June at the Galapagos Islands, and left them a month later.*) There we fitted and provisioned the *Pilgrim*, with orders to remain another season for the purpose of procuring a cargo of skins. She was left under the command of my brother Samuel, with him my brother William as first officer, and twelve men. She remained on the coast until 4th September 1807, during which time they experienced many hardships and privations. But they procured between twelve and thirteen thousand skins, with which they arrived safe at

A PERUVIAN BALSA, MADE FROM SEALSKINS.
(FROM THE COLLECTIONS OF THE LIBRARY OF CONGRESS)

Canton, though some of the skins were damaged by being wet, in consequence of the schooner being upset while entering the China seas. After discharging the skins at Canton, the *Pilgrim* was sold, and my brothers safely returned to Boston after an absence of five years, during which long and tedious voyage they encountered many dangers and vicissitudes of fortune. William was again upset on his return to America in the brig *Peacock* off the Straits of Sunda.

The *Perseverance* proceeded on her voyage toward Canton, and arrived at the Hawaiian Islands on the 8th of September, where we took in fresh provisions and water, and sailed again on the 30th.

WE ARRIVED AT MACAU on the 10 November, took a Chinese pilot and passport, and proceeded up to Canton. On going up we passed the English frigate *Phaeton*, commanded by Commodore Wood, with several other men of war under his command. We were boarded from the squadron, and treated politely, they offering us any assistance we might be in want of. Shortly after my arrival at Canton, some misunderstanding took place between Commodore Wood and the Americans at that place which was in consequence of an American vessel passing the squadron with English deserters on board, and deceiving the Commodore, as he said, with false reports concerning them. This transaction caused much difficulty between the English commander and the Americans then at Canton. The conduct of the Americans, in my opinion, was not very wise or judicious, as it is always a maxim with me not to engage in a quarrel without possessing some means whereby I could be able to redress myself when I had received an injury; but in this case there was no possible ground on which the Americans could maintain the position they had taken, as the English possessed the power if they had not the right on their side.

The Chinese empire is said by some to be the largest in the world. This however cannot be very well ascertained, but there is no doubt that it contains the greatest number of inhabitants of any. When the Europeans first visited this country they were received by the Chinese with great kindness and hospitality, granting them every indulgence in the pursuits of commerce which were reasonable. They at first had full liberty to go where they pleased, but the strangers soon began to abuse this indulgence, and conduct themselves in such a manner, by taking liberties with their women, and other gross improprieties which a Chinese can never overlook, that the government were obliged to curtail their liberties and confine them to the port of Canton only, where they are permitted to reside for the express purpose of commerce. Foreigners are not admitted into the city of Canton, but are allowed the suburbs to erect their factories and transact business.

China in modern times has been found to be foremost in the arts and sciences and in agriculture. It is one of the best regulated governments in the world. The laws are just, and are maintained with such strict impartiality, that the guilty seldom escape punishment, or the injured fail to obtain prompt justice. In punishing with death, there is no people on earth more scrupulous than they are. Under certain circumstances, if a man is accused of a crime by which his life is forfeited, he has the advantage of fifteen tribunals before he can be sentenced to death; but there is one law in China which will be condemned by the people of countries where there is more freedom enjoyed, which is that if a person kills another, the laws require that his life should be taken as the only atonement. There is no difference made between killing with premeditated malice, or by accident, or through the influence of passion.

For smaller crimes they are not very ceremonious as to the punishment. Flogging is very common, and frequently very severe. Imprisonment is considered as an impolitic measure, for, say they, men are only made more wicked by confinement, and those that are free have to work to maintain those that are in prison; and if people cannot be made to do right by flogging, let them be banished to the cold northern regions of China for life.

Merit is rewarded by the emperor of China, in some cases very liberally, and as far as I have been able to know generally, where it is deserved and he can be informed of the fact; but this is frequently very difficult, on account of the jealousy which exists among the officers, who are always envious at seeing others rise into notice with their sovereign, and this of course will keep them from letting him know of any thing that might tend to lessen their own importance.

Marriages are much respected by the Chinese, and are celebrated by them with great solemnity. It is the custom of the country for every man to marry one woman who is his equal in rank, and that his parents think suitable for him. "A man can have only one lawful wife, and her rank and age must be nearly equal to his own; but he may receive into his house, on certain conditions, several concubines or wives of the second rank, who are wholly subject to the lawful spouse. Their children are considered as hers, they address her as mother, and can give that title to her only." I have known some Chinese who have four or five wives, but it is uncommon for them to have more than one.

The marriage is first contracted between the parents, when the likeness of the woman is shown to the young man, and sometimes that of the man is sent to the woman, but the women do not have so much attention paid in this respect as the men, for there is seldom much difficulty in gaining the consent of the woman if her parents approve of it. Neither the man or the woman ever see each other till after the marriage is consummated, and the wife is never permitted after marriage to see any man except her husband.

The last time I was in China, in 1806, the son of Conseequa, my hong merchant, was married, in consequence of which I had the privilege of knowing how the courtship and marriage was conducted, as both the father and son were very friendly to me. The bridegroom was about twenty years old, and the bride seventeen or eighteen. Conseequa informed me that the father of the bride was a particular friend of his, and likewise well known to me. He was a man well disposed and generally esteemed in Canton. He had fixed upon the marriage with his friend, and when the contract was drawn between them, it took place as soon as the parties were reconciled to have the nuptials celebrated. The bridegroom told me that he never saw his bride till after all the writings were signed by the parties, when he received her at his door; but that he had before had her likeness sent to him for his inspection, which he said was very handsome.

I have been often informed that it is not a common custom with the Chinese to put two wives into one house, as it is not agreeable to them to live together. Also, a man cannot have more than one wife unless he gives satisfactory evidence that his circumstances enable him to maintain them. The custom of marrying their children at a very early age does not prevail in China as it does among the Hindus, who marry theirs when not more than five or six years old. The former permit their children to arrive at years of puberty before they are married, and make use of very different arguments on the subject from what are used by the latter, who say that the male and female who are destined to pass their lives together as man and wife cannot be too soon introduced to each other, and be made constant companions. The Hindus hold that the sexes should be early accustomed to be together, as it will tend to habituate them to each other's temper and manners, and will be more likely to cause them to live happily together when they come to a maturer age.

The funeral ceremonies in China are very solemn and splendid. Nothing is held more sacred with a Chinese than the death, the funeral obsequies, and the place of deposit of the remains of a parent. The mandarins that hold high offices expend large sums of money on such occasions. They make splendid feasts, and clothe a great number of people in white, which is the colour of their mourning. They form a column of people of half a mile in length to attend the corpse to the grave, most of whom receive in a direct or indirect manner some present or consideration.

Their tombs or places of interment are always chosen in places that are not public, and on land that is not fit for cultivation, it being a maxim with them not to occupy for any other purpose than agriculture land that is capable of producing any kind of verdure. The tomb is shaped according to the fancy of the owner, though they are generally round, but sometimes square, oblong, or oval. Those that are round have an elevation in the center of the circle, raised two or three feet, being shaped like the top of an oven, and the door by which they enter them is made in the same manner as that of an oven. The platform is twenty or thirty feet in diameter, with the floor level and smooth, and round the outside they are raised one or two feet. They are built with a cement of stone and lime mortar. One tomb serves for a family for many ages, and they are scattered singly over all the barren grounds. There are several of them on Dean's Island, which forms one side of the river below Huangpu. Some of the mandarins and wealthy people have soil placed round their tombs, and trees planted, which gives them a very pleasant appearance.

(Some of Delano's Dutch friends who had been on an embassy to Peking gave a lengthy report of the proceedings, from which the following is excerpted.)

THEY LEFT CANTON IN beautiful covered boats, and proceeded on through the canals. Some of the party would go on shore, and walk near the water whenever they chose, along by the side of the canal, while the others remained on the boats. When they came to a place where the canal did not carry them in the most direct course, or to where it was frozen, they left their boats and proceeded on horse-back. It was in the winter season when they made the journey, and the country of course did not appear to so much advantage as it would had it been in the summer. The mandarins, who accompanied them, indulged them in every thing they asked that was reasonable, and showed them every curiosity worthy of their attention.

When the embassy arrived at Peking great parade was made. It was said in Canton that there was more attention paid to the Dutch than there was to the English in their embassy, which was thought to be in consequence of the Dutch not asking any favours of them.

Their amusements in which they joined consisted of a kind of theatrical performance, music and dancing, and skating on the ice. These theatrical performances I have frequently seen at Canton. They put boys into the skins of different animals, and sometimes dress them up with feathers, with the wings of birds attached to them. I have seen lions, tigers and ostriches represented on a Chinese stage, which appeared nearly as natural as life. My friends informed me that while their embassy was at Peking, parties were frequently formed to skate on the ice, in which the Emperor always joined. Of the Chinese who formed skating parties, some were archers, and performed some extraordinary feats on skates with bows and arrows. One of the exploits was shooting arrows through hoops suspended in the air. The hoops were about the size of those on sugar hogsheads, fifteen to forty feet high, suspended from poles about twenty feet distance from each other, three or four in a line, so that an arrow correctly aimed would pass through all of them. The archers would pass the line of hoops on their skates with the greatest speed, and shoot their arrows with such correctness that they would pass through all the hoops.

It has been asserted by writers that Chinese women are in the habit of drowning a certain portion, say one third, of their female offspring in the rivers; but from the information that I have on the subject, I am fully convinced that it is not correct. I have frequently conversed with very respectable Chinese merchants on the subject, who appeared to revolt at the idea, and denied it altogether. The story most probably has arisen from the circumstance of the lower class of women in the suburbs of Canton having children by European or American fathers, and have exposed them in this manner to conceal it from their countrymen. I have on two instances seen infants floating down the river at Canton, and on viewing them was convinced that they were of this description.

There is one law of China which I will mention, though it may be well known to many. It is a fixed and unalterable law of the Empire that no foreign woman can be admitted into the country, on any account whatever. The consequence of a violation I do not exactly know, but am led to believe that if they were caught there, they would be put to death. The following account I had from good authority, and believe to be true. The captain of an English ship took his wife with him to Canton, disguised in man's dress. He managed the business with such secrecy that not one on board the ship knew anything of it, but considered her as a young man that was a passenger on board. While lying in Canton the captain invited several of the supercargoes with others to dine, and his wife was introduced to them as a young English gentleman who had come from Macau as a passenger. While sitting at dinner, it being very warm, she imprudently took off the handkerchief from her neck and threw open her shirt collar. When in the act of drinking, leaning her head back, something seemed to excite considerable surprise among the Chinese attendants, and caused much conversation between them, which the English captain, being ignorant of their language, could not find out the cause of, till one of them, who was his friend, asked him to step out, when he told him that the person he had introduced as an English gentleman was a woman. On the captain's expressing his surprise at the discovery, the Chinese told him that they were certain of the fact, for she had no protuberance in her throat — Adam's apple — and that there must be something done with her immediately or the mandarins, who had already been informed of it, would cut off her head. The English captain ordered his barge to be instantly manned and armed, and brought close along side of the ship. In the meantime, he contrived to have his wife leave the cabin when not observed by the company, and go into the gun-room, where he put her out of one of the ports into the boat, and they started for Macau, which is out of the Chinese jurisdiction. The mandarins in the two boats which were guarding the ship, immediately pursued them with all haste, but the Englishmen by their superiority in rowing were enabled to escape, and arrived at Macau, although the mandarins followed them for miles down the river before they gave up the pursuit.

There is one custom among the Chinese that heretofore

I have omitted to mention, which is the remarkably small feet of their women, caused by putting them in iron shoes when very young, which prevents their feet from growing. They are so crippled by this that it is with the greatest difficulty that they can walk. The first cause of this custom, I was told by the Chinese, arose from its being inflicted on the women as a punishment, on account of an attempt made by them in some early period of the nation to interfere with the affairs of government. It afterwards became a mark of honour among them, and remains so to the present day. None of their women except those who are of pure Chinese blood are permitted the honour of having small feet. It is not a custom among the Tartar women that reside within the Chinese empire.

I shall finish my remarks by saying that China is one of the most fertile and beautiful countries on the globe. It affords the fruits and vegetables of almost all climates; abounds with most of the manufactures that are useful to mankind; is favoured with the greatest conveniences by water transportation of any country; and finally, is the first for greatness, riches, and grandeur of any country ever known.

Departure from Canton; Trials at Sea; Capetown; The Boers, Hottentots, Bushmen, Kaffirs; Manners of the Dutch Colonists; Wild Beasts; Return to America

ON THE 27th of January, 1807, we left Macau Roads on our homeward passage by way of the Cape of Good Hope, off which we were beating from the first to the 12th of May before we rounded the Cape. On the latter date, and in sight of Table Hill, we were spoken by the celebrated Captain Surcouff, who has been so notorious in the East Indies for privateering out of Mauritius during the French revolution. He was then from St. Maloes (*Saint-Malo*) in France, and bound to Mauritius in a fast new sailing ship, mounting twenty twelve-pound cannon and had two hundred men.

Having been previously acquainted with him in Mauritius, I went on board his ship and spent several hours, and was treated very politely. He gave me false information that England and America were at war with each other, and advised me by all means to avoid all English ports. It was undoubtedly his policy to prevent my informing the English of his cruising about in those parts. With no certain news to the contrary at the time, I accordingly ran down for the coast of America in latitudes between 20° and 30° south, to avoid St. Helena. I was very much alarmed at the thought of being taken prisoner and losing all my property after such a long and tedious voyage, and consequently used every requisite precaution. We frequently met with westerly winds that lasted for many days together, which is very uncommon in these seas.

The false information which I received from Capt. Surcouff caused me a great deal of anxiety, and kept my mind in such a perpetual agitation that my spirits became depressed, and I lost my appetite to such a degree that I could scarcely eat any thing. My limbs became so benumbed that they were almost useless. Our vegetable and fresh provisions were exhausted, and the crew were worn down with fatigue and suffering incident to such a long voyage. Besides, they were all sick with a very troublesome and alarming disorder, the nature and cause of which was entirely unknown to me. They were in such a feeble state, that it was with the greatest difficulty they performed the common duties of the ship. My reflections at the time, and after my arrival home, were that I should rather prefer an honourable death than undergo such hardships and severe trials as I experienced during this passage.

We attempted to speak with every vessel that we saw to get information concerning the war, but they all appeared to shun us as much as possible, and we were unable to gain any intelligence till the 8th of July, when we saw a sail to the north east. We at first thought her to be a Bermudian privateer and called all hands to quarters, but on coming up with her, she proved to be the schooner *Eliza-and-Margaret* from Teneriffe, bound to Norfolk. From her we obtained the pleasing intelligence that there was no war, which news enlivened and animated our spirits very much. The captain treated us with every mark of politeness and humanity, and supplied us with a share of what little refreshments he had on board. We proceeded on our voyage in much better spirits, and on the 14th of July, when in latitude 33° 2' north and longitude 56° 37' west, we spoke the schooner *Hamilton* from Freeport,

Maine, Captain Luffden, who was very kind to us. He divided one bushel of potatoes with us, which was all he had, and gave us five or six pounds of butter which was likewise half he had, besides supplying us with every article in his power to make us comfortable. For these and all similar favours, I shall always hold myself bound in honour and gratitude publicly to acknowledge.

(Prior to the long Atlantic voyage home, Delano stopped at Cape-town. His report includes this final visit as well as several others made previously to the town and coast of the Cape of Good Hope.)

THE CAPE IS AN EXCEEDING GOOD PLACE to procure supplies on a passage either from or to India. The port afforded every sort of refreshment of the very best kind, and at very reasonable prices before the English took possession of it. Since then the maintenance of a numerous garrison and supplying provisions for the navy has contributed to make almost everything very dear. Yet the inhabitants of Capetown seem throughout better fed and housed than is generally the case in seaports.

Capetown is very regularly built, the streets being straight and spacious; the houses are genteel, most of them being white-washed, with their doors painted green, and are generally two stories high, flat-roofed, with an ornament in the centre of the front, and a platform before the door.

The established religion is Calvinist, or reformed. The Lutherans have a church, likewise the Moravians, and there is also a Methodist chapel. The Malay Mahometans being refused a church, perform their worship in the stone quarries at the head of Capetown. There are eleven hundred forty-five dwellings in the town, occupied by five thousand five hundred whites, and ten thousand blacks. The whole colony is estimated at twenty-two thousand Christians, who chiefly consist of Dutch, and have settled the country from six to eight hundred miles back of the Cape. The native Hottentots are mostly domesticated, and are chiefly servants to the Dutch.[45]

The citadel, which is at present called the Castle of Capetown, is a regular pentagon fort, with two outworks surrounded by a wet ditch. It is itself commanded by a rising ground, regularly sloped to the Devil's Hill. The English have filled the entire space of this slope with redoubts, batteries, and block-houses, and other improvements. A small battery commands the entrance of the bay, and a bastion runs along the water's edge within which are the powder-houses, ammunition, and other military store houses.

The inhabitants are in general an idle and ignorant set of men, very gross in their manners and behaviour, and books are very seldom a part of their household furniture. I do not wish by this assertion to be thought partial, for although this is the general trait of the inhabitants of this colony, yet there are many among them who would be an honour to any nation whatever. The inhabitants are composed of Europeans, mostly Dutch, Hottentots, Malays, and other natives of the East Indies. The proportion of slaves of both sexes to whites is two to one, but male slaves to male whites are five to one. The Dutch prefer the Malays and Kaffirs to the Hottentots for their service, which must arise from some unaccountable prejudice, as the two former are inferior in talents, and more capricious, cruel and revengeful than the latter.

The free coloured people of the town are chiefly mechanics and fishermen, and are industrious, supporting their families very comfortably.

The Dutch are very fond of dealing, and auctioneering appears to me to be carried on there by way of amusement. A person will buy in the morning, and put up the same article for sale in the afternoon, a great many of them spending their time sauntering from one public sale to another. They have retained their native fondness for gardening, and have transplanted almost every species of the fruit trees of Europe and the East Indies to the vicinity of the Cape with considerable success. As the climate is mild in the winter, there seldom being any frost, the most they have to fear is the sultry south east winds in the summer which parch the soil and blast all the leaves and fruit on the trees. To alleviate this, they plant oak fences round their vineyards, gardens and plantations.

During the periodical winds the town seems to be abandoned, all the doors and windows being shut to keep out the particles of dust and gravel which fly in suffocating clouds sometimes for twenty-four hours together until they are blown out to sea. These winds are likewise very detrimental to both man and animal. They weaken body and mind, and deaden the power of energy and activity. In the winter it rains in torrents, and in summer there is scarcely a shower to refresh the earth. An English officer remarked that the people who inhabit the valleys about Table Bay "were either in an oven, or at the funnel of a pair of bellows, or under a water spout."

Almond trees grow here in the most barren soils, and are reckoned very good. Tobacco that is planted here, if properly prepared, would fall little short in goodness to that of Virginia. All the male inhabitants of every station, and almost every age, smoke, for which reason the American tobacco is very dear, that of their own growth being only used by the most inferior classes of men.

The colony is divided into four classes, namely, the people of Capetown who are chiefly in the commercial line; the vine cultivators, who are of French extraction and have introduced the vine at the Cape, and have the best estates and houses; the grain farmer; and the grazier. The two latter are called boors (*Boers*), and are a wretched set of slothful, indolent men, living in miserable hovels, one apartment being often occupied by the family, cattle and Hottentot servants, and serving at the same time for parlour, kitchen and stable. The Boers themselves will not work any more than they can possibly help, but are very fond of hunting, and are generally attended by Hottentot boys to carry their muskets as the masters wish to enjoy their pipes on the way. The women are great drudges, as all the domestic concerns are entirely left to them. They are far from being neat and clean, either in their persons or households.

They have all kinds of quadrupeds. The black cattle are very good, and the sheep are remarkable for the size of their tails, one of which will commonly weigh seven or eight pounds.[46] I have seen boys of seven or eight years of age riding on their backs, four or five in a company. I was told this breed had been very good, but that the English had introduced the common kind among them shortly after they first took possession of the Cape during the last wars, which must have contaminated the breed, for I found the mutton to be coarse, rather ill flavoured, and the wool of an inferior quality. They use the skins chiefly to clothe their Hottentot and Malay slaves. The town carries on some small trade with the inhabitants along the coast, eastward and northward of the Cape, but it is inconsiderable, as the natives in the vicinity of the town have but few articles of traffic, and are savage and treacherous.

There are plenty of fish about the Cape a little distance off the coast. The whales that have been caught on this coast were all females of a small kind, yielding from six to ten tons of oil each. The bone is small and consequently not worth much. Other trade consists in the exportation of dried fruits, ostrich feathers, skins of wild beasts, and some ivory. This article has become rather scarce at the Cape as the elephants have been so hunted down within the limits of the colony that there are but few remaining; and the sea-cow, called by some the hippopotamus, the teeth of which is the best ivory, is still more scarce.

The people are very much in want of some of that enterprising spirit which signalizes the northern mercantile nations, to enable them to benefit by the many advantages which nature has given them. Education is very much neglected, as neither the civil nor ecclesiastical funds have as yet been sufficient to afford a public school. The lower class are destitute of any instruction, and the higher class send their children to be educated in Europe.

Their amusements consist generally in eating, drinking and smoking, and sometimes dancing and riding. They have been pretty free from taxes or assessments. On their first settling, a tax was introduced called the lion and tiger money, to pay the expenses of hunting down those animals who were at that time very obnoxious neighbours, harrassing their flocks, and used frequently to come into the town at night and endanger the lives of the people. But since these animals have become scarce, the money is allotted for the building of streets, roads and public edifices.

The Boers, even from the most distant parts of the colony, generally visit the town once a year to settle their business with their agents, and buy a supply of goods to serve them until their next visit. The Jews, who are numerous in the town, make a good business of taking the advantage of the credulity and stupidity of the Boers, and often cheat them in the most bare-faced manner. The inhabitants of Capetown are very courteous and hospitable to strangers, especially to English or Americans for whom they evince a great partiality.

I have made several excursions with ladies and gentlemen of the town who never failed in making their society very agreeable, and showing every advantage their vicinity afforded, especially their gardens which were elegantly planned and filled with the handsomest and most curious shrubs and flowers, and the choicest fruits, not even omitting the pine apple.

One of the most remarkable of my excursions was round the mountain called the Lion's Rump, in a waggon with two horses, by a road that runs parallel with the shore in a south and west direction, and skirting round the mountain almost to the summit. Whilst proceeding up this serpentine ascent, I calculated myself to be a thousand feet above the level of the sea, which appeared to be directly beneath us, and that if we were to slip we would seemingly have tumbled into it without stopping. In this manner the Dutch driver jolted us along, sometimes on the very brink of the mountain, and sometimes through openings cut through the rocks, several yards into the side of the mountain. I was extremely gratified by the extensive and majestic prospect of the ocean and the adjacent country, which appeared to the best advantage, and seemed more like a chart laid out under my feet than reality.

After spending some time in contemplating this sublime and awful scene, we made preparations to return to town. Down some of the descents the waggon would roll with great swiftness in spite of the exertions of the horses to prevent it, jolting at an incredible rate. Not being used to this species of riding, I got very uneasy, and told the driver to desist, as I would get out and walk; but he would occasionally tell me by way of comfort that we had not yet come to the worst places. At last I got out of the waggon for fear of being thrown down the hill. The Dutchman then fastened the wheels with chains so that they could not turn round, and let the waggon slide slowly down the steepest parts, whilst I followed on foot.

Excursions into the most distant parts of the colony, into Kaffir Land, and the part of the country inhabited by the Bosjesmans (*Bushmen*), are the greatest felicities of the Dutch peasantry, to accomplish which they are at considerable expense to procure waggons sufficiently strong, and stout oxen, to cross the deserts, ford rivers, and go through all the fatigues of travelling the most wild parts of the country. The brutality with which they use their oxen on some occasions is unparalleled even in the most uncivilized nations. On ascending steep places, or when the wheels of the waggon sink in mud, or between fragments of rocks, if the oxen do not immediately extricate themselves, the savage and impatient Boer deliberately takes out his knife and slashes away on the flanks and hind legs of the beasts, cutting scars of several inches in length, laying almost all the ribs bare, until the poor animals, in convulsive agonies, start the waggon and proceed on their way, where many of them drop down dead, after having for three or four hours marked their tracks with blood. Those that recover retain the scars of almost every cut they have received. This brutality is evident on all their team oxen. Some even boast of their being able to start their oxen by only whetting their knives on the wheels, their cattle having so frequently experienced this brutal practice. A Boer was recently displaying this experiment to some company he had in his waggon. The beasts started on hearing the knife clashing against the edge of the wheel and overturned them. One of the company had a leg broken, which unfortunately happened not to be the owner of the team. The dangers and difficulties of the roads even in the most frequented parts of the colony are but very little attended to — every one getting over them as well as he can, without troubling himself any further.

THE HOTTENTOTS, THOUGH VERY LOW in the scale of humanity, have often been misrepresented, and made worse than they really are. They are a mild, quiet and timid people, perfectly harmless, and though very phlegmatic, they are very affectionate to each other. They have little of the kind of art and cunning that most savage nations possess, and their indolence seems to be a disease, of which terror alone can cure them. Though they are great gluttons, they stand hunger with patience; and when they cannot procure victuals they console themselves by sleeping.

The external appearance of the Hottentots is far from being prepossessing. Their faces are ugly, having high prominent cheek bones, and a narrow pointed chin, forming a triangle. Their eyes are long and narrow, at a great distance apart, and their eye-lids, instead of forming an angle next the nose like Europeans, are rounded into one another like the Chinese. Their colour is a yellowish brown, similar to that of a faded leaf; their teeth are very white, but their hair is of a singular kind, growing irregularly in lumps on the head, and when cut short is not unlike a hard shoe brush. When it is allowed to grow it twists into small curls, and hangs like coarse fringe down their necks. The rest of their bodies are well proportioned and slender; their feet and hands small. They have, when young, a weak and effeminate appearance, but grow old very soon.

It is seldom the case that a Hottentot lives to the age of sixty. They are almost all within the district of the colony in the service of the Dutch peasantry, who in the remote parts use them in the most barbarous manner, flogging them most brutally with thongs of hides, and firing small shot into their legs and thighs on the most trivial occasions. Nor is it infrequent that the Boer punishes a Hottentot with death when enraged. Some have a very ridiculous manner of punishing them, by flogging not by the number of strokes, but by time, reckoning as many pipes of tobacco as he deems the crime deserves, which he deliberately smokes whilst inflicting the punishment. Those that hire themselves out from year to year as labourers, are not much better situated than those in actual servitude. Their salary is pitiful, consisting of an ox or a dozen sheep of about six or eight dollars value for the whole year; and this trifle is withheld from them on the most frivolous occasions. If an ox or a sheep is missing, the Hottentot must replace it, and dares not leave the service until he has earned the value of it. And frequently a bill for tobacco or brandy is brought against him to the whole amount of his income. This treatment most naturally contributes in a great measure to their depopulation.

Their marriages are scarce and seldom produce more than two or three children, and many of their women are barren. Probably the time is not very distant when this wretched and oppressed tribe will be totally extinct. I was told that they are very voracious. After the animal they fix upon is slain, they cut it up into large steaks, into which they place the edge of their knife and cut in a spiral manner to the centre, producing strings of meat two or three yards long, which they coil up and broil on the ashes; this at the same time serves in lieu of salt. When the meat is hardly warmed through, each takes a string in both hands, and soon gets through a yard of flesh. In this manner it is not infrequent for ten of them to devour a middle sized ox, and after the meal highly improve the polish of their skins by wiping their hands on their bodies. These frequent greasy baths, together with the dust and dirt they gather, at length covers the body with a thick coating of black, which entirely hides the real colour of the skin. The young peasantry very frequently make free with the Hottentot women. These illicit connections have produced a numerous and strong set of men called bastards. These are not ill featured, are active and industrious, and generally good drivers.

THE BUSHMEN ARE VERY MUCH LIKE the Hottentots, excepting that they are more active and alert both in mind and body, and not so much inclined to idleness. Although they are in continual dread of being surprised and taken by peasants, they are cheerful and lively, often spending their nights in dancing, and keeping close in their huts in the day time. They neither cultivate the ground or keep cattle, but show great sagacity in their manner of catching game. This they effect by digging pits and covering them over with small sticks and bushes, piling stones on each side of these traps, and placing sticks with black ostrich feathers in rows, to hinder the game from going any way than the one leading to the pit.

The Dutch are greatly prejudiced against them. The name Bushman seems universally to excite disagreeable sensations, and is the terror of the women and children. A peasant talks as coolly of shooting a couple of Bushmen as he would of a pair of partridges. These wretched creatures, when oppressed by hunger, sally forth in bodies, and at the peril of their lives, seize cattle to supply the wants of their little families, and often fight most courageously with poisoned arrows and darts, as they know if they are taken, they are put to death without judge or jury, whether guilty or not. Their plundering expeditions are conducted with regularity. They divide themselves into two parties, one to seize the cattle and the other to harrass the pursuers; and if the latter party is defeated, the former pierce as many of the cattle as they can get at with their spears and arrows. Both Hottentots and Bushmen are, like other savages, remarkably quick-sighted in discovering game or anything at a distance. This may arise from continual practice, just as the experienced seaman will distinguish a sail long before a passenger can see any thing of it.

THE KAFFIRS ARE VERY DIFFERENT from their neighbours in colour and manners. They are of a glossy brown, verging on black, their face and head as well proportioned as an European's; only they have thick lips and flat noses, and are a species of negroes. The men are tall, athletic and manly in their appearance, with open good natured countenances, indicating their being strangers to suspicion and treachery. Their women are shorter and stouter than the young female Hottentots, and not so delicately formed; but their lively and good natured faces, and sprightly manners make them by far the most agreeable. The people are warlike and industrious, and manufacture all their arms and utensils themselves, and smaller articles such as beads and trinkets that would not disgrace an European market.

They are very much attached to their cattle and dogs, with whom they converse very affectionately. These in turn are much attached to their respective owners. Their dress is similar to that of the Hottentots, consisting only of a skin hung over their shoulders, and some trifling ornaments, with a narrow belt, generally of a jackal skin; the women wearing, beside a calf skin over their shoulders, an apron of about nine inches long and four or five broad, which is always adorned in their grandest manner with brass buttons and trinkets. And on their heads they wear close leather caps, which they take great pains to decorate with buckles, shells and buttons. The men paint their faces with red ochre, and tattoo their skins. They are good hunters, but what is most singular, that though they inhabit the sea coast, they have not the least idea of building canoes or rafts for fishing or trade.

In 1796 a vessel from India cast away on a part of the coast occupied by the colonists. The peasantry from all the neighbouring parts flocked to the wreck, not to assist the unfortunate sufferers, but to plunder everything they could get to shore; and it is a fact that they even killed one of their own party who was striving to save a few things for the captain and officers.

In June 1797, an American ship ran ashore on the coast of Kaffir. When the crew and passengers, about sixty in number, got on shore, they were surrounded by the Kaffirs, and expected every minute to be slaughtered by these savages, when to their great astonishment, they gave orders for an ox to be roasted and distributed among the sufferers. But the Kaffirs could not withstand the temptation of cutting off their metal buttons, which they did without much ceremony. They then conducted them to the houses of the colonists, and never touched any of the rest of their property except a just demand of five or six dollars from the captain for their trouble, and an equal sum from each of the crew. It would be an object greatly to be wished that some of the more civilized inhabitants of sea coasts would follow this example of the Kaffirs.

Yet their generosity is not to be trusted any more than other savages. When I was in India I saw an account of the ship *Grosvenor* that was wrecked on this coast on her return from India. She split on a rock, and the greatest part of the crew and passengers got on shore; among the latter were several ladies of distinction, who were returning to England. The Kaffirs stripped them of almost everything they had on after some resistance from the crew who were soon overpowered and cut to pieces by the Kaffirs, excepting four or five, who after many difficulties and dangers got to the Cape where they related the particulars of that unhappy circumstance.

They said the ladies had tried to conceal their jewels in their hair, but the Kaffirs soon found out this stratagem and cut every lock of their hair off; and after stripping them naked, dragged them off with them, probably to their kraals or villages where they kept them to cohabit with. Several waggons were fitted out from the Cape to go in search of them, but all their inquiries and searches were in vain, for they were never after heard of. I have since heard that about fifteen years after the *Grosvenor*'s shipwreck, several grown up mulatto boys had been seen about that coast, and it was strongly conjectured that these lads were sons to the above mentioned ladies by their Kaffir gallants.

I VISITED THE VINEYARD of Constantia in one of my excursions into the country, and was very much delighted with the neatness and elegance of the buildings, and the manner the lands were laid out, both for utility and pleasure. The vintners had all the appearance of opulence, were polite and hospitable, and knew better how to enjoy life than their fellow colonists, the grain farmers and graziers. I drank of the wine on the spot, and found it the most exquisite I had ever tasted. It is of an oily nature, so rich that more than one or two glasses would satiate, and can only be used sparingly as a choice liquor, and not as a beverage. This plantation is celebrated all over the world for its wines.

Wood is very scarce in the vicinity of Cape Town. Some families have two or three slaves constantly employed in gathering faggots for the kitchen, which is the only fire they keep in the house. This method, or buying it by cart loads, is equally expensive, and will amount in a moderate family from a hundred to a hundred and fifty dollars annually. But in the interior there are many useful sorts of wood and timber growing in extensive forests, but it is very dear on account of the difficulty and expense of the land carriage.

I have seen many wild beasts at the Cape, such as lions, tigers, leopards, zebras, and several different species of antelope, and many others. The elephant, the largest and most docile of the quadrupeds, was once very numerous, but now they are very scarce within the limits of the colony. They generally keep in droves, each having its female to which they are very much attached. When a male or female is killed or taken, its companion becomes mournful, and even comfortless; it leaves the drove and rambles about by itself, and often dies of grief. These animals are chiefly caught in pits covered with branches, and some of their favourite fruits or leaves are placed in the center to entice them to walk over and fall into the pit. By this means they become a less dangerous game than by hunting them, which had often proved fatal to the hunters; for as soon as one is wounded, it faces round and furiously strikes about with its trunk, and though clumsy in appearance, is considerably active. They can likewise be taken by stratagem and domesticated, by letting a tame female go among a drove of wild ones. She will seldom fail of coaxing a male back with her to her stable, in which the visitor is immediately secured and reduced by hunger to obedience.

There is a little brown bird of the species of the cuckoo, called by the farmers the honey bird, from its pointing out and conducting people to the nests of bees by a chirping and whistling noise. It flies from bush to bush and flutters its wings until the discovery is made, for which service it receives a part of the booty, which it could not procure himself. This unaccountable bird is used with the same deference by the colonists as the robin red breast is with us, and appears to be conscious of this patronage, showing no timidity on the approach of a person.

There is another bird which is held sacred both by the

colonists and Hottentots. This bird is called the secretary bird, from the feathers on its crest, which they say looks like a pen stuck in the side of its head, like a merchant's clerk.

Snakes are numerous and more or less poisonous, and some are very large. When one of them has coiled itself around any thing, the Hottentots will dip the end of a stick in a dark brown liquid, extracted from tobacco, which they call tobacco oil, and hold it to the mouth of the snake, who always puts its tongue out when enraged, and as soon as it takes the liquid it falls into convulsions and dies, appearing shrunk and hard as if dried in the sun. The Hottentots say the strongest poison may be extracted from tobacco, but they do not rub it on the points of their arrows as it loses its strength by being exposed to the air.

The poison with which the Kaffirs and wild Hottentots envenom the points of their arrows, is extracted from a spider of a very large and ugly species, which lives in the holes that it makes in the earth, and covers over with a strong web, like a trap door, which it opens to watch for its prey, and shuts at the approach of noise.

ON THE 26TH OF JULY 1807, we arrived safely in Boston harbour, after an absence of nearly four years. Myself and crew were so much worn out that it was with the greatest care and attention that we were enabled to recover our health again. They all recovered however, except one, who died soon after he landed with a languishing complaint.

It is worthy of being remarked that during the three voyages of the *Perseverance*, and in three times circumnavigating the globe, which occupied more than seven years, she never touched the ground.

Voyage to the Island of St. Bartholomews in 1810; Hurricane; Passage Home

CHAPTER XXVIII

(The voyage to the West Indies concerned an "alleged violation" of revenue laws. The difficulties encountered appear to stem either from misunderstandings and omissions on both sides, or more likely, from an attempt on the part of local officials to swindle the American ship, taking her and her cargo. The Perseverance *was seized, but escaped from St. Bartholomews (St. Barthelemy, Leeward Islands) under fire while sustaining damage to sails and rigging, but with no loss of life. The final segment of this voyage is included here.)*

AFTER WE got clear of the port, and sent the people and every thing that did not belong to us on shore, we steered for what is called the Sambraro Passage, repairing the damages we had received as we proceeded on. It was a very fortunate circumstance for us that the king's schooner, which guarded the island, sailed the day before on a look-out to windward, and there was no vessel of force in the harbour to follow us. These considerations were taken into view at the time of fixing on the plan of going to sea. They, however, on finding that we had got clear of the batteries, armed a schooner in the best manner they could, and put on board her thirty-five men and sent in pursuit of us; but either by accident or by design, I do not know which, they missed us.

On the fourth day after we left St. Barthelemy we experienced a tremendous hurricane, which was more terrible to us than the fire of the batteries we had escaped from. We were in latitude between 24° and 25° when it commenced, the wind being at that time east-north-east. The gale increased gradually, and the wind hauled to the eastward and south-ward, continuing to freshen till twelve o'clock in the day, when it hauled to the south-east, and blew with such violence as to reduce us to a two reefed main topsail, fore-sail and foretopmast-staysail, the ship right before the wind, and two good men at the wheel. The wind hauled, so that at four o'clock, it was south, and increased to such a degree that it was thought not safe to start tack, sheet, or brace. About this time the ship took a proud yaw, and the foretopmast-staysail was suddenly filled with wind and split into many pieces. This deprived us of the best sail we had to keep the ship be-fore the wind. The wind kept hauling and increasing till sun-set, and there was no abatement till after twelve o'clock at night, when I think it was hardest. At four a.m. the wind be-gan to abate, and at eight the weather was moderate. I consid-ered it almost a miracle that the fore-sail and maintopsail stood through the gale, but they were both nearly new, and the latter was very small. This was almost the only time that I ever commanded a vessel at sea when I had no other resort in my mind if the course we were pursuing should fail. For had the ship broached, that is, come to the wind against the helm, she must inevitably have gone to the bottom. During the gale the whole crew performed their duty in every thing that was required in the best manner that men could do.

After we had weathered this gale, we proceeded on our passage and arrived safe in Boston in October. I entered a pro-test in the custom-house against the conduct of the govern-ment of St. Barthelemy, on which evidence, a new register and other necessary papers were granted for the ship.

(Delano concludes his chronicle with a brief narrative of his earliest voyage, going back to September 1779, when he was 16.)

I SAILED FROM BOSTON ON a cruise in a privateer ship called the *Mars*, mounting twenty-two guns, fitted out by Mr. David Sears of Boston, and commanded by Captain Gilbert Ash. The first lieutenant was Josiah Roberts, my fellow officer in the *Massachusetts*.

In seven days after leaving port, we experienced a distressing gale of wind which wrecked almost every vessel that was afloat from Jamaica to the Western Islands. We lost our mizenmast, sprung the mainmast below the top, and the foremast below the deck, hove overboard nine of our waist guns, which were fortified nine pounders, and many other heavy articles, and cut away four anchors from the bows, in order to make the ship scud before the wind. After the gale was over, all the repairs that could be were made at sea, and the ship continued to cruise till winter, when an attempt was made to get into the port we sailed from. We beat about on the coast of America the greatest part of that terrible winter of 1779–1780, losing sails, rigging, spars and men almost every day. The latter part of the winter, we took a privateer snow of fourteen guns, belonging to Liverpool, England, which was the first and only prize we took during the cruise. We then steered for Martinico, one of the West India islands (*probably Martinique, Windward Islands*), where we arrived after suffering every hardship that was possible for men to endure. It will ever be my wish that all privateers may be as unsuccessful as the *Mars* was.

(*Delano notes several other voyages to the West Indies, Spain, Ireland, and Portugal in his youth.*)

My first voyage as commander was from Duxbury in 1786, in a schooner belonging to my uncle, Joseph Drew. He was always kind and friendly to me, and I shall ever acknowledge my obligations, gratitude, and sincere regard for him as

THE SALEM PRIVATEER *GRAND TURK*, AS DEPICTED ON A LIVERPOOL
WARE PUNCH BOWL. (COURTESY OF THE PEABODY ESSEX MUSEUM)

long as I live. He was benevolent in the extreme, to all descriptions of people, and died eight or nine years since, the most universally beloved, perhaps, of any man of the age in Duxbury. I sailed for Cayenne (*in French Guiana*), made the north cape of the river Amazon, steered down the coast in from seven to fifteen fathoms of water, and from five to ten miles off shore, till we arrived at Cayenne, which is an island separated from the continent by a narrow belt of water not more than half a mile broad. The country along this coast abounds with the greatest variety of wild beasts, beautiful birds, serpents and reptiles of any country I was ever acquainted with.

I afterwards sailed in command of several vessels in voyages to the West Indies, during which I visited Cayenne, Demerara, Issiquibo, Trinidad, Tobago, St. Eustatia, Cape Francais, Puerto Rico, St.-Martin, and several other ports in the West Indies.

Capt. Amasa Delano.

Selections from a Biographical Sketch

BY AN ANONYMOUS FRIEND OF AMASA DELANO

MASA DELANO was born in Duxbury, Massachusetts, one of the oldest towns in the late colony of New Plymouth, on February 21st, 1763. His parents were respectable, and connected with the ancient families of that place. His mother was a Drew, and his maternal grandmother a Soule, both of which are among the oldest and most influential families of that ancient town. His father, Samuel Delano, was, with his brother Amasa, in the military service under George II in the war with the French and Indians in 1757–1759. This Amasa was an officer in Rogers' Rangers, a corps well known in those days. Though very young, he was much esteemed for his bravery and good conduct, and at the age of twenty was honoured with a lieutenancy. He was with a party of rangers on an expedition near the Canada lines, which being led astray by their guides, were lost in the wilderness. They were obliged to separate and to hunt for food.

The party commanded by Amasa consisted of eighteen privates and one officer besides himself. They were reduced to the greatest extremity, and were compelled to eat an Indian child which they met in the woods. They soon came to an Indian settlement, and their conduct with regard to the child being known, they were massacred in a most horrid manner. The writer of this journal was named for this unfortunate uncle.

His father, Samuel, was the youngest of the two brothers, and was a sergeant in Captain Gamaliel Bradford's company in Nova Scotia, Ticonderoga, Crown Point, Fort William Henry, etc. After the peace of 1763 he worked at the ship carpenter's business, and was a master builder for many years. He was with our army at Roxbury in 1776 when the British troops had possession of Boston.

In early life, Amasa, whose adventures are here related, was much accustomed to the salt water, and by the frequent practice of swimming, became almost amphibious. At the age of five or six years he could swim and dive under water in a most surprising manner. Even in the coldest season, he has been known to dive into the water like a sea fowl sporting in its natural element, and it was said he was more expert and daring in the water than the natives of the West Indies, islands he often visited between the ages of 15 and 35.

We are obliged to state that Captain Delano, when very young, was averse to school and study. His fondness for active scenes will account in part for this aversion, but the idle gossiping stories of domestics of the severity of schoolmasters had a share in giving him a dislike to these nurseries of useful knowledge and good morals. When he came to years of reflection, he regretted his early prejudices, and is entitled to much credit for applying himself afterwards to those branches of ordinary learning which are necessary to render a man qualified for the common and active pursuits of the world.

At an early age Delano was particularly fond of fishing and gunning, and was considered very expert, both as matter of sport and business. Sea fowl are numerous about the beach and bay and salt-water creeks in Duxbury, and young Delano was generally successful as well as enterprising in attacking the game.

In 1772 the family removed to Braintree where his father attended to ship building, supposing that the vicinity of the place to Boston would render the business more certain and lucrative. There they remained only about two years, as the interruption of navigation, occasioned by the disputes between Great Britain and the colonies, operated unfavourably to his employment. They returned to Duxbury.

The citizens of Duxbury were unanimously opposed to the measures of the British ministry, and discovered a great ardour in the cause of liberty. Delano would not rest easy at home. Though only about 12 years of age, he visited the camp at Roxbury, and spent much time there, witnessing the military movements of our infant army.

In the summer of 1777, at a time when his father was a prisoner on board the *Rainbow*, a British man-of-war, information was received that Burgoyne had advanced from Montreal to Lake Champlain with a large army, had taken Ticonderoga, and was marching towards Albany, probably with a plan to join the British army from New York, somewhere on the Hudson River. The people in the northern states were greatly and justly alarmed. New recruits were called for by the provincial congress, and great numbers marched to join the army under General Gates to oppose Burgoyne. Young Delano, then only fourteen years, came forward to enlist.

At this time he marched to Boston with many others of his fellow townsmen, under the command of Captain Joseph Wadsworth of Duxbury, then of the Continental Army, a brave and meritorious officer. But on his arrival in Boston, he met his father returning from captivity at Halifax, who, to the boy's great mortification, insisted on his leaving this military corps and accompanying him home to Duxbury. Being under age, he was obliged to submit. He was very much disappointed and mortified in being thus deprived of an opportunity of performing the daring feats of a true blooded Yankee.

It is believed he passed the winter in attending a private school, for at this age he had become ambitious of acquiring information from books as well as from the world. The following summer, at age fifteen, he served several months in the militia, under General Heath, and belonged to the troops who guarded some captured British soldiers at Prospect Hill in Cambridge.

In the summer of 1779, in company with several other young men, Delano went to Boston, and entered on board the privateer *Mars*, and sailed one cruise in her which continued till the following spring. The inclemency of the season was the cause of much exposure and suffering, and great complaint was made, we know not how justly, of the severity and cruelty of the officers of the privateer. His spirits and constitution seemed to be broken down, and his health was so much injured that it was many months after his return before he recovered his former strength and activity. For a considerable period he remained at home, more contentedly than formerly. Afterwards, his wishes led him again to the ocean. He was very averse, however, from privateering, and always spoke with decision against the practice.

He now, in 1781, entered on board a merchant ship, the *Russell*, belonging to Messrs. R. & J. Leach of Salem, and made a voyage to Cape Francois in the West Indies. The French fleet, under command of Count D'Grasse was then in that port, and he assisted in towing the fleet out of that place, when it sailed to the Chesapeake. An embargo had been laid on all merchant vessels then at Cape Francois, which lasted for six weeks. The season proved very sickly, and great numbers died of the prevailing fever. It was supposed that all tropical fruit was injurious, and, if used at all, on this account, was eaten with great caution and very sparingly. But Delano is said to have subsisted almost entirely on it, and to have eaten it in great quantities at all times without any bad effects. He was alike careless in guarding against wet and cold, exposing himself to the severest weather without additional garments. And this manner of living seemed rather to strengthen than to impair his constitution.

Upon his return from another voyage to the West Indies that year, Delano laboured with his father in ship building. They built the brig *Peacock* in 1782, for E. Parsons Esq. of Boston, and in this vessel he afterwards sailed to Martinique and Puerto Rico in the West Indies, to Virginia, and to Bilboa in Spain. While on board the *Peacock* in the harbour of Boston, he narrowly escaped drowning, having fallen overboard in the night, as he was on deck endeavouring to keep the vessel secure during a very violent storm. The *Peacock* was loaded and nearly ready for sea. The wind, high in the latter part of the day, increased to a gale, so that a third anchor was taken on board from the wharf, and the topmasts and yards were taken down; and as there was no apparatus or materials for cooking, the captain and all the crew, except Delano, and one other hand, went on shore for the night. It was supposed the brig was securely anchored and that it would not be necessary for any more crew to remain on board.

After Delano and the other man had been asleep a short time, they were awakened by a violent shock against their vessel, which they found, on going up deck, was occasioned by a cartel sloop then lately from Halifax running against them. The gale had increased and the sloop had been driven from her moorings. The anchor of the sloop caught hold of the *Peacock*'s, and she rode alongside. Every attempt was made to disengage the cartel from the brig, but without effect. The people belonging to the sloop, however, did not offer to assist.

When it was found that the brig could not be parted from the sloop, Delano placed fenders between the vessels to prevent all damage possible. He determined they should keep a watch on deck through the night, and he offered to take his turn first. The force of the wind was so great that the ropes which fastened the fenders were broken repeatedly. Delano stepped on the gunwale of the sloop and replaced them.

By the violence of the gale, the sloop several times sheered off and then came alongside the brig again with a great shock. Delano was standing on the gunwale of the *Peacock* and had hold of a rope which was fast behind him, waiting for the cartel to approach, and intending to jump onto her bow. As he was about to do this, on her being driven near again, the rope he had in his hand gave way and he was precipitated head foremost into the water under the bows of the sloop; and in this fall he lost his hold of the rope. He had on at the time a great coat and thick heavy boots. His great exertion was to keep above water; and he says he was particularly careful not to open his mouth so as to take in salt water. He could think of no assistance to be had from any quarter. His companion was in bed, and probably asleep. The people belonging to the cartel were also probably asleep, as they had not been on deck for some time. The wind was so violent that he knew it would be in vain to arouse them by his voice. And he also feared to shout lest the water should fill his mouth and throat.

Whilst thus tossed about by wind and waves, his hand struck a rope which was the stopper for the anchor, and was fastened to the sloop's cat-head, so he could keep himself above water long enough to cry out. He remained in this precarious situation some time, but he found himself unable to make anyone hear. Nor could he get on board either vessel, though he attempted to haul himself up by the rope in his hand: his clothes were too heavy, and his boots filled with water. After some time, however, with his feet against the bow of the sloop, he swung himself so as to catch hold of the brig's main chains, and thus reached the deck of his own vessel again. This was, indeed, a wonderful escape.

After this he sailed in the *Peacock* again to the West Indies and back. During the winter, the *Peacock* was frozen up and lay at Fredericksburg. As soon as possible she came down the Rappahannock River and the bay of Chesapeake in company with the brig *Thomas* of Boston, and the private armed ship *Iris* of Salem. They were chased into Yorktown by the *Eagle*, an English sixty-four gun ship, and a frigate. There they beheld the awful devastations of war. This was the place occupied by the British troops under Lord Cornwallis when they were captured in October 1781. Though Delano was fond of adventure, yet he did not delight in the misery of his fellow men, nor was he indifferent to the evils and calamities of war.

In March, the *Peacock*, *Thomas*, and *Iris* left the harbour and passed Cape Henry. The British ships of war could not fetch by the cape on account of a high northerly wind, and the Americans returned and anchored in Hampton Roads. Two days after they left the cape, they experienced a very heavy gale, and the *Iris* was probably foundered, as she was never heard of afterwards. Off Cape Finistiere, the *Peacock* spoke a Swedish ship from which they first received the news of peace.

(*From 1783–1886, Delano worked as a ship builder.*) Sometimes he wrought with his father, and sometimes was alone the master builder. In this time he built several vessels at Duxbury, and at Brunswick in the District of Maine. (*Delano made several successful voyages in 1786 to the West Indies, and the following year he took command of the ship Jane bound for Cork, Ireland, and thence to St. Ubes, Portugal. The ship's owner-merchant and supercargo were, apparently, less than honest, and young Delano encountered many difficulties in carrying out his mission.*) On his return from St. Ubes to Boston, he was cast away on Cape Cod on December 28, 1788. He lost everything he had; his people were destitute and penniless, and it was not in his power to afford them any pecuniary assistance. He was greatly distressed and mortified at his situation, for he was generous, humane and honest. He was soon after engaged in another undertaking, which was also attended by disappointment and mortification. He undertook to raise and repair a vessel lying in Taunton river for some merchants in Boston. It was found that the vessel had lain a long time under water and was more damaged than he had supposed. His employers were not very well satisfied with the proceedings. But their dissatisfaction was not greater than his regret that they were disappointed. It was a most fatiguing job to him, and it was believed he omitted nothing on his part to make the affair profitable. Though conscious of no immorality of conduct, he was so affected by the disapprobation of those by whom he had been employed, that he appeared greatly discouraged, and was almost ready, he has said, to give up all enterprize of the sort.

Fortunately for him, however, the ship *Massachusetts* was soon to be launched and sail for Canton in China. It was a large ship of 900 tons, built at Quincy. Here begins the journal of his voyages and adventures as given in this volume.

Notes

CHAPTER I

1. (p. 5) "The ship *Massachusetts* [was] almost eight hundred tons burthen, the largest vessel constructed to that date in an American shipyard." *The Maritime History of Massachusetts, 1783–1860*, Samuel Eliot Morison (Boston: Houghton Mifflin Company: 1941), p. 52.

2. (p. 7) For more information about Amasa Delano and crew, see *Seafaring America*, Alexander Laing (New York: American Heritage Publishing Co., 1974).

CHAPTER II

3. (p. 25) The "large blue pigeon" is possibly the Wompoo Pigeon, the Rose-crowned Pigeon, or the Purple Crowned Pigeon. These three are also found in the Molucca Islands and New Guinea; the Rose-Crowned in Timor as well. See *What Bird Is That? A Guide to the Birds of Australia*, Neville W. Cayley (Sydney: Angus and Robertson, Ltd., 1935), p. 20. It may also be the Crowned Pigeon (Goura victoria). "The largest surviving pigeon is the Goura, or Crowned Pigeon, of New Guinea, ...the home of the three species of crowned pigeons; the lacy crowns were hunted as much as the Birds of Paradise." *Living Birds of the World*, E. Thomas Gilliard (New York: Doubleday, 1958), p. 199. From an illustration on p. 39 of *The Doomsday Book of Animals*, David Day, Viking, 1981, one also wonders if Delano may have seen an immature or female Choiseul Crested Pigeon (Microgoura meeki), extinct c. 1910, known in the Western Pacific, in the Solomon Islands, Melanesia.

CHAPTER III

4. (p. 42) The "flying fox" is also called Fox Bat, any of numerous tropical Old World bats belonging to the family Pteropodidae (q.v.). See also Fruit Bat. *The New Encyclopedia Britannica*, Vol. 4, Micropedia, Ready Reference, 15th ed.

CHAPTER IV

5. (p. 48) "The inhabitants of New Guinea are Melanesians, Negritos, and Papuans." *New Columbia Encyclopedia*, 4th ed.

6. (p. 49) Bird of Paradise: "Family, Paradisaeidae; 43 species in 18 genera. They are found in the Moluccas, New Guinea, Australia." *The Encyclopedia of Birds*, Perrins and Middleton (New York: Facts on File Publications, 1986), p. 436.

7. (p. 50) The Rhea is "frequently called the South American ostrich. Ana-

tomically and taxonomically rheas are quite distinct from the ostrich" of Africa. Perrins and Middleton, *The Encyclopedia of Birds*, p. 21.

8. (p. 60) McClure's Inlet or Gulf, West New Guinea, is now known as Teluk Berau (*National Geographic Atlas of the World*, 6th ed.)

9. (p. 68) William Dampier (1652–1715). English navigator, hydrographer, buccaneer, pilot. *Chamber's Biographical Dictionary*, rev. ed. See also notes 35 and 36, Chapter XVII.

10. (p. 76) See *Physician For Ships; Containing Medical Advice for Seamen and Other Persons at Sea on the Treatment of Diseases and on the Preservation of Health in Sickley Climates*, Usher Parsons, M.D. (Boston: Charles C. Little and James Brown, 1842). A great many fevers are discussed, ameliorating methods described, but there were no cures. If a person were already weak or malnourished, death was not infrequent. According to Parsons, "The 'intermittent' fever…is the most common fever in tropical climates. It is not frequent at sea, but generally attacks men when they got into harbor, particularly such as are sent on the business of *wooding* and *watering*, and are thus exposed to the noxious effluvia by which it is produced." (p. 14).

The transmission of malaria by the Anopheles mosquito was not recognized for nearly 100 years after Delano's day. Many other illnesses also described as "fevers" were various forms of dysentery. Typhoid was common, as was cholera. Public sanitation and knowledge of public health were still primitive nearly everywhere, even up to the late nineteenth century.

CHAPTER V

11. (p. 79) See also *Voyage of H.M.S.* Pandora*, Despatched to Arrest the Mutineers of the* Bounty *in the South Seas, 1790–91*, being the narratives of Captain Edward Edwards, R.N., commander, and George Hamilton, surgeon; with an introduction and notes by Basil Thomson (London: Francis Edwards, 1915).

12. (p. 81) For a full account see *The Mutiny on Board H.M.S.* Bounty, William Bligh, Lieutenant (New York: The New American Library of World Literature, Inc., 1961). On the subject of the *Bounty* there are fiction and nonfiction writings too numerous to mention.

13. (p. 91) Australia's Great Barrier Reef. *Pandora*'s wreck was found in 1957 by the National Geographic Society's Luis Marden. See "In *Bounty*'s Wake: Finding the Wreck of H.M.S. *Pandora*," *National Geographic Magazine*, Vol. 168, no. 4, October 1985, pp. 423–451.

14. (p. 93) See also Pandora*'s Last Voyage*, Geoffrey Rawson (London: Longmans, 1963). This book details the search for *Bounty*, the persons involved, and elaborates on the history of the Pitcairn colony.

Notes

15. (p. 116) For illustrated modern references to Pitcairn Island and its people, see *National Geographic Magazine* issues Jan. 1942, Jan. 1949, Dec. 1957, Oct. 1983, Oct. 1985.

CHAPTER VI

16. (p. 124) See Dea Birkett, "Fletcher Christian's Children," *New York Times Magazine*, 8 December 1991, p. 66. Subtitle: "For descendants of the famous mutineers, life on Pitcairn Island is far from paradise."

CHAPTER VII

17. (p. 131) 1983 estimated population of Jakarta city: 7,636,000. *Concise Columbia Encyclopedia*, 2nd ed.

CHAPTER VIII

18. (p. 134) Borneo is the third largest island after Greenland and New Guinea. Australia is classified as a continent.

19. (p. 139) Jolo or Sulu Island. The town of Jolo, a walled city, was long the capital of Sulu chieftans, and Mohammedan since the 14th century. *Columbia Lippincott Gazetteer of the World*, 1962.

CHAPTER IX

20. (p. 141) Birds' nest soup: The nest of various small swifts (genes Collocalia) of southern Asia and neighboring islands that is made chiefly of the dried glutinous secretion of the salivary glands of the birds and is used in making soup. *Webster's Third New International Dictionary*, unabridged, 1986.

21. (p. 142) In *Voyages* there are numerous references to provisioning of turtles and tortoises. These animals became a major source of protein for colonies of people, seafarers, and commercial processors, early in history. In many places, such as Cayman Islands and others in the West Indies, rookeries have become extinct, the few remaining turtles moving in search of nesting sites. The survival of many turtle species now depends upon the education of human populations and tough laws to control all forms of commercial exploitation.

For example, "the major international markets for meat and soupstock are the Federal Republic of Germany, the United Kingdom, and Japan....The major consumers of leather are France, Italy, and Japan....The Hawksbill turtles have been variously exploited for thousands of years as one culture after another coveted the horny scutes of their shells for making tortoiseshell jewelry and objects of art....[It is] also hunted for its eggs, leather, and for immature specimens which are stuffed, lacquered, and sold to tourists." *Biology and Conservation of Sea Turtles*, ed. Karen A. Bjorndal (Washington, D.C.:

Smithsonian Institution in cooperation with World Wildlife Fund, Inc., 1981), pp. 185–186.

See also *New York Times* articles by Keith Schneider, March 21, 1991, p. 12A; and by Keith Bradsher, May 17, 1991, p. 1A. Stories report on continuing harvests of hawksbills, cruel and inhumane methods of harvest, international commercial disagreements, particularly between the United States and Japan, and the need for action to prevent possible extinction of hawksbills and other species of turtles.

See also James Brooke, "Brazilians Take Pains To Save Sea Turtles," *New York Times*, Environment Section, 17 December 1991, p. C4. Subtitle: "Former poachers now gather eggs for hatching." A report on the 11-year history of Project Tamar at Praia do Forte.

CHAPTER XI

22. (p. 169) In the entry Delano, Amasa, the 5th edition of *The New Columbia Encyclopedia*, 1993, erroneously implies that Delano's career was as a sea captain *and* a privateersman. He became the former in due course, but the fact is that his single experience sailing on a privateer vessel was when he was 16 to 17 years of age, aboard the ship *Mars*, from the fall of 1779 through the winter of 1780. See Chapter XXVIII.

23. (p. 170) 1990 estimated population of Mauritius: 1.1 million. *1993 Britannica Book of the Year*.

CHAPTER XII

24. (p. 176) 1991 estimated population of Bombay: 12.57 million. Census of India 1991 Provisional Population Totals, quoted in "India's Population Put at 844 Million," *New York Times*, 26 March 1991, p. A6.

25. (p. 182) Elephanta, an island in Bombay harbor, is noted for six Brahmanic caves, carved in the 8th century from solid rock some 250 feet above sea level. The Great Cave contains gigantic pillars supporting its roof and colossal statuary, especially the famous three-headed bust of the Hindu god Siva. The caves are much visited by Hindu pilgrims. The statue of an elephant, now removed to Bombay city, gives the island its English name. The Indian name is Gharapuri. *The New Columbia Encyclopedia*, 4th ed.

CHAPTER XIII

26. (p. 187) 1990 estimated population of Sri Lanka: 17.8 million. *1993 Britannica Book of the Year*.

27. (p. 189) 1991 estimated population of Madras: 3,795,028. *1993 Britannica Book of the Year*.

Notes

28. (p. 196) 1986 estimated population of Bangladesh (only), officially the People's Republic of Bangladesh, formerly East Pakistan: 102,563,000. *Concise Columbia Encyclopedia*, 2d ed.

29. (p. 198) 1991 estimated population of Calcutta: 10.86 million. Census of India, *New York Times*, 26 March 1991, p. A6.

30. (p. 210) At the time Delano's *Voyages* was published in 1817, world population was estimated to be somewhat less than one billion. "By the mid-nineteenth century, however, it had grown to about one billion, and by 1930 it had risen to two billion; it is expected to double again by 1980." *The New Columbia Encyclopedia*, 4th ed.

"The world's population was about 4.4 billion in 1980, having increased from less than 3.7 billion in 1970 and 2.5 billion in 1950." *The Concise Columbia Encyclopedia*, 2nd ed.

The 1991 edition of "The State of World Population," a report of the United Nations Population Fund (UNFPA) gives the current figure of 5.2 billion. See a summary of the report by Anne Rickert for "The Inter-Dependent," published by the United Nations Association of the U.S.A., Vol. 17, No. 3, June-July 1991.

CHAPTER XV

31. (p. 215) Fur Seal: Any of various eared seals that have a double coat with a dense soft underfur highly valued for clothing and trimmings, and that are now nearly extinct except at a few protected breeding places. Hair Seal: A seal whose coat lacks underfur. Sea Lion: Any of several large-eared seals native to the Pacific Ocean related to the fur seals but lacking their valuable coat and including several largely coastal members of the genera Zalophus, Australian, Californian, and South American. *Websters Third New International Dictionary*.

32. (p. 216) There are 13 species of albatross in the world. The largest of seabirds, the albatross is capable of long sustained flight of months over ocean, alighting only on the surface to feed or when becalmed by lack of wind. They can drink salt water. The long narrow wings are inefficient at flapping flight, but they are masters of gliding on the winds of the world's oceans. Species range in length from 28 to 53 inches. The Wandering Albatross, for example, is from 42 to 48 inches long, about the same as a Royal Albatross, and with a wingspread among males of from 10 to 11½ feet — the largest wingspread, along with the Royal, of any living seabird. *The Audubon Society Encyclopedia of North American Birds*, John K. Terres (New York: Knopf, 1980), p. 8–11.

CHAPTER XVI

33. (p. 224) 1991 estimated population of Concepción: 217,756. *1993 Britannica Book of the Year.*

CHAPTER XVII

34. (p. 237) Más Afuera Island, the Chilean island Delano often refers to, is now known as Alejandro Selkirk Island. With Robinson Crusoe Island — Delano's Juan Fernández Island — they are the principal islands of what is known as the Juan Fernández group. Undoubtedly, Delano's "Goat Island" is the much smaller Isla Santa Clara.

35. (p. 237) "Woodes Rogers...with William Dampier as one of his officers, came to the Pacific on a privateering expedition with ships named the *Duke* and the *Duchess*....They rested and stocked up on wood and water at Juan Fernandez. ...On this occasion the ships found the most famous of marooned sailors, Alexander Selkirk, not famous for himself — he had a creditable but undistinguished naval career — but as the model for Robinson Crusoe. When the *Duke* and *Duchess* called, Selkirk received them in goatskins, looking, according to Rogers 'wilder than the first owners of them.' Rogers took him on board as a mate....Other men had lived alone on Juan Fernandez. William, a Mosquito Indian from Darien, survived there alone for three years, having been abandoned accidentally, whereas Selkirk had been put ashore deliberately." *The Wind Commands: Sailors and Sailing Ships in the Pacific*, Harry Morton (Vancouver: University of British Columbia Press, 1975), p. 350.

36. (p. 238) "At a time when plagiarism was routine and copyright laws nonexistent, writers commonly copied and elaborated the accounts of others until it became nearly impossible to distinguish truth from fiction, even in books ostensibly based on fact....

"Daniel Defoe was the quintessential master of this genre. His most famous work, *Robinson Crusoe*, based on the adventures of Alexander Selkirk and Will, was published as a deliberately imaginary account, although he followed the conventions commonly used by real-life voyagers in writing about their travels....

"William Dampier and his men rescued a Central American native known only as Will, several years before he and Woodes Rogers found Selkirk. (Will and Dampier both would eventually provide grist for adventure writers, notably in Daniel Defoe's *Robinson Crusoe*.)" *Voyages of Discovery: Captain Cook and the Exploration of the Pacific*, Lynne Withey (New York: Morrow, 1987), pp. 30–36.

CHAPTER XVIII

37. (p. 245) It is this encounter with the slave ship *Tryal* that is the inspira-

tion for Herman Melville's story "Benito Cereno" in *The Piazza Tales*, first published in 1856. See Introduction.

CHAPTER XXI

38. (p. 287) "Vaccina, or cow-pox: Although this singular disease has been known for more than half a century, in some districts in England, and in Germany, as affecting the udder of cows, and also the extraordinary fact of its being a preventative of small-pox, it was not till 1797 and 1798, that the intelligence was promulgated and the disease artificially propagated among mankind. Dr. Edward Jenner, an eminent English physician, was the first who made it a subject of medical investigation....[S]ores on [cows'] teats and udders...occasionally communicated to the hands and arms of those who were employed in milking them, producing ulcerous sores and some degree of fever, and from the hands thus affected, the same disease was frequently communicated to other cows by the operation of milking. Hence the disease obtained the name of kine, or cow-pox; and it was...ascertained that the person who has once undergone the disease so communicated, is ever after secure against the infection of the small pox." *American Modern Practice; or a simple method of prevention and cure of diseases, etc.*, James Thatcher (Boston: Cottons and Barnard, 1826), pp. 449–450.

CHAPTER XXIII

39. (p. 315) Kangaroo: A name for a variety of hopping marsupials found in Australia, Tasmania, and New Guinea. There are many species of wallabies, classified in several genera. Tree and rat kangaroo are also members of this large family. The Kangaroo Rat is a small desert rodent found throughout the arid regions of Mexico and the south and west United States. *The New Columbia Encyclopedia*, 4th ed.

In Australia, the "kangaroo rat" is probably the Desert Rat-Kangaroo, a small mammal. Only a single small population is known, and was last sighted in 1935. The nearest existing relative is the Rufous Rat Kangaroo. Of the many species of Wallaby, three are considered technically extinct (not sighted in more than 50 years). Twenty species are potentially threatened with extinction. *Australia's Vanishing Mammals: Endangered and Extinct Species*, Timothy Fridtjof Flannery (Surry Hills, New South Wales, Australia: RD Press, 1990), pp. 27–32; pp. 183–184.

CHAPTER XXIV

40. (p. 327) "It was the custom of the sealers to fight, or be prepared to fight, for possession of a particularly promising sealing ground. The relations between the Australians and the Americans at the Bass Strait grounds deterio-

rated to the point where violence took place between Americans led by Amasa Delano (President Franklin Delano Roosevelt's ancestor) and Australians led by Joseph Murrell. This collision took place in October 1804 and the event is copiously documented, for both Delano and Murrell wrote accounts of it, but they are so contradictory that any impartial assignment of blame for taking the initiative is now impossible." *The United States and the Southwest Pacific,* C. Hartley Grattan (Oxford: Harvard University Press, 1961, American Foreign Policy Library), pp. 79–80. Information courtesy of historian Frank B. Poyas.

41. (p. 329) "The candor of this narration is exceptional in a period when self-sacrificing heroism was a dominant theme in fiction and poetry." *The American Heritage History of Seafaring America*, Alexander K. Laing (New York: American Heritage Publishing Co., 1974), p. 211.

42. (p. 332) Amasa Delano. *A Narrative of a Voyage to New Holland and Van Diemen's Land.* A facsimile extract of chapters 23 and 24 from Delano's original 1817 volume was published in Hobart, Tasmania: Cat and Fiddle Press, 1973.

CHAPTER XXV

43. (p. 342) 1990 estimated population of Lima and Callao metropolitan area: 6,115,700. *1993 Britannica Book of the Year.*

44. (p. 363) "Peruvians say the nation's peasants have grown coca for hundreds of years, using it as a mild stimulant and a hot beverage, and that it is Western industrialized countries that have turned its chemical base into a powerful drug....Some Peruvians also argue that proceeds from the sale of coca leaf, estimated at $500 million to $1 billion a year, are desperately needed in a country where more than 80 percent of the population lives in poverty." Nathaniel C. Nash, "Peru Takes Bigger Role in Production of Cocaine," *New York Times*, 29 July 1991, p. A2.

CHAPTER XXVII

45. (p. 380) 1985 estimated population of Capetown metropolitan area: 1,911,521. *1993 Britannica Book of the Year.*

46. (p. 382) "Most of the sheep kept in tropical Africa are what are known as *Persians*. These tails are the device of a desert animal to store energy in times of plentiful food for the lean times that are sure to follow. By the end of the wet season these tails are huge — great wide bags of fat. We used to kill about one sheep a week, and the surplus fat was always turned into excellent soap." *The Forgotten Crafts*, John Seymour (New York: Knopf, 1986), p. 187.

Glossary

ANTIMONY: A silver-colored metalloid used in medicine.

ARECA NUT: Fruit of a genus of palm; it may be rolled up in betel leaves and chewed.

AZIMUTH COMPASS: A compass designed to take into account the variation between magnetic north and true north.

BAIZE: Woolen or cotton fabric resembling felt.

BANGUE (bang): A narcotic drug derived from hemp; hashish.

BEACH-LE-MAR (bêche-de-mer): The holothuria, or sea-slug, or sea cucumber, esteemed in China and the Far East as a delicacy; known there as trepang. Also called swalloo.

BEAM, TO: To stretch a hide or cloth over a beam, a wooden form, for scraping or shaving.

BEAM ENDS: The ends of the transverse deck beams of a vessel. A ship "on beam ends" is heeled so far on one side that the deck is practically vertical.

BEAT, TO: The operation of sailing to windward by a series of alternate tacks across the wind.

BEEFWOOD: Any of several hard heavy reddish chiefly tropical woods used especially for cabinetwork.

BEND, TO: To join a rope to another or some other object, originally with a "bend" or hitch; on a square-rigged ship, a sail is bent to a yard.

BENZOIN, BENJAMIN: An aromatic balsamic resin from trees of the genus Styrax of southeastern Asia used in medicine, as a fixative in perfumes, and as incense.

BOATSWAIN: The officer in charge of rigging, anchors, cables, sails, etc.

BOBSTAY: A chain or heavy wire rigging running from the end of the bowsprit to the stem or cutwater.

BOHAN UPAS (Malay *pohon upas*, poison tree): A tall Asiatic and East Indian tree (*Antiaris toxicaria* of the mulberry family) that yields a latex that contains poisonous glucosides used as an arrow poison; a shrub or tree of the same region (*Strychnos tieuté* of the family Loganiaceae) also yielding an arrow poison.

BOLLSY (balsa): A raft or float used chiefly for fishing in coastal waters off the Pacific coast of South America, usually made of two cylinders of buoyant wood, but also made of inflated floats of animal skins.

BOOBY: A gannet of the genus Sula having a bright bill and/or feet; a sea-bird.

BOTTOMRY: A mortgage on a ship executed by the captain of a merchant vessel who is out of touch with the owners and needs to raise money for repairs or to complete a voyage. If money is raised on the cargo, it is known as a respondentia bond.

BOWER ANCHOR: The two largest anchors in a ship carried permanently attached to their cables, one on either bow, ready for letting go in an emergency.

BOWSPRIT: A spar projecting from the upper end of the bow of a sailing vessel.

BRACE, TO: The operation of swinging round, by means of braces, the yards of a square-rigged ship to present a more efficient sail surface to the direction of the wind.

BRACE: A rope by which a yard is swung about and secured horizontally.

BROACH, TO: To veer to windward.

CAJEPUT, CAJUPUT: (Malay *kayu*, wood or tree; *puteh*, white): An East Indian tree (Melaleuca leucadendron) of the myrtle family that yields a pungent medicinal oil

CAMPHOR: A gummy fragrant compound obtained from the wood and bark of the camphor tree, used in medicine.

CAPSTAN: A vertical windlass for winding in ropes or cables.

CARRONADE: A short piece of ordnance, usually of large caliber, having the chamber for the powder like a mortar; chiefly used on shipboard. Made in Carron, Scotland.

CARTOUCH, CARTOUCHE: A gun cartridge with a paper case.

CASSIA: A variety of cinnamon derived from the cassia-bark tree.

CAT-BLOCK: A two- or three-fold block forming part of the tackle which raises the anchor to the cat-head.

CAT-HEAD: A projecting timber to which an anchor is hoisted and secured.

CHRONOMETER: "An instrument for measuring time; specifically applied to time-keepers having a special escapement and a compensation balance, used for determining longitude at sea, and for other exact observation." (1735 definition from *Oxford Universal Dictionary*, 3d ed.) John Harrison, b. 1693, son of a carpenter, was first to solve the problem of determining accurate longitude at sea. "The problem...is one of chronometry, for it depends on making a time-piece that will show the time at the port of sailing, at any moment, not withstanding all the vicissitudes of a sea voyage. On comparing this time with local time at any place, it is easy to find the difference in longitude..." Harrison's No. 1 chronometer (there were a number of later ones) is still in going order at the National Maritime Museum, Greenwich, England. *Scientific Instruments in Art and History*, Henri Michel (New York: Viking, 1967), p. 166.

COPPER, TO: To sheathe the bottom and sides of a ship below the waterline with copper, for protection against damage by weeds, barnacles, or worms.

COWRY: A brightly colored shell of a marine gastropod of the genus Cypraea, used as money in Asia and Africa, also used as ornament.

CROSS-JACK YARD: The lower yard on the mizen-mast of a square-rigged ship.

CROSS SEA: A sea running in a contrary direction to the wind. During a gale in which the direction of the wind changes rapidly, the direction of the sea, whipped up by the wind, lasts for some hours after the wind has changed, creating an irregular wave pattern dangerous for ships.

CURRIER: A person who dresses leather after it is tanned.

CUTTER: A small decked ship, relatively fast, with one mast and bowsprit; used as an auxiliary ship.

EARING: A rope attached to a grommet or loop and used for attaching a corner of a sail to a yard or boom.

EAST INDIAMAN, INDIAMAN: A ship of the various East India companies, particularly those of England and Holland, noted for their size and magnificence.

EPHEMERIS: An astronomical almanac containing tables showing the positions of a heavenly body in a number of dates in a regular sequence.

FACTOR: An agent entrusted with goods to sell for others.

FACTORY: An establishment for factors and merchants carrying on business in a foreign country.

FRIGATE: A fast naval vessel, generally having a lofty ship rig, and heavily armed on one or two decks.

GANG CASK: A water cask used on board ship.

GERMAN-COUSIN (usu. cousin-german or brother-german): Having the same parents or grandparents on either the paternal or maternal side.

GILL: Unit of liquid measurement equal to one-quarter pint.

GO-DOWN (from Malay *gudang*): A warehouse or other storage place in India and other Asian countries.

GRAIN: A fishspear or harpoon with two or more "grains" or prongs.

GRAPE SHOT: A cluster of small cast iron balls, used as a charge for a cannon.

GRAPNEL: A small anchor with three or more flukes, used for grappling or dragging, or for anchoring a small boat.

GUNWALE: The upper edge of the side or bulwark of a vessel.

GYAL, GAYAL: A semi-domesticated ox found in India.

HACMETAC: The American larch or tamarack tree.

HAND, TO: The act of furling the square sails of a ship to the yards.

HAUL, TO: The seaman's word meaning to pull; a ship also hauls its wind when it is brought nearer to it after having been running with the wind free.

HAWSE: The distance between the ship's head and anchor as it lies on the bottom.

HONG MERCHANT: One of a corporation of Chinese merchants in Canton who, before 1842, had the monopoly of trade with Europeans.

HUBBLE-BUBBLE: A kind of hookah where the smoke bubbles through water.

INSTANT: Of the present or current month.

INTENDENCY: District under the charge of a government official known as an intendant.

JOLLY BOAT: A light boat carried at the stern of a sailing vessel.

LATEEN SAIL: A triangular sail set on a long sloping yard.

LAUNCH: A large utility boat carried by a warship.

LAURUS: A genus of trees or shrubs in the laurel family, including cinnamon and sassafras.

LEAD, LEAD LINE: A weighted rope for determining depth at sea.

LIGHT: Lighthouse.

LORY (Malay *nuri*, *luri*): Any of numerous parrots of Australia, New Guinea, and adjacent islands, particularly of the genera *Domicella*, *Trichoglossus*, *Chalcopsitta*, and *Eos*.

LUFF, TO: To bring a ship's head up closer to the wind by putting the helm down, or to leeward.

MACARONI: A fop or dandy, called "macaroni" because of a preference for foreign food; the macaroni penguin was so called because its crest was thought to resemble the coiffure of a "macaroni."

MANCHINEEL: A West Indian tree with a poisonous and caustic milky sap, and acrid fruit resembling an apple.

MANI: A South American earth nut.

MATÉ, MATTA, MATTE: The leaves and shoots of a South American holly (*Ilex paraguayensis*) used for making a tea-like beverage.

MINUTE GUN: A cannon fired at intervals of a minute, especially as a signal of distress or in a military or nautical funeral.

MIZEN, MIZZEN: The name of the third, aftermost, mast of a square-rigged ship.

MOTHER CARY'S CHICKENS: Any of various small petrels, especially the stormy petrel.

NANKIN, NANKEEN (from Nanking, China): A durable brownish yellow cotton fabric originally made in China.

NAUTICAL ALMANACK: A publication containing information for working out the position of a sailing vessel by celestial navigation.

NODDY: Any of several dark-bodied terns found on the coasts and islands of warm seas, often so tame as to seem stupid.

PAINTER: A rope, usually at the bow, for fastening a boat to a ship, stake, etc.

PARBUCKLE: A kind of tackle for raising or lowering a cask or similar object, consisting of a rope looped over a post with its two ends passing around the object to be moved.

PAWLS: A series of bars at the bottom of the barrel of a capstan that engage with scores in a pawl-ring around the capstan at deck level to prevent it from recoiling.

PINNACE: a ship's boat rowed with eight or sixteen oars and sometimes equipped with sails.

PROW (Malay *prau*): A small sailing vessel with a large triangular sail and an outrigger.

PULSE: The edible seeds of various leguminous crops, such as peas, beans, lentils; the plants yielding pulse.

QUADRANT: An instrument used in navigation for measuring altitudes.

QUARTERMASTER: An officer on a ship in charge of the helm and navigational instruments.

REEF, TO: The operation of shortening sail (to roll and tie down) in a vessel by reducing the area exposed to the wind, an operation required when a vessel begins to labor because of the strength of the wind.

REQUISITE TABLE: A set of tables used with a nautical ephemeris, to facilitate navigational calculations.

RESPONDENTIA: A loan upon the cargo of a vessel to be repaid only if the goods arrive safe at their destination.

RIDE, TO: To lie moored or anchored.

ROUND SHOT: Spherical balls of cast iron or steel for firing from smooth-bore cannon.

ROYAL: The sail set next above the topgallant sail in a square-rigged ship; the fourth or fifth sail in ascending order.

SCUTTLE, TO: To sink a ship deliberately by opening seacocks or making openings in the bottom.

SEPOY: A native of India employed as a soldier in the service of Europeans.

SEXTANT: A navigational instrument for measuring vertical and horizontal angles at sea, and is capable of measuring angles up to 120° (a quadrant can measure angles up to 90°).

SHADDOCK: A large yellow or orange citrus fruit of a tree of southeastern Asia, also called a pomelo; named after Captain Shaddock, a 17th-century English ship commander, who brought the seed to the West Indies from the East Indies.

SHAG: A small cormorant.

SHEER, TO: To turn or alter direction, swerve.

SHEET ANCHOR: An additional anchor carried in a large ship for security in case the bower anchors fail to hold the ship.

SHEET: A line or pulley used for trimming a sail to the wind.

SISSOO-WOOD: A valuable timber-tree in India.

SLOOP: A smaller auxiliary naval vessel.

SNOW: A European two-masted merchant vessel, rigged as a brig.

SPEAK, TO: To communicate with a passing vessel at sea, by signal, speaking trumpet, etc.

SPECIE: Coined money.

STAYSAIL: A triangular fore-and-aft sail attached to a stay, which is part of the rigging that supports a mast.

SUBAHDAR: The chief native officer of a native company in the army of the British Empire.

Glossary

SUPERCARGO: An abbreviation of cargo superintendent. "The only approach to a privileged class in the Massachusetts fleet was the supercargoes. This position — the business agent of the owners on shipboard — was often reserved for Harvard graduates, merchants' sons, and other young men of good family who had neither the taste nor the ruggedness for the rough-and-tumble of forecastle life." *The Maritime History of Massachusetts, 1783–1860*, Samuel Eliot Morison (Boston: Houghton Mifflin Co., 1920, 1941).

SWALLOO: See beach-le-mar (bêche-de-mer).

SWIVEL: A swivel gun; a gun mounted on a pedestal so that it can be turned from side to side or up and down.

TACK, TO: To change the course of a sailing vessel by bringing the head into the wind and then causing it to fall off on the other side.

TAFFRAIL, TAFFEREL RAIL: The after rail at the stern of a ship, but formerly the curved wooden top of the stern of a sailing man-of-war or East Indiaman, usually carved or otherwise decorated. Taffrail is a contraction of taffarel, the original name for this adornment. In its modern meaning it is often used to indicated the deck area right at the stern of a vessel.

TARRA OR TARO ROOT: An edible tuber of the Pacific Islands.

TENDER: An auxiliary ship employed to attend one or more other ships.

THRUM, TO: A sail or piece of canvas is thrummed by sewing lengths of rope to it, and then used to cover a damaged part of a ship's hull.

THWART: The transverse wooden seat in a rowed boat on which the oarsman sits.

TIMBER HEAD: The top end of a timber, rising above the deck and serving for belaying ropes.

TIME KEEPER, TIME PIECE: Chronometer (see definition above).

TOP: A platform at the top of the mast of a ship.

TOPGALLANT: The mast in a square-rigged ship set above the topmast to form the third and top part of a complete mast.

TUTENAG: A nickel silver containing copper, nickel, and zinc.

WAIST: The central part of a ship, between the forecastle and the quarterdeck.

WARP, TO: To move a ship by hauling with warps, or ropes, that have been fastened to something fixed, as a buoy or anchor.

WATER PIPE: A large water cask.

WEAR, TO: To put a ship about, bringing the stern windward.

WEATHER: Applied to anything which lies to windward. The "weather-head" is the windward side.

WHORTLEBERRY: The edible black berry of a Eurasian shrub of the heath family.

WINDSAIL: A canvas funnel, the upper end of which is guyed to face the wind, used to ventilate a ship by deflecting the wind below decks, the funnel being led below through a hatchway.

YAW: A deviation from a straight or chosen course, produced by a following wind or sea.

YAWL: A ship's small boat, rowed by a crew of 4 or 6.

Glossary sources: *Oxford Universal Dictionary*, 3d ed.; *Oxford English Dictionary*, 1971 two-vol. ed.; *The Oxford Companion to Ships and The Sea*, ed. Peter Kemp (London: Oxford University Press, 1966); *Webster's Seventh New Collegiate Dictionary*; *Random House Dictionary of the English Language*, Unabridged, 2d. ed.; and other sources as noted.

Illustration Sources

PAGE 9: The ship *Three Sisters*, built in Charlestown, in 1795. Owner, 1796: Thomas Russell of Boston; Master, John Cathcart. Painting by J.E. Toulza, 1802. Courtesy of the Peabody Essex Museum.

PAGE 12: *Quincy Patriot Ledger* 26 July 1940. Courtesy of the Peabody Essex Museum.

PAGE 18: Whampoa Pagoda. From Thomas Daniell, *A Picturesque Voyage to India by Way of China*. London, 1810. From the collections of the Library of Congress.

PAGE 35: Abba Thulle, King of Pelew; Ludee, one of the Wives of Abba Thulle. From George Keate, *An Account of the Pelew Islands, Western Part of the Pacific Ocean, Composed from the Journals and Communications of Captain Henry Wilson....*London, 1788. From the collections of the Library of Congress.

PAGE 43: View of Part of the Town of Pelew, and the place of Council. From George Keate, *An Account of the Pelew Islands*. From the collections of the Library of Congress.

PAGE 53: Malaye Proas and Canoes. From Thomas Daniell, *A Picturesque Voyage*. From the collections of the Library of Congress.

PAGE 64: The *Thames*, East Indiaman, 1424 Tons, Built for, and Employed by The Honble. East India Compy. E. W. Cooke, *Sixty-five Plates of Shipping and Craft*. London, 1829. From the collections of the Library of Congress.

PAGE 86: Model of a ketch, *Eliza*, built in Salem, Massachusetts, in 1794 by Enos Briggs for Elias Hasket Derby. Courtesy of the Peabody Essex Museum.

PAGE 165: Port Louis. From T. Bradshaw and William Rider, *Views in the Mauritius, or Isle of France*. London, James Carpenter, 1832. From the collections of the Library of Congress.

PAGE 189: *Eliza*, brig of Providence. A watercolor by J.E. Toulza, 1802. Vietor Collection. Courtesy of the Peabody Essex Museum.

PAGE 203: Old Fort Gaut, Calcutta. From Thomas Daniell, *A Picturesque Voyage*. From the collections of the Library of Congress.

PAGE 292: *Attatant*, brig of Boston. Gouache, unsigned, attributed to Michele Felice Corne. Vietor Collection. Courtesy of the Peabody Essex Museum.

PAGE 295: The ship *Columbia*, built at North River, Massachusetts, 1773; with sloop *Washington*, off the mouth of the Columbia River, 1792. From a lithograph of American ships by George C. Wales. Courtesy of the Peabody Essex Museum.

Delano's Voyages of Commerce and Discovery

PAGE 301: Chinese Trading & Fishing Vessels. From Thomas Daniell, *A Picturesque Voyage*. From the collections of the Library of Congress.

PAGE 308: *Samuel*, a schooner of Boston. Unsigned, attributed to Michele Felice Corne. Vietor Collection. Courtesy of the Peabody Essex Museum.

PAGE 334: Chinamen Working Guano — Great Heap — Chincha Islands. From *Rays of Sunlight from South America*. Photographed by Alexander Gardner. Washington, D.C.: Philip & Solomons, 1865. From the collections of the Library of Congress.

PAGE 337: Panorama of North Island, Chincha Islands, with Part of Fleet Waiting for Guano. From *Rays of Sunlight*. From the collections of the Library of Congress.

PAGE 344: Municipality Building, Great Plaza, Lima. From *Rays of Sunlight*. From the collections of the Library of Congress.

PAGE 347: Old Avenue of Pizarro, Lima. From *Rays of Sunlight*. From the collections of the Library of Congress.

PAGE 355: Church of San Francisco (Mosaic), Lima. From *Rays of Sunlight*. From the collections of the Library of Congress.

PAGE 358: A lady of Lima in her full Dress. From Joseph Skinner, *The Present State of Peru*. London: Richard Phillips, 1805. From the collections of the Library of Congress.

PAGE 365: The *Balza*. From Antonio de Ulloa, *A Voyage to South America.* … London, 1758. From the collections of the Library of Congress.

PAGE 367: Plan dune Balse faite de peaux de loups marins cousues et pleines d'air. From A. François Frezier, *A Voyage to the South Sea along the Coast of Chile and Peru, in the Years 1712, 1713, & 1714*. London: Jonah Boyer, 1717. From the collections of the Library of Congress.

PAGE 397: Detail of Liverpool ware punch bowl, showing ship *Grand Turk*. Courtesy of the Peabody Essex Museum.

PAGE 398: Captain Amasa Delano. From *A Narrative of voyages and travels in the Northern and Southern hemispheres*. Boston, 1817. From the collections of the Library of Congress.

ELEANOR ROOSEVELT SEAGRAVES has been a librarian, educator, bibliographer, and researcher in the humanities. She lives in Washington, D.C.

WILLIAM T. LA MOY is Director of the James Duncan Phillips Library at the Peabody Essex Museum in Salem, Massachusetts, and is editor of *Peabody Essex Museum Collections.*